S0-BZO-528

COMPUTER ORGANIZATION AND PROGRAMMING

WITH AN EMPHASIS ON THE PERSONAL COMPUTER

McGraw-Hill Series in Computer Organization and Architecture

Bell and Newell: Computer Structures: Readings and Examples
Cavanagh: Digital Computer Arithmetic: Design and Implementation
Gear: Computer Organization and Programming: With an Emphasis on the Personal Computer
Hamacher, Vranesic, and Zaky: Computer Organization
Hayes: Computer Architecture and Organization
Hayes: Digital System Design and Microprocessors
Hwang and Briggs: Computer Architecture and Parallel Processing
Kogge: The Architecture of Pipelined Computers
Siewiorek, Bell, and Newell: Computer Structures: Principles and Examples
Stone: Introduction to Computer Organization and Data Structures
Stone and Siewiorek: Introduction to Computer Organization and Data Structures: PDP-11 Edition

McGraw-Hill Computer Science Series

Ahuja: Design and Analysis of Computer Communication Networks
Barbacci and Siewiorek: The Design and Analysis of Instruction Set Processors
Ceri and Pelagatti: Distributed Databases: Principles and Systems
Debry: Communicating with Display Terminals
Donovan: Systems Programming
Filman and Friedman: Coordinated Computing: Tools and Techniques for Distributed Software
Givone: Introduction to Switching Circuit Theory
Goodman and Hedetniemi: Introduction to the Design and Analysis of Algorithms
Katzan: Microprogramming Primer
Keller: A First Course in Computer Programming Using Pascal
Kohavi: Switching and Finite Automata Theory
Liu: Elements of Discrete Mathematics
Liu: Introduction to Combinatorial Mathematics
MacEwen: Introduction to Computer Systems: Using the PDP-11 and Pascal
Madnick and Donovan: Operating Systems
Manna: Mathematical Theory of Computation
Newman and Sproull: Principles of Interactive Computer Graphics
Payne: Introduction to Simulation: Programming Techniques and Methods of Analysis
Révész: Introduction to Formal Languages
Rice: Matrix Computations and Mathematical Software
Salton and McGill: Introduction to Modern Information Retrieval
Shooman: Software Engineering: Design, Reliability, and Management
Tremblay and Bunt: An Introduction to Computer Science: An Algorithmic Approach
Tremblay and Bunt: An Introduction to Computer Science: An Algorithmic Approach, Short Edition
Tremblay and Manohar: Discrete Mathematical Structures with Applications to Computer Science
Tremblay and Sorenson: An Introduction to Data Structures with Applications
Tremblay and Sorenson: The Theory and Practice of Compiler Writing
Tucker: Programming Languages
Wiederhold: Database Design
Wulf, Levin, and Harbison: Hydra/C. mmp: An Experimental Computer System

COMPUTER ORGANIZATION AND PROGRAMMING

WITH AN EMPHASIS ON THE PERSONAL COMPUTER

FOURTH EDITION

C. William Gear

Department of Computer Science
University of Illinois at Urbana-Champaign

McGRAW-HILL BOOK COMPANY

New York St. Louis San Francisco Auckland Bogotá
Hamburg Johannesburg London Madrid Mexico Montreal New Delhi
Panama Paris São Paulo Singapore Sydney Tokyo Toronto

This book was set in Times Roman by Beacon Graphics Corporation.
The editors were Eric M. Munson, Kaye Pace, and Sheila H. Gillams;
the production supervisor was Diane Renda.
New drawings were done by Danmark & Michaels, Inc.
Halliday Lithograph Corporation was printer and binder.

COMPUTER ORGANIZATION AND PROGRAMMING

With an Emphasis on the Personal Computer

1 2 3 4 5 6 7 8 9 0 HALHAL 8 9 8 7 6 5

ISBN 0-07-023049-8

Library of Congress Cataloging in Publication Data

Gear, C. William (Charles William), date
Computer organization and programming.

(McGraw-Hill series in computer organization and architecture)
1. Electronic digital computers—Programming.
2. Computer architecture. 3. Microcomputers—Programming.
I. Title. II. Series.
QA76.6G38 1985 001.64′2 84-20180
ISBN 0-07-023049-8

CONTENTS

PREFACE

This book is intended for a course in programming at the machine level and is aimed at students who have taken one or two earlier courses in a procedure-oriented language. The material covered is essentially that in Association for Computing Machinery Curriculum '78 courses SC3 and CS4, although it does not cover as much logical design as CS4. The intent of the book is to let the student see the principles behind various machine-language features and understand the alternatives available to the computer designer. I do not view this as a course for training assembly-language programmers; indeed, few such programmers are needed any more. However, there are many reasons for knowing something about the machine at this level: a high-level language programmer can produce better code when there is an understanding of the processes occurring at the machine level; occasionally, some inner part of a high-level language program must be written at the machine level, either to gain efficiency or to gain access to devices at the bit level; computer designers need to understand machine-level programming and how it is used in the implementation of high-level language constructs; and future microprogrammers certainly need to understand the concepts of machine-level programming!

The objective of this book continues to be presentation of the basic concepts of machine-level architecture and programming, so that all ideas are discussed in a non-machine-specific setting. The objective I state to students taking this course is that at the end they should be able to pick up the assembler and principles-of-operation manuals for a computer and be able to find out how to program it in assembly language. The machine- or system-specific information in this book is not intended to be a complete reference for the computer or its system, but to introduce the student to the computer's use. The student should have copies of the reference manuals for the particular hardware and operating system in use. Unfortunately, those manuals are mostly unreadable, so one purpose of this text is to show the student the underlying principles to make it possible for her or him to use the reference manuals.

I place heavy emphasis not on learning details of a particular machine but on understanding concepts. However, I have found that it is necessary to teach students a particular assembly language at first and neither leave them in the air with vague generalities nor confuse them with the details of more than one computer. Therefore, I introduce each new topic (such as index registers) by first discussing the general principles and giving some motivation for their use. Then I illustrate with the particular computer being used for homework assignments. I do not discuss other computers until late in the course when the basic ideas are fairly well understood and confusion is less of a problem.

This fourth edition has been rewritten to reflect the fact that the majority of instructional use is now interactive, and reorganized considerably to present the material in a more top-down manner. The introduction now includes a brief overview of typical operating systems, some specifics on actual operating systems, and a quick look at editors. Most students will have had some experience with the use of systems in an earlier class, but if not, this material is intended to make it possible for them to start using a computer as soon as possible. Chapter 2 starts with a quick look at machine-level programming of the simplest type and then presents an initial look at assembly so that the student can start to try out simple programs. It also looks at debugging systems, since these can be used to watch the execution of simple machine-language code interactively. I strongly recommend that this method be used in the early stages of instruction, as it bypasses all problems of input and output. In fact, with some absolute debuggers it even allows avoidance of the assembler, as the debuggers permit direct assembly of code with absolute addresses, and this is sufficient for the initial experiments with machine code.

In this version of the fourth edition, specific examples are taken from the INTEL 8080 and 8086/88 hardware with the CP/M and IBM PC DOS operating systems, respectively. There are enough similarities between the two architectures and systems that the student can see the ideas in a real setting without the confusion of too many different implementations. At the same time, the two architectures and systems include many of the ideas of modern computer and system design.

I supplement the book with additional material on the computer being used. I have found that some locally prepared short summaries of the key information, coupled with manufacturers' documentation, offer a good compromise, as one of the skills to be learned is the use of typical computer reference documentation.

It is important to assign a number of programs as homework during the course. I have found it helpful to provide the students with a simple, working assembly-language program and to ask them to make minor changes to it as their first assignment. This allows them to gain some experience while the beginning ideas are covered in class. By the time some of Chapter 2 has been covered, a second assignment that requires more independent work can be made. Material in Chapters 3 and 4 can be covered at almost any time, and many instructors prefer to get into procedures in Chapter 5 as soon as possible. The amount of material covered in Chapter 3 should be determined by the interests and backgrounds of the students—it is not essential to cover more than the initial overview of twos complement. Chapter 4 can be left as a reading assignment; it is included for the sake of completeness. Chapters 6, 7, and 8 are the last that I view as essential to cover in a course of this type. Chapters 9 through 12 are optional; each can be omitted without affecting later discussions. Chapter 9 can be used for engineering-oriented classes. Chapter 10 can be given as a reading assignment. Chapter 11 can be used to give a better insight into the assembler or to illustrate a large programming problem. Chapter 12 can be used as a source for programming problems as well as for some low-level data structure discussions.

There are a variety of questions at the end of the chapters, including some programming problems. Many of these can be modified to provide additional questions or homework.

C. William Gear

COMPUTER ORGANIZATION AND PROGRAMMING

WITH AN EMPHASIS ON THE PERSONAL COMPUTER

CHAPTER 1

INTRODUCTION

Computer programs can be written with no knowledge of the underlying *architecture* (that is, the hardware organization) of the computer system that will be controlled by the program. Indeed, modern programming practice stresses the desirability of making programs *machine-independent*. For most purposes, the programmer can view a program as a step-by-step description of a computational *process* without any regard for the computer to be used. Any suitably precise language can be used to describe the process, and a computer can be viewed as a device that is capable of understanding that description by following the steps in the specified order in the same way a human reader might. The only restriction imposed by the computer that the programmer need be aware of is one of *representation*: the program and data have to be represented in a form acceptable to the computer system to be used.

At the the other extreme, computer architecture can be designed with little attention to programming languages. As long as the architecture is capable of representing common data and of performing the fundamental operations (communication, data manipulation, such as subtraction, and decision making by comparison, such as "Is X greater than Y?") we know that the computer can be programmed to perform any computation. However, what is important in the architectural design is the ease and speed with which common programs can be processed, and what is important in programs for some large, difficult problems is the way in which they make the best use of the computer structure.

In this book we will study the representation of programs and data in computers and the organization of computers. Our goal is to understand how programs should be written so that they can be efficiently processed, and how computers can be organized to aid in attaining that goal. The emphasis will be on current computer architectures and programming styles, so we will examine several popular examples of computers. In this study we will stress the view that the program is a process that is to be executed on a computer. The data associated with the program and the current point of execution of the progam is the *state* of the process. As the computer ''reads'' through the program, following the instructions specified in each step, the data values change as the computer moves from step to step, and thus the state of the process changes. The computer organization only affects the way in which the process is represented internally; the average programmer is free to think of the process as represented in Pascal or any other language, but internally it is represented in the form understood by the architecture, called machine language. To understand the interplay between architecture and programs, we must study *machine-level languages,* which include actual machine languages and simple representations of them, called *assembly languages,* that are more comprehensible to people.

It is often fruitful to glance over the historical development of a field to gain an understanding of why things are the way they are, even in a field such as computer science, in which most developments have occurred since 1945. The digital computer was developed in answer to the need for quicker and more efficient ways of handling large numerical computations. Those computations arose in practical situations, as in the solution of engineering problems such as the design of a bridge or plane and the choice of heating-cooling strategies to minimize fuel consumption, as well as in the course of theoretical endeavors, such as the attempt to locate prime numbers. (Locating prime numbers is not a task of great economic value, but related problems are of intellectual interest to mathematicians, and excess time on early computers was used in such calculations.) Tasks such as these *could* have been doen without the help of computer technology, but in many cases their value would have been negated by the cost in human time and stress, not to mention the high probability of error in human calculation.

However, some fairly large calculations had to be done before the development of the automatic digital computer, and these were handled in the following way: They were split into many sections — each relatively independent of the others — which were then computed separately. Each section was broken down into a set of instructions and the data to which it was to be applied. The various sections were then handed on to a number of assistants who performed the indicated computations using hand calculating devices. Now, the instructions and data are given to the digital computer; it performs the routine tasks previously done by these assistants. (No matter how fast computers are, it appears that society will always have problems that exceed the capacity of computers. Today, some extremely large problems are broken into relatively independent parts, and each part is solved on a separate computerlike device, although these devices may be interconnected so that data and program can be transferred between them. This is called *parallel processing*.)

After the initial use of computers in numerical problems, workers began to explore other areas of application. It was noted that any finite class of objects could be related to the sets of numbers that the computer could handle and could be manipulated in the same way. *Nonnumeric* data processing became important. (Even before the automatic digital computer, nonnumeric data processing had become available for some business applications through the use of punched-card machines.)

Nonnumeric processing is basically similar to numeric processing in that various logical processes, or *algorithms*, which manipulate finite sets of objects (either numbers or other data) can be prepared for the same computer used to solve numerical problems. At first, this was viewed as the numerical representation of nonnumerical data. As an example, the letters of the alphabet could be assigned numeric values 1 through 26, with a space represented by 0. (Space, or *blank*, as it is usually called in computer usage, is one of the possible characters that a computer must be able to "print" on a page.) A machine capable of manipulating 8-digit decimal numbers could then be used to manipulate four–or–less–letter words by replacing each letter by its equivalent number and adding spaces (zeros) if there were less than four letters. Thus, MOTH would be represented as 13 15 20 08 and MAT as 13 01 20 00. In this scheme, words could be arranged alphabetically by arranging their numerical representations in numerical order. MAT preceded MOTH because 13012000 is less than 13152008.

Through such techniques, business data processing, frequently involving the manipulation of large amounts of character data, was automated for computers. Nonnumeric processing has been extended to applications involving the manipulation of abstract mathematical quantities, such as groups; to the problems of natural language translation, such as Russian to English; to graphical or pictorial data processing, such as the matching of fingerprints or the examination of x-ray pictures for disease indications; to the control of complex processes, such as those involved in running oil refineries; and to the control of robots.

Programs for the first computers were written directly in machine-level languages by people who were familiar with the inner structure of the computer. As computer applications grew in number and variety, the computer became available to people with little knowledge of the details of its inner structure. A typical user now wants to specify only the steps in a computational task, not the details of the way those steps are to be executed in a particular computer, just as a person asking another person to retrieve a letter from a file, for example, does not want to also describe how the file drawer should be opened or how to alphabetize letters. Therefore, to the basic computer *hardware* (that is, the physical parts of the computer) was added the *software* of *system programs*, which handle many common operations for the user and which translate the language of the user into that of the computer. The hardware and system programs together constitute the *computer system*. The hardware provides the ability to do basic operations, the software the ability to specify the job in a convenient notation and to move from one job to another without delay. The user sees the combination and does not need to distinguish the two parts. Indeed, as technology changes, things once done by software in early systems are done by hardware in later systems.

This book discusses computer organization by describing various ways in which the basic hardware and software components of the computer are logically connected, the reasons for the different organizations, and the advantages of each. This material is then used as background for a discussion of the basic principles of machine-level programming. These principles are illustrated by a discussion of some aspects of (1) the translation of programs written in a language applicable to a task, called a *source language*, into an equivalent program expressed in machine language; (2) the scheduling of these user programs by other programs, usually referred to as *kernel*, *executive*, and *supervisor* programs; and (3) providing assistance to the program in execution by system subprograms, which are typically concerned with input-output and other communication.

A computer system should provide a tool for solving problems quickly—in terms of the computer's time as well as that of the user. The hardware should be designed to operate as fast as possible within given cost limits. The software should be designed to minimize the amount of wasted computer time and yet provide as flexible a means of controlling the operation as possible. Computer functions that can be expected to be fixed throughout the life of the machine should be provided by hardware where possible. Functions that will change—by increases in capabilities without the negation of earlier properties—should be controlled by software. The objective of system design must be one of minimum cost for the whole job, including the cost of programming as well as execution on the computer. These considerations are as important for the large central computers that process a great variety of jobs as for the microcomputers that allow placement of a separate computer on everybody's desk.

The programmer who programs at the machine level may be a *system programmer*, that is, one who writes programs that will help other users access the computer system; an *application programmer* who finds it necessary to work at the machine level in sections of very large application programs where high speed is important; or a designer faced with the development of a microcomputer for a single application. This book is directed at all of these types of programmers.

1.1 THE BASIC CAPABILITIES OF COMPUTERS

A digital computer is capable of basic operations of finite sets of objects such as numbers. These include the usual arithmetic operations of *addition*, *subtraction*, *multiplication*, and *division*. In addition, a computer has the important ability to compare two numbers or nonnumeric quantities in order to take one action if the comparison is successful or another if it fails. These comparisons usually include tests for *greater than or equal to*, *equal to*, *less than*, etc. In additon to operating on information, the computer must be able to read the initial data from the user, retain it for later computations, and write the answers for the user. Therefore, in addition to the operational power, it has facilities for *storing* data and for reading and writing it in a useful form. This form can be a human interface (such as keyboards, or printed output) or the sampling of data signals and control signals to devices such as those used in automatic flight control. The next few subsections will trace briefly the historical development of these facilities and the importance of each new feature.

1.1.1. The Hand-Operated Calculator

The mechanical, hand-operated calculator was one of the first computing tools. With its ability to perform the basic arithmetic operations it replaced a lot of tedious human calculation. However, human intervention was still needed, both to control the steps in the calculation and to retain intermediate results (by writing them on scratch paper). In order to use a hand calculator effectively, the steps of a problem must be carefully organized; that is, the sequence of calculations must be specified carefully. This specification is a progam that describes a process for the hand calculator. The process can be executed by pushing the control keys specified for each step. Modern electronic, hand-held calculators provide a number of *storage registers* that eliminate the need to copy intermediate results, but the speed of a hand-operated calculator is limited by the speed with which a human operator can issue instructions in the process by manually pressing keyboard buttons.

1.1.2 The Stored-Program Computer

The step to *stored-program* computers, which bypassed the speed limitation imposed by human control of processing, occurred in two stages. The first stage was marked by the introduction of sequence-controlled calculators.[1] A fixed cycle of steps, that is, a program, was prepared ahead of time, encoded, and stored on a punched tape or a plugboard. The calculator got its sequence of operations from this storage device and repeated the cycle of steps indefinitely. The capabilities provided by such mechanisms were equivalent to those of a computer in which programs consisting of only one or two simple assignment statements were executed repetitively.

These techniques were used for repetitive operations, such as summing numbers punched in cards. With the addition of auxiliary cycles of steps that were activated under certain conditions (and with a lot of ingenuity), quite sophisticated jobs were tackled. The sequence-controlled calculator was limited by its inability to modify its cycle of steps in any significant way because the cycle was stored in a semipermanent memory such as a plugboard. Today, the more expensive hand-held calculators can store programs.

The limitation of sequence-controlled calculators was overcome by the introduction of the stored program computer,[2] in which the sequence of steps was stored in the same memory as the data instead of in a separate memory such as a plugboard. Because

[1]Although sequence-controlled calculators were designed as early as 1812, when Charles Babbage designed his "Analytical Engine" (he was unable to complete it because of technological difficulties), the first calculator capable of performing long sequences of calculations was the Harvard Mark I, designed by Howard Aiken in 1937, built by IBM, and donated to Harvard University in 1944. It was essentially mechanical. The first electronic calculator was the ENIAC (Electronic Numerical Integrator and Calculator), designed by J. P. Eckert and J. W. Mauchly of the Moore School of Electrical Engineering, University of Pennsylvania. It was completed in 1945.

[2]The first design for a stored program computer was by Eckert and Mauchly of the University of Pennsylvania. Many of the ideas resulted from the work of John von Neumann, a person who contributed greatly to both mathematics and computer science. This computer, the EDVAC, was not finished until 1951. Separate efforts of design and construction were occurring simultaneously in the United Kingdom. Alan Turing, then at the National Physical Laboratory (NPL), had proposed a design for the Automatic Computing Engine (ACE). That design was quite different from other designs and was heavily modified by others before finally being built in a prototype version called the Pilot ACE. Manchester University and Cambridge University were undertaking separate efforts. The EDSAC, designed at Cambridge in 1946 and operational in 1949, was probably the first operational stored program computer, but a prototype machine at Manchester University was operational on June 21, 1948, and was probably the first stored program computer to be operational. The latter was the basis for a subsequent design that was put into production by the Ferranti company and became the first commercial computer, beating the better-known UNIVAC I by a short period. The UNIVAC I was also designed by a team led by Eckert and Mauchly. For a brief historical summary see the opening chapters in M. V. Wilkes, *Automated Digital Computers*, J. Wiley & Sons, New York, 1956. For an interesting view of an unusual and important figure in those times, see Andrew Hodges, *Alan Turning: The Enigma*, Simon and Schuster, New York, 1983.

operations could be performed on the contents of the memory, this computer was able to modify its own programs during execution. This feature made it possible to vary the program according to need. It was first thought that this would be an important step toward operating efficieny, but subsequent developments (for example, indexing, to be discussed in later chapters) have made it possible to avoid program modification. For reasons to be discussed later, program modification is now viewed with disfavor.

1.1.3 Operating Systems and Translators

After the introduction of stored program computers, complex tasks could be tackled. However, many errors could be made during the preparation of a program. In the early days, the programmer sat at the console of the machine to run a program. The computer would often stop on errors, and the programmer would then have to examine the content of the computer to locate the errors. As machines increased in speed, this correction process became uneconomic. A program that would execute for 1 second could take 5 minutes of human intervention. Therefore, the *operating system* was introduced. This is a program that regains control of the machine when an error is committed by the user program. It attempted to provide the user with diagnostic information at computer rather than human speeds.

The operating system provided additional capabilities by means of *commands* and *system calls*. These are, in fact, programs, but to the user they appear to be machine enhancements. This was the beginning of the development of the modern computer system as a series of layers, each layer adding capabilities to the layer below, as indicated in Figure 1-1.

With increase in speed it also became necessary to simplify the drudgery of rote programming. Large volumes of code had to be produced, much of it repetitious and similar—if not identical—to code previously written. Conventions for writing standard codes and ways for using these codes were adopted for each machine, so that any user had access to a *library* of codes generated by the users' groups. To the user, these library programs could also be viewed as an additional layer providing further capabilities in the computer system. To simplify the programming of a piece of code that could not be obtained from other sources, *high-level languages* were designed. Each machine executes code in its own machine language, which is more detailed than is necessary for human statement and understanding the underlying problem being programmed. High-level languages are oriented toward solving a problem rather than detailing the work of the machine.[3] Programs were developed to translate from these user-

[3]Large numbers of high-level computer languages have been implemented, but few are ever more than experimental. The first successful language was Fortran. It was issued by IBM in 1957 as Fortran I, but this was replaced by Fortran II a year later. A brief historical summary can be found in W. P. Heising, "Fortran," *Comm. Assoc. Computing Machinery*, March 1963, pp. 85–86. A more recent view can be found in J. Backus, "A History of Fortran I, II, and III," *ACM SIGPLAN Notices*, August 1978, pp. 165–180. About the time that Fortran appeared, an international committee released a preliminary report on a language for specifying algorithms. This was known as Algol 58 (A. J. Perlis and K. Samelson, "Preliminary Report: International Algorithmic Language," *Comm. Assoc. Computing Machinery*, December 1958, pp. 8–22). In 1960 an updated version appeared called Algol 60. The report on that was later corrected and appeared as P. Naur (ed), "Revised Report on the Algorithmic Language Algol 60," *Comm. Assoc. Computing Machinery*, January 1963, pp. 1–17. Historical notes on many languages can be found in the ACM SIGPLAN notices cited above. These are the preprints for a conference on the history of programming languages.

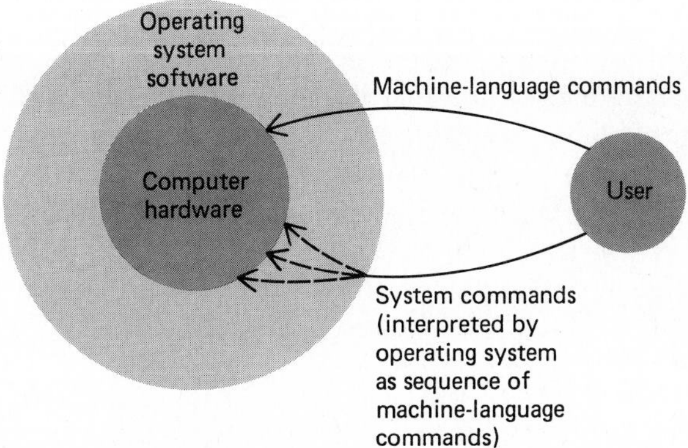

FIGURE 1-1 Layers of a computer system

oriented languages to machine-oriented languages. (These programs are examples of the nonnumeric processing that occurs every day in even the most scientifically oriented computer department. Because up to 50 percent of the time of many computers is spent in translations and analogous system activities, it is very important that efficient techniques be integrated into such programs.) With the advent of high-level languages, the user was removed one layer further from the basic operations and inner structure of the computer, but saw a corresponding increase in flexibility and power.

1.1.4 Timesharing and Remote Terminals

Initially, operating systems seemed to satisfy the desire of management to have the most efficient computer organization in terms of actual versus possible running time. These systems took the programmer out of the computer rooms so that costly interaction with a program during execution was no longer possible. Although this certainly eliminated much nonsense, ironically, it did slow down the rate at which a single program could be developed. Long *turnaround times*, the periods between handling a job in for processing and receiving the output, and the inevitable occurrence of unexpected conditions, left the programmer sitting idle, waiting to correct minor faults. It also led to many inefficiencies not immediately apparent to management. Because the programmer could no longer interact with the program during execution and could not predict the types of errors that would be encountered, it was necessary to have enough data printed so that all probable contingencies were covered. During test runs of programs, a lot of time saved by the efficient operating system was lost to excessive printing.

In order to allow the user to interact with a program while it was being executed and also to request only the output that was of significance, many consoles, called *remote terminals*, were attached to a single computer.[4] Programs for each programmer were stored in different parts of the computer memory, and the processing section of the

[4]One of the first large timesharing systems was the CTSS (Compatible Time-Sharing System) developed at the Massachussets Institute of Technology. It was in regular use in 1963. It was described in F. J. Corbato et al., *The Compatible Time-sharing System: A Programmer's Guide*, MIT Press, Cambridge, MA, 1963.

computer switched from one program to another as it switched from one console to another. While one program was being executed for a brief period, other programmers could be examining their results and preparing further input. The timesharing systems were organized so that each user seemed to have access to a separate computer. Initially, the consoles were typewriterlike devices (teletypewriters). Now most terminals use alphanumeric cathode ray tubes (CRTs), also called video display units (VDUs). They are frequently connected to the computer by telephone lines so that they can be placed at great distances from the computer.

1.1.5 Microcomputers

The early computers were physically very large because their electrical circuits were constructed out of large components such as vacuum tubes. Each of these components performed no more than a single, simple function. The invention of the transistor, followed by major technological developments that permitted large numbers of transistor-like devices to be manufactured as a single, small component called an *integrated circuit*, or *chip* (because it is usually made on a small chip of silicon metal), permitted complex computer circuits to be constructed in a very small space. By 1975 this miniaturization permitted the manufacture of low-price computers called microcomputers. These were initially used in applications such as experimental control in which the computer followed a fixed program to perform a single task. This is called a *dedicated* use of a computer. In 1977 the first of these microcomputers was marketed as a general-purpose device in the $500 price range by Commodore. It was called the PET computer and was the first *personal computer* on the market. It had the computing capacity and nearly the same memory capacity as the earliest computers, but its price was about one two-hundredth of their price. The wheel had turned full circle and once again the programmer could sit at the console of a private computer. However, the microcomputer provides many of the additional features found in a large modern system. While it might be slower in executing large tasks, the microcomputer can provide immediate service for small requests, avoiding the waits that occur in some large timesharing systems when they are fully loaded with users. For this reason, many terminals for large systems contain microcomputers so that some tasks can be handled locally. Terminals that are capable of doing simple screen editing functions are called *intelligent terminals*, whereas those that provide many local computation functions are called *workstations*.

1.2 COMPUTER ORGANIZATION

The hardware components of a computer system are classified into three groups:

1 Memory
2 Central processing unit (CPU)
3 Input-output (I/O)

These units are shown connected together in Figure 1-2. The I/O units are for communication between the internal representation of information by electrical signals used in the computer and the external representation, such as terminals, printed paper, other

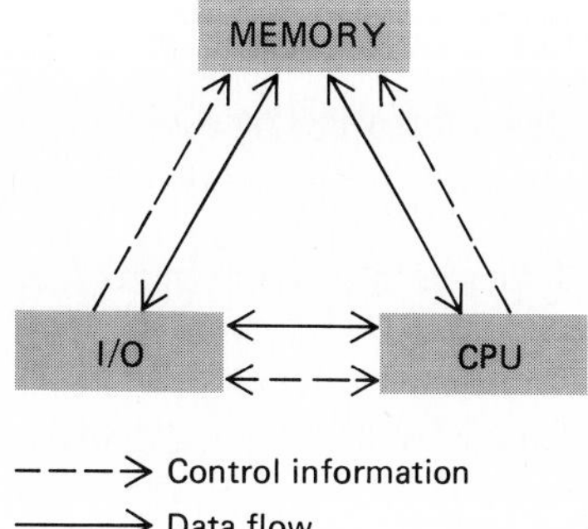

FIGURE 1-2 Computer organization

hard copy media, and sensing and control devices. The program is stored in memory and executed by the CPU. The CPU reads (*fetches*) the description, or *representation*, of each program step from the memory, fetches the data needed in that step, *executes* or *processes* that step, and returns the results to memory as appropriate. The CPU is sometimes referred to as *the* processor because it processes the program steps and, in most systems, ultimately controls everything. On some very small systems, the CPU directly controls the I/O units and information passes through the CPU on the way between memory and I/O units, but in many systems I/O units are controlled by separate processors, naturally called I/O processors, as shown in Figure 1-3*a*. When

FIGURE 1-3 (*a*) Single processor with I/O processors; (*b*) multiprocessor system

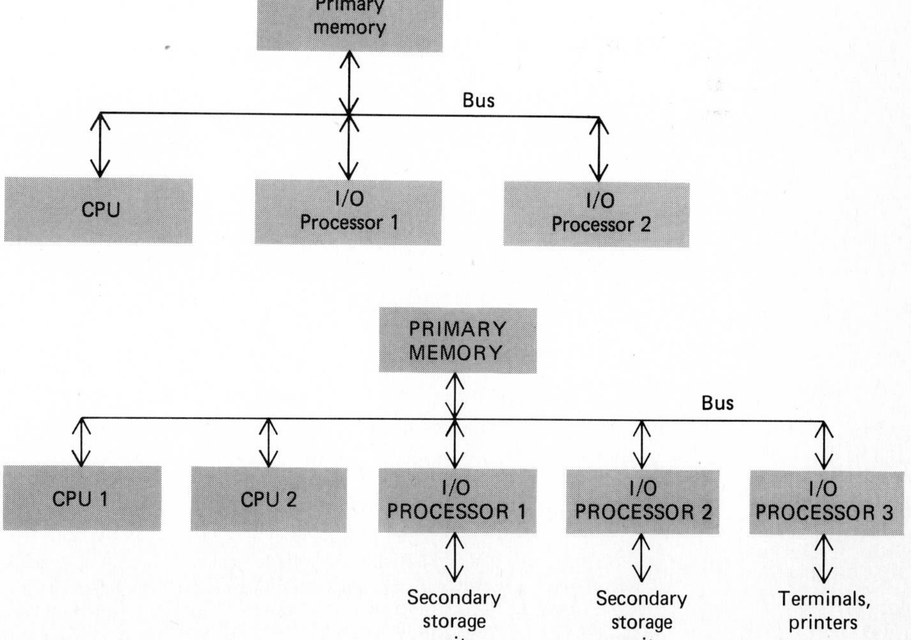

there is more than one processor in a system, it is possible for two or more processes to be executed simultaneously, perhaps one for computation and one for I/O. For example, many systems let a user request the printing of a file at the same time that another program is being executed. The former process is executed by an I/O processor, the latter by the CPU. Large systems often have more processors — several I/O processors and possibly more than one CPU, as shown in Figure 1-3*b*. In these systems, the various units are often interconnected by a *bus*, which is a set of wires along which data and control information can be passed between any pair of units connected by the bus. When there is more than one CPU, programs for more than one user can be processed at the same time, or a user's problem can be organized into more than one process that can be executed simultaneously. The latter requires careful partitioning of the data among the different processes to avoid conflict.

Some types of units connected to I/O processors are used to store large amounts of information for long periods of time. These units are called *secondary storage* units to distinguish them from the *primary storage* or *primary memory*.

The CPU, the primary memory, and their controls contain the hardware necessary to perform the arithmetic and logical operations on numeric and nonnumeric data. There are many different methods for performing these operations, but there are many similarities among different machines. For any given machine, there are a number of programming tricks that can be used to provide shortcuts. Some of these are deliberately built into the computer by the designer; others are "discovered" at a later date by programmers. Some of these tricks are important in the fast and effective programming of a given computer, whereas others are a hindrance, leading to code that is hard to follow and difficult to debug. These tricks are beyond the scope of this book, since they depend on the particular machine. They are best learned by direct experience. The theme of this book is that no one machine constitutes the "ultimate" in machine design. Each machine represents the idiosyncrasies and beliefs of one design team, with the result that some machine features may become drawbacks because of changing needs. However, there are many ideas common to all machines, and certain types of functional elements, such as adders and registers, are found in all computers. We shall discuss the various functional elements that make up a computer in order to trace the way in which instructions are executed by the hardware. However, this is not a text in machine design,[5] but rather a study of the interactions between computer organization and the design of programs.

Computers are frequently classified by their size. You will hear talk about largescale computers, minicomputers, and microcomputers. Large-scale computers frequently occupy one or more large rooms and provide service to a large number of users with diverse needs. Minicomputers are more frequently used by a few people, or they may be dedicated to a particular set of tasks, such as experimental process control and data gathering. Microcomputers occupy a very small space and are the basis for very small, usually single-user systems such as personal computers. However, in spite of the great

[5]If the student is particularly interested in this subject he may refer to such texts as T. C. Bartee, *Digital Computer Fundamentals*, 4th ed., McGraw-Hill Book Company, New York, 1977; D. Siewiorek, G. Bell, and A. Newell, *Principles of Computer Structures*, McGraw-Hill Book Company, New York, 1982; and A. S. Tannenbaum, *Structured Computer Organization*, Prentice-Hall, Englewood Cliffs, NJ, 1983.

difference in size, price, and speed (as much as 10,000 to 1) the underlying principles are the same—if you can drive a Volkswagen, you can drive a Rolls Royce!

The general ideas will be illustrated with examples drawn from a number of popular computers, both large-scale, mini, and micro. Many different microcomputers available today use the same type of central processor, called a *microprocessor*. One series of computers will be emphasized in this version of the text, the INTEL 8080 and its descendants, the Zilog Z80 and the INTEL 8088 and 8086. Many program examples will be written for the 8080, as these can be used directly on some of its descendants. (This is called *upward compatibility* by manufacturers. It is a way of introducing new equipment that can be used—and bought—by people with a heavy investment in programs for earlier computer models.) Other examples of programs will be taken from those written for the 8088. This is the microprocessor used in the IBM Personal Computer.

1.3 LANGUAGES FOR USING COMPUTERS AT DIFFERENT LEVELS

Many people use computers, but relatively few program them. For example, many automatic household gadgets, such as microwave ovens, video tape recorders, and video games, have built-in computers dedicated to a particular task. These are used by giving direct *commands* to the device, usually by pressing control buttons, just as a hand-held calculator is operated. In the same way, the travel agent uses a computer when commands are typed into a terminal to request information on flight availability, make reservations, etc. This is not programming, but the use of a computer by specifying only the task to be solved. The details of the method of solution are left to the device—the travel agent doesn't need to know how the reservation information requested is determined or updated when a reservation is made, and the video tape recorder user normally does not care how the recording mechanism functions. Strictly speaking, programming is the preparation of a sequence of steps yet to be carried out by a computer (or other device), although in popular usage the word "program" often encompasses the direct use of computers described above. In this section we will look briefly at the way computers are used, starting from direct usage and moving through various levels of programming.

Some devices, computer-controlled or otherwise, can only be used at a single level. The typical alarm clock, even though it may have a simple computer-like chip inside, permits only a few direct commands to set the clock and alarm times. However, some computer-controlled devices, and virtually all computers can be used at a number of levels. At the "highest" level, direct commands can be given. For video tape recorders, the commands are specified by pressing buttons; for terminals to an airline reservation system, they are specified by typing lines of characters. In either case, we can view them as statements in a *language* understood by the computer. Statements in this language specify the problem to be solved. We call such a language a *problem-oriented language*. At the next level, we may wish to specify a sequence of steps to be carried out—that is, we may want to specify a *procedure* for solving a problem. The language in which the sequence is specified is called a *procedure-oriented language*. In many cases, the individual steps in a procedure are not directly executable by the hardware, but are converted by the software system into longer sequences of basic steps in the machine. These longer sequences are in a language directly understandable to the machine; that language is called *machine-oriented language*. Thus there are three principal levels of computer language:

1 Problem-oriented
2 Procedure-oriented
3 Machine-oriented

At the highest level, the problem is described; at the next level, the method of solution is also described; at the bottom level, the detailed use of the machine is specified. As we progress to the lower levels, additional detail must be provided, so naturally we wish to stop at the highest level at which we can handle the job we want to do on a computer.

If a program has already been written to handle the job we want to do, we can use that program directly. All that is necessary is to provide the data. That data can be viewed as a description of the problem to be solved, that is, as a statement in a problem-oriented language. For example, if an instructor has written a program to add student scores on homework and exams, to rank order the students by total score for grade assignment purposes, and to print the class list in alphabetical order for use in record keeping, another instructor could use that program if it had been designed to work for a variety of class sizes, numbers of homework assignments, etc. The program would have to accept input describing the class size, scores, etc. An efficiently organized system makes it possible to share many programs in this way, so much processing can be done at the problem-oriented level.

A program of the type discussed in the previous paragraph can be called a problem-oriented language processor. Many very large, problem-oriented language processors have been written for frequently occurring tasks, such as structural analysis of airplanes, buildings, and bridges and the analysis of electrical circuits. The input language for these systems is very complex, as it must permit the description of a complete problem such as the design of a bridge. If a problem-oriented processor is not available or does not provide the options needed for a particular problem, it is necessary to drop to the next level, the procedural level. If, in the grading example given above, the program does not allow for certain options that the second instructor needs (for example, the ability to ignore the lowest of the homework grades), that second instructor will have to modify the program by specifying, in a procedure-oriented language, how to find the lowest homework grade and how to remove it from consideration. The only other reason for dropping to the procedural level is to overcome some deficiencies of the problem-oriented processor, such as its slowness. In a typical data processing environment found in business, the majority of computer jobs are handled by existing software. Unfortunately, even the best of computer systems has problem-oriented processors for only a few of the jobs that need to be done in a typical research environment, so many programmers are needed at the procedural level.

At the procedural level, jobs are specified as a sequence of steps. The sequence is called a procedure. The steps may be relatively elementary, or they may themselves involve the use of a problem-oriented processor. For example, a computer system may provide some commands that permit sets of data to be printed in a variety of formats or to be sorted according to various characteristics. Thus the system might permit the user to specify

```
PRINT <format specification> <name of set of data>
```

for printing, where "<format specification>" is a description of the printing format and "<name of set of data>" indicates where the data is located. We can view these descriptions as statements in a problem-oriented language. Sorting might be requested by entering

```
SORT <sorting description> <name of set of data>
```

in a similar way. The sequence

```
SORT ···
PRINT ···
```

is a simple program that prints a set of data in sorted form. Each statement in this program uses a rudimentary problem-oriented processor.

A flexible computer system permits the user to construct procedures as sequences of any operations available in the computer. It also provides some common procedural languages that are useful for particular classes of jobs. For example, it may provide BASIC, which is popular for elementary programming, Pascal, which is used in teaching computer science, FORTRAN, which is common in numerical scientific calculations, and COBOL, which is used in many commerical data processing applications. Almost any computer job could be specified in any one of these languages; the differences between them concern the ease with which tasks common to a particular area can be described. For example, very little knowledge is needed to write a simple BASIC program. Pascal, on the other hand, is far easier to use for the description of logically complex tasks. COBOL permits the description in a relatively simple way of jobs involving a large amount of input and output in complex formats. However, all these languages allow simple data manipulations to be expressed in a convenient manner. For example,

```
A = B * C + D
```

or something very similar can be written to cause the product of B and C to be added to the variable D and assigned to A in almost all procedural languages.

At the machine level, computer jobs are also specified as sequences of steps, but each step must take the form of one of the operations that can be executed directly by the hardware, such as an addition or comparison. For example, the machine may permit operations of the form

```
ADD B and C to get A
```

and

MULTIPLY D and E to get A

to be executed in single steps. A procedural language statement such as

A = B * C + D

must be converted into several machine-level steps, such as

MULTIPLY B and C to get A
ADD A and D to get A

Actual machine language consists of the internally coded form of these steps. The form we have written above is a form of assembly language. Programming in a procedural language is faster and easier than at machine level, although the resulting program may sometimes be slightly less efficient. However, the resulting loss of computer time is usually more than offset by the saving of people time. The vast majority of jobs can be adequately described in one of the common procedural languages, so there is seldom reason to drop down to the machine level. This is necessary only when those few parts of a job that cannot be handled with sufficient efficiency at the higher level must be programmed or when access to particular hardware operations not directly accessible via a procedural language is needed. Thus a typical job will not be programmed at the machine level, although a small section of it that is extremely time consuming might. Programs to, for example, print data in a variety of formats will be programmed at the procedural level, although the section of code called on by the procedural program to send the appropriate electrical signals to the ouput printer may be written at the machine level. This code however, is a part of the operating system available to all users. Therefore, relatively few people need to program at the machine level, although knowledge of the way the computer operates internally can be valuable in using the computer at any level.

1.3.1 Program Development and Style

A machine-level program can be written using very few different types of computer operations, but modern computer sytems contain a large variety of operations designed to make the program more efficient. A procedure-oriented language also provides many language constructs for expressing common actions such as loops, selection, and input-output (I/O). Again, a program could be written using very few different constructs, but the use of the variety available makes a program easier to write and understand. Consequently, there are many ways in which even a simple algorithm can be coded for a computer. When the number of different algorithms is also taken into account, we find a confusingly large number of programs that could be written to solve a single problem. One of these programs must be chosen—preferably the best program or a close approximation to it. Since computers exist to do a job (and not to test the ingenuity of programmers), the "best" solution is the solution that is most economical when all economic factors are taken into account.

Programming is often spoken of as an art whose works are judged, at least in part, subjectively. Such statements are made mainly because no way has yet been found to evaluate objectively all the criteria of an economical program. However, in the final analysis the value of the program depends on its cost, not its beauty. The programmer may easily be carried away by the fascination of the inner structure of a program, forgetting that the ultimate user of the program, who cares nothing about programming per se, is interested only in getting correct answers as rapidly and as inexpensively as possible.

The cost of a program is determined by a combination of many factors. In addition to the obvious costs of programming and execution, there are the costs of documentation and future changes. Almost no large program remains constant throughout its lifetime. Errors are found long after a program has been pronounced working, and additional functions invariably must be added to existing software. Many changes will be made after the original programmer has left, so that it must be possible for another programmer to understand the design and implementation of a program so that it can be updated. Therefore, the yardsticks by which a program must be measured include:

Programming time
Debugging time
Speed of execution
Size of program and data
Flexibility and expandability
Portability to other computers
Clarity
Documentation

At first sight, it may seem that we have listed these in order of importance. After all, the major concern to us, the programmers, is the time it takes us to get the program running. Next, we are certainly concerned about the speed of execution, and the space the program and its data will occupy in the computer will be an imporant economic factor in its extended use. However, we will immediately dismiss the speed and size questions from consideration. That is not to say they are not important, but the choice of the algorithm has far more effect on these properties than clever programming. *If we pay attention to the other considerations, the program is more likely to be fast and occupy a reasonable amount of space than if we concern ourselves solely with these questions*. The exceptions to such a sweeping statement include a few "key" subprograms used by large numbers of people. These may be part of the center of the operating system — the kernel — or simple library subroutines used by almost all other library subroutines, such as square root. Since such codes are used so frequently, their size and space are clearly the most critical considerations. However, they are so short that many of the other considerations are unimportant.

What about flexibility and expanability, that is, the freedom to use the program for a wide variety of problems and the ease with which it can be changed? If we want the program to be used by others, or by ourselves at a later time, to solve a problem similar to the one currently being solved, we should attempt to write a program that is as flexible as possible. Where it is pointless to provide additional features, because they are not needed for the current job, we should be careful to design the program in such a way that they can be added later.

What about portability—the ease with which a program can be moved to another computer or computer system? The computer we are using today will not be with us always, so we had better concern ourselves with this. At the machine level, it is unlikely that there will be much portability to other systems, except for those using identical processors. However, different installations with the same processors may not have the same I/O equipment, so we should write programs in which code dealing with particular devices is separated from the bulk of the code so that the former can be changed easily.

Now we come to clarity and documentation, two aspects that most beginning programmers ignore, although these are the keys to good programs—if a program is clear and well documented, it is easily changed and moved to another computer. Chances are that if it is slow, finding out why will be easy. Furthermore, a program is almost certain to be easier to program and debug if it is clear what everything does. Consequently, these are the most important aspects of a good program; if it has these characteristics, the others will follow. To obtain clarity and make documentation simple, we must develop a clear programming style that is easy to *apply* and *follow*. The key buzzwords[6] are

Top-down development: planning the method to be used first at a global level, then at the detailed level

Stepwise refinement: first expressing the program at a macroscopic level as a sequence of very high-level operations, then refining each macroscopic statement as a sequence of simpler statements

Structured programming: using a fairly rigid, carefully organized program structure whose form matches well with the program meaning

These are similar ideas that naturally augment each other. They are also a natural complement to the desire to program at the highest level practical. The first step in preparing a problem for a computer is to prepare a careful description of the problem. This requires a precise description of the initial data available (the input) and the final results needed (the output). This is the first level of development. If a problem-oriented language processor is available for the class of problem we have, the description of the problem can be prepared in that language and the problem will be ready for computer processing. If such a processor is not available, we must be concerned with determing a method for solving the problem. We can determine some intermediate results that would make the task easier, describe these (this is top-down development), and then describe the solution procedure as a sequence of steps proceeding from the initial input via the intermediate results to the final answer. This is the first level of refinement, expressing the job as a sequence of simpler jobs. In an earlier example, we expressed

[6]A buzzword is a word in the jargon of a subject that is currently in vogue but is vague and is frequently used solely to convince the reader of the writer's position in the forefront of the field.

the job "Print a set of data in sorted order" as the two steps "SORT" and "PRINT." Having done that, we can use available computer commands to sort and print, provided that the input data, intermediate results, and final results are compatible with the available commands. If suitable commands are not available, we must refine the program further by expanding each step after planning additional intermediate results. This process continues until the program is in a form that can be executed by a computer. Usually we can stop at the procedure-oriented language level, but occasionally some of the steps must be refined down to the machine-oriented level.

Each level of refinement replaces a single step in the program with a sub-sequence of simpler steps, suggesting that a program is a linear sequence of steps, which we know is not true in programs for most problems that require loops and selection among alternatives. However, we can introduce these constructs if we permit a single step to be refined to a loop around a single step or to a selection among alternate single steps. This is the simplest view of structured programming, that it is a style of programming in which the structure of the program at each stage in the refinement is a linear sequence of steps, where each step is either a simple action, a loop containing an action, or a selection among different actions. However, many writers have very strong opinions of just what structured programming involves, and these opinions are not always consistent. The person responsible for the principal ideas and name is Dijkstra, so a definition, if one is wanted, should properly be taken from his work,[7] which is a major contribution to the art of programming. The underlying concept is extremely important, referring to the use of rules of programming style that tend to make programs easier to write, debug, and change.[8]

1.4 PROCESSING THE PROGRAM

The programming process has been completed once the job has been described in a language acceptable to the system. From the user's viewpoint, this language is the language obeyed by the machine. The computer can be viewed as a processor that processes the steps in the program one at a time. Thus the process being executed is described by the program, and its state is determined by the values of any data used by the program and knowledge of the next step to be executed.

We saw in the previous section that the programming process will typically stop at the first level of refinement at which it is expressed in terms comprehensible to the computer system, although this is typically not a machine-oriented language but a procedure- or problem-oriented language. Since the computer cannot execute such programs directly but must use software that is part of its operating system to understand them, one of two things must happen: either the programs written by the user must be translated into a machine language (the actual language understood by the hardware) or each statement in the program must cause a particular program in the operating

[7]E. W. Dijkstra, "Notes on Structured Programming," in O-J Dahl, E. W. Dijkstra, and C. A. R. Hoare, *Structured Programming,* Academic Press, New York, 1972.

[8]Other books on program style that are important reading for every programmer are N. Wirth, *Systematic Programming: An Introduction,* Prentice-Hall, Englewood Cliffs, NJ, 1973; E. Yourdon and L. L. Constantine, *Structured Design,* Prentice Hall, Englewood Cliffs, NJ, 1979; and B. W. Kernighan and P. J. Plauger, *The Elements of Programming Style,* 2d ed., McGraw-Hill, New York, 1978.

system to be executed. The latter is the technique normally used when a simple program such as

```
SORT ···
PRINT ···
```

is executed by the computer. It is called *interpretation*. On the other hand, most of the common procedure-oriented language programs are translated into machine language by translation programs called *compilers*. Similarly, assembly-language programs are normally translated into machine language by a translator called an *assembler*. These translations could conceivably be done by a programmer, who would effectively be performing further stages of refinement, but it would be a tedious and error-prone task for a human and is precisely the type of task that computers can handle effectively. The program prepared by the programmer is called the *source program*. It is the input to a translator or interpreter. If it is translated, the resulting form output from the translator is called the *object program*. In some cases, different parts of the program are written in different languages. In this case the object code for each of the translated sections is combined with any required library programs and *loaded* into the computer memory. The first phase of the loading process, called *link-editing*, links together all of the elements of the job and assigns them space in the computer memory. Then the loader puts the resulting program in memory. In the final step the user program is executed, or processed, by the computer processor.

If parts of a job are interpreted rather than translated, the source language is read into memory and stored there. The statements in the source language are examined by the interpreter program one at a time and cause execution of appropriate programs in the computer system. The combination of the interpreter program and the machine simulates a machine that executes the source language directly.

The distinction between translation and execution on the one hand and interpretation on the other is not clear cut. We can draw a simile from the translation of natural languages. The translator is a professional language expert who accepts input in one language, say French, and produces output in another, say English. For example, if the text to be translated is in a technical field such as mathematics, the translator does not have to understand the text. That is read afterwards, by an English-speaking mathematician. If the mathematician wishes to reread a section for closer understanding, the already translated version can be reread. Interpretation, on the other hand, is similar to the work done by an English-speaking mathematician who can read English directly but to read French must first translate sentence by sentence, into English. If such a person attempts to read a mathematical work in French and wishes to reread a particular section, each sentence (statement) in the source language must be retranslated in order to reread. If the work is to be read just once, interpretation is as efficient and may have some advantages, because the interpreter can refer to the original source if questions arise. On the other hand, if the work is to be read many times, translation is more efficient.

In practice, both translation and interpretation are involved in reading a foreign-language book. In the same way, computer systems use a mixture of translation and interpretation to get the best balance of speed and flexibility.

1.5 OPERATING SYSTEM SOFTWARE: AN INTRODUCTION

The objective of an operating system is not only to make it possible to execute programs rapidly, but also to make it possible to prepare programs rapidly. The operating system is a set of programs that is in control of the system except when a user program is executing. During a typical interaction with a computer, the user issues commands to the operating system requesting it to perform actions on the user's behalf, such as to compile or assemble a program, to print a set of data, or to put a user or another system program into execution.

Files The operating system works with sets of data called *files*. A file could be a collection of input lines from a terminal or card reader or the set of output information generated during the execution of a program. In the course of an interaction with the computer, such files will be stored in the computer memory, usually on a secondary storage device such as a disk (to be described in a later chapter). Files may also be left on a disk or other secondary storage device between computer sessions. Files are given identifiers as names so that users can refer to them in the system commands. These identifiers are usually character strings, perhaps restricted to alphabetic and numeric characters, although some systems permit any printing characters to be used in file identifiers. (Nonprinting characters, including space, tab, and similar characters, are never allowed in identifier names.) For example, a file name could have the form MYPROG. The maximum length of the name (the maximum number of characters in the name) is usually restricted, but it may be unlimited.

Commands When a single-user system is turned on, the user has immediate access to the operating system. In a multiuser, timeshared system, the first action that a user must take is to *login* to the system. This is done in interaction with a system program called the login program. It asks for the programmer's name (or other identification) and a secret password. Only then does the system allow the user access to other operations.

The user is informed that the computer is ready for input by a *prompt*, which is one or more characters typed by the computer on the screen at the start of a line. For example, some systems issue the prompt

```
>
```

The user responds by typing a line containing a command. Each line input by the user is scanned by the operating system by means of a *command scanner*. In most cases, the computer does not examine the line until it has been completely typed and a carriage return has been typed.[9] A typical command format is

```
>command-name      operand(s)
```

[9]This allows the user to correct typing errors within one line by use of the backspace key and overtyping, and by use of characters that delete complete lines. Most systems use a number of the *control characters* for this. These are nonprinting characters input by pressing the *control key* at the same time another key is pressed. The control key is similar to a shift key, but it causes a different character to be sent to the computer. Systems interpret these control characters in various ways, although some are standard. For example, control-H is the same as backspace and control-I is the same as Tab.

Here we have assumed that the prompt character, ">", is typed by the system. The user types the rest of the line. The operands specify the data to be used by the command or where the results of the command are to be placed. The operands to commands are also called *arguments* to the commands. The command names are names of programs known to the system. These programs implement the commands. For example, there might be a command PRINT, so that typing

```
PRINT MYFILE
```

causes a system program named PRINT to be executed to print the file "MYFILE". The operands to system commands are usually the names of files of data, as in the PRINT example above.

Many of the operating system commands are concerned with manipulating files of data. For example, there are usually commands to do the following file maintenance operations:

```
Copy     file 1 to file 2
Delete   file(s)
Rename   file 1 to file 2
Print    file(s) (on a line printer)
Type     file(s) (on the terminal)
List the current file names (the directory of files)
Concatenate two or more files to get a single file
```

Examples of these commands in a typical system include

```
>COPY    MYPROG SAVEMYPROG
```

which creates a new file named SAVEMYPROG whose content is the same as that of MYPROG,

```
>ERASE   MYOLDPROG
```

which removes a file named MYOLDPROG from the disk or other secondary storage;

```
>RENAME  SAVEMYPROG MYOLDPROG
```

which changes the name of the file SAVEMYPROG to MYOLDPROG;

```
>DIR
```

which lists the *directory* of file names, that is, the list of files currently saved by this user; and

```
>CONCAT  PROG3 = PROG1, PROG2
```

which creates a new file, PROG3, consisting of PROG1 followed by PROG2.

Files are created in the first place by direct input of data from another source, by use of an editor, which is a program that permits the user to type information into a file and edit the previously typed information to make corrections, or by program generation of data at execution time. If, for example, a user has a set of data or a program on tape or cards from another computer, it is usually possible to read that information into the computer and store it in a file. Some operating systems have programs to do that job. Other systems use a scheme that permits input and output devices to be treated as files, so that a command such as

```
>COPY     CONSOLE  MYPROG
```

would read data from the device CONSOLE (which would be a reserved name) into a file named MYPROG. For example, if CONSOLE refers to the terminal (keyboard or screen for input or output, respectively), this command would read all subsequent information from the terminal keyboard into the file until an *end-of-file* character were typed. This is a special character. It varies from system to system. (Control-D or Control-Z are used in a number of systems.)

A system can contain a *subsystem* that can be brought into execution by issuing an appropriate command. This places the subsystem in control until the user *exits* to the main system. For example, many computer systems provide a BASIC subsystem for the BASIC language. In these systems, typing the command BASIC brings the BASIC subsystem into operation. The subsystem then interprets commands input by the user until the user exits from the subsystem back to the main system by means of a suitable command. In this type of system, the commands recognized by the various subsystems may be different from those recognized by the main system.

Some systems use file-naming conventions that are related to the use of a file. In these systems, the name of a file consists of two parts: a primary name and a suffix, or secondary name. The secondary name indicates the type of use and is usually separated from the name with a period. Thus, if assembly-language files have the suffix ASM, a file name might take the form MYPROG.ASM if it consists of assembly language statements. In such a system, the assembler might require all files that are to be assembled to have this suffix, whereas a compiler such as Pascal might require all Pascal programs to use the suffix PAS.

Typical operating systems include translators for a number of languages. These convert files in the source language to files in the object language. The file containing the source program consists of a sequence of lines, each line containing a step in the program. For example, if an assembly-language program includes

```
        MPY     A, B, C
        ADD     A, D, A
```

meaning "Multiply B by C and put the result in A" followed by "Add D to A, putting the result back in A," the assembler translates these lines to object language form and puts the result in another file called the object file. The user must prepare a file containing the assembly language program and assemble the file by issuing a command of the form

```
>ASMBL    MYPROG
```

If the system expects file names for assembly to have the suffix ASM, this command will cause the information in file MYPROG.ASM to be assembled. The result would be put in another file, perhaps named MYPROG.OBJ.

The object file will not yet be ready for execution, but must be *loaded*. Therefore, a system includes commands for loading. If the system uses suffixes on file names to indicate file use, a command such as

```
>LOAD     MYPROG
```

will load a file named MYPROG.OBJ, assuming that it contains the output of an assembly (or other translator). The loading program creates a file that is ready to be executed as a program, typically under another name, such as MYPROG.EX (indicating an executable file). All that remains to be done is to tell the operating system that the program should be executed. In many systems it suffices to type the name of the program itself, namely MYPROG, to cause execution of MYPROG.EX.

Thus we see that the sequence of commands

```
>ASMBL    MYPROG
>LOAD     MYPROG
>MYPROG
```

might be sufficient to assemble, load, and execute a program named MYPROG. Note that if the system permits files named <name>.EX to be executed by entering nothing but <name>, the identifier <name> in effect becomes another command, a command that causes the execution of a user-written program rather than a system program.

We have discussed a system in which suffixes on the file names determine the type of file. In these systems, commands to assemble and load can be provided with the first part of a file name and can create as many files as needed for different uses. For example, an assembler may have one input file, suffix ASM, and create two output files, suffix OBJ for the object and suffix LST for a listing file. (A listing from an assembler is a copy of the source program, perhaps with some additional information from the translator, such as error messages.) Other systems use a prefix rather than a suffix, but the principles are identical. Some systems do not use either, but require the user to provide file names for every file used. In such systems, the assemble command may require three file names: a source, an object, and a listing file. In some cases the names can be omitted and a *default* file can be used, either one with a fixed name such as OBJECT or a *null file*, which means that the particular output is discarded, as might be desired in the case of an assembler listing.

File names are kept in a directory that is itself stored on disk and is, therefore, a file. As a file it has a name, and some systems let the user refer to the directory directly by name. In such systems it is possible to have more than one directory of files, each containing different files. The user can then group files into directories according to the use of the files or any other arrangement valuable to the user.

Systems that permit multiple directories have a *current directory*, which is the one in current use, and a *home directory*, which is the one current when the user first logs in. File names given with no other qualifications are assumed to be in the current directory. System commands allow the user to change the current directory. However, that is not sufficient, as, on occasion, the user must refer to files in different directories in the same command. For example, suppose that the file SOURCE is to be copied from the directory COMPILER into a directory called BACKUP under the file name OLD-SOURCE. In this case, *path names* must be used to indicate the path to the files. Path names are constructed by concatenating the directory name with the file name to specify how to get the actual file from the current directory. A character is placed between the file names to indicate this concatenation. The character used depends on the system. Among the characters used on different systems are ":", ">", and "/". Path names for the example above are COMPILER/SOURCE and BACKUP/OLDSOURCE if "/" is the character used. The copy command to make the copy would be

```
>COPY     COMPILER/SOURCE      BACKUP/OLDSOURCE
```

If the current directory contains a file, it is not necessary to specify a path name for that file, so that, for example, if SOURCE is in the current directory, the foregoing command could be written

```
>COPY     SOURCE               BACKUP/OLDSOURCE
```

Batch Systems The discussion above has centered on interactive systems. Historically, batch systems were developed first, but today it is simpler to view a batch system as a special case of an interactive system in which all system commands are prepared ahead of time and then submitted in a single *batch* for processing by the system. Modern systems make little distinction between the commands executed in batch mode and those executed in interactive mode.

1.5.1 An Introduction to the CP/M Operating System

CP/M is a popular operating system for microcomputers. It is available for many different systems, in particular for most INTEL 8080- and ZILOG Z80-based systems. We will illustrate some operating system features in the CP/M system. Details can be found in the supplier's manual[10] as well as in a number of other publications, such as those by Hogan and Zaks.[11, 12]

Files in CP/M have two-part names: a one- to eight-character primary name and a zero- to three-character secondary name. None of the characters may be < > . , ; : ? * [ ], although it is usually better to restrict names to alphabetic and numeric characters entirely. The form of a name is PPPPPPPP.SSS where PPPPPPPP is the primary name and SSS is the secondary name. If the secondary name has no characters, the period

[10]*An Introduction to CP/M Features and Facilities,* Digital Research, Pacific Grove, CA, 93950.
[11]Thom Hogan, *CP/M User Guide,* Osborne/McGraw-Hill, New York, 1982.
[12]Rodnay Zaks, *The CP/M Handbook with MP/M,* Sybex, Berkeley, CA, 1980.

can be omitted. The secondary name is used to indicate the type of file in some cases (for example, as input to the assembler), but it is not required in all cases. In the standard system, types include ASM (assembler input), HEX (hexadecimal object code generated by the assembler), and PRN (a printer file produced by the assembler for listing purposes).

A typical 8080-based system running under CP/M has one or more disk drives. They are named A, B, C, . . . , up to P, for a maximum of sixteen drives. When the computer is started, drive A is automatically selected and remains the *default* drive until another is selected. We can think of the file system on drive A as the home directory for the user. Selecting another drive is equivalent to changing directories to the one on the new drive. When the system is ready for a command to be typed, it prompts the user with a line

```
A>
```

The initial A indicates that drive A is the current default drive. If the user responds by typing, for example, D:, followed by a carriage return, drive D becomes the default drive and the prompt becomes D>. In the sample commands below, we will assume that the default drive is A. If the user wants to access a drive for a specific file, the file name can be preceded by the drive name and a semicolon. For example, C:MYPROG.ASM refers to file MYPROG.ASM on drive C. Thus CP/M allows a path name consisting of exactly two components: drive name followed by file name.

The user can type any command after the prompt. Until the carriage return is typed, the command is not examined by the system. Until that time, several control characters can be used to edit the line to correct errors. Backspace moves the cursor backwards and erases the last character typed. Rubout (called "delete" on some terminals) has a similar effect on the typed information, but it doesn't backspace; rather it echos the previous character a second time. Control-U deletes the whole line typed thus far, so that the line can be retyped from the start.

After a complete line has been typed, it is examined by the CP/M command processor. Commands that deal with disk files include

DIR	List the file names in the directory
ERA	Erase (delete) a file from the directory
REN	Rename a file in the directory
TYPE	Type the content of a file on the terminal
SAVE	Save an area of primary memory as a disk file

Because each drive has its own directory, DIR lists the file names on the current drive unless an argument x: is given, where x is one of the letters A to P corresponding to an active drive. Use of a drive name as a prefix to a file name does not change the default drive, so that future file names without a drive name prefix continue to refer to the old default drive. Thus

```
A>ERA      C:OLDPROG.PRN
```

deletes the file OLDPROG.ASM on disk drive C, but leaves the current disk at A.

REN renames a file using the syntax REN newfilename = oldfilename. A drive name may be given, but if it is given for both files it must be the same, as the file cannot be moved by this operation. TYPE simply types a file at the console. Thus

```
A>TYPE     E:ABC.PRN
```

types the file ABC.PRN from drive E.

Other commands in CP/M are connected with processing the data in files. ASM assembles a file. The command

```
A>ASM      PROGAB
```

assembles the program in file PROGAB.ASM on disk drive A.

This creates two new files, a listing in file PROGAB.PRN and an object in file PROGAB.HEX. The latter can be loaded using the command

```
A>LOAD     PROGAB
```

which leaves the binary form in file PROGAB.COM. The program can then be executed by the command PROGAB (the suffix COM is not necessary). Thus PROGAB becomes a new command in the system. Any of these file names can be preceded with a drive name in the usual way.

The command PIP (Peripheral Interchange Program) invokes the PIP subsystem, which allows the copying and concatenation of files and the movement of data between files and I/O devices. PIP has its own set of commands. PIP can be invoked to execute a single command by entering

```
A>PIP command
```

which causes the PIP command to be executed.

The form of a PIP command is

```
<destination>=<source.1>,<source.2>,···,<source.n>
```

where the destination and each source is the name of either a file or one of the recognized I/O devices. The source files are concatenated and placed in the destination. Thus

```
A>PIP B:PROG.ASM=C:PROG.BAK
```

copies file PROG.BAK on drive C to a new file named PROG.ASM on drive B. The PIP system can be entered by simply typing the command PIP with no arguments. Thereafter, PIP commands can be typed, one to a line, until an empty line (that is, nothing but a carriage return) is typed. The empty line is a command that exits (returns control to the outer level of CP/M). While the PIP subsystem is in control, the prompt character is "*". Thus the sequence

```
A>PIP
*BOTH.XXX=ABC.PRN, DEF.PRN
*B:ALL.XXX=BOTH.XXX, GHJ.PRN
*(carriage return)
```

has the result of first concatenating files ABC.PRN and DEF.PRN and putting the result in file BOTH.XXX, all on the default drive, and then making file ALL.XXX on drive B equal to BOTH.XXX followed by GHJ.PRN from the default drive.

I/O devices are referenced using the names

```
CON:        Console
RDR:        Reader
PUN:        Punch
LST:        Printer
PRN:        Printer (but tab characters are expanded to spaces)
```

The precise nature of these devices depends on the units attached to the system. However, the CP/M system takes care of the minor differences, so that these names can be used in place of file names in PIP commands. For example,

```
A>PIP PRN:=MYPROG.ASM
```

sends a copy of the file MYPROG.ASM from the default drive to the printer, thus listing it, whereas

```
A>PIP B:NEWFILE=CON:
```

reads from the console keyboard to the file NEWFILE on drive B. After such a command has been typed, all characters typed on the keyboard except for the special control characters are sent to the file NEWFILE. This process stops when the *end-of-file* character, control-Z, is typed. For example, the lines

```
A>PIP C:MYPROG=CON:
Now is the time for
all good persons to
come to the aid of the computer.
Control-Z
```

will cause the file MYPROG on disk C to be created, consisting of the three lines of text shown above.

1.5.2 An Introduction to DOS for the IBM PC

DOS, the Disk Operating System, is an operating system for the IBM Personal Computer. We will illustrate some operating system features in the DOS system. Details can be found in the supplier's manual.[13] Files in DOS have two-part names: a one- to eight-character primary name and a zero- to three-character secondary name, also called an *extension*. Names can consist of alphabetic and numeric characters and some special characters, although it is usually better to restrict names to alphabetic and numeric characters entirely. The form of a name is PPPPPPPP.SSS, where PPPPPPPP is the primary name and SSS is the secondary name. If the secondary name has no characters, the period can be omitted. The secondary name is used to indicate the type of file in some cases (for example, as input to the assembler), but it is not required in all cases. In the standard system, types include ASM (assembler input), OBJ (object code generated by assembler), and LST (a printer file produced by the assembler for listing purposes). The names CON, AUX, COM1, LPT1, PRN, and NUL may not be used as file names because they are reserved as the names of devices or special files.

A typical IBM PC running under DOS has one or two disk drives; they are named A and B. When the computer is started, drive A is automatically selected and remains the default drive until another is selected. We can think of the file system on drive A as the home directory for the user. Selecting another drive is equivalent to changing directories to the one on the new drive. When the system is ready for a command to be typed, it prompts the user with the line

```
A>
```

The initial A indicates that drive A is the current default drive. If the user responds by typing "B:" followed by a carriage return, drive B becomes the default drive and the prompt becomes B>. If the user wants to access a drive for a specific file, the file name can be preceded by the drive name and a semicolon. For example, B: MYPROG.ASM refers to file MYPROG.ASM on drive B. Thus DOS allows a path name consisting of exactly two components: drive name followed by file name.

The user can type any command after the prompt; until the ENTER key is typed, the command is not examined by the system. (The ENTER key is equivalent to the carriage return key found on many terminals and is in about the same position.) Until that time, several control characters can be used to edit the line to correct errors. Backspace (labeled ← on the keyboard) moves the cursor backwards and erases the last character typed. ESC (escape) deletes the whole line typed thus far, so that the line can be retyped from the start. Other editing commands make it possible to correct any character in the line before it is processed as a command. Details are discussed later in this chapter.

[13] "*Disk Operating System*," IBM Personal Computer, Personal Computer Language Series, IBM, Boca Raton, FL, 1981.

After a complete line has been typed, it is examined by the DOS command processor. Commands that deal with disk files include

DIR	List the file names in the current directory
ERASE	Erase (delete) a file from the directory
RENAME	Rename a file in the directory
TYPE	Type the content of a file on the terminal
COPY	Copy one file to another

Because each drive has its own directory, DIR lists the file names on the current drive unless an argument x: is given, where x is one of the letters A or B, corresponding to an active drive. Use of a drive name as a prefix to a file name does not change the default drive, so that future file names without a drive name prefix continue to refer to the old default drive. Thus

```
A>ERASE    B:OLDPROG.ASM
```

deletes the file OLDPROG.ASM on disk drive B, but leaves the current disk at A.

RENAME renames a file using the syntax

```
A>RENAME         oldfilename newfilename
```

A drive name may be given for the old file, but the file cannot be moved by this operation in such a way that the new file will not be on the same drive. TYPE simply types a file at the console. Thus

```
A>TYPE    B:ABC.LST
```

types the file ABC.LST from drive B.

The COPY command has two arguments: the old file name and the new file name. For example,

```
A>COPY    B:MYPROG.ASM YOURPROG
```

copies file MYPROG.ASM on drive B into file YOURPROG (with no extension) on drive A. Either of the file names can be one of the reserved names

CON:	Console
NUL:	Nothing (a permanently empty file)
PRN:	Printer
LPT1:	Also the printer
AUX:	A device connected to a communication line
COM1:	The same device

The colon following the name is optional. The precise nature of these devices depends on the units attached to the system. These names can be used in place of file names in the COPY command. For example,

```
A>COPY     MYPROG.ASM PRN
```

sends a copy of the file MYPROG.ASM from the default drive A to the printer, thus listing it, whereas

```
A>COPY     CON B:NEWFILE
```

reads from the console keyboard to the file NEWFILE on drive B. After such a command has been typed, all characters typed on the keyboard except for the special control characters are sent to the file NEWFILE. This process stops when the *end-of-file* character, control-Z, is typed. For example, the lines

```
A>COPY     CON B:MYFILE
Now is the time for
all good persons to
come to the aid of the computer.
Control-Z
```

will cause the file MYFILE on disk B to be created, consisting of the three lines of text shown above.

Other commands in DOS are concerned with processing the data in files. ASM assembles a file. The command

```
A>ASM     PROGAB
```

assembles the program in file PROGAB.ASM on disk drive A.

This can create several new files, depending on additional input that will be requested from the user. Normally, an object file is created in PROGAB.OBJ. The user has the option of changing this because the assembler outputs the line

```
Object filename [PROGAB.OBJ]:
```

If the user responds by pressing the ENTER key, the name in brackets is the one used. Alternatively, the user can specify a different name. If no extension is given, the default extension OBJ is provided; otherwise the one specified is used. A listing is available if wanted, but is not normally saved. The assembler outputs

```
Source listing [NUL.LST]:
```

If the user presses ENTER, the listing is sent to the NUL file, which is the system name for a bottomless pit—that is, the listing is discarded. If the user wishes to get a listing, a file name must be specified in response to this output line. The extension LST is provided by the system unless the user overrides it. A fourth file called a cross-reference file can also be generated if needed. It contains some information about variable names used in the program and will be discussed in a later chapter.

After a file has been translated, it can be combined with other files for loading by using the command

```
A>LINK
```

This program requests the names of the file(s) to be loaded and the name of the final executable file. If we had previously produced a translated file in PROGAB.OBJ, we could respond to the request for "Object Modules" with the name PROGAB. Then we would be asked for the "Run File," to which request we can reply with any file name. This name is given the extension .EXE. This is the file that will be executable when the link (loading) process has been completed. The LINK program will also ask for other information, which we can ignore initially by pressing ENTER in response to each question. Any of these file names can be preceded with a drive name in the usual way. The final run file (which contains our program ready for execution) can be executed by typing its name without the .EXE suffix.

1.6 AN INTRODUCTION TO EDITORS

An editor is a program that allows the user to modify the content of a text file. The reader should use a particular editor to understand the details of its use, as different editors implement the operations in different ways. In this section we will discuss a few of the ideas underlying editors and take a brief look at editors provided with CP/M and DOS.

The types of operations allowed in an editor include:

Insert new information typed on the keyboard.
Delete existing information.
Move information from one place to another.
Search for particular information.
Change information.

These operations work entirely on the content of a single file. In addition, there may be operations that allow the contents of other files to be involved. These operations include:

Write part of the current file being edited into another file.
Read all or part of another file into a position in the current file.

As indicated above, editors operate on a particular file, called the current file. The version that is being modified is usually a copy of the current file, so that if unwanted changes are made, the prior version is still available. During the editing process, the copy is updated, and when the user wishes to finish the editing process, the original version can be replaced by the copy. In some editors, the original version is automatically saved as a backup file, perhaps under the name <filename>.BAK, where

<filename> is the first part of the name of the file being modified. In other systems, it is the responsibility of the user to first make a copy of the original file before it is modified if it is thought wise to keep a copy (as it is if major changes are to be made).

An editing operation consists of a number of parts, much like an operating system command. These parts are the operation, where it should be performed, and other data. For example, if the operation is to delete a line, the line to be deleted must be specified. If some data is to be inserted after a given line, the operation, the line, and the data must be specified. If a set of lines is to be moved, the operation, the range of lines involved, and the place to move it to must be specified.

There are a number of editors in popular use, and they can be classified into two general categories: line-oriented editors and screen-oriented editors. In a line-oriented editor, the file being modified is thought of as a set of lines, and the user can "address" any line or set of lines. In a screen-oriented editor, the display screen can be thought of as a window on the file. The window can be moved around to different positions in the file, so that the user can see what is in the file "through" the window. A VDU screen has a cursor (it is usually a flashing box, underline, or inverted-color character) that indicates a position on the screen. As the user moves the screen cursor around, its position indicates a corresponding position in the text file. Changes can be made at the cursor position, and those changes are displayed on the screen at the same time they are stored in the file. The underlying principle of a screen-oriented editor is "What you see is what you get." At all times, the window displays exactly what is in the file under the window. Many line-oriented editors have a concept similar to the cursor position called the current line or current character pointer. This is a position in the text file remembered by the editor and is the place in the file at which the next change will be made unless the user specifies otherwise.

Some editors, typically line-oriented editors, have two or more *modes*. In the *command mode,* input from the user is interpreted as a command to the editor. One or more of the commands, such as the Insert command, switch the system to the *input mode,* in which all input is entered directly into the file until a special end of input is encountered. This end of input might be a control character, such as end-of-file; a blank line; or a line that does not appear in typical text, such as a line with nothing but a period in column 1. Once the end of input has been sensed, the editor is back in the command mode.

Line-oriented editors allow individual lines to be addressed. The simplest form of address is numeric. The lines in the file are numbered, and a specific line can be indicated by its numeric address. A range of lines can be indicated either by the address of the first and last lines or by the address of the first line and the number of lines involved. Two types of numeric address have been used in editors: fixed line numbers and relative line numbers. Fixed line numbers do not change unless the user makes a change. Relative line numbers give the position of the line within the file, so that the number of a given line will change whenever the number of preceding lines is altered. For example, if the user refers to the seventy-third line of the file and then deletes line 72, the line previously referred to as line 73 will become the new line 72.

Early editors, especially those used in BASIC language subsystems, use the fixed line number technique. They assign a line number to each line in the file at the time it is generated. The numbers are attached to the line permanently and can be used to reference the line. For example, the lines

```
250 LET A = 3
260 INPUT B
280 PRINT A, B, A + B
```

might be input. The line numbers 250, 260, and 280 are now allocated to these lines. Line 260 can be deleted by specifying the delete command and the line number 260. The lines in the file are ordered by line number, but the numbers do not have to be contiguous, so that it is possible to insert a line between any two lines by assigning it a number between the numbers of the two lines. A RENUMBER command allows all of the lines to be renumbered when there are no longer enough spaces between the existing numbers.

Most current line-oriented editors use relative line numbers. The user can specify a line by its relative number and then specify an operation to be done on it. To illustrate, in the UNIX editor *ed,* the command d means "delete the current line," so 34d means "go to line 34 and delete the current line" (that is, delete line 34).

Ranges of lines in editors are usually indicated by two line numbers. For example, the UNIX *ed* command

```
34,67m105
```

moves all lines from 34 to 67 inclusive. The line number 105 following the m command indicates that the moved lines should be placed after line 105 (the numbering referring to the state of the file before any movements are made).

Editors that use relative line numbers often allow the current line pointer to be named in a command. In many editors, its name is the period character, so that a command such as

```
.,105d
```

means to delete all lines from the current line to line 105 inclusive.

When the user works with more than one editing system, it is wise to be aware of differences in interpretation of similar-looking commands. For example, in some editors, a range is indicated by a construct of the form 34:67 (lines 34 to 67), and in those editors the construct 34,67 might mean "starting at line 34 for 67 lines."

An important feature of editors is the ability to search for specified information. For example, if the user notices that there is a misspelled symbol (for example, COEFICENT) in a program that must be changed (to COEFFICIENT), a search command is a fast way to find it. (A misspelled symbol is of no concern to an assembler or compiler, but all uses of a symbol should involve the same spelling!) A search command looks for a specified *string* of characters and moves the current pointer to that position. In this example, the string COEFICIENT could be the *object* of the search, although the shorter string EFI might be sufficient to find it alone. (The string COEF would not work because all correct spellings would also be located.) An important adjunct to the search command is the string replace command. This command accepts two strings: the search string and the replacement string. The search string is located (if present), removed from the text, and replaced with the replacement string. For example, we might replace EFI with EFFI to correct the spelling of COEFICIENT. Search commands can usually be constrained to work on a single line, over a range of lines, or even over the whole file. If, for example, the user wants to replace all instances of the symbol XCOEF with ZCOEF, such a *global* string replacement could be used. However, care has to be taken, because in such a change the symbol MAXCOEF would be changed to MAZCOEF. Some editors are sensitive to the syntax of the material being edited. In such editors the problem above can be avoided by requesting that only *symbols* named XCOEF be changed.

Screen-oriented editors do not usually have modes, but interpret all control characters as commands. In these editors, entering printing characters and the *white space* characters such as space, tab, and carriage return from the keyboard causes the characters to be inserted directly into the file at the current cursor position. Usually the screen is split into a command area and one or more *windows*. (If multiple windows are permitted, each window may give a view of a different file). The command area is used to communicate with the user and to display the current command.

Some editors provide additional features that permit the user to write short sequences of editor commands and execute them repeatedly, like small programs. For example, a user might need to find all lines that start with the word Tab, delete the word Tab, and join those lines to their previous lines. Such operations are very tedious by hand; some editors permit them to be done with a single line of input.

1.6.1 The CP/M Editor

The CP/M editor is invoked by executing

```
A>ED <filename>
```

If the file name does not exist, it is created; otherwise the file of that name is prepared for reading by the editor. Because this system is designed for microcomputers with small primary memories and slow disks, the whole of a file is not accessible to the editor at any particular time unless it is a small file. Instead, a part of the old file is copied into a *memory buffer,* as shown in Figure 1-4. When the user is happy with the changes to that part, lines from the beginning of the buffer can be copied out to a temporary file and new lines can be brought in from the old file. The A command (Append) is used to bring lines in from the old file, and the W command is used to write them out to the temporary file. Thus, 40A reads the next 40 lines from the old file to the end of the memory buffer, whereas 20W writes the next 20 lines out from the memory buffer to the temporary file. The E command (End) completes the edit, moving the rest of the lines from the buffer and the old file to the temporary file. If the name of the old file being edited were EXAMP.TYP, the temporary file would be named EXAMP.$$$, that is, the name would consist of the primary name and a secondary

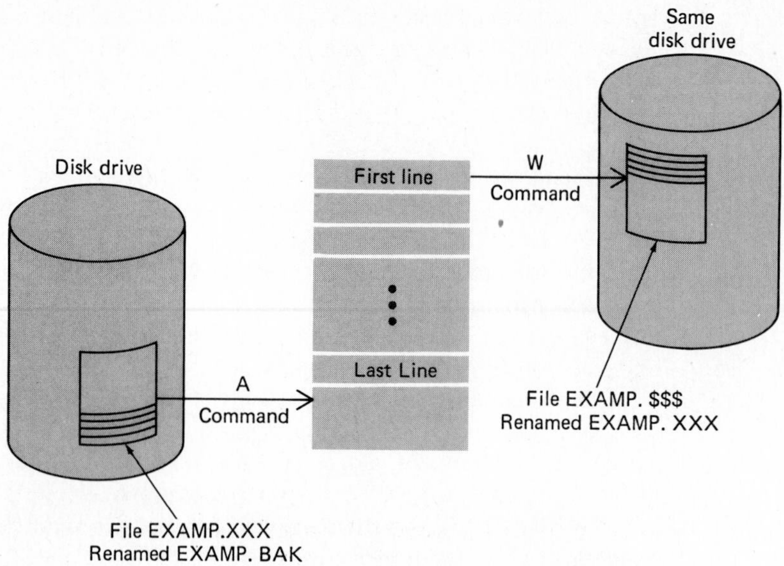

FIGURE 1-4 Use of temporary files and memory buffer in CP/M and DOS editors

name consisting of three dollar signs. At the end of an edit, the secondary name of the old file is changed to BAK, so that the old file's name would be EXAMP.BAK in this example. If there were already a filed named EXAMP.BAK, it would first be deleted. The temporary file assumes the name of the old file, EXAMP.TYP in this case, at the end of the edit.

Within the memory buffer, the user has a fairly conventional line-oriented editor. The commands are single letters preceded by an optional signed integer indicating the number of characters or lines involved. There is a current character position pointer that can be placed between any pair of adjacent characters on any line. The current position can be moved back or forward by a number of characters (C) or a number of lines (L). Thus 5L or +5L moves the current position forward five lines to the beginning of the fifth line, whereas −3L moves it to the beginning of the line three lines earlier and 7C moves the current position seven character positions forward. (The end of a line has two characters, carriage return and line feed, which must be counted in such a move.) Any number of lines before or after the current position can be typed (T) or deleted (K), and any number of characters before or after the current position can be deleted (D). For example, 3K deletes the rest of the current line from the current position on, plus the next two lines, whereas −2K deletes the characters before the current position in the current line and the preceding line.

The editor has an input mode that is entered with the I command. After the I command, further input is placed immediately before the current position. All input is placed into the memory buffer until the end-of-file (control-Z) is typed. This returns the editor to the command mode.

The search command F (Find) takes the form

$$\text{nF}c_1c_2 \ldots c_k$$

which searches the memory buffer for the *n*th occurence of the *k* character string $c_1c_2 \ldots c_k$, starting from the current position. The N command is similar, but searches through the whole file, moving additional lines into the buffer from the old file and from the memory buffer to the temporary file as necessary. The string replace command is S. It takes the form

```
nS<string1><end-of-file><string2>
```

which locates the next *n* occurrences of <string1> and replaces them with <string2>.

A single command line can contain a sequence of individual commands. This sequence can then be repeated a number of times by prefixing the line with the *n*M command, which executes the rest of the line *n* times. For example,

5M1L1K

deletes the lines 2, 4, 6, 8, and 10 from the current position. It does this by repeating the 1L1K sequence five times. 1L moves the current position forward to the beginning of the next line, and 1K deletes one line.

Any numeric value in a command can be replaced with the # character. It is interpreted as the integer 65,535 ($2^{16} - 1$), which is effectively infinity. Thus #A reads all of the old file into the memory buffer (if there is space), whereas the command

```
#M2A1L1K1W
```

given immediately after the editor has been entered will delete every second line starting from line 2 in the whole file—it moves two lines from the old file to the memory buffer (2A), moves the current position down one line (1L), deletes a line (1K), and then writes the first line (1W). This is repeated until the old file has been emptied (#M).

Text from another file can be copied into the file being edited by using the R command. R<filename> copies all the content of a file named <filename>.LIB at the current position. (This is intended to be used for inserting library code into a program being written; hence the suffix.)

1.6.2 The DOS Editor for the IBM PC

The DOS editor, EDLIN, is invoked by executing

```
A>EDLIN    <filename>
```

If the file name does not exist, it is created; otherwise the file of that name is prepared for reading by the editor. The whole file is not accessible to the editor at any given time, unless it is a small file. Instead, a part of the old file is copied into a *memory buffer* when the user wants to modify it, as shown in Figure 1-4. When the user is happy with the changes to that part, lines from the beginning of the buffer can be copied out to a temporary file and new lines can be brought in from the old file. The A command

(Append) is used to bring lines in from the old file, and the W command is used to write them out to the temporary file. The A command copies lines from the old file until the memory buffer is 75 percent full. This normally leaves enough space for the user to insert additional material. If the memory buffer fills up, lines can be written to the temporary file with the W command, which moves information until the memory is only 25 percent full. The user can also control the number of lines appended (A) or written (W) by specifying the number involved in front of the command. Thus 40A reads the next 40 lines from the old file, whereas 20W writes the first 20 lines out to the temporary file.

The E command (End) completes the edit, moving the rest of the lines from the buffer and the old file to the temporary file. If the name of the old file being edited were EXAMP.TYP, the temporary file would be named EXAMP.$$$, that is, the name consists of the primary name with a secondary name consisting of three dollar signs. At the end of an edit, the secondary name of the old file is changed to BAK, so that the old file's name would be EXAMP.BAK in this example. If there were already a file named EXAMP.BAK, it would first be deleted. The temporary file assumes the name of the old file, EXAMP.TYP in this case, at the end of the edit. The Q (Quit) command terminates the editing without rewriting any files, so that any changes made are lost.

Within the memory buffer the user has a fairly conventional line-oriented editor. The commands are single letters preceded by an optional signed integer indicating the number of lines involved. There is a current line position pointer that can be placed at the start of any line or at the end of the file. Its name is the period character. Lines can be printed at the terminal with the List command L. Thus

```
10,25L
```

types the lines from line number 10 to 25 inclusive, whereas 15L starts typing at line 15 for 23 lines (a full screen for a typical monitor). The command L without any line numbers prints from 11 before to 11 after the current position. Lines can be deleted using the D command. Thus 23D deletes line 23, whereas 11,17D deletes lines 11 through 17 inclusive.

The editor has an input mode that is entered with the I command. After the I command, further input is placed immediately before the current line position. When the I command is preceded by a line number, the insert lines appear before the old line with that number; in other words, for the first line entered the line number will be specified in front of the command. Thus

```
21I
Some new lines
go in here
control-Z
```

causes the two lines to be placed in the file with line numbers 21 and 22, respectively. (If there were less than twenty lines in the file before the change, the new lines would be put on the end.) All input is placed in the edited file until the end-of-file (control-Z) is typed. This returns the editor to the command mode.

Intraline editing, that is, making changes within a single line, is performed by entering a line number with no other information. This causes the contents of that line to be printed on the screen followed by a line with just the line number. For example, if line 5 contains "Now is the time", the command

5 (ENTER)

causes

5:*Now is the time
5:*

to appear on the screen. (The "*" indicates that 5 is the current line.) The *function* keys, F1 to F5, the INS (insert) key, and the DEL (delete) keys can be used to move characters from the upper line, called the *template*, to the lower line. Key F1 moves one character down from the template to the lower line. DEL skips over one character in the template without changing the lower line. INS permits characters to be typed from the keyboard into the lower line until INS is pressed again. F2 followed by a character—say, "x"—copies characters from the template to the lower line until the first "x" character. F4 skips characters in the same way. F3 causes the remaining characters in the template to be copied to the lower line. Pressing ENTER replaces line 5 (in this example) with the content of the lower line, that is, with the edited form. (If ENTER is pressed before any editing of the template has been done, the line is not changed.) If the line needs to be edited further, key F5 can be pressed instead of ENTER. This moves the lower line into the template position for further editing.

The intraline editing described above can also be used to correct any line entered into the terminal under the control of DOS. If, after a command has been typed, key F5 is pressed instead of ENTER, the line is placed in the template position and the same editing operations can be performed.

The search command S takes the form

line1,line2?S$c_1c_2 \ldots c_k$

which searches the memory buffer for the next occurrence of the k character string $c_1c_2 \ldots c_k$ starting from the line1. If line1 is not given, the start of the file is assumed. The search continues until the string is found or line2 is reached. If line2 is not given, the search continues to the end of the file if the string is not found earlier. The "?" character is optional. If it is not present, the search stops at the first occurrence. If it is present, the user is queried to see whether this is the desired occurrence. An answer of N (No) lets the search continue. Y (Yes) stops the search. The string replace command is R. It takes the form

line1,line2?R<string1><end-of-file><string 2>

which locates all occurrences of <string1> and replaces them with <string2> between the lines indicated. The line numbers are interpreted as in the S command. When the option "?" is specified, the user is queried before each replacement and can answer Y or N to allow or disallow the change. The end-of-file character is control-Z; the F6 function key can also be used.

1.7 SUMMARY

Computer programs are written in a machine-independent way when possible, so that knowledge of the architecture of the computer is not necessary. A program is a step-by-step specification of a computational process. Its state consists of the current values of its data and its point of execution. The computer understands, or executes, machine language, although programmers work with assembly language if they have to work at the machine level. Computers at first performed only numerical calculation, but they were used to perform nonnumeric work very early, including manipulation of character data. Computer hardware provides basic operations such as addition, subtraction, multiplication, and division, and comparisons such as greater than or equal to, equals, and less than. It also has the ability to store and recall information. In modern computers, the program is stored in the memory. The operating system consists of system programs that supplement the hardware operations. The combination is called a computer system. System programs include the kernel, executive, and supervisor programs, which schedule and monitor a job's execution on a computer, and translation programs, which convert source language programs written by the user into machine-language object code. The operating system is used by issuing commands. These commands invoke sections of the program in the operating system. Other bodies of code are gathered into program libraries for general use.

In time-sharing systems, remote terminals are used to interact with computer programs so that many users can be preparing and using programs at the same time. Developments in the last decade have led to microprocessors built out of a few integrated circuits, each on a single chip of silicon. Such processors may be dedicated to a particular application, or part of a microcomputer. A personal computer is a microcomputer designed to be used by one person at a time. Intelligent terminals have built-in microprocessors that can perform simple functions such as editing. They are used as terminals to other computer systems. If the built-in microprocessor can perform full computing activities, the terminal is called a workstation.

A computer consists of a memory, a CPU, and I/O units, usually connected via a bus. The I/O units may be controlled by an I/O processor. Secondary storage units may also be connected via I/O processors to supplement the primary memory.

High-level languages simplify the use of computers. At the highest level, problem-oriented languages can be used to describe a problem for solution. At the next level, the method of solution is specified in a procedure-oriented language, but none of the detail of machine-oriented language is present. A program is a procedure for solving a problem. The steps in a program may be interpreted by system programs or translated into machine language by compilers and assemblers. The object program resulting from translation is loaded into memory after it has been link-edited with the object program from other translators (if more than one is used). The result is executed.

The operating system allows the user to create and process files of data. The files have identifiers that are used to name them in commands. The files are usually stored on disks. If a file contains a program in a language, it can be translated into machine language by executing the appropriate translator. The file name is typed after the command as an argument. The translator puts the object code into another file and puts a listing of the input, together with error messages and other useful information, into a third file. A loader converts the object file or set of files into a machine language program ready for execution in yet another file. That file can be put into execution by specifying its name to the operating system.

Commands exist to copy, rename, print, concatenate, and delete files. Editors can be used to create and modify files. There are two principal types of editors, line-oriented editors in which the user can reference groups of lines numerically, and screen-oriented editors in which the content of the file being edited is displayed on a terminal screen and editor commands permit a cursor to be moved around the file to places where the user wants to make changes by typing or retyping information.

CHAPTER 2

MACHINE-LEVEL PROGRAMMING: PRIMARY MEMORY AND THE CPU

The CPU processes information obtained from the primary memory and returns the results to primary memory. There is usually a block of information that the programmer sees as being processed in any one operation and moved to or from memory. This is called a *word.* A word may represent a number to be used in numerical calculations or one or more characters of nonnumeric information. The length of the word differs from machine to machine. On most machines, however, a word consists of a number of *bits,* the most common lengths being between 8 and 64 bits.

The word "bit" is a contraction of "binary digit," meaning a digit that can take one of the two values 0 or 1, just as a decimal digit can take one of the ten values 0, 1, . . . , 9. Although human beings commonly use decimal digits to represent numbers, machines commonly use binary digits because most physical devices used in machines can retain one of two states most reliably, for example, an on or off switch, a positive or negative voltage, north or south magnetization.

2.1 INTEGERS AND CHARACTER CODES

A word, consisting of a number of bits, may be used to represent anything that the user cares to have it represent. Each bit of an N-bit word can be a 0 or a 1 independently, so that a word can assume any one of 2^N different states. With one word, the user can represent one out of not more than 2^N different objects, such as numbers, letters, species of trees, etc. The most common use of a word is for number and character representation. Much of today's computer terminology reflects the fact that, in the early days, computers handled mainly numbers. If a word consists of N bits, it is usually drawn as in Figure 2-1. The bits have been numbered arbitrarily from 0 to $N - 1$. Bit $N - 1$ is often referred to as the *left-hand bit* or *most significant bit* and bit 0 as the *right-hand*

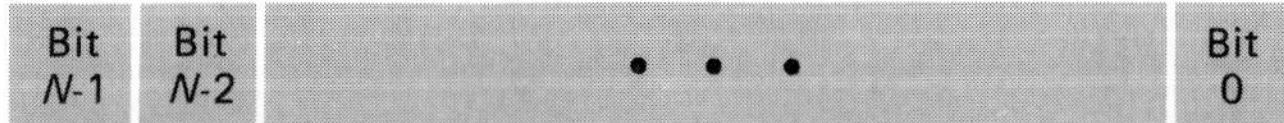

FIGURE 2-1 A computer word

bit or *least-significant bit*. The word is referred to as being N bits long. (Some machine designers prefer to number the bits in the other direction, so that bit 0 is the left-hand bit.)

When a group of bits is used to represent a number, the so-called *natural binary-coding scheme* is usually employed. Because a single bit can represent only two states, the value, or *weight,* of each bit or digit in a word is a power of two—thus the bits in a word, starting from the right-hand side, indicate the number of 1's, 2's, 4's, 8's, etc., in the number. Thus if 7 bits, say

$$b_6b_5b_4b_3b_2b_1b_0$$

are used to represent a number, the value of that number is

$$b_6 * 2^6 + b_5 * 2^5 + b_4 * 2^4 + b_3 * 2^3 + b_2 * 2^2 + b_1 * 2 + b_0$$

The largest value that this can take is the binary number 1111111, representing the decimal value 127, that is

$$1 * 2^6 + 1 * 2^5 + 1 * 2^4 + 1 * 2^3 + 1 * 2^2 + 1 * 2 + 1 * 2^0$$

The smallest value is the binary number 0000000, representing the value 0. Obviously, such a representation handles positive integers only, but one common way of handling negative numbers is to use one more bit to indicate the sign. This is frequently the leftmost bit, with a 0 indicating a positive number and a 1 a negative number. Thus numbers between -127 and $+127$ could be represented in 8 bits, the first being used for a sign and the remaining 7 for the magnitude of the number. This is called the *sign/magnitude* system. Examples are shown in Table 2-1. Notice that there are two representations for 0, one positive and one negative. If the bits of the word are

$$b_7b_6b_5b_4b_3b_2b_1b_0$$

where b_7 is the sign bit, then the value of the number is given by

$$(1 - 2b_7)(b_6 * 2^6 + b_5 * 2^5 + b_4 * 2^4 + b_3 * 2^3 + b_2 * 2^2 + b_1 * 2 + b_0)$$

Other ways to handle negative numbers will be discussed in detail in Chapter 3. One of these, called twos complement, is used in many computers. Fortunately, we can often view twos complement numbers as positive integers and simply ignore the sign information, so for this chapter we will not concern ourselves with the way signed information is handled in detail.

TABLE 2-1 SIGN/MAGNITUDE BINARY REPRESENTATION

Decimal number	8-bit sign/magnitude representation
−127	1111 1111
−126	1111 1110
−125	1111 1101
...	...
−1	1000 0001
−0	1000 0000
+0	0000 0000
+1	0000 0001
...	...
+125	0111 1101
+126	0111 1110
+127	0111 1111

Besides representing numbers, words are often used to represent nonnumeric data such as alphabetic characters. In program translation, business data processing, and work such as the differentiation of algebraic expressions or word-frequency studies, it is often necessary to represent natural language text such as English or American. To do this, each character (letter, digit, punctuation mark, etc.) is represented by a different bit pattern. The number of bits needed to represent a character is determined by the number of different characters. N bits can represent up to 2^N characters. For example, 64, 128, or 256 characters can be represented with 6, 7, or 8 bits, respectively.

If 8 bits are used to represent each character, but the word length is much greater than 8, say 32, it is clearly inefficient to store just one character in each word. In this case, several characters are *packed* into a word. Thus four 8-bit characters may be packed into a 32-bit word. If 6-bit characters are used, similar packing can occur. For example, the CDC CYBER 170 series packs ten 6-bit characters into its 60-bit words.

Modern computers need to represent more than sixty-four characters because it is convenient to represent upper- and lower-case letters, decimal digits, and a number of special characters. Because 7 turns out to be an awkward number of bits, 8 bits are used. One such code is known as ASCII (American Standard Code for Information Interchange). It uses only 7 of the bits for information. Table 2-2 gives the ASCII character set. Single character entries in this table are printable characters (on those devices that have all such characters available). The two-letter and three-letter entries represent *control characters* and other nonprinting characters that cause various actions on typical terminals. For example, *sp* and *bs* represent space and back space, respectively, whereas *cr* represents carriage return. The left-most (number 7) bit is not shown: it is usually a 0. Sometimes it is set so that the total number of 1 bits is odd (odd parity) or even (even parity). Parity is discussed in Chapter 3. Not unusually, the largest computer manufacturer has its own standard, known as EBCDIC (Extended BCD Interchange Code). It is an outgrowth of an earlier, very common representation of the uppercase letters, the ten digits 0 to 9, and the twelve special characters + − * / , . ( ) $ = ' and space (forty-eight characters altogether) that used 6 bits. That code was known as the BCD code (Binary Coded Decimal). With a few variations, it was

TABLE 2-2 ASCII CHARACTER SET

Bits 6 to 3	Bits 2 to 0							
	000	**001**	**010**	**011**	**100**	**101**	**110**	**111**
0000	*nul*	*soh*	*stx*	*etx*	*eot*	*enq*	*ack*	*bel*
0001	*bs*	*ht*	*nl*	*vt*	*np*	*cr*	*so*	*si*
0010	*dle*	*dc* 1	*dc* 2	*dc* 3	*dc* 4	*nak*	*syn*	*etb*
0011	*can*	*em*	*sub*	*esc*	*fs*	*gs*	*rs*	*us*
0100	*sp*	!	"	#	$	%	&	'
0101	(	)	*	+	,	-	.	/
0110	0	1	2	3	4	5	6	7
0111	8	9	:	;	<	=	>	?
1000	@	A	B	C	D	E	F	G
1001	H	I	J	K	L	M	N	O
1010	P	Q	R	S	T	U	V	W
1011	X	Y	Z	[	\	]	^	_
1100	`	a	b	c	d	e	f	g
1101	h	i	j	k	l	m	n	o
1110	p	q	r	s	t	u	v	w
1111	x	y	z	{	|	}	~	*del*

standard for many computers and could be found in many machine manuals. The EBCDIC code is an 8-bit code that can handle lower-case alphabetic characters and many other special characters in addition to those in the BCD code.

Although each pattern of bits in these codes represents a particular character, it also retains a numerical value. Thus an important feature of a code is the *collating sequence* it implies. This sequence is given by sorting the characters according to the numerical value of the code. Naturally, we expect the alphabetic characters to be ordered alphabetically and the other printing characters to be placed in a reasonable position. The accepted collating sequence places blank before any character and the digits after the letters. EBCDIC has this ordering. A sort using the ASCII coding places the digits before the letters, but otherwise the results are as expected.

2.1.1 Hexadecimal and Octal

It is frequently necessary to describe the bit pattern in a word. Because words contain many bits, it is tedious and error-prone to write out a full word in binary. Instead, a condensed notation is used. Two such notations are in common use, *hexadecimal* and *octal,* meaning base 16 and base 8, respectively. It is easiest to think of these as ways of grouping bits—3 bits per group for octal and 4 bits per group for hexadecimal. Consider the 24-bit word

110011101001110001010111

Arrange it as eight groups of 3 bits, that is, as 110 011 101 001 110 001 010 111. Each group can now be repaced by its value as an integer between 0 and 7, that is, as a base-8 digit. We get 63516127. This is the octal representation of the word. Alternatively, we can arrange the word in groups of 4 bits as 1100 1110 1001 1100 0101 0111. Each group can now be replaced by its value as an integer between 0 and 15, or a base-16 digit. The values between 0 and 9 can be written as the usual decimal digits, but we must use other symbols for the values 10 through 15. Usually we use the letters A through F. Thus the 24-bit word can be written as CE9C57 in base 16. This is the hexadecimal representation of the word. If there is any doubt about which representation is being used when a number is being written, it must be stated explicitly. In mathematical writing we do this by writing the base as a subscript after the number. Thus 4032_8 means 4032 base 8 or octal. Machine-level languages frequently use letters to indicate the base of a number, so that 3023D would mean 3023 decimal, 3023X or 3023H would mean 3023 hexadecimal, and 3023O or 3023Q would mean 3023 octal. (Because the letter O and the digit 0 are easy to confuse, many systems permit Q to be used instead of O.) Binary values are often indicated by a trailing B. Thus 10000B is equivalent to 16 decimal. Since numeric values are expected to begin with a digit, many systems require hexadecimal values to start with a numeric digit. If the first digit of a hexadecimal value is A through F, the representation can always be preceded with a 0 digit without changing its value. Hence the binary value 11111111B (the largest value of an 8-bit byte) is given by the two hexadecimal digits FF, but it can be written as 0FFH.

2.2 MEMORY

Some uses of a single word have already been discussed. A typical job will involve many thousands of words, be they numbers or strings of characters. Therefore the memory must store many words and have some way of getting at them when they are needed. The memory can be likened to the boxes at a post office. Each box holder has a box with a unique number that is its *address*. This address serves to identify the box. Each box or *location* in a memory has a unique number, called the *address,* associated with it. This serves to identify it for storage and retrieval. Usually, addresses are integers between 0 and $M - 1$, where M is the number of locations in memory. Usually M is a power of two, that is, 2^R for some R. Each location can store one word of N bits, where N is normally the same for all locations. Thus the memory may be asked to store the bit pattern 1011 . . . 0 in location 1027. Later on, if it is asked what is in location 1027, it is expected to reply "1011 . . . 0". Here the analogy with the post office box breaks down. If the post office customer fetches the contents from box 342, then box 342 is empty. A computer location cannot be empty. It consists of hardware capable of being in one of 2^N states or bit patterns, and it is always in one of them. Hence, if the contents are fetched from a location in memory, the memory retains a copy of the word. That is, its state does not change. Thus a better analogy is a set of switches. Storing is equivalent to placing the switches in the positions appropriate for representing the bit pattern being stored. Reading is equivalent to making a copy of the positions of the switches without changing them.

Earlier we defined a word as the minimum amount of information that could be transmitted between the memory and its environment at one time. Most of today's computers allow the user to refer to different amounts of information in different instructions. It then becomes difficult to define a word precisely. Physically, the memory may have a certain width, and this could be said to be the word size. However, the physical width may have no effect on the instructions available to the user. Indeed, the IBM 370 is available in various models with different physical memory widths, but the models are identical from the programmer's point of view. A very important property of a computer is the amount of information that can be addressed in an instruction, so a second definition that could be adopted would involve equating the word size to the minimum amount of information that is addressable. On most machines, one can find at least one instruction that allows a single bit to be specified, so this definition could lead to a 1-bit-word characterization. As usual with computers, we must compromise and say that the word size is that number of bits used in the majority of instructions and therefore probably the most efficient to use in a calculation. With this definition, the IBM 370 can be said to be a 32-bit-word machine, although it can address 8-, 32-, or 64-bit quantities for fixed-length arithmetic, and it can manipulate strings of n 8-bit bytes for any n from 1 to 256. The CYBER 170 is a 60-bit machine and the PDP-11 is a 16-bit machine, but its descendant, the VAX system, is a 32-bit machine. The INTEL 8080 is an 8-bit machine, but the 8086/88 machines can operate on 16-bit words. (The only difference between the 8086 and the 8088 is the "width" of the data path to memory. The 8086 has a 16-bit path, whereas the 8088 has an 8-bit path. Consequently, the 8088 is slightly slower when 16-bit data has to be fetched, because 2 bytes have to be read consecutively.) Another important property of a memory is the smallest amount of information that can be addressed as a unit. Today, most systems allow any 8-bit byte to be addressed. We say that such memories are *byte-addressable*.

2.2.1 Symbolic Addressing

Information to be processed is stored in the memory and brought to the CPU for processing. For example, it may be necessary to add two numbers together and to save the result for later processing. These two numbers are in two locations in memory and the result is to be put back into memory. In high-level languages, this operation might be written as

$$X \leftarrow Y + Z$$

We think of X as a variable that is assigned the result of adding values of two variables Y and Z. Corresponding to each of these variables is a memory location. Perhaps location 10571 corresponds to X, location 10732 to Y, and location 27501 to Z. The contents of locations 10732 and 27501 are to be added together and the result stored in location 10571. We shall use the notation (10732) to mean the contents of location 10732.

The high-level language statement

$$X \leftarrow Y + Z$$

is equivalent to the operation

$$(10571) \leftarrow (10732) + (27501)$$

It is not always convenient to use numerical addresses when talking and writing about the computer, because the action of an operation is not dependent on the particular locations used. In the above example, the important information (to the user) is that X, Y, and Z are the variables involved. Therefore, we shall write

$$(X) \leftarrow (Y) + (Z)$$

instead. This is a confusion of variable names and location names that is in common use, so the student should endeavor to become clear on the different uses of X, Y, and Z above. In the high-level language statement $X \leftarrow Y + Z$, we must think of X, Y, and Z as the *names* of variables, not as the variables themselves. The value of variables named Y and Z are to be added and the result is to be stored as the value of the variable named X. In machine-level languages, X, Y, and Z are the names of locations that contain the values of the variables. Therefore, two pieces of information are associated with the name Z: first, the content of the location, which we have written as (Z), and second, the actual address of the location, which we have written as Z. To avoid pedantry, we usually refer simply to Z; the context makes it clear whether the content or the address of the location is intended. Because a name, such as Z, has an associated address, this name is often called a *symbolic address*.

2.2.2 Multibyte Data Addressing

Computer instructions deal with varying amounts of data. It is not unusual for a computer to have instructions that will add 8-, 16-, or 32-bit quantities. If the computer is byte-addressable, that means that it must reference 1, 2, or 4 bytes in a single instruction. Therefore, several bytes are grouped together to form a larger unit. For example, in the IBM 370, a 2-byte group is called a half word, a 4-byte group a word, and an 8-byte group a double word. The same terminology is used in the VAX, which also permits a 16-byte quad-word group. In the 8088/8086 systems, a 2-byte group is called a word. The set of bytes in a group are stored in memory location with consecutive addresses, and the lowest address is used as the address of the group. There are two schemes in use for allocating the bytes to consecutive cells. In VAX computers, the 8080 and its descendants, and others, the bytes are stored in increasing addresses from right to left, as shown in Figure 2-2. In the IBM 370, the bytes are stored in increasing addresses from left to right, as shown in Figure 2-3. (The bits are also numbered from left to right in this scheme.) The scheme used is of no concern to programmers in most cases, but if multibyte data is stored by means of an instruction that works with a multibyte group and then accessed 1 byte at a time, care has to be taken. We will refer to the two schemes as *right-end* addressing and *left-end* addressing, respectively, because the address used for a multibyte item is the address of the right-most or left-most byte, respectively.

Since the memory in many computers is physically several bytes *wide,* so that, for example, 4 bytes can be read in one memory read operation of a 32-bit word to achieve speed, there is often an advantage in *alignment* of multibyte data. A group of 2^s bytes

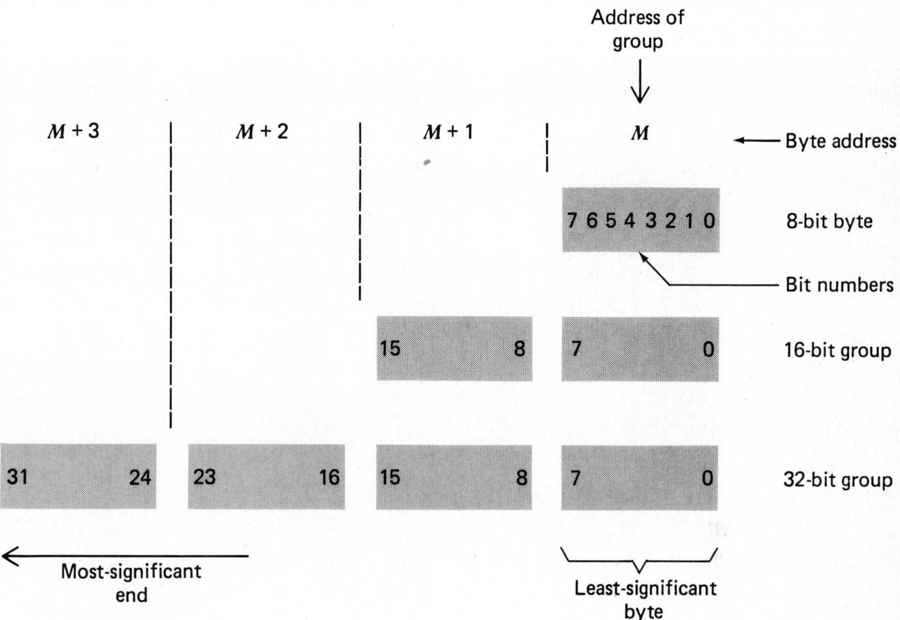

FIGURE 2-2 Right-end addressing

FIGURE 2-3 Left-end addressing

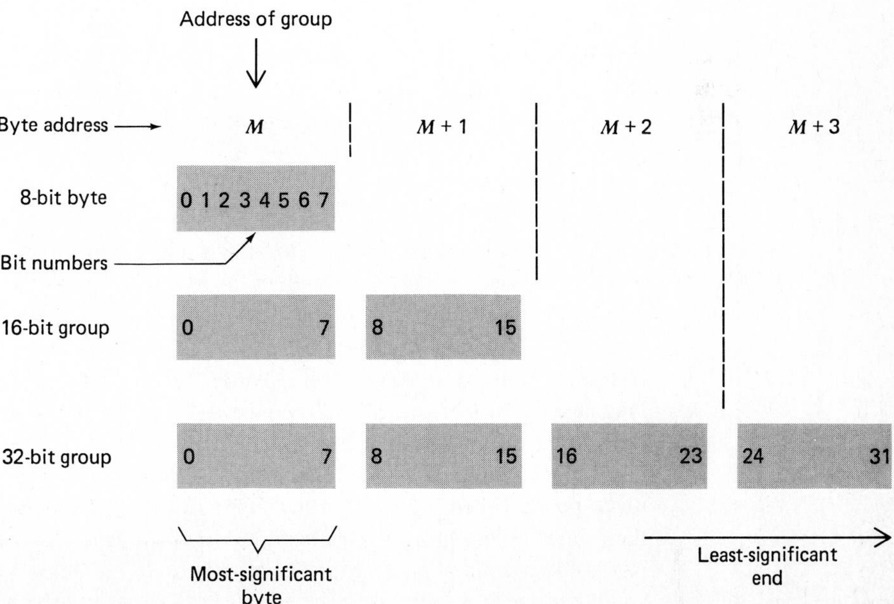

is aligned if it starts on a byte address divisible by 2^s. Thus a 32-bit word is aligned if it occupies bytes with addresses $4m$, $4m + 1$, $4m + 2$, $4m + 3$. An operation using aligned data is frequently faster than one using unaligned data; indeed, on earlier machines such as the IBM 360, the use of aligned data was required.

Instructions are also stored in memory using varying numbers of bytes, depending on the number needed for the particular instruction. These instruction bytes are stored in increasing addresses in all common computers and are also addressed by the smallest byte address. If the instruction includes an address that needs more than 1 byte, it will also be stored in the form used in that computer—right to left in the INTEL 8080 and VAX computers, and left to right in IBM. The computer keeps track of the memory address of the first byte of the next instruction to be executed.

2.3 THE CENTRAL PROCESSOR AND ITS OPERATIONS

The CPU fetches program statements from memory one at a time and executes them. It is capable of a number of elementary operations, such as addition and subtraction. All but the smallest computers also include multiplication and division operations, although these can be programmed using more elementary operations. Most machine-language statements involve just one elementary operation, such as addition, so that a complex calculation that could be a single statement in a high-level language, such as

```
X ← B * (C + D * E - F/G)
```

must be *compiled* into a sequence of elementary operations. This can always be done. The above example can be written as

```
T1 ← D * E
T1 ← C + T1
T2 ← F/G
T1 ← T1 - T2
X ← B * T1
```

whereby each statement uses exactly one elementary operation. (The variables T1 and T2 are used to store intermediate results.) The majority of arithmetic operations require two *operands,* that is, two numbers on which to operate. The result also has to be placed somewhere. An *instruction* is a specification of an operation such as addition, the location of the operands, and the place to put the result. Each machine-language instruction can be executed directly by the CPU. It keeps track of the location of the next instruction by storing the memory address of the next instruction in a special storage cell in the CPU called the *program counter* (PC). Special storage cells of this type are called *registers.* They function very much like memory locations in that they can store the same type of data, but they are usually much faster. The state of the process in execution is determined not only by the content of memory, but also by the content of this register and of other registers to be discussed later.

Computer instructions can be classified in many ways. Machine manuals usually group them into categories based on the type of operation involved, for example, arithmetic, data movement, and testing. Such classifications are useful for reference purposes. Another important property of instructions is the way in which they use operands and machine registers. In the next four subsections we will examine four important subclasses of instructions from this viewpoint. Many machines have instructions in most of these classes, although machines predominantly use those from one class.

2.3.1 Three-Address Instructions

We saw that a simple assignment statement that involved the calculation of an expression and assigning its value to a variable could be written as a sequence of assignment statements, each using a single arithmetic operation. A CPU can be designed to execute instructions that specify an operation and the addresses of its two operands and the result—three addresses in all. Such an instruction is called a *three-address instruction*. It allows for the direct execution of single-operation assignment statements. To make possible the evaluation of arithmetic expressions involving addition, subtraction, multiplication, and division, three-address instructions for each of these operations can be provided. The instructions

```
Add        (ADD)        X,Y,Z
Subtract   (SUB)        X,Y,Z
Multiply   (MPY)        X,Y,Z
Divide     (DIV)        X,Y,Z
```

perform the indicated *diadic* or *binary* operation (that is, an operation on two operands) on the contents of locations X and Y and store the result in location Z. Thus

```
DIV     P,Q,R
```

is equivalent to (R) ← (P)/(Q). The Fortran assignment statement

$$X \leftarrow B * (C + D * E - F/G)$$

is equivalent to

```
MPY     D,E,T1
ADD     C,T1,T1
DIV     F,G,T2
SUB     T1,T2,T1
MPY     B,T1,X
```

Note that there are five operations indicated in the expression $B * (C + D * E - F/G)$, and that it takes exactly the same number of three-address instructions. This will be true for all expressions using only the diadic operations provided by the computer, regardless of parenthesization.

2.3.2 Two-Address Instructions

For cost reasons, the simple three-address instruction is not used in many machines. If $X \leftarrow B + C + D + E + F + G$ is to be programmed, the shortest three-address code is

```
ADD    B,C,X
ADD    X,D,X
ADD    X,E,X
ADD    X,F,X
ADD    X,G,X
```

All but the first instruction needed only two different addresses, but the programmer had to provide three. The *two-address instruction* permits the unnecessary address to be omitted. It has the form

```
ADD    X,Y
```

which means $(X) \leftarrow (X) + (Y)$. The four basic arithmetic operations are usually provided by the instructions

```
ADD    X,Y
SUB    X,Y
MPY    X,Y
DIV    X,Y
```

meaning

$$(X) \leftarrow (X) + (Y)$$
$$(X) \leftarrow (X) - (Y)$$
$$(X) \leftarrow (X) * (Y)$$
$$(X) \leftarrow (X)/(Y)$$

respectively. Note that the first address provides the first operand and that the result replaces the first operand.[1] Because subtraction and division are not commutative, that is, $(X) - (Y)$ is not $(Y) - (X)$ and $(X)/(Y)$ is not $(Y)/(X)$, it is useful, although not necessary, to have *inverse* subtraction and division operations available. An inverse operation, as the name implies, produces the "other-way-around" of the result. Say that

[1]Some computers, in particular the VAX, reverse the position of the two addresses. That is, SUB X,Y performs $(Y) \leftarrow (Y) - (X)$.

a two-address subtraction, SUB X,Y, performs (X) ← (X) − (Y). A two-address inverse subtraction would perform (X) ← (Y) − (X), and a two-address inverse division would perform (X) ← (Y)/(X).

The equivalent of the three-address instruction MPY X,Y,Z can be performed by the two-address instructions as

```
SUB     Z,Z
ADD     Z,X
MPY     Z,Y
```

The effect of the first two instructions is to move the contents of location X to location Z by first *clearing* Z, that is, setting it to 0 and then adding (X). Since moving data is a very common operation, it is usual to have a single two-address instruction MOVE X,Y, which puts (Y) in location X. Then

```
X ← B + C + D + E + F + G
```

can be implemented by

```
MOVE    X,B
ADD     X,C
ADD     X,D
ADD     X,E
ADD     X,F
ADD     X,G
```

Note that this sequence contains one more instruction than operations in the expression. In general, the equivalent two-address code will contain at least one additional instruction in order to move one of the operands into position. Let us consider the assignment statement X ← B ∗ (C + D ∗ E − F/G) again. This can be performed by means of the two-address code

```
MPY     D,E
DIV     F,G
SUB     D,F
ADD     D,C
MOVE    X,B
MPY     X,D
```

Notice, however, that this destroys the contents of locations D and F. In fact, F now contains F/G and D contains C + D ∗ E − F/G. In general, this is not permissible, because the variables stored in these locations may be needed in the evaluation of other expressions. Therefore, additional move instructions must be used, resulting in the code:

```
MOVE    X,D
MPY     X,E
MOVE    T1,F
DIV     T1,G
SUB     X,T1
ADD     X,C
MPY     X,B
```

This is the shortest code that will evaluate this expression without changing any of the variables on the right-hand side, assuming that all of the symbolic addresses X, B, C, D, E, F, and G represent different locations. If there is a possibility that X could represent the same location as B, C, . . . , or F, then X must be replaced by a temporary location, say T2 in the above code and the additional instruction MOVE X,T2 must be appended.

In many calculations a *unary minus* is used. This is a subtraction operation with only one operand. It is called a unary or *monadic* operation. Thus the subtraction in $X \leftarrow -Y$ is monadic. It can be implemented either with the two-address instruction MOVE-NEGATIVE X,Y or the one-address instruction SET-NEGATIVE X, which performs $X \leftarrow -X$.

2.3.3 One-Address Instructions

In addition to saving the programmer work by requiring only two addresses rather than three, two-address instructions can result in a lower overall cost, since less information has to be used to represent each instruction in memory. If the cost can be reduced by decreasing the number of addresses, we naturally look for ways to reduce the number of addresses even further. If we examine the simplest hand-held calculators, we will see that they have just one register whose content is displayed. Operations such as addition add a number entered on the keyboard into this register. It is called an *accumulator*. See Figure 2-4. In a similar manner, the CPU of a computer can be provided with an accumulator that will always contain one operand of a diadic operation. The four basic arithmetic operations can now be provided in a one-address form as

FIGURE 2-4 Addition on a desk calculator

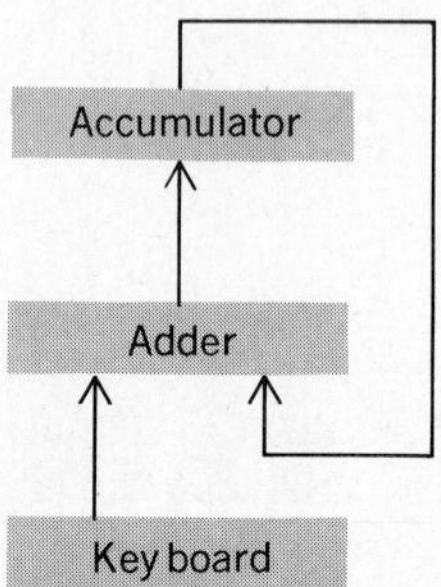

```
ADD     X
SUB     X
MPY     X
DIV     X
```

SUB X performs (AC) ← (AC) − (X), where AC is the name of the accumulator. Because of the noncommutativity of the subtraction and division operations, it is convenient to have the inverse instructions available as well. Whereas DIV X performs (AC) ← (AC)/(X), INVERSE-DIV X performs (AC) ← (X)/(AC).

The accumulator of the one-address machine can be used as a scratch working register to evaluate expressions. The equivalent of the two-address MOVE operation is needed to place the contents of a memory location into the accumulator. This is often called LOAD. LOAD X performs (AC) ← (X). B + C + D + E can be calculated in the accumulator by the sequence

```
LOAD    B
ADD     C
ADD     D
ADD     E
```

If the result is to be stored back in memory, a MOVE from the accumulator to the memory is needed. This is called STORE X, meaning (X) ← (AC). The assignment statement X ← B * (C + D * E − F/G) can be calculated by

```
LOAD    F
DIV     G
STORE   T1
LOAD    D
MPY     E
ADD     C
SUB     T1
MPY     B
STORE   X
```

Here T1 is a memory cell for an intermediate result. Note that this took two LOAD and two STORE instructions, just as the two-address form took two MOVE instructions plus an additional one if X could be the same as one of the right-hand side operands. This is always true: a one-address code using only diadic operations can be transformed into a two-address code with one more MOVE instruction than the number of LOAD or STORE instructions, and vice versa.

Corresponding to the two-address MOVE-NEGATIVE instruction is the one-address instruction LOAD-NEGATIVE. Because the names of some of these instructions are unduly long, they are abbreviated in use to a form determined by the system. On many systems, LOAD is replaced by a name such as L or LD to save the programmer time. We shall use LOAD in this book, except when discussing specific machines.

2.3.4 Stack (Zero-Address) Instructions

If a saving is effected by reducing the number of addresses in instructions, it is natural to examine *zero-address instructions*. Since a diadic operation requires two operands, both must be in known places prior to the execution of the instruction. These places could be specified registers. In some machines it is necessary to specify which of the several CPU registers are to be used as accumulators, so that an address is needed after all. However, there is one type of design in which arithmetic instructions do not require any addresses. It uses a *stack*. A stack, also known as a *last-in-first-out* (LIFO) *queue* or a *push-down list,* can be thought of as a set of registers, one on top of another. Each register can store one value. We refer to the top register as the top level, the second register as the second level, and so on. A stack is a data structure with two principal operations, PUSH and POP. A *push* operation places another register on top of the stack of existing registers and puts a value in the new top level. The prior top level becomes the new second level. A *pop* operation does the opposite. It reads the value from the top level, then removes the register so that the prior second level becomes the new top level. (Of course, registers are not physically moved around; rather the information in them is moved. However, conceptually we should take the view given above.) A simple analogy to use is a stack of file cards. A push operation is equivalent to writing a value on a card and placing it on top of the stack. A pop is equivalent to removing the top card, reading the value, and discarding the card.

A binary operation such as ADD pops two values out of the stack, adds them, and pushes the result back in. This is illustrated in Figure 2-5. In the card analogy, addition is equivalent to removing the top two cards, adding the values on them, writing the result on another card, and placing that card back on top. Another way of describing this operation is to say that it adds the second level to the top level, puts the result in the second level, and discards the top level, thus leaving the result as the new top level.

A machine that uses this organization is called a *stack machine*. It is obvious that if a word is to be fetched from memory or stored in memory an address must be provided, so a stack machine will have some instructions with addresses. Two essential instructions are LOAD and STORE. LOAD X fetches a word from memory location X and pushes it into the stack. STORE X pops a word from the stack and puts it into location X. The six basic operations for a stack machine are therefore:

```
LOAD    X    PUSH (X) into top of stack
STORE   X    POP (TL) and store into (X)
ADD          (SL) ← (SL) + (TL); POP
SUB          (SL) ← (SL) − (TL); POP
MPY          (SL) ← (SL) * (TL); POP
DIV          (SL) ← (SL)/(TL); POP
```

SL and TL stand for second level and top level, respectively. As with two-and one-address machines, an inverse subtract and an inverse divide are useful instructions, although not necessary.

An assignment statement can be performed by code in many ways for any type of machine. There is always a way of coding a simple statement for a stack machine such

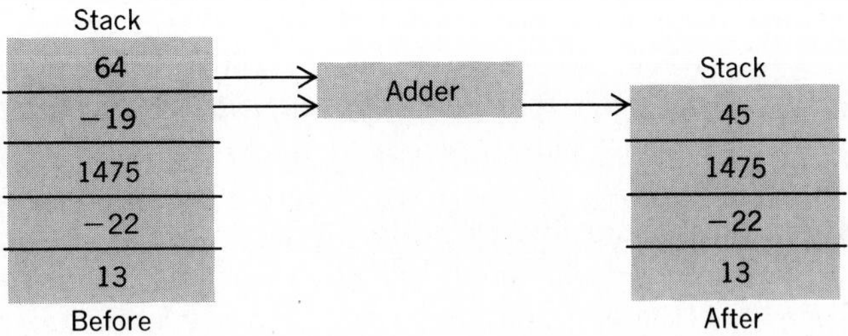

FIGURE 2-5 Addition on a stack

that only one STORE instruction is used. (That one is needed to complete the assignment.) For example, the statement X ← B ∗ (C + D ∗ E − F/G) is equivalent to the zero-address code

```
LOAD    B
LOAD    C
LOAD    D
LOAD    E
MPY
ADD
LOAD    F
LOAD    G
DIV
SUB
MPY
STORE   X
```

This form is obtained by writing LOAD VAR in turn for each variable VAR that appears in the expression and by inserting an arithmetic instruction into the code at the first opportunity, that is, when the top two levels of the stack contain the operands for the operation.

There must be a zero-address instruction for each operation in the original expression, a one-address LOAD instruction for each operand on the right, and a one-address STORE instruction for the assignment. Since there is one more operand than binary operation in the expression, an N-operation assignment statement will use N zero-address instructions and $N + 2$ one-address instructions.

2.3.5 CPU Registers

If we look back over this and the previous three sections, we see that the example X ← B ∗ (C + D ∗ E − F/G) was coded using each of the four structures. It required 5 three-address instructions, 7 two-address instructions, 9 one-address instructions, or 12 stack-machine instructions, (5 zero-address and 7 one-address). A computer designer is concerned about many different costs. There is the construction cost of the computer, the cost (in programmers' time) of writing programs, and the costs that increase if it takes longer to compute a result because one particular design is slower than another. Therefore, a design is chosen that, one hopes, will keep all these costs reasonable. A multiaddress instruction appears to be better, because fewer instructions are used to perform a given computation (in general). However, a multiaddress instruction is also usually executed more slowly than a one- or zero-address instruction, for two reasons: it takes more time to deal with the additional addresses, and the time it takes to get information from the memory is typically much greater than the time it takes to get information from CPU registers. Furthermore, the instructions themselves have to be read from memory. If they have more operand addresses, they tend to occupy more space, so reading them takes longer.

For these reasons, the design of a computer represents many trade-offs between cost and speed and involves many judgments by the designer. Consequently, there are many differently organized computers on the market. However, they all use the basic principles discussed here. Modern machines provide many registers in the CPU to reduce the number of memory references for data. These registers are usually organized in one of three ways:

1 As a stack
2 As a set of general registers, each of which can be used as an accumulator
3 As a set of "special" memory locations that can be referenced directly in any instruction

A number of computers in the past have used stack organizations, most notably Burroughs and English Electric, but the design is no longer common. General register machines include the IBM 370, VAX, PDP-11, and Cyber computers. Since each register can function as an accumulator, its "address" has to be specified in each instruction needing an accumulator. For example, if the sixteen registers have the names R0 to R15, an ADD instruction might be written as

```
ADD     R5,X
```

meaning that the content of location X is to be added to register R5. The IBM 370 uses this type of instruction (although ADD is abbreviated to A). This is, in effect, a two-address instruction, but it only has to fetch one operand from memory. The INTEL 8080 has an accumulator plus a number of registers that can be used in place of memory to provide an operand in a one-address instruction. These registers are assigned the names B, C, D, . . . , and can be used as addresses. Thus

```
ADD     B
```

adds the content of the B register to the accumulator in the INTEL design. The INTEL 8086/88 is a hybrid of an accumulator-plus-special-register machine and a general-register machine.

The advantage of the general-register format is that a number of moves of data may be saved. For example, if we want to form U * V + X * Y in a general-register machine, we can form U * V in one register, form X * Y in another, and then add them using a *register-register* operation such as

```
ADD        R5,R7
```

which does not have to access memory for data at all. In an accumulator machine, the product U * V would have to be formed in the accumulator and then moved to another register so that the accumulator could be used to form X * Y before being added to the first product. The advantage of the accumulator-plus-special-register machine is that the standard instructions require only one address and therefore may take less space in memory.

Multiplication and Division Addition and subtraction of a pair of values usually leads to a result of about the same size—that is, if we add two values, with each represented in ten digits, the answer is normally representable in ten digits. Since a computer normally has a fixed number of digits for representing a value, this means that we can usually represent the answer in the same space. (If the answer is too big, we have an *overflow,* which will be discussed in the next chapter.) The same is not true of multiplication and division. If two 10-digit numbers are multiplied, the result usually requires 20 digits to be represented correctly. We say that the result is a *double-length* quantity. In a computer, the multiplication of a pair of values, whether from registers or from memory, normally requires two registers or memory locations for the double-length result. Frequently, a pair of registers is used.

Division is the inverse of multiplication, so it normally starts with a double-length dividend. The divisor is divided into this value to get a *single-length* (that is, one register or memory location) *quotient* as a result. The division operation may also produce a remainder, which is also left as a single-length result in another register or location.

2.3.6 INTEL 8080 Data Registers and Instructions

We will describe the structure of the INTEL 8080 and its instructions. The registers and instructions found in the 8080 are found in its derivatives, such as the Z80 and INTEL 8085, although these also have additional registers and instructions. The instructions we will discuss are all covered in the manufacturer's manual[2] and the CP/M introduction.[3] They can also be found in the Macro Assembler manual.[4]

The INTEL 8080 is principally a one-address machine using a single 8-bit accumulator. For example, we can load and store information through the accumulator using

[2] *INTEL 8080 Assembly Language Programming Manual,* Intel Corp., Santa Clara, CA, 1975.

[3] *An Introduction to CP/M Features and Facilities,* Digital Research, Pacific Grove, CA, 1978.

[4] *CP/M MAC Macro Assembler: Language Manual and Applications Guide,* Digital Research, Pacific Grove, CA, 1977.

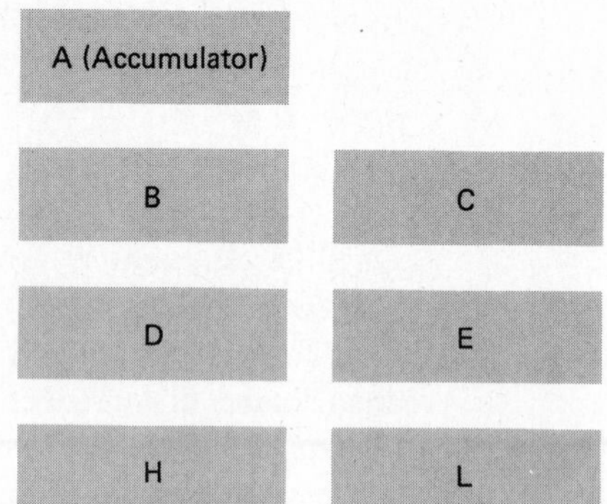

FIGURE 2-6 Data registers in the INTEL 8080

```
LDA     P     Load Accumulator from location P
STA     Q     Store Accumulator into location Q
```

It also has six additional 8-bit registers. They are called B, C, D, E, H, and L, as are shown in Figure 2-6. Addition and subtraction can get information from these registers directly. For example,

```
ADD     C
SUB     D
```

adds the content of register C to the accumulator, then subtracts the content of register D from it. Because some alphabetic identifiers, including A, B, C, D, E, H, and L, are used as register names, they should not be used as symbolic addresses for memory locations.

Two-address instructions can be used to move information between the registers. For example,

```
MOV     B,C
```

copies the content of C into B. The accumulator can also function as a register in move operations. Its name is A. For example,

```
MOV     A,C
MOV     C,D
MOV     D,A
```

switches the contents of registers C and D, using the accumulator as a temporary location.

The 8080 has no multiply or divide instructions; these must be programmed using the instructions we will describe in the next few sections.

2.3.7 INTEL 8086/88 Instructions and Registers

The INTEL 8086/88 is described in the manufactuer's manual[5] and IBM PC manuals.[6] The 8086/88 uses a 16-bit word and is principally a two-address machine, with the general registers shown in Figure 2-7, although some instructions (for example, multiply and divide) are one-address instructions that assume that one operand and the result are in a known register. In this sense, the AX register is an accumulator.

The 16-bit registers shown in Figure 2-7 are named AX, BX, CX, and DX. Each can be viewed as a pair of 8-bit registers. Thus AX is the pair AH and AL, standing for A-High byte and A-Low byte, respectively. The 8086/88 can also perform 8-bit arithmetic with all of these registers. Thus

```
ADD        AX,BX
```

is a 16-bit addition of the BX register to the AX register, and

```
ADD        BL,CH
```

is an 8-bit addition of the CH register to the BL register. The SUB and MOV operations are similar, working on 8-bit or 16-bit data, depending on which registers are specified. Either of the operands, but not both, in ADD, SUB, and MOV instructions can be obtained from memory. Thus, if DATA is the symbolic address of a word in memory, the following are valid instructions:

```
ADD        CX,DATA      Register-from-memory
SUB        DATA,AX      Memory-from register
MOV        BX,DATA      Register-from-memory
```

[5]*The 8086 Family User's Manual,* Intel Corp., Santa Clara, CA, 1979.

[6]*IBM Personal Computer Hardware Reference Library, Technical Reference, Document 6025008,* IBM, Boca Raton, FL, 1981; *IBM Personal Computer: Computer Language Series, Macro Assembler, Document 6172234,* IBM, Boca Raton, FL, 1981.

FIGURE 2-7 INTEL 8086/88 arithmetic registers

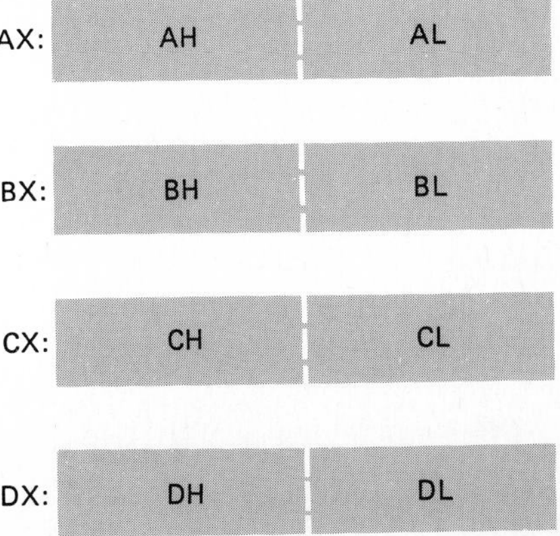

The XCHG (exchange) instruction is similar to a move, but it switches data between two registers, or between a register and memory.

Multiplication operates on data in the accumulator, which is AX for 16-bit arithmetic and AL for 8-bit arithmetic. Since the answer is a double-length result, it requires 32 or 16 bits, respectively. For 16-bit multiplication, the answer is in DX,AX (that is, the two registers can be considered as connected end-to-end to form a 32-bit quantity). For 8-bit arithmetic, the answer is in AX. Thus the product of the two 8-bit values BYTE1 and BYTE2 in memory can be formed in AX as a 16-bit quantity by

```
MOV     AL,BYTE1
MUL     BYTE2
```

If the answer is small enough to fit in 8 bits, the result can be taken from AL. Similarly, two 16-bit quantities, WORD1 and WORD2, can be multiplied to get a 32-bit quantity by the sequence

```
MOV     AX,WORD1
MUL     WORD2
```

The result is in DX,AX, although if the result is small enough to be represented in 16 bits, DX is 0 and AX contains the answer. Division operates on the 16-bit or 32-bit dividend in AX or DX,AX, respectively. Hence it can be used following a multiplication. If WORD1, WORD2, and WORD3 are the addresses of 16-bit words in memory, the value WORD1 * WORD2/WORD3 can be computed using

```
MOV     AX,WORD1
MUL     WORD2     WORD1 * WORD2 in DX,AX
DIV     WORD3     Result in AX
```

The quotient is left in the accumulator—AX for 16-bit arithmetic or AL for 8-bit arithmetic. The remainder is left in DX or AH as a 16-bit or 8-bit quantity, respectively. The single operand in MUL and DIV can be obtained from memory or from a general register. Thus MUL CX multiplies AX by CX, whereas MUL BH multiplies AL by BH.

The identifiers AX, AH, AL, etc., refer to the registers, so the programmer must be careful not to use them as symbolic addresses.

2.4 INSTRUCTION REPRESENTATION AND SEQUENCING

We have seen zero-, one-, two-, and three-address instructions. Some complex instructions for handling strings of characters may have even more addresses. Since memory is usually addressed by a positive integer between 0 and $M - 1$, A bits, where 2^A is at least M, are needed to represent each address used in an instruction. Further, some bits are needed to distinguish among the various operations. The representation of an instruction may be divided into a number of *fields,* with one field representing

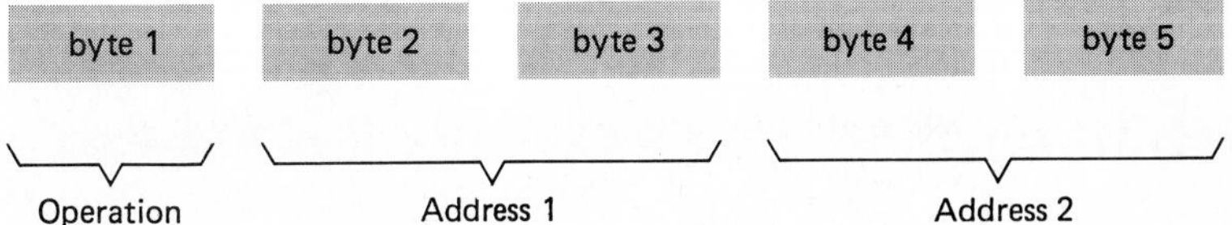

FIGURE 2-8 A two-address instruction format

the operation and other fields representing addresses in the instruction and other information. For example, if M is 65,536 = 2^{16} and there are no more than 256 different instructions (which can be represented in 8 bits, since 2^8 = 256), a two-address instruction could take 40 bits, or 5 bytes, and could have the format shown in Figure 2-8. In practice, a machine may have both one- and two-address instructions, so that more than one format must be used for instructions. In byte-addressable computers, this means that different instructions use different numbers of bytes. For example, some microcomputers and minicomputers, such as the 8080 and PDP-11, have instructions as short as 1 byte. Since the 8080 is essentially a one-address computer, its longest instruction is 3 bytes, but the PDP-11, which is essentially a two-address computer, can have instructions of up to 5 bytes. The more varied instruction sets of larger computers and of more recent minis and micros give rise to much longer instructions. In long-word-length machines, such as the CDC Cyber with its 60-bit word, several instructions can be packed into one word. The Cyber uses 15-bit instructions with no memory addresses and 30-bit instructions with one memory address. Up to four of these can be packed into a single word.

The program counter, also called an *instruction counter* or a *control counter,* is a register in the CPU containing an address-length number, which is the address of the next instruction to be obeyed. Each time an instruction is fetched from memory, the program counter is incremented by the length of the instruction. The action of sending the address contained in the program counter to memory, incrementing the content of the program counter, and reading the instruction addressed is called the *fetch cycle*. Note that the control counter contains the address of the *next* instruction to be executed during execution of the current instruction.

The automatic incrementing of the program counter allows for the sequential execution of instructions, one after another. If the statements of a high-level language are compiled into machine language, this sequencing provides for the sequential execution of statements. However, in a high-level language, we also have control statements such as **if** that determine the path of control on the basis of data values. Machine instructions must be provided that change the path of control when needed. The BRANCH instruction (it is called a JUMP instruction in some systems) is a one-address instruction that causes the next instruction to be fetched from the address specified in the instruction. BRANCH X is a command to execute the next instruction from location X by putting X into the program counter. Since the program counter contains the address of the next instruction to be executed, the next instruction will come from location X.

The BRANCH instruction provides a machine-level implementation of the high-level language statement **go to**. (The use of this statement is discouraged in high-level programming, but it cannot be avoided at the machine level.) A machine-level implementation of a selection, as with an **if** statement, requires a test. This is done with a *conditional branch* instruction. It tests an internal machine condition or even an external condition, such as a switch.

In high-level programs we want to test for conditions such as equality and sign. At the machine level these require that we be able to test the value of variables to see if they are zero, positive, etc. Two different designs of conditional branches can be found in computers. In the first design, the conditional branches test the contents of either specific registers or designated registers. For example, in a machine with an accumulator, instructions may be provided to test the state of the accumulator. These would be one-address instructions whose address is the *branch address*. A typical one-address conditional branch instruction is BPL (Branch if PLus). BPL X causes X to be placed in the program counter if the accumulator is positive or 0. Similar instructions include "branch if minus but not zero," "branch if zero," and "branch if nonzero." If the condition is met, the next instruction is taken from the branch address; if not, it is taken from the next location in sequence.

Two-address organizations often provide two-address instructions to test one location and branch to another if the test is successful. Stack machines usually test the top level of the stack and branch with a one-address instruction. (Usually, they do not pop the top of the stack in case the operand is needed subsequently.)

Conditional branches can be used to construct program loops. If, for example, we want to execute a sequence of instructions a given number of times, say N, a counter can be set to N initially and decreased by 1 after each execution of the loop. It will be 0 after the Nth pass through the loop. A high-level description of a code to form 2^N is shown in Program 2-1. A stack machine version of this code is shown in Program 2-2. In this program the BZ (Branch if Zero) instruction is assumed to branch if the top of the stack is zero but not to pop the stack, so that COUNT remains in the top of the stack. The locations to which control are transferred—in this example, LOOP and DONE—are indicated by writing the symbolic address in the branch and on the left of the instruction, which is the *object* of the branch. It is evident that each symbolic address should appear on the left of exactly one instruction. This program also uses a shorthand notation for constants. The instruction LOAD =1 means that the operand to be loaded from memory is the constant 1. This constant must be stored in some location in memory and its address placed in the instruction. This will be explained in more detail later.

In the second design for conditional instructions, a special register of *flags,* whose values indicate the state of previous operations, is provided, and the conditional in-

Program 2-1 High-level code to compute 2^N

```
Set COUNT to N
Set RESULT to 1
do while COUNT > 0
   Multiply RESULT by 2
   Decrement COUNT by 1
   enddo
```

Program 2-2 Stack code to form 2^N

```
              LOAD      NN         NN is the address of a
                                   location containing N.
                                   COUNT is in top of stack.
              LOAD      =1         =1 is address of location
                                   containing 1.
              STORE     RESULT
LOOP            BZ        DONE     Branch if COUNT zero
                LOAD      RESULT
                LOAD      =2       Load constant 2.
                MPY                Double RESULT.
                STORE     RESULT
                LOAD      =1       LOAD constant 1.
                SUB
                BRANCH             LOOP     Repeat loop
DONE            ...                Continuation of program...
```

structions test these flags. For example, there will be a flag that indicates whether the result of the last arithmetic operation was 0, a flag that indicates the sign of the result of the last arithmetic operation, and other flags to be discussed later. The register holding the flags is sometimes called a *condition register* and is usually part of the *program status word,* which is a part of the process state held in the CPU. In this design, the conditional branch instructions execute or do not execute a branch according to the state of the flags. In this type of design, not all instructions affect all of the flags, so the programmer simply has to refer to a machine manual to determine the effect of each instruction on the flags.

2.4.1 INTEL 8080 Control

The INTEL 8080 executes instructions in order of increasing address under control of a 16-bit program counter PC. The PC contains the address of the first 8-bit byte of the next instruction. The PC is incremented by 1, 2, or 3 during instruction execution, depending on the length of the instruction. The JMP instruction breaks the sequential processing by changing the contents of PC. Thus

```
JMP      S
```

sets the value of PC to S. Conditional branches in the INTEL 8080 are made on the basis of the 4 condition bits shown in Table 2-3. These condition bits are set by most of the arithmetic instructions. The Z (Zero) bit is a 1 if the result of the last operation was 0. The S (Sign) bit is a 1 if the last result was negative. The other bits will be discussed in the next chapter. For example, the ADD and SUB instructions set all of the bits appropriately. The one-address CMP instruction compares the accumulator with

TABLE 2-3 CONDITIONS AND CODES IN THE INTEL 8080

Condition	Mnemonic to test for on	Mnemonic to test for off
Zero (Z)	JZ (Zero)	JNZ (Non Zero)
Sign (S)	JM (Minus)	JP (Positive)
Parity (P)	JPE (Parity Even)	JPO (Parity Odd)
Carry (CY)	JC (Carry)	JNC (No Carry)

another value by computing the difference between the accumulator and that value and setting the condition bits. It does not change the accumulator. Thus

```
        CMP     D
```

compares the content of register D with the accumulator and sets all of the condition bits appropriately. After its execution, the condition bits have exactly the same value as if the instruction

```
        SUB     D
```

had been executed. The condition bits can be tested by the eight instructions shown in Table 2-3. Each of these tests a single condition bit for on or off. For example, to place the larger of registers C and D into register A, we can execute the code

```
        MOV     A,C         Move content of C to A.
        CMP     D           Set condition of C − D.
        JP      DONE        If positive, C is larger.
        MOV     A,D         If not, move D to A.
DONE    ...                 Next instruction.
```

The use of these instructions is illustrated in Program 2-4, which forms the greatest common divisor using the technique described at a high level in Program 2-3. (This is the Euler algorithm. It continually subtracts the smaller of the two values from the larger until they are the same, at which time their value is the greatest common divisor.

Program 2-3 Greatest common divisor

```
Program to compute GCD of X and Y
 all values are positive integers
do while X ≠ Y
  if X < Y then switch X and Y endif
  X ← X − Y
  enddo
GCD ← X
```

Program 2-4 Greatest common divisor on INTEL 8080

```
        LDA        Y
        MOV        B,A         ;Put Y in register B
        LDA        X           ;X is kept in Accumulator
LOOP      CMP        B         ;Compare X and Y
          JZ         ENDLP     ;Exit loop if X = Y
          JP         XHIGH
            MOV        C,A     ;Switch X and Y using C reg.
            MOV        A,B
            MOV        B,C
XHIGH       SUB        B       ;X = X - Y
          JMP        LOOP
ENDLP   STA        GCD         ;Store result back in memory
```

Understanding algorithm is not important; the reader can compare the high-level and the machine-level descriptions given.)

2.4.2 INTEL 8086/88 Control

The INTEL 8086/88 executes instruction in order of increasing address under control of a 16-bit program counter called the *instruction pointer,* or IP register. IP contains the address of the first 8-bit byte of the next instruction. The IP is incremented by from 1 to 5 during instruction execution, depending on the length of the instruction. The JMP instruction breaks the sequential processing by changing the contents of IP. Thus

```
JMP        S
```

sets the value of IP to S. Conditional branches in the 8086/88 are made on the basis of a number of condition flags. The condition flags are set by most of the arithmetic instructions. The ZF (Zero) flag is a 1 if the result of the last operation was 0. The SF (Sign) flag is a 1 if the last result was negative. The other flag bits will be discussed in the next chapter. All flags are given in Table 2-4 for completeness. The two-address CMP instruction compares the value in a register with another value from a register or memory by computing the difference between the first value and the other value and setting the condition flags on the basis of the result. It does not change either of the values. Thus

```
CMP        DX,AX
```

compares the content of register DX with the content of register AX by subtracting a copy of the value in AX from a copy of the value in DX and sets all of the condition flags appropriately. After its execution, the condition flags have exactly the same value as if the instruction

TABLE 2-4 CONDITION FLAGS IN THE INTEL 8086/88

Flag name	Meaning if flag on	On name	Off name
ZF	Result zero	ZR	NZ
SF	Sign negative	NG	PL
OF	Overflow occurred	OV	NV
CF	Carry	CY	NC
AF	Auxiliary carry	AC	NA
PF	Parity even	PE	PO
TF*	Trap (used for debugging)	—	—
IF*	Interrupt enabled	EI	DI
DF*	Direction down	DN	UP

*This is not a condition flag; it controls processor actions.

```
        SUB     DX,AX
```

had been executed. The condition flags can be tested by a number of instructions, including

```
        JS      Jump on Sign (Branches if SF=1)
        JNS     Jump if Not Sign (Branches if SF=0)
        JZ      Jump on Zero (Branches if ZF=1)
        JE      Jump if Equal (Same as JZ)
        JNZ     Jump if Not Zero (Branches if ZF=0)
        JNE     Jump if Not Equal (Same as JNZ)
        JAE     Jump if Above or Equal
```

There is more than one name for some instructions. For example, tests for Zero (JZ) and equality (JE) are the same. Following an arithmetic operation, JZ determines whether the result is 0. Following a comparison, JE determines whether the compared values were identical. Since a comparison is based on an airthmetic operation (subtraction), there is no difference, but it may be easier for a person to read a program that uses the appropriate name. There are a number of additional conditional branches that will be covered in the next chapter after we have looked at the representation of negative numbers. One example is given above—JAE, Jump if Above or Equal, which branches if the result is above or equal to 0 considered as an unsigned value. For example, to place the larger of the values in the BX and CX registers into AX, we can execute

```
        CMP     BX,CX
        JAE     B_BIG
        MOV     AX,CX
        JMP     DONE
B_BIG   MOV     AX,BX
DONE    ...             Next instruction
```

Program 2-5 Greatest common divisor on INTEL 8086/88

```
         MOV      AX,X      ;X kept in AX
         MOV      BX,Y      ;Y kept in BX
LOOP       CMP      AX,BX   ;Compare X and Y
           JZ       ENDLP   ;Exit loop if X = Y
           JAE      XHIGH   ;Skip if X >= Y
             XCHG     AX,BX ;Switch X and Y
XHIGH        SUB      BX    ;X = X - Y
           JMP      LOOP
ENDLP    MOV      GCD,AX    ;Store result back in memory
```

The use of these instructions is illustrated in Program 2-5, which forms the greatest common divisor using the technique described at a high level in Program 2-3. (This program is also given for the INTEL 8080 as Program 2-4. See the comment at the end of the previous section.)

2.5 ASSEMBLY LANGUAGE

We have been using a form of assembly language to describe instructions. Without it, we would not have been able to describe machine instructions other than by specifying the actual binary form. The latter form is no more necessary to the writing of instructions than it is to the understanding of machine language. In assembly language we have the capability of describing the form of the instructions to be executed by the computer exactly, but we can use easy-to-remember names for the operations (called *mnemonics*), and symbolic names (called *symbols* or *identifiers*) instead of actual numerical memory addresses. We can also describe values to be placed in the computer memory for use by the program as constants and initial values of variables. These descriptions are given in *pseudo instructions,* which look very much like regular instructions. Pseudo instructions can also be used to allocate space in memory for variables to be used by the program. Finally, the programmer can give instructions to the assembler on matters such as where the program is to be placed. This is done in *directives,* which are also called pseudo instructions by some writers. The purpose of this short section is to give a quick overview of assembly language so that we can use it to discuss additional machine instructions and to try some very simple programs on the machine. More details will be given in Chapter 6.

2.5.1 Assembler Representation of Instructions

The assembly-language version of a program consists of a sequence of lines each containing an instruction or other information. The assembler converts each line containing an instruction into the equivalent machine instruction and assigns it space in memory, called the *location* of that instruction. Consecutive instructions are allocated to consecutive locations in memory. The assembler usually provides a listing of the translated form of the code alongside the assembly language. A typical listing takes the form

```
1 0000      03 1234      START LOAD      BASE
2 0003      22 1235            ADD       OFFSET
3 0006      41 0321      LOOP  STORE     POINTER
4 0009      23 0017            SUB       DECR
   ...                         ...
```

The listing consists of a number of columns. In this example, the first is a line count. The second indicates the location where the instruction for that line will be loaded. (The first of several locations in the case of multibyte instructions.) The next two columns give the internal form of the instruction, usually the operation followed by the operand address(es). In this example, we have assumed that the LOAD instruction is represented internally by 03 (in fact, the internal form is binary, so this is an alternate numerical form for the binary, usually hexadecimal or octal). The operand address for the LOAD is 1234 in this example. The remainder of the line contains the original input. From this listing the programmer can see that the symbols START and LOOP are associated with locations 0000 and 0006, respectively. The assembler will often provide a listing of all symbols used and their equivalent addresses.

In each instruction, the programmer has to be able to specify the name of an instruction and its operand address or addresses, and to indicate whether a symbolic address is associated with the location containing the instruction. *Fields* of the input line are associated with each of these items. Many of the early assemblers used *fixed-format* input in which each field occupied a fixed position in the input line. This was convenient when punched cards were used, as was the case on many early computers, but is less convenient for terminal input and does prevent the use of indentation in display structure. Consequently, most current assemblers use variable-format input. In variable-format input, each field is separated from the next by one or more separator characters. Virtually all assemblers use a format in which the four items are specified in the following order:

1 Location symbol, if present (also called a label)
2 Operation
3 Address(es)
4 Comment

For example:

```
SYMB5     ADD       SYMB1,SYMB2       Comment
          SUB       SYMB2,SYMB3       No comment
```

One or more of the fields may be empty. The way these fields are distinguished from each other varies from assembler to assembler, but there are two principal methods. In the first, typically used on the larger computers, such as the IBM 370 and CDC Cyber, the fields are separated by one or more blanks. If the first (or first few) columns are blank, there is assumed to be no location symbol. This is the format illustrated above. The first line defines SYMB5 to refer to the ADD instruction. It has all four fields present, separated from each other by blanks. The second line has no location symbol. This is indicated by the additional blanks in the early columns. If an instruction has no operand address, the field can be blank; the assembler knows which instructions cannot have addresses and thus knows that in an instruction such as

```
SYMB       SET-NEGATIVE              Change sign of accumulator
```

there is no address, therefore the third field must be comment. The comment field can be left blank, as its use is entirely at the discretion of the programmer, but it *should* be used for comment so that the program will be easy to understand. If a line containing only comment is required, this type of assembler usually requires a special character in column 1, often an asterisk.

In the second type of assembler format, the various fields are separated from each other by special characters. A very common form of assembler requires the location symbol, if present, to end with a colon and 0 or more blanks, the mnemonic to end with one or more blanks, and the comment field to be preceded by a semicolon. The two instructions above would appear as follows in this type of input:

```
SYMB5:     ADD        SYMB1,SYMB2        ;Comment
           SUB        SYMB2,SYMB3        ;No comment
```

A line with nothing but a comment is allowed; the first nonblank character must be a semicolon.

Since only one column or separator character is needed to separate fields, it is possible to write a program "squeezed to the left." For example,

```
GCD LOAD FF1
  SUB X2
  BZ XT
  BPL Y
  SMI
  STORE X2
  BR YNOT
Y STORE F1
YNOT BR GCD
XT LOAD F1
  RET
```

This is a terrible piece of code for several reasons, not the least of which is that nothing is lined up, so it is almost impossible to tell where the various fields begin and end. The assembler does not care how many blanks are in the input, or what variable names are used, so these degrees of freedom should be used by the programmer to make the program as clear as possible to the human reader. What is not clear should be told in comment (which is noticeably missing from the code above). Symbols for variables and instruction locations should be chosen for their informative value, not at random or for their "cuteness." Thus we could, and should, rewrite the fragment of code above as follows:

```
*            THIS SECTION OF CODE COMPUTES THE GREATEST
*            COMMON DIVISOR OF FACT1 and FACT2. IT IS
*            CALLED AS A SUBROUTINE. THE RESULT IS LEFT
*            IN THE ACCUMULATOR. FACT1 AND FACT2 ARE
*            CHANGED. EULER'S ALGORITHM IS USED.
*            REFER TO ··· FOR A DESCRIPTION OF THIS METHOD.
*
 GCD          LOAD       FACT1        Start of loop
              SUB        FACT2        Compute difference
              BZ         DONE         Terminate if FACT1 = FACT2
              BPL        F1LARGE      If FACT1 < FACT2 then...
*                                     (FACT2 is the larger)
                SMI                     Change sign to get
*                                         FACT2 - FACT1
                STORE      FACT2        Set FACT2 = FACT2 - FACT1
                BR         IFEND
*                                       else (FACT1 is the larger)
F1LARGE         STORE      FACT1        Set FACT1 = FACT1 - FACT2
IFEND           BR         GCD          Repeat loop
DONE          LOAD       FACT1         Result to accumulator
            RET                       Return to calling program
```

Note that probably nobody but the author of the code could have made this change, as it is doubtful that anybody else could have understood the original code! (This is still not a good piece of code, as the algorithm functions only for strictly positive integers. The code should really check to see that the initial data satisfies this requirement. As it stands, the code could easily get stuck in an infinite loop for invalid data.)

Assemblers place restrictions on the form of symbols used. These are similar to the restrictions on identifiers in higher-level languages. Usually, they must start with a letter and contain nothing but alphanumeric characters (the letters and decimal digits, although some systems define additional characters as alphanumeric). The length is often restricted, typically to somewhere between five and eight characters as a maximum, although more recent assemblers have relaxed this requirement in line with modern high-level programming languages. Most assemblers allow expressions to be used in place of any address. For example, if the symbol BLK1 were to represent memory address 105, BLK1+2 would represent address 107. Expressions may involve the usual arithmetic operators and possibly some additional ones, but the form allowed is very dependent on the assembler. Other restrictions are placed on expressions by system requirements that will be discussed in later chapters.

2.5.2 Definition of Data and Storage by Pseudo Instructions

The assembler converts lines containing assembly language instructions into the internal form of the instructions. In the same way, it converts lines containing pseudo instructions defining data into the internal representation of the data. Typical of these pseudo instructions (or pseudos for short) are those that allow for the definition or declaration of numerical values and character strings. Early assemblers provided a different pseudo for each data type. Some more recent assemblers use a single pseudo and determine the data type from the format of the data. General forms of pseudos are illustrated in the following examples:

```
NUMB     WORD     10,-43,1234H,1111B
PIECE    BYTE     143,23Q,34H,-1
NAMES    CHAR     'ABCDEFGHIJK'
```

The pseudo looks very much like a regular instruction. It has a location symbol, a mnemonic, and an operand address field. It can also have a comment field, if desired. The assembler knows the names of the mnemonics and thus knows that these are pseudos. The first, WORD, assembles a sequence of words of data into consecutive cells. The symbolic address in the location field NUMB is associated with the address of the first word loaded. In this example, four words are loaded; each word is specified by an item in the address field. Items are separated with commas. Most but not all assemblers expect decimal numeric values unless specified otherwise. In this case, decimal is called the *default* base. In this example, the first two words are decimal values, the third is hexadecimal, and the last is binary. Some allow the default base of numbers to be set by the user. The second example above, BYTE, appears in some computers that have byte addressing. It allows individual bytes to be loaded with 8-bit data quantities. Otherwise, it is similar to WORD. The symbol PIECE is assigned the address of the first byte loaded. CHAR loads character strings into consecutive bytes. In the example above, 11 characters are loaded into consecutive bytes of memory (or into whatever unit of memory is used to hold 11 characters). The symbol NAMES is assigned the address of the first character. The address field in CHAR is a string surrounded by single quotes. Just those characters inside the quotes are loaded. If the string is to contain a quote as a character, it must be input as two quotes. For example:

```
QUOTE    CHAR     'USE '' TO GET A SINGLE QUOTE'
```

Note that two single quote characters must be used, not the double-quote character.

Pseudos cause data to be assembled into consecutive locations just as instructions are assembled into consecutive locations. For example, for a byte-addressable machine, an assembler given the input

```
VALS     BYTE     13,15,255
         BYTE     21
         BYTE     45,22
```

will assemble the 6 bytes 13, 15, 255, 21, 45, and 22 into six consecutive locations. If the address of the first is 100, the symbol VALS will correspond to address 100, and the last value, 22, will assemble into location 105.

In addition to allowing the user to specify constants via pseudos, many assemblers allow the use of *literals*. These are constants that are written in the address field of an instruction that refers to them. In most assemblers, they are preceded by the character "=". The assembler places the constant following the literal character (=) in a storage cell at the end of the program and generates a symbolic address by which to refer to it. For example,

```
        LOAD    =6
```

might be translated by the assembler to

```
        LOAD    \0001
        . . .
\0001   WORD    6
```

Note that the assembler generates a symbol for the literal of a form that is unlikely to be used by the programmer. In fact, in many assemblers, the generated symbol will have a form that is not permitted to the programmer. The assembler keeps a list of all literals specified and generates a table of them in cells following the program. Whenever constants are used, it is preferable to use literals; the code is easier to read, and many assemblers check to see whether the same literal is used twice so that only one copy need be kept. Needless to say, one should not write an instruction such as STORE =6, even if the assembler allows it! The reason for this can be seen in the code segment

```
        LOAD    =3
        STORE   =6
        LOAD    =6
        STORE   RESULT
```

Execution of this will store the value 3 in RESULT, a fact not apparent if one reads only the last two lines!

2.5.3 Assembler Directives

Directives are used to place code into memory locations out of normal sequence, to reserve blocks for multiword items, to define symbolic addresses and other identifiers, and to pass information to the assembler. Typical of directives are BSS, EQU, ORG, and END, which are directives found in almost all assemblers. For example,

```
QARRAY  BSS     100
```

reserves the next 100 words of memory for a block of data. The address, QARRAY in this example, is identified with the first of these words. The BSS (Block Started by

Symbol) pseudo above causes 100 memory locations to be set aside, so that the next instruction or pseudo will be assembled 100 locations beyond the previous one. For example, the sequence

```
VAL1      BYTE     25
X15       BSS      100
VAL2      BYTE     12
```

uses 102 memory locations. If the value 25 from the first line were assembled into location 300, X15 would correspond to location 301 and VAL2 would correspond to 401, which is the location into which the byte 12 is assembled. The address field of a BSS instruction can usually be an expression depending on other, previously defined symbols.

Whereas BSS is used to allocate space, the ORG (origin) directive indicates that subsequent code is to be assembled starting at a new location or *origin*. For example,

```
          ORG      200
```

sets the origin to the value of the expression 200, that is, the next item to be assembled will be placed in location 200. For example,

```
          ORG      100
VAL1      BYTE     22
VAL2      BYTE     23,24
```

assembles the bytes 22, 23, and 24 into locations 100 to 102 inclusive. The address field of an ORG pseudo can often contain an expression. Thus the two following constructions have the same effect:

```
          ORG      100
QARRAY    BSS      1
          ORG      QARRAY+100
VAL3      BYTE     5

          ORG      100
QARRAY    BSS      100
VAL3      BYTE     5
```

Both make the symbol QARRAY equivalent to location 100, make VAL3 equivalent to 200, and will cause the nest item to be assembled into location 201.

EQU (EQUivalent to) is used to assign the value of a symbol directly. For example,

```
N         EQU      100
```

states that the value of the symbol N is 100, so that N is a symbolic name for 100. The principal use of EQU is in defining the values of *parameters* of programs that are known prior to assembly. For example, if one is writing a program to sort blocks of data, it will need arrays of space in which to manipulate that data. If the program needs, say, two arrays, one twice the size of the other, it should be written with a parameter, say N, that gives the size of one array. It might start with the statements

```
N       EQU     100
REG1    BSS     N
REG2    BSS     2 * N
```

which allocate the two blocks. If it becomes necessary to change the size of the arrays, one need only change the EQU statement.

The last line in an assembly language program has to be indicated. The usual way is with the directive END. The END directive is allowed an address field in some assemblers. The value of the address indicates the starting address for execution of the program. (In high-level languages, execution is usually required to start at a predetermined place, the start of the body of the main program. In assembly language we can usually specify the place at which execution is to commence after the program has been loaded into memory.)

2.5.4 The CP/M Assembler

There are a number of assemblers for 8080 computers, and there are slight differences between them. We will discuss the one available in the CP/M operating system.[7] It is a good example of an assembler for a microcomputer. The four fields of the assembler statements are standard. They are

Label: Terminated by semicolon or blank
Operation: Terminated by blank
Address: Terminated by semicolon or end of line
Comment: Terminated by end of line

Additional blanks may appear with the terminators. The exclamation mark is interpreted as an end of line if it is not part of a character string. This allows several instructions to appear on one physical line. For example:

```
MOV A,C ! MOV C,B ! MOV B,A ;Switch B and C contents
```

Symbols may not be the names of the registers (A, B, C, D, E, F, H, L, M, SP, or PSW) or of operation codes. They must start with an alphabetic character and contain only alphanumeric characters or embedded $ characters (which can be viewed as blanks for breaking up long symbols, but are otherwise ignored). Symbols can be up to sixteen characters in length. Constants must start with a decimal digit. If they are not terminated with the letter B (Binary), H or X (Hexadecimal), or Q or O (Octal), they are decimal constants. (The letter D may also be used at the end to indicate decimal

[7] *An Introduction to CP/M Features and Facilities*, Digital Research, Pacific Grove, CA, 1978.

integers.) A constant may also have embedded $ characters, which are ignored. A character string constant is formed in exactly the way described in Section 2.5.2.

The data loading pseudos are

```
        DB                      ;define bytes
        DW                      ;define words
```

DW can be used to specify a sequence of 16-bit words. It takes the form

```
        DW        item1,item2,· · ·,itemn
```

If this is preceded by a symbol, that symbol will be equated with the address of the first byte loaded. Each item is translated into a 16-bit quantity and loaded into 2 consecutive bytes; the least significant byte of the item is stored in the location with the *lower* address, because right-end addressing is used. For example, the pseudo

```
VALS        DW        1234H,5678H
```

stores words or 4 bytes. VALS is a symbol whose address is the location of the first byte loaded. If that address is location 100, the locations and contents of the 4 bytes are

```
        100       34H
        101       12H
        102       78H
        103       56H
```

Note how the bytes are reversed from the word order: the *word* starting at location 100 contains the value 1234H.

The pseudo instruction DB is similar except that 8-bit quantities are loaded and therefore the items must evaluate to 8 bits. The address field of a DB pseudo may also be a string of characters surrounded by single quotes, for example,

```
MSG:        DB        'END OF INPUT'
```

This generates the ASCII encoding of the character string in a set of consecutive bytes. MSG is the address of the first byte, and the characters are stored from left to right in locations with increasing addresses.

Space is allocated with the DS (Define Storage) pseudo. For example,

```
W:          DS        4*KW
```

allocates a block of 4*KW bytes. All symbols in the address field must have been defined earlier so that the assembler knows how many bytes to allocate.

The INTEL 8080 assembler includes a minimum set of directives, including ORG, EQU, and END. These are as described in Section 2.5.3. The CP/M operating system

Program 2-6 Sample CP/M Assembly Language Program

```
        ORG     100H    ;Start assembly at location 100H
        LDA     BYTE1
        MOV     B,A     ;BYTE1 to B
        LDA     BYTE2
        ADD     B       ;BYTE1 + BYTE2 to A
        STA     BYTE3   ;Result to BYTE3
        JMP     0       ;A way to stop progam in CP/M
BYTE1   DB      34H
BYTE2   DB      2EH
BYTE3   DS      1
        END     100H    ;Begin execution at 100H
```

normally expects code to be assembled starting at location 100 hexadecimal, so the first line of an assembler code is usually ORG 100H. The last line is usually END 100H, so that execution begins at the first line of the user code. Program 2-6 gives a short sample code for the CP/M 8080 assembler. We will see how to watch this execute a step at a time in Section 2.6.

2.5.5 The IBM PC Assembler

This assembler[8] is similar to the INTEL assembler for the 8086/88 and bears many resemblances to the CP/M assembler for the 8080. The four fields of the assembler statements are standard. They are:

Label: Terminated by a colon in instructions or a blank and/or tab in pseudos and directives
Operation: Terminated by blank and/or tab
Address: Terminated by semicolon or end of line
Comment: Terminated by end of line

Additional blanks and tabs may appear with the terminators. Symbols may not be the names of the registers (AX, AH, AL, BX, BH, BL, CX, CH, CL, DX, DH, DL, SP, BP, SI, DI, CS, DS, ES, or SS). They must start with an alphabetic character or a period and contain only alphanumeric characters or the special characters ?, @, _, or $. Symbols can be of arbitrary length, but only the first thirty-one characters are recognized. Constants must start with a decimal digit. If they are not terminated with the letter B (Binary), H or X (Hexadecimal), Q or O (Octal), they are decimal constants. (The letter D may also be used at the end to indicate decimal integers.) A character string constant can be surrounded by either single- or double-quote characters. Whichever is used, the other can appear inside the string.

[8]*IBM Personal Computer: Computer Language Series, Macro Assembler, Document 6172234*. IBM, Boca Raton, FL, 1981.

Two of the data loading pseudos are

```
        DB                      ;define bytes
        DW                      ;define words
```

DW can be used to specify a sequence of 16-bit words. It takes the form

```
        DW          item1,item2,· · ·,itemn
```

If this is preceded by a symbol, that symbol will be equated with the address of the first byte loaded. Each item is translated into one or more 16-bit quantities and loaded into pairs of consecutive bytes; the least significant byte of each pair is stored in the location with the *lower* address because right-end addressing is used. For example, the pseudo

```
VALS    DW          1234H,5678H
```

stores 2 words or 4 bytes. VALS is a symbol whose address is the location of the first byte loaded. If that address is location 100, the locations and contents of the 4 bytes are

```
        100         34H
        101         12H
        102         78H
        103         56H
```

Note how the bytes are reversed from the word order: the word starting at location 100 contains the value 1234H.

The pseudo instruction DB is similar except that 8-bit quantities are loaded and therefore the items must evaluate to 8 bits. The address field of a DB pseudo may also be a string of characters surrounded by single or double quotes, for example,

```
MSG:    DB          "THE FOLLOWING IS A 'QUOTED STRING'"
```

This generates the ASCII encoding of the character string in a set of consecutive bytes. Note that the string in this example can contain single quotes because the string is surrounded by double quotes. MSG is the address of the first byte, and the characters are stored from left to right in locations with increasing addresses.

Space is also allocated with the DB and DW pseudos. If an item is specified as by ?, the item is initialized to an indeterminate value. Any item can be surrounded by a repeat factor, written <repeat factor> DUP (<item>), to cause several values to be assembled. For example,

```
SPACE   DB          100 DUP(?)
```

allocates a block of 100 bytes that are not initialized, whereas

```
GARRAY     DW          100 DUP (1234H)
```

generates a block of 100 words, each initialized to 1234 hexadecimal.

The IBM PC assembler includes a large number of directives. We will mention only those needed to assemble the simplest program here. Many of them are necessary because the INTEL 8086/88 chip has a number of complexities that we will not discuss for a while but that require the programmer to specify a large amount of information to the assembler. Some of these directives are illustrated in the assembly code for the IBM PC shown in Program 2-7. This code also uses some instructions that will not be covered until later chapters. These should be ignored for the present. The reader should use the directives, pseudos, and instructions shown in any code to be executed on a PC. This example contains only three instructions of interest to us: MOV, ADD, and MOV, which add the values in WORD1 and WORD2, putting the result in WORD3. WORD1 and WORD2 are defined by hexadecimal constants using the DW pseudo. (These lines of code and data can be replaced by other examples to try out assembly language programs.) In the next section we will see how to watch the execution of this program a step at a time.

2.6 DEBUGGERS

A debugger is a program that helps the user locate errors (*bugs*) in programs using a number of interactive techniques. Debuggers are very powerful tools for tracking down some types of errors, particularly those resulting from a misunderstanding of the way in which instructions operate. A debugger is not only a valuable debugging tool, it is also a valuable learning tool, especially at the machine-language level, because it can be used to watch the execution of a program a step at a time. The beginning student is urged to experiment with a debugger as a way of becoming familiar with a machine. Debuggers allow the user to execute a single section or a single statement of a program and then pause to examine the effect of that statement or section immediately after it has been executed. During the pauses in execution, the values of variables, the contents of registers, or the code that has just been executed or is about to be executed can be displayed. In a *trace*, the values of key variables or registers can be displayed as each statement is executed, whereas in the *breakpoint mode*, the program can be executed until the next breakpoint is encountered. A breakpoint is simply a named statement. At

Program 2-7 Sample IBM PC Assembly Language Program

```
TITLE     SAMPLE PC ASSEMBLY PROGRAM
COMMENT*  ANY INFORMATION FROM HERE TO THE LINE THAT
     ENDS IN AN ASTERISK IS COMMENT AND HAS NO EFFECT      *
;
COMMENT*     THE FOLLOWING LINES ARE TYPICAL OF THOSE THAT
     MUST APPEAR IN ALL PROGRAMS                            *
;
```

```
STACK      SEGMENT   PARA STACK 'STACK'
           DB        64 DUP('STACK  ')
           ENDS
WKAREA     SEGMENT   PARA PUBLIC 'DATA'
;
COMMENT*      NORMALLY SPACE FOR CONSTANTS AND VARIABLES
       ARE PLACED IN THE SEGMENT NAMED WKAREA. IN THIS
       EXAMPLE WE ARE USING TWO CONSTANTS, WORD1 AND
       WORD2, AND A VARIABLE, WORD3.                        *
;
WORD1      DW        1234H
WORD2      DW        5432H
WORD3      DW        ?
;
COMMENT*      THE NEXT FEW LINES SEPARATE THE SEGMENT
       USED FOR DATA AND THE PROGRAM AREA USED FOR CODE *
;
WKAREA     ENDS
CSEG       SEGMENT                  PARA PUBLIC 'CODE'
START      PROC      FAR
           ASSUME   CS:CSEG,DS:WKAREA,SS:STACK,ES:NOTHING
           PUSH      DS            ;THESE ARE SOME
           SUB       AX,AX         ;INSTRUCTIONS THAT ARE
           PUSH      AX            ;NECESSARY TO SET UP
           MOV       AX,WKAREA     ;INFORMATION NEEDED
           MOV       DS,AX         ;BEFORE THE PROGRAM
                                   ;CAN BE EXECUTED
                                   ;IN CONJUNCTION WITH THE
                                   ;OPERATING SYSTEM DOS.
;
COMMENT*      FINALLY WE COME TO SOME ACTUAL CODE!          *
;
           MOV       AX,WORD1
           ADD       AX,WORD2   ;WORD1 + WORD2 TO AX
           MOV       WORD3,AX   ;STORE RESULT IN WORD3
;
COMMENT*      AND NOW TO RETURN CONTROL TO THE OPERATING
SYSTEM AND TELL THE ASSEMBLER THAT EVERYTHING IS DONE   *
;
           RET
START      ENDP
CSEG       ENDS
           END       START      ;END OF PROGRAM. BEGIN AT
                                ;START
```

any time, values of variables, the content of registers, or even the code in memory can be changed before execution is continued for further tracing or to the next breakpoint. Thus the programmer can watch the progress of program execution to see whether the values being computed are those expected.

A debugger is a subsystem. It accepts commands from the user and executes those commands, one at a time, interactively. The commands tell the debugger what is wanted. For example, there will be commands to display the values of variables or memory, to set breakpoints, to trace a number of statements, etc. Many operating systems have debuggers for different languages. A debugger for machine language is called an *absolute debugger;* it can be used on the object code of any translator, whereas a *symbolic debugger* works with a program written in a particular language.

In an absolute debugger, the user must refer to data by means of its memory address and must know which locations are used to store which data and which program instructions. The contents of memory and/or registers can be displayed in one of a number of formats, for example, as hexadecimal, integer decimal, or character values. They can also be displayed as machine instructions using a *dis-assembler,* which interprets the binary content of each cell as an instruction and converts it back to an assembly language format in which the instruction mnemonic is given in a familiar form, although the address has to be in numeric form because no symbolic information is available.

A symbolic debugger obtains information about the location of variables, their type, and the external form of statements from the source code at translation time. Typically, a debug option has to be requested of the translator, causing it to provide tables of symbolic information for the debugger. The details of this do not concern the user, who sees a system in which the value of various named variables can be requested or changed interactively and in which statements can be viewed and perhaps modified in source form. As with most system programs, details vary from system to system, so the best way to understand a debugger is to use a particular version rather than read about generalities. In the next sections we will look briefly at some absolute debuggers.

2.6.1 DDT for the INTEL 8080

The CP/M system has an absolute debugger, DDT. It is invoked by executing

```
DDT        PROG.HEX
```

(Recall that the .HEX suffix file is the output from the assembler.) It can also be given the name of a executable file (.COM suffix) with the same effect. Once in the debugger, the user can enter one of a number of commands. Commands that display information are:

```
D          Display memory in Hexadecimal and ASCII
L          Display memory in Assembler Format
X          Display the state of the CPU registers
```

The D and L commands display twelve lines from the last place listed unless a hexadecimal starting point is given after the command. Thus L100 displays twelve lines starting at location 100 hexadecimal in assembler format. An L with no argument lists the next twelve lines. X with no arguments gives a list of the contents of all registers. All numeric values are entered and printed in hexadecimal in DDT. The output takes the form

```
CbZbMbEbIb A=hh B=hhhh D=hhhh H=hhhh S=hhhh P=hhhh iiii
```

where b is a bit (0 or 1), h is a hexadecimal digit, and iiii is a mnemonic instruction. C, Z, M, E, and I stand for the Carry, Zero, Sign, Parity, and Auxiliary (Intermediate) carry flags. A stands for the accumulator. The remaining registers are grouped in pairs. B stands for the register pair BC. Hence, if we see that B = 1234 we know that B contains 12 hexadecimal, whereas C contains 34 hexadecimal. Similarly, D stands for DE and H stands for HL. S stands for the stack pointer (to be discussed later). P is the program counter (which is 16 bits long and is therefore printed as four hexadecimal digits). The value of each status flag and register is given after the name. If the name of a register is given as a parameter to the X command, the content of only that register is displayed and the user has an opportunity to change it. For example, XA displays the content of the accumulator. If a two-digit hexadecimal value is typed in response, the accumulator is changed to that value. XP displays the program counter. Changing it allows execution to be restarted at any point.

Memory values can be changed in hexadecimal with the S*n* command. It displays location *n* in hexadecimal and allows it to be changed. If no change is required, a period should be given; otherwise a two-digit hexadecimal value should be typed. It will be stored in the addressed cell. The value in the next location is then typed so that it can also be changed. This process is repeated until a single period is entered. Code can be put into memory with the A*n* command, which starts assembling into location *n* (hexadecimal) until an empty line is input. All assembly-language statements must use hexadecimal addresses except for the names of the registers.

The trace command, T, causes the next instruction to be executed and the new state of the registers to be displayed, whereas T*n* causes the next *n* instructions to be executed with a display of the registers after each.

The student just starting to use an 8080 system should try checking out a few simple programs using DDT with the trace command to see what is happening at the machine level. The A command allows simple programs to be entered directly into memory. Initial data can be entered with the S command. The registers can be set with the X command, and the results of execution can be observed using the T command and the L command. For example, to observe execution of Program 2-6 we could assemble that program and apply DDT to it, or we could input it directly, as shown in the following example of DDT use. (Information in the left column is printed by the computer, and that on the right is entered by the user. Lower case text is comment that is neither output by the computer nor to be input by the user.

Computer	User	Comment
	DDT	Enter the DDT system.
DDT VERS 2.2		Message from the system.
–	A100	– is the prompt from DDT; user asks to start assembly in location 100H.

```
100            ADD      B  Some instructions to test.
101            STA      110
104            JMP      0
107                     A null line indicates end of assembly.
-              XP       Examine Program Counter.
P=0100                  It is already set to 100H.
XA                      Examine and set A register to
A=00           55       binary 01010101.
-              XB       Examine and set BC register.
B=0000         1F00     B becomes binary 00011111.
-              X        Display registers to check that we have
                        set them correctly. The next instruction
                        to be executed is from location 100H.
C0Z0M0E0I0 A=55 B=1F00 D=0000 H=0000 S=0100 P=0100 ADD B
-              S110     Examine location 110.
110 28         .        It is 28H. No more input.
-              T        Trace one step. All of next line is
                        printed by computer to give status.
                        The status is given before the next step
                        is executed. The next instruction to be executed is
                        also displayed, followed by the address of the
                        subsequent instruction (101).
C0Z0M0E0I0 A=55 B=1F00 D=0000 H=0000 S=0100 P=0100 ADD B*101
-              T        Now trace to the next instruction.
                        Note that program counter has advanced
                        by one, the ADD has been executed,
                        and the accumulator has changed.
                        The last item printed is the address of the following
                        instruction, which is to be executed.
C0Z0M0E0I0 A=74 B=1F00 D=0000 H=0000 S=0100 P=0101 STA 0110*104
-              T        Trace next step.
C0Z0M0E0I0 A=74 B=1F00 D=0000 H=0000 S=0100 P=0104 JMP 0000*0000
-              S110     Examine location 110 for the answer
110 74         .        There it is!
```

2.6.2 DEBUG for the IBM PC

The IBM PC DOS has an absolute debugger, DEBUG. It is invoked by executing

```
DEBUG     PROG.EXE
```

(Recall that the .EXE suffix file is the executable file from LINK.) Once in the debugger, the user can enter one of a number of commands. In this section we will describe the simplest use of DEBUG. Further details can be found in the IBM DOS manual referenced earlier. Commands that display information are:

```
D      Display memory in Hexadecimal and ASCII (Dump)
U      Display memory in Assembler Format (Unassemble)
R      Display the state of the CPU registers
```

The D and U commands can be followed by an optional address or address range. If an address is given, the D command prints 128 bytes in both hexadecimal and ASCII, starting from the address specified. If no address is given, the next 128 bytes are dumped. (If the VDU monitor displays only 40 columns across rather than the usual 80, only 64 bytes are dumped at a time.) The address must be specified in hexadecimal. It indicates an address in the *data* region of the program. (INTEL 8086/88 programs are divided into different *segments,* which occupy different regions of memory. These will be discussed in more detail later in this chapter. The segment named WORKAREA in Program 2-7 contains the data. If you assemble this program and look at the listing, you will find that this part of the program is listed as

```
0000           WKAREA    SEGMENT   PARA PUBLIC 'DATA'
0000 1234 WORD1     DW        1234H
0002 5432 WORD2     DW        5432H
0004 ???? WORD3     DW        ?
```

If the DEBUG command D 0 is given, 128 bytes, starting with the bytes corresponding to WORD1, will be printed.) If a range of addresses (in hexadecimal) is given, all bytes in that range will be output. Thus D 10 2F prints all data segment bytes between addresses 0010 and 002F.

The U command is similar to the D command, except that the program region of memory is output in assembler format with addresses in hexadecimal. The address given in the U command refers to the addresses that will be found alongside the assembler listing for the code segment of the program (the information following the line containing CSEG SEGMENT . . . in Program 2-7). R with no arguments gives a list of the contents of all registers. The output takes the form

```
AX = 1234 BX = 5432 CX = FF00 DX = 8000
SP = 04A2 BP = 0002 SI = 0400 DI = 111A
DS = 04AA ES = 04AA SS = 04AA CS = 04B0
IP = 0004 NV UP DI PL NZ NA PO NC
04B0:0004 03060002        ADD AX,0002
```

(On some displays, this may be collapsed to three lines.) The registers on the first line are ones we have already discussed. The registers on the second and third lines will be discussed later in this chapter. The IP register on the fourth line is the *Instruction Pointer* or program counter (also called PC). The remaining entries on that line are the states of the flags listed in Table 2-4. The last two columns in that table show the names listed according to the states of the flags. (The Trap flag is not listed.) The final line gives the address of the next instruction to be executed (the content of IP). It is preceded by another hexadecimal value, which is actually the content of the CS register; it will be discussed in later sections. It is followed by the hexadecimal contents of that location and a few of the subsequent bytes. The last item is the assembler mnemonic form of the next instruction to be executed.

If the name of a register is given as a parameter to the R command, the content of only that register is displayed and the user has an opportunity to change it. For example, R AX displays the content of the AX register. It is printed in the format

```
AX 1234
:_
```

The screen cursor is shown as an underlined character. The user can now enter a new value for the AX register (in hexadecimal). Doing nothing (just pressing ENTER) leaves it unchanged. The flags can be changed by displaying them with the R F command. It outputs the current values, and the user can type the new values of the flags that need to be changed by using the names in Table 2-4 in any order.

Memory values can be changed in hexadecimal with the E (Enter) command. When followed by a hexadecimal address, it displays the content of that location in the data segment of memory and permits the user to change the value. A block of locations can be changed by following the address with a list of hexadecimal and/or string values.

The trace command, T, causes the next instruction to be executed and the new state of the registers to be displayed, whereas T*n* causes the next *n* instructions to be executed with a display of the registers after each. The display is exactly as for the R command, except that if the next instruction to be executed references memory, the content of the referenced quantity will be displayed at the end. The instruction shown on the last line is the next instruction to be executed.

The student first starting to use an IBM PC system should try checking out a few simple programs using DEBUG with the trace command to see what is happening at the machine level. For example, if Program 2-7 is assembled under the name PROG and DEBUG is applied to it, we can observe the results by executing the sequence

```
DEBUG PROG.EXE
-T5                                      The DEBUG prompt is -. The T5
                                         command executes the first five
                                         instructions, which do not concern
                                         us at the moment. A register
                                         printout occurs after each. The
                                         last is shown.
AX=04D1 BX=0000 CX=0000 DX=0000
SP=01FC BP=0000 SI=0000 DI=0000
DS=04D1 ES=049F SS=04B1 CS=04AF
IP=0009 NV UP DI PL ZR NA PE NC
04AF: 0009 A10000 MOV AX,[0000] DS:0000 = 1234
-T                                       Execute the MOV AX, WORD1
                                         instruction. Observe that AX
                                         changes. Only the first and last
                                         lines of output are shown.
AX = 1234 BX = 0000 CX = 0000 DX = 0000
. . .
04AF: 000C 03060200 ADD AX,[0002] DS:0002 = 5432
-T                                       Execute the ADD AX,WORD2
                                         instruction.
```

```
AX = 6666 BX = 0000 CX = 0000 DX = 0000
04AF:0010 A30400 MOV [0004],AX DS:0004 = 0000
-T                                     Execute the MOV WORD3,AX
                                       instruction.
. . .                                  Another register printout.
-D 0                                   Examine the data. Observe that
                                       locations 4 and 5 have changed
                                       to the answer.
04D1:0000 34 12 32 54 66 66 00 00      4.2TFF..
04D1:0008 00 00 00 00 00 00 00 00      ........
. . .
```

2.7 ADDRESS STRUCTURE

A digital computer is designed to execute programs rapidly. This means that it must be possible to express frequently occurring tasks in a simple way with few instructions. Therefore, although a task can be coded using only the simplest of instructions, such as those discussed in Sections 2.3 and 2.4, computers usually have a variety of instructions designed to speed processing. For example, neither addition, multiplication, nor division are necessary, as they can all be coded using subtractions (multiplication and division are not even provided on some small microcomputers, such as the INTEL 8080), but without them an arithmetic task takes longer to program and execute. Allowing flexible access of data from memory is one way in which a careful computer design can speed the processing considerably. This section will examine some classes of instructions and related hardware that help to gain speed.

2.7.1 Index Registers

It is frequently necessary to process arrays of data in a sequential fashion. For example, it may be necessary to execute the equivalent of A(I) = B(I) + C(I) for values of I from 1 to 1000. Let us assume that the variables A(1), A(2), . . . , A(1000) are in locations A, A + 1, . . . , A + 999 in memory, and that similar arrangements exist for the arrays B and C. The task can be executed for I = 1 by the one-address program

```
LOAD    B
ADD     C
STORE   A
```

but it is certainly not desirable to repeat this a further 999 times! Most early computers stored one instruction in each word, and the operand address in an instruction was on the right-hand side of a word. The typical one-address instruction set previously discussed can be used to modify such instructions by making use of the fact that instructions and data are in the same memory. Thus the one-address code

```
X       LOAD    B
Y       ADD     C
```

```
Z       STORE   A
        LOAD    X       Copy of "LOAD B" in accumulator
        ADD     =1      Add 1 to it to get "LOAD B + 1"
        STORE   X
        LOAD    Y
        ADD     =1      Form "ADD C + 1"
        STORE   Y
        ...     etc.
```

first handles A(1) = B(1) + C(1), then modifies the first few instructions so that they contain

```
        LOAD    B + 1
        ADD     C + 1
        STORE   A + 1
```

If we add a counter to this code and embed it in a loop to be executed 1000 times, we can accomplish the objective. However, we must be aware that after execution, the first three instructions have been changed to LOAD A + 1000, etc., so they must be reset before reexecution. Program 2-8 presents about the fastest well-structured code that can be written with the general one-address instructions covered so far.

Many machines now on the market provide simple instructions that can be used to reduce the length of this program. Two examples are the instructions ADD TO MEMORY, which performs an addition leaving the result in the addressed memory location rather than the accumulator, and INCREMENT MEMORY BY ONE, which adds 1 to a specified memory cell.

Program 2-8 has thirteen instructions inside the loop and one further outside, and it requires five additional storage locations. Only three of the thirteen instructions contribute directly to the arithmetic being performed, so in a sense the loop is less than 25 percent efficient. Recognizing that what is needed is an efficient scheme to modify addresses in a sequential fashion, the machine designer provides one or more *index registers*. An index register is functionally similar to the accumulator in that it is a device for storing a number in the CPU. Each index register is named with an address that must be distinguishable from a memory address. Since there are only a few index registers (for example, eight to sixteen), an index register address is a small integer that can be represented in a few bits. The function of an index register is to provide a *displacement* to the operand address in an instruction, that is, it changes the actual address by displacing it by the amount in the index register. In a computer with index registers, each operand address may have an index register address associated with it. The *effective operand address* is the sum of the actual operand address and the contents of the index register specified. Figure 2-9 shows a typical instruction format for a 3-byte instruction in a computer with fifteen index registers and a 16-bit memory address. In this hypothetical case, the index registers are numbered 1 to 15. The effective address is Y + (RX), where (RX) is the content of index register RX if RX is between 1 and 15. If RX is 0, the effective address is simply Y; that is, it is unindexed. We can indicate this in our program by writing Y to mean the unindexed

Program 2-8 Indexing through an array with instruction modification

```
*Initialize  COUNT to   -1000
             LOAD       =-1000
*            DO UNTIL COUNT=0
LOOP         STORE      COUNT
             ADD        =(LOAD B+1000)
*            Accumulator now contains binary form of LOAD B+I
*                                      where I=COUNT+1000
             STORE      X
             ADD        =(ADD C-LOAD B)
*            Accumulator now contains binary form of ADD C+I
             STORE      Y
             ADD        =(STORE A-ADD C)
*            Accumulator now contains binary form of STORE C+I
             STORE      Z
X            LOAD       B              The next three
Y            ADD        C              instructions are set
Z            STORE      A              above.
*            Increment  COUNT
             LOAD       COUNT
             ADD        =1
             BMI        LOOP
```

In this program, the address =(LOAD B) indicates the address of a word containing the instruction LOAD B. Similarly, the address =(ADD C − LOAD B) indicates the address of a word containing the difference between the instruction ADD C and the instruction LOAD B.

address and Y(RX) to mean the address Y indexed by register RX. (Some assemblers use other notations for this.) Now the principal part of our code is

```
LOAD     B(RX)
ADD      C(RX)
STORE    A(RX)
```

It is only necessary to arrange for register RX to be stepped through the values 0, 1, . . . , 999 and we have completed the problem. This requires a set of instructions to

FIGURE 2-9 Three-byte instruction format with indexing

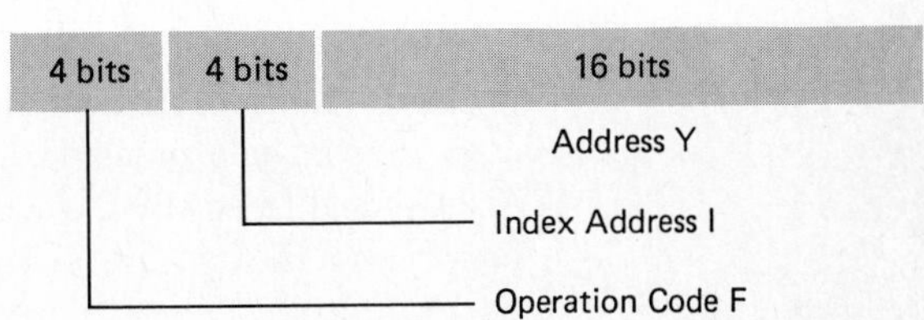

set and modify the index registers. There are a number of approaches to this problem. Many of the multiple-register machines, in particular the IBM 370, VAX, and CYBER 170, sidestep the problem by using the general registers as either accumulators or index registers. Other computers have special instructions for manipulating index registers.

There are five items of information to be specified in a loop:

1 The address of the first instruction in the loop
2 The initial value of the index
3 The increment
4 The end condition
5 The address of the last instruction in the loop

If testing for termination is done at the start of the loop, so that zero executions of the loop are possible, there must be a branch from the beginning to the end of the loop in addition to a branch back from the end of the loop to the beginning. If testing is not done until the end of the loop, there need be only one branch instruction from the end of the loop back to the beginning. This type of code can always be converted to a "test first" code by simply branching to the end test before entering the loop, as shown in the example that follows, which is a typical one-address implementation of the high-level code:

```
do for I ← M to N by K
  <body of loop>
  enddo
```

The machine-level language version of this for a one-address machine is

```
          LOAD      M
          STORE     I
          BRANCH    RPLOOP
LOOP      <body of loop>
          . . .
RPLOOP    LOAD      I
          ADD       K          Increment counter I
          STORE     I
          SUB       N
          BGE       LOOP       Repeat loop if I<=N
```

In fact, this is usually the best organization of the branches, since it puts just one branch inside the loop. The last five instructions of the code above indicate the inefficiency that is possible unless special instructions are included for index handling. If I is in an index register, it can be incremented by K in one instruction rather than the three here. Many computers include an instruction with the action "Increment index register RX by K." The operand is usually the address itself; that is, the quantity K is added to the index register, not the contents of location K. Thus we write "Increment index register RX by K." Such instructions are supplemented with other instructions, such as "Load index register RX with K," and "Compare index register RX with K." This reduces the five instructions, terminating the loop to three namely

```
Increment index register RX by K
Compare index register RX with N
BRANCH to LOOP if condition less than or equal
```

Frequently, computer designers make efforts to reduce this to two or one instruction. It can easily be reduced to two by storing I − N instead of I in the index register, provided that the operand address takes the form A + N(RX). (This means that N cannot be a variable.) In this way, the final value of RX is 0, so no comparison is needed. Through use of an additional register to hold the increment K, or through assuming that it is 1, some computers have a single counting and testing instruction that increments (or decrements) an index register and branches if the result is nonzero. Such an instruction can be used to control N passes through a loop by setting the register to −N (or +N) prior to entering the loop and terminating it with this one instruction. On machines with multiple address instructions, it is relatively simple to design single-loop control instructions, because the different quantities can be specified in the various operand fields.

Some computers allow for multiple indexing of an address; that is, the contents of more than one index register can be added to a single address. The IBM 370 and many modern machines (such as the INTEL 8086/88) are in this class.

2.7.2 Base and Segment Registers

The purpose of an index register is to provide a displacement to an address to allow the effective address to be changed during the calculation. An alternative use of such a register is to hold a *base address,* which is the starting address of a set of data. For example, suppose we need to process a set of table entries, and each table entry consists of a set of 15 words, and among other processing we need to sum the first, seventh, and twelfth words in each table entry. In that case we could set an index to hold the address of the *base* of the table entry (word 0 of the current entry) and use the code

```
LOAD    1(X)
ADD     7(X)
ADD     12(X)
```

This can be done using index registers, but in this case we refer to the register X as a *base register* and call the numeric offsets from the start of the table (1, 7, and 12 in this example) *displacements*. Because displacements are frequently much smaller than the maximum memory address, they can be restricted in size by the computer design (thus saving bits in the instruction). For example, although IBM 370 addresses are 24 bits long, displacements are restricted to 12 bits in that architecture. This means that fewer bytes need to be read from memory for each instruction fetched, resulting in increased speed.

As long as registers are long enough to hold a full memory address, operand and instruction addresses can be held partially or completely in registers. Indeed, many modern architectures permit an operand address to be obtained from a register entirely, thus saving even the bits of a short displacement quantity. However, in some minicomputers and microcomputers, the length of a register is shorter than the length of an address. For example, there are many 16-bit computers whose memories are byte-addressable. They can address a maximum of 2^{16} (=65,536) bytes. This is inadequate for many modern computers, so a large *address space* is needed. Some of these machines use the idea of *segment* addressing. This employs one or more segment registers, which contain additional bits of the address. For example, if a 20-bit address is needed in a 16-bit machine, a segment register will have to provide 4 additional bits on the left of the 16-bit quantity available from a register, as shown in Figure 2-10. At any given time in this example, the program can address 2^{16} bytes directly, but it must change the segment register to reach the remainder of the 2^{20} (=1,048,576) bytes addressable in memory. The advantage of this design is that the word size of the machine can be relatively small (which reduces cost) without limiting the memory size. The disadvantage is that programs that use more than a single segment of memory (2^{16} bytes in the example) are more complex.

2.7.3 Indirect Addressing and Immediate Operands

In the usual addressing mode, the instruction contains the operand address; that is, bits in the instruction specify the address of the cell containing the actual operand. In *indirect addressing*, the instruction specifies a cell that contains the address. We will indicate this by enclosing the address in parentheses. The instruction ADD (Q) first fetches the content of location Q from memory and then uses the content as the address of the operand for the addition. This is called *single-level indirect addressing*. Indirect addressing is often indicated by means of a bit in the instruction. If this bit is 0, the address in the instruction is used as the operand address directly. If it is a 1, the address in the instruction is used to read a word from memory that will contain the operand address. The *effective address* is the address finally obtained for use by the instruction. This is illustrated in Figure 2-11 for single-level indirect addressing. Since the word fetched from the memory location may have fields besides the address field, it could

FIGURE 2-10 Segment register and address

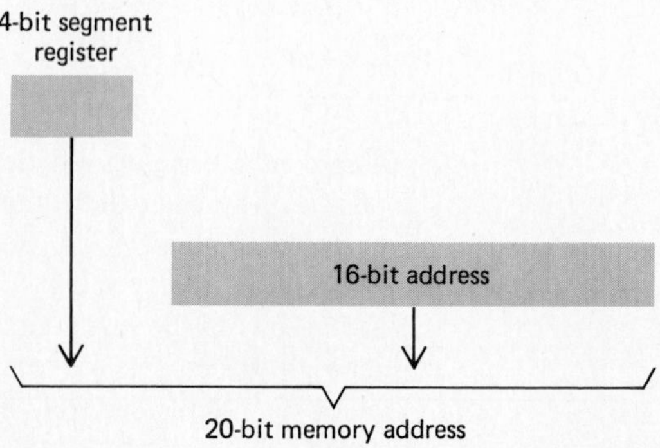

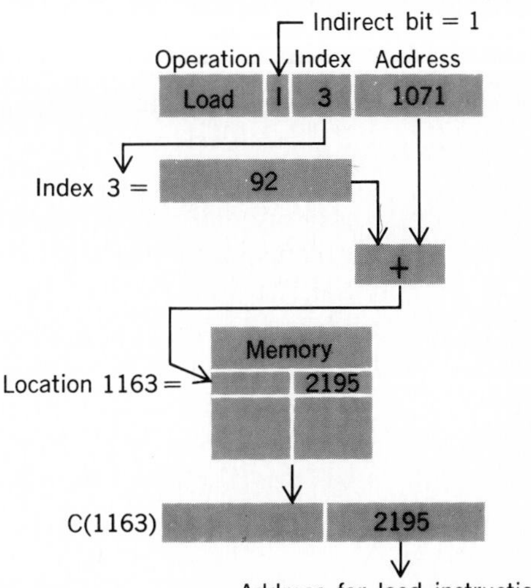

FIGURE 2-11 Single-level indirect addressing

contain another indirect address bit. This would allow *multiple-level indirect addressing*.

An important application of indirect addressing is parameter transfer in subroutines. This will be discussed in Chapter 5. Indirect addressing can also be used to supplement the number of index registers. If several instructions use the same element of an indexed array, say A(I), the address of A(I) can be kept in a memory cell, say P, and each instruction can refer indirectly through P. Suppose, for example, that we wish to square the contents of A(I) for I ← 1 to 1000 inside a loop, but are short of index registers (or are using a small computer with no index registers). We can code

```
            Set count to 1000
            Set location P to address A
LOOP        LOAD      (P)
            MPY       (P)
            STORE     (P)
            LOAD      P
            ADD       =1            Increment P by 1
            STORE     P
            ...                     Rest of loop body
            Decrement count and branch if nonzero to LOOP
```

Clearly, this is not as "clean" as indexing, so it should be avoided if at all possible, but on some small computers it may be the only effective way to achieve indexing.

If the word fetched from memory for indirect addressing is longer than the length of an address, additional levels of indexing are possible as well as additional levels of indirect addressing. Figure 2-11 shows indexing being performed before the address in the instruction is sent to memory. If an index-register address can also be stored in the word fetched from memory, the address in that word can be indexed again. Thus in

Figure 2-11 we could also examine the index bits in (1163) and modify the address (2195) by the specified index register.

The concept of an *immediate operand* is, in a sense, the inverse of indirect addressing. Many instructions call for the use of simple integer operands such as 0, 1, 2, and 10. We have already seen, this need in the index-register instructions described in a previous subsection. Many computers have options on some of the arithmetic instructions for immediate operands. For example, the ADD-IMMEDIATE N instruction adds the value of the integer N to the accumulator, not the content of the cell with address N. This has two benefits: less space is used for data, and one less memory reference is needed to execute an immediate instruction because data does not have to be fetched from memory. However, immediate instructions should be used with care, because if the operand N ever has to be changed, the program must be changed, whereas if simple direct addressing (the normal case) is used, only data has to be changed.

2.7.4 INTEL 8080 Address Structure

The INTEL 8080 uses a 16-bit address, whereas most of the arithmetic is on 8-bit bytes. The design of the 8080 places a great emphasis on the reduction of the amount of space used for instructions. This is done by using very short register addresses of 3 bits in many instructions. The format of the MOV instruction is shown in Figure 2-12. It occupies only 1 byte. The 3-bit address specifies one of the six registers, B, C, D, E, H, or L, or the accumulator. This uses seven of the combinations of the 3 bits. The eighth combination specifies that the register pair HL contains a 16-bit quantity to be used as an address for the operand. This is indicated in an assembler instruction by specifying the operand M. Thus

```
MOV     B,M
```

means that the register B will be loaded with the byte stored in the location whose address is in HL. We can view HL as a type of index or base register in this usage. The address M may be used as either a *source* or a *destination* address in the MOV instruction, and it may be used as an address in the one-address arithmetic instructions that operate on the accumulator. Thus the effect of

```
MOV     M,A
SUB     M
```

is to store the content of the accumulator in the locations whose address is in the HL pair and then to subtract that quantity from A, thus clearing A to 0.

The register pair HL can be loaded with an address by means of the LXI (Load Immediate) instruction. It takes the form

FIGURE 2-12 Format of MOV instruction in INTEL 8080

Op-code 2 bits	Address 1 3 bits	Address 2 3 bits

Register/Register pair		Address as 8-bit register		Address as 16-bit register	16-bit name
B	C	0	1	0	B
D	E	2	3	2	D
H	L	4	5	4	H
	A	–	7	–	–
SPH	SPL	–	–	6	SP

FIGURE 2-13 Registers in the INTEL 8080

```
LXI        H,MEM
```

where MEM is a memory address. The first address, H, is the address of one of the four register pairs shown in Figure 2-13. Any of these can be loaded directly, using the names, B, D, H, or SP. For example, to implement X $\leftarrow$ Y + Z − W, we can program

```
LDA     Y       ;Value (Y) to Accumulator.
LXI     H,Z     ;Address Z to HL.
ADD     M       ;Add (Z) to Accumulator.
LXI     H,W     ;Address W to HL.
SUB     M       ;Y+Z-W in Accumulator.
STA     X
```

There are no conventional index registers in the 8080 (although the Z80 does have some). However, the three register pairs B, D, and H may be used in a fashion analogous to indexing—the memory address may be obtained from a register pair rather than from the instruction. We have already seen that the register pair named H can be used in the move and arithmetic instructions. Besides these, the accumulator can be loaded and stored using the address in register pair B or D. For example, the code

```
LDAX    B       ;LoaD Accumulator using indeX B
STAX    D       ;STore Accumulator using indeX D
```

loads the byte whose address is in BC and stores it in the address held in DE. Some 16-bit arithmetic is provided on the 16-bit registers. DAD (Double ADd) adds any of the four 16-bit registers shown in Figure 2-13 to HL. INX and DCX increment and decrement, respectively, any of the four 16-bit registers by 1. INR and DCR do the same for 8-bit registers. Their use is illustrated in Program 2-9, which moves a string of N bytes from locations Q through Q + N − 1 to locations R through R + N − 1.

Program 2-9 Move a string of *N* bytes in the INTEL 8080

```
        LDA     NN       ;NN is location containing N
        MOV     L,A      ;Put N in register L
        LXI     B,Q      ;Load indeX Immediate, puts
                         ;address Q in register pair B.
        LXI     D,R      ;Address R in register pair D
LOOP:     LDAX    B      ;Move byte from location Q+i
          STAX    D      ;to location R+i.
          INX     B      ;INcrement indeX by 1
          INX     D      ;Increment D by 1.
          DCR     L      ;DeCrement Register L by 1.
          JNZ     LOOP   ;Repeat loop if count not zero.
```

Only register pairs B and D may be specified in the LDAX and STAX instructions. However, the same effect can be obtained for the register pair HL in the MOV instructions. Register pair SP cannot be used as an "index"; it is reserved for a special use to be described in Chapter 5.

The INTEL 8080 does not have indirect addressing as such; it must be programmed. In some situations, the instruction LHLD (Load H and L Direct) can be used. For example, LHLD Q picks up the pair of bytes from locations Q + 1 and Q and places them in register HL. Thus

```
        LHLD    R
        MOV     A,M
```

loads the accumulator with the byte whose *address* is in memory locations (R + 1,R). If it is necessary to go through further levels of indirection, more extensive code is needed. For example, to load HL with the pair of bytes whose address is currently in HL, we can execute

```
        MOV     E,M     ;Move the least significant byte to E
        INX     H       ;Increment register pair H
        MOV     D,M     ;Move most significant byte to D
        XCHG            ;eXCHanGe HL with DE
```

As in all computers, there are many ways to program even the simplest task. For example, we could also execute the pair of instructions

```
        SHLD    R + 1   ;Store HL Direct
R:      LHLD    0       ;Load HL Direct. The address is set
                        ;by the preceding instruction.
```

to perform the same task. SHLD stores the value in register pair HL in locations R + 1 and R + 2. Since R is the address of the next instruction (LHLD), whose format is

```
byte 1:      op-code
byte 2:      low-order byte of operand address
byte 3:      high-order byte of operand address
```

the operand address in the LHLD instruction is set to the content of HL. At first sight, this code may seem superior, consisting of half the instructions and not changing register pair D. However, it takes 6 bytes of code, versus 4 in the former, and needs nearly 50 percent more execution time because of additional memory references.

There is an immediate operand option on move, add, and subtract operations. Each uses its 1-byte address as immediate data. The instructions

```
MVI     A,7     ;Move Immediate of 7 to A
ADI     5       ;Add Immediate of 5 to A
SUI     7       ;Subtract Immediate of 7 from A
```

are all 2 bytes long; the second byte contains the immediate operand (which is 8 bits long). The MVI instruction can be used to load any register or any memory cell with an arbitrary 8-bit byte. For example,

```
MVI     A,0FFH
LXI     H,P
MVI     M,'G'
```

sets the accumulator to FF hexadecimal and then moves the binary form of the ASCII character "G" into location P. There is also an immediate option on the compare instruction. CPI n forms the difference A $-$ n and sets the condition bits accordingly; n is a 1-byte immediate operand.

The INTEL 8080 instruction set may seem to be full of anomalies and missing options, but it must be remembered that the basic instruction is only 8 bits long. That does not allow for a great variety, but it does give a very concise representation for many programs. If very complex tasks are to be programmed, some of the operations that are not available in the INTEL 8080, such as multiplication, must be programmed. This will be described as an example in the next chapter.

2.7.5 INTEL 8086/88 Address Structure

The INTEL 8086/88 provides two index registers, a base register, and four segment registers. These are shown in Figure 2-14, along with some other registers. (The numeric values in parentheses are the addresses of these registers in various instructions. They are there for later reference.) These registers are all 16 bits in length, although the first four, which we have already discussed, can be viewed as eight 8-bit registers for byte arithmetic. In some instructions their use is specialized, as indicated by the names on the right of the figure. The second group of four registers can be used in many instructions as general registers, but their main purpose is indicated by their name. SI and DI are index registers. BP is a base pointer. SP is a stack pointer, to be discussed later. The instruction pointer, IP, is the program counter. It cannot be referenced

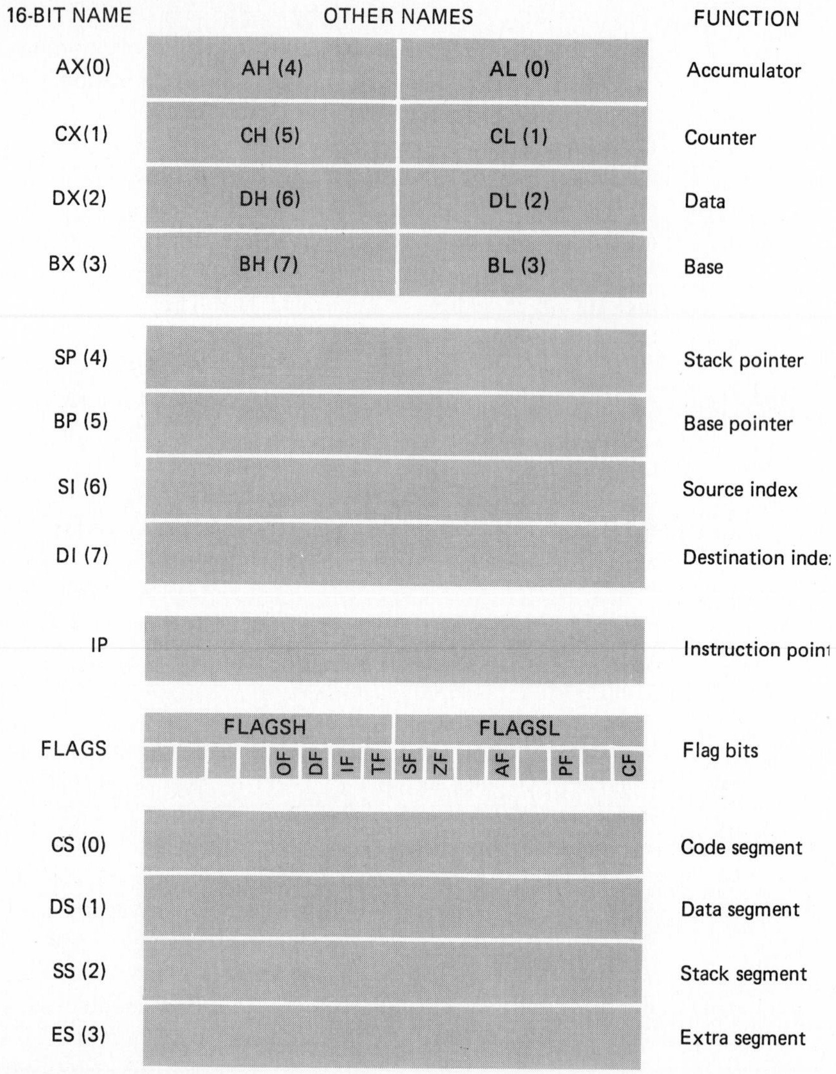

16-BIT NAME	OTHER NAMES		FUNCTION
AX(0)	AH (4)	AL (0)	Accumulator
CX(1)	CH (5)	CL (1)	Counter
DX(2)	DH (6)	DL (2)	Data
BX (3)	BH (7)	BL (3)	Base
SP (4)			Stack pointer
BP (5)			Base pointer
SI (6)			Source index
DI (7)			Destination inde
IP			Instruction poin
FLAGS	FLAGSH: OF DF IF TF	FLAGSL: SF ZF AF PF CF	Flag bits
CS (0)			Code segment
DS (1)			Data segment
SS (2)			Stack segment
ES (3)			Extra segment

FIGURE 2-14 INTEL 8086/88 registers

directly by instructions. The FLAGS register consists of the flag bits given in Table 2-4. The last four registers are segment registers used to extend 16-bit addresses to 20 bits.

The design of the 8086/88 places a great emphasis on the reduction of the amount of space used for instructions. This is done by using very short register addresses of three bits in many instructions. For example, a few instructions, such as XCHG AX,BX (exchange AX and BX) use only 1 byte. The instruction is actually called "exchange register with accumulator" and has one 3-bit register address in the instruction. It is illustrated in Figure 2-15. Many instructions occupy only 2 bytes and contain two

	Reg Bx
1 0 0 1 0	0 1 1

	W		Reg Bx	Reg Cx
1 0 0 0 0 1 1	0	1 1	0 1 1	0 0 1

FIGURE 2-15 (*a*) XCHG AX,BX; (*b*) XCHG BX,CX

register addresses. For example, XCHG BX,CX, illustrated in Figure 2-15*b*, has two register addresses, BX and CX in this example. This second format has many options, some of which we will discuss below. For example, if we wish to exchange bytes as in XCHG BL,DH, we can also use the format in Figure 2-15*b* with the w bit set to 0 (it indicates bytes or words) and appropriate register addresses (which are shown in Figure 2-14). Fortunately, the user does not have to be concerned with these addresses, as the assembler accepts an instruction such as

```
XCHG        CX,AX
```

realizes that it is an exchange between the accumulator and a register, and uses the short form in Figure 2-15*a*, while the instruction

```
XCHG        AL,CH
```

is converted to the longer form. (Whereas the assembler removes many problems of this sort from the user, it does make it harder to know which registers may be used in which instructions. As a general rule, the first eight 16-bit registers in Figure 2-14 may be used in general operations expecting a 16-bit register operand, whereas the last four may only be used in operations referring specifically to segment registers—these will be discussed at the end of this section.) Similarly, any of the first eight 8-bit registers may be used in general operations that have a byte option.

Indexing is provided by the DI and SI registers. Either of these can be added to a memory address, if desired. In assembler language, this is indicated by enclosing the index register name in brackets. The displacement can precede the bracketted register name or be placed inside, as shown below:

```
MOV         AX,12[SI]
MOV         AX,[SI+12]
```

These two instructions are identical in machine language. They move the information from the word whose address is found by adding the content of register SI to 12. For example, to sum the words in locations LIST to LIST+10 (six locations because of byte addressing for 16-bit words), we can execute

```
MOV         AX,LIST     ;First word to AX.
SUB         DI,DI       ;Clear index DI.
```

```
LOOP1:    ADD    AX,LIST+2[DI]    ;Add a word.
          ADD    DI,2             ;Increment DI by 2. (This is an
                                  ;immediate operand
                                  ;discussed below.)
          CMP    DI,10            ;Compare DI with immediate
                                  ;operand 10.
          JNE    LOOP1            ;Continue loop if not equal.
                                  ;Result in accumulator AX.
```

This code advances the index register through the sequence 0, 2, 4, 6, and 8. When it reaches 10 the loop is not repeated again.

Note that the immediate addresses, which are permitted in the general register operations, are indicated by writing a numeric address. Internally, in machine language, there is a special format for immediate addresses. This is generated by the assembler for the user. The assembler decides whether the address is immediate or not on the basis of the form of the address—if it is numeric, it is immediate.

The registers BX and BP can be used as base registers (which can be viewed as additional index registers). The options allowed in effective address construction are

{BX or BP} + {SI or DI} + {Displacement}

where any of the items in braces may be absent. To the assembler, the addresses can be indicated in a variety of forms, provided that the base and index registers are in brackets. The IBM assembler manual cited earlier lists all of these forms. The user is advised to select one form and stay with it to reduce confusion. The one that uses fewest characters in most cases is the one given in the following examples.

```
          MOV    CX,DISP[BX+SI]
          ADD    CX,DISP+2[DI]
          MOV    DISP+4[BX]
```

Counting through loops can be handled with the Loop until count complete (LOOP), Loop if Equal or Zero (LOOPE or LOOPZ), and Loop if Not Equal or Not Zero (LOOPNE or LOOPNZ) instructions. These use the CX register as a counter. They decrement it by one and branch if the count is nonzero. The second instruction also requires the Zero Flag, ZF, to be one. The previous example, which adds a list of words, can be coded as

```
          MOV    AX,LIST          ;First word to AX.
          MOV    CX,5             ;Count to CX.
          SUB    DI,DI            ;Clear index DI.
LOOP1:    ADD    AX,LIST+2[DI]    ;Add a word.
          ADD    DI,2             ;Increment DI by 2. (This is an
                                  ;immediate operand
                                  ;discussed above.)
```

```
        LOOP      LOOP1      ;Decrement CX and loop until
                             ;zero.
                             ;Result in accumulator AX.
```

The INTEL 8086/88 uses a 20-bit address, whereas the registers hold 16-bit quantities and the displacements are 16-bit quantities. First the effective address is formed by adding, in 16-bit arithmetic, the displacement and the contents of the index register and base register if either is specified. Then the 20-bit address is generated by adding the contents of one of the segment registers shifted left four bits, as shown in Figure 2-16, to get a 20-bit memory address. The content of a segment register is added to all addresses sent to memory. The segment register used is determined by the source of the address. Instruction addresses from the instruction pointer (IP) have the content of the code segment register, CS, added. Most operand addresses have the contents of the data segment register, DS, added, although some use the extra segment, ES. The stack segment, SS, is added to addresses from the stack pointer SP, whose use is discussed in Chapter 5. It is possible to cause a different segment register to be used for most data addresses. In machine language this is done by a special instruction *prefix* that modifies the subsequent instruction. In assembly language it is done by prefixing the operand address with a segment register prefix, as in ES:TABLE. In most cases the user does not have to be concerned about the segment registers, because the assembler takes care of preparing the machine language form. If the program occupies less than 2^{16} bytes and the data is similar, it is not necessary to change segment register values during execution, so it is necessary only to set them up at the start of execution, as was done in Program 2-7. If the program is longer than 2^{16} bytes, it is possible that a branch from one segment to another will be needed. There are several versions of the unconditional jump instruction, JMP, for this. A *far* jump changes the code segment register to a value that enables the new address to be reached, whereas a *near* jump remains within a segment. Again, the assembler determines which form to use.

FIGURE 2-16 8086/88 Memory address generation

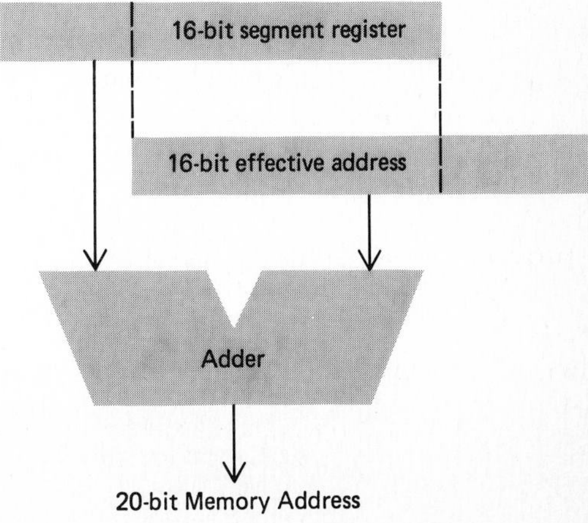

2.8 LOGICAL OPERATIONS

The logical instructions are bit-wise operations; that is, they treat each bit separately and identically. The three basic logical operations are AND, OR, and NOT. If a binary 1 is thought of as corresponding to *true* and a binary 0 is thought of as corresponding to *false*, then the result of X AND Y is true if both operands X and Y are true individually. X or Y is true if either operand is true, whereas NOT X is true if X is false. Thus we have the *truth tables*

```
0 AND 0 = 0      0 OR 0 = 0
0 AND 1 = 0      0 OR 1 = 1      NOT 0 = 1
1 AND 0 = 0      1 OR 0 = 1      NOT 1 = 0
1 AND 1 = 1      1 OR 1 = 1
```

Furthermore, the EOR (EXCLUSIVE OR) operation is often available. It has the truth table

```
0 EOR 0 = 0
0 EOR 1 = 1
1 EOR 0 = 1
1 EOR 1 = 0
```

In most computers, the logical instructions take the same form as the arithmetic instructions. Thus, in a one-address computer, we can expect to find an AND instruction that ANDs a word from memory with the accumulator contents, bit by bit. Logical instructions are useful for testing the state of bits within words. For example, to see if the second bit from the left end of a word is a 1, the word can be ANDed with a word containing 0100 . . . 0 in binary. If the result is 0, the second bit was a 0.

Shifts can be viewed as another class of logical instruction. A shift "moves" bits in a word to the left or right. For example, if a byte contains the bit pattern 00111100, a *right shift* of that pattern changes it to the pattern 00011110. This is called a *1-bit right shift*. Similarly, a 3-bit left shift of the pattern 00001100 results in the pattern 01100000. Computers have shift instructions that move bits in the accumulator or other registers. In the two examples above, we did not have to worry about what happens if nonzero bits are "shifted-out" of the register. However, if we consider a one-bit right shift of the pattern 00001111, we have to ask, "What happens to the rightmost 1 bit that is shifted off the end of the register?" There are several different kinds of shifts. In a simple *logical* shift, such bits are simply lost. Notice that the bits on the left-hand end are being set to 0 during the right shift and vice versa. A *rotate* or *circular shift*, on the other hand, is a type of shift in which the bits shifted off one end are inserted in the other end, as illustrated in Figure 2-17 for a left rotate. Thus a 1-bit right rotate of the pattern 00001111 results in 10000111, because the bit (whose value is 1) shifted off the right end is inserted in the left end. Similarly, a 3-bit left rotate of the pattern 11110000 results in the pattern 10000111 (and is the same as the result of a 5-bit right shift). Rotates do not lose information—the bits of the shifted word are just in a different place.

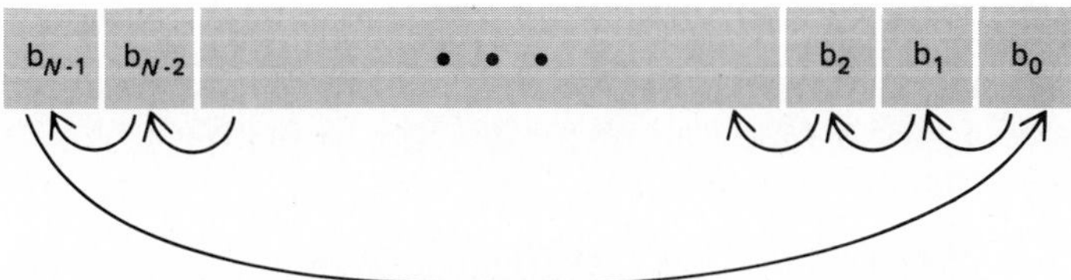

FIGURE 2-17 Left circular shift

A shift or a rotate is also a convenient way of testing particular bits in a word. The bit can be shifted until it is in the sign position so that a conditional branch on the sign can be made. This is usually preferable to using an AND to extract the bit if the computer provides an N-bit shift, because it is possible to follow this test with tests of other bits by performing additional shifts already tested. On the other hand, ANDing a word with a constant to extract certain bits for testing is usually better when several bits have to be tested at once. For example, if we want to know whether the bottom 4 bits of a value in an 8-bit accumulator are 1011, we can code the following:

```
AND         the quantity 00001111
SUB         the quantity 00001011
```

At this point the accumulator is 0 if the condition is true. The constant used to select the bits by ANDing, in this example 00001111, is called a *mask*. It *masks out*, or sets to 0, the bits of no interest corresponding to the 0 bits in the mask.

2.8.1 Logical Operations in the INTEL 8080

The INTEL 8080 has AND, OR, and EXCLUSIVE OR operations that take the same form as the ADD instruction. For example:

```
ANA    B   ;ANDs B register and accumulator,
           ;result left in accumulator.
XRA    M   ;EXCLUSIVE OR of memory cell whose
           ;address is in HL with the accumulator.
ORA    E   ;OR E register with accumulator.
```

Each of these has an immediate operand option; ANI, XRI, and ORI perform the same operations as the above but use their 1-byte address as the operand. The logical operations set the Zero, Sign, and Parity flags, but do not change the Carry flags. The content of the accumulator can also be *complemented* with the CMA instruction. This performs a NOT of each of the 8 bits.

2.8.2 Logical Operations in the INTEL 8086/88

The AND, OR, and XOR (exclusive or) operations are two-address instructions, either between a pair of registers or a register and memory. That is, they have the same addressing options as the ADD and SUB operations. They can operate on word or byte operands. The NOT instruction has one operand; it is inverted. Thus

```
NOT    CS
NOT    AL
NOT    WORD[SI]
```

invert the word in CX, the byte in AL, and the word in location WORD + [SI], respectively.

The rotate instructions rotate a word or byte *through* CF, that is, the CF flag is considered as a seventeenth (or ninth) bit appended to the end of the operand, and the rotate instructions operate on these extended operands. This can be used to leave a bit in CF for testing in a conditional branch instruction such as JC (Jump if Carry). The ROL (Rotate Left) and ROR (Rotate Right) rotate either one bit position or a number of bits given by the value in the CL register. Thus

```
ROR    AL,1
ROL    DX,CL
```

rotates the byte in AL right 1 bit and the word in DX left [CL] bits.

2.9 IMPLEMENTATION OF PROGRAM STRUCTURES

Even though the purpose of programming in a machine-level language rather than a high-level language is for reasons of efficiency, it is still important to adopt a reasonable program style so that the code can be debugged and modified when needed. Since most computers now have an adequate amount of memory, it is not necessary to go to extremes to try to save memory space in most applications, and so a reasonable program structure can be adopted at the expense of a small amount of space. (Space may be at a premium in some special applications, such as on-board flight-control computers for space applications, where every additional gram of weight increases costs tremendously.) Speed, however, is normally quite important, so it is desirable to keep the number of unnecessary instructions to a minimum. In this section we will mention a few simple guidelines and ideas to help in this goal.

Program loops were discussed in Section 2.7.1. We saw there that some machines have special loop instructions that do the counting, testing, and branching in a single instruction. Whatever instructions are available in a machine, it is almost never necessary to have more than one branch instruction in a simple loop. That instruction should be at the end and return control to the beginning. If it is necessary to implement a **while** type of loop, there should be an initial branch from before the start of the loop to the test at the end, so that only one branch instruction has to be executed in each passage through the loop. That was illustrated in Section 2.7.1.

The "cleanest" way to implement an if-then-else construct is to use two branch instructions, the first of which is a conditional branch to test the condition and the second of which is used to skip over the else clause, as in the following implementation of the high-level statement "**if** A = B **then** C ← D **else** E ← F".

```
          COMP      A,B        Compare A and B.
          BNE       ELSE10     Branch on opposite of condition
                               (Not Equal) to else clause.
          MOVE      D,C        Then clause
          BRANCH    ENDF10
ELSE10    MOV       F,E        Else clause
ENDF10    <continuation of code>
```

However, if speed is critical and one value of the condition is much more likely than the opposite, it is worth placing the infrequently used clause "out of line" in such a way that the other clause needs no branch. For example, if it is most likely that A is not equal to B, the else clause is most likely to be executed in the example above. Hence the following code is faster, on the average:

```
          COMP      A,B
          BE        THEN10     Branch to then clause.
          MOV       F,E        Else clause
ENDF10    <continuation of code>
          . . .
THEN10    MOV       D,C        Then clause is at end of code.
          BRANCH               ENDF10
```

This encoding saves a branch most of the time. (A branch is sometimes a slow operation, particularly in very-high-speed computers, because it interrupts the smooth flow of the program and prevents the CPU from doing some of the instruction fetching ahead of time. A conditional branch that does not cause an actual branch is usually faster.)

Another program structure that is frequently used in machine-level programming is the equivalent of a case statement. Suppose, for example, that a program is to input one character and then to execute one of a considerable number of different sections of code, depending on the character input. This is the type of situation typically handled by a case statement. The fastest machine-level code for handling this is obtained by using a table of branch addresses. Suppose that there are 256 different input characters with integer values from 0 to 255. A table of 256 addresses is constructed, so that the address in the I-th entry is the starting address of the code to be executed when the character with binary code I is read. If an indexed indirect branch instruction is available, it can be used to accomplish the branch to the appropriate code section; that is,

```
          LDINDEX RX,CHARACTER_CODE
          BRANCH (TABLE(RX))
```

does what we want, where the table of branch addresses starts in TABLE, the character input is placed in index RX, the expression TABLE (RX) means the address TABLE indexed by RX, and the expression (TABLE(RX)) is the address found in location TABLE(RX). This is illustrated in Figure 2-18. Note that if byte addressing is used, the

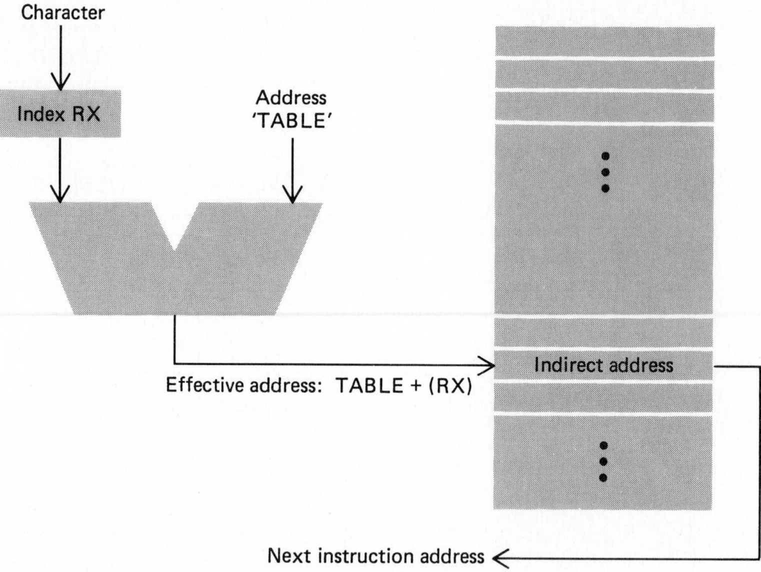

FIGURE 2-18 BRANCH (TABLE(RX))

index RX will have to be multiplied by a suitable amount to account for the number of bytes used to hold each address in the table. This can usually be done by a shift, because addresses are usually 2 to 4 bytes long and a shift in binary halves or doubles a value. (This will be discussed in the next chapter.) If indirect addressing is not available, a *branch table* can be used, that is, each entry in the table can consist of a branch instruction that branches to the desired section of code. Then two branches have to be executed; the first is BRANCH TABLE(RX), which goes to the RXth entry in the table, and the second is the branch instruction found in that RXth entry. In some machines it may be simpler to load the address from the table into another register and then perform an indexed branch.

2.9.1 Coding in the INTEL 8080

The 8080 has no instructions specifically for handling counting loops, but this can be done quite economically using the DCR instruction to decrement a count in one of the registers, followed by a conditional branch. It is better to set the register initially to the number of times the loop is to be executed and to count down, because counting up from 0 and comparing would take an extra instruction for the compare.

An indexed branch to a branch table can be implemented using the PCHL instruction, which places the content of the HL register into the program counter. Because a double-precision addition can be done on the HL register, the 16-bit indexed branch instruction can be constructed there. Suppose, for example, that a character code has been read to the accumulator and that the two hundred fifty-six 16-bit words starting at location TABLE contain the two hundred fifty-six addresses corresponding to each input character. The following code branches to the corresponding address in the table:

```
        LXI     H,TABLE
        MOV     C,A
        MVI     B,0          ;BC contains character
        DAD     B
        DAD     B            ;Add character twice
        MOV     A,M          ;Least significant part of branch
                             ;address
        INX     H
        MOV     H,M          ;and most significant part
        MOV     L,A          ;HL now contains branch address
        PCHL                 ;move it to PC to get a branch
```

2.9.2 Coding in the INTEL 8086/88

The INTEL 8086/88 has a relatively "rich" instruction set for a microcomputer, providing a number of options for the implementation of common program structures. However, its address structure, with an emphasis on using as few bits as possible in each instruction, sometimes requires the use of additional instructions. This is particularly true with the conditional branches and looping instructions, which are all 2 bytes long. The first byte is the operation code and the second byte is a displacement from the current value of the instruction pointer. The displacement represents a signed quantity in the range -128 to $+127$ (using the twos complement representation to be described in the next chapter), so a conditional branch is limited in the "distance" it can cover. If the *object* of the branch (the location to be transferred to) is more than 128 bytes from the branch instruction, a direct conditional branch is not possible. Instead, a combination of a conditional branch and the unconditional branch (which can go anywhere) must be used. Thus, to branch to location LOOP2, with the AX register equal to 25, we can execute

```
        CMP     AX,25
        JE      LOOP2
NEXT    ...
```

provided that LOOP2 is within the range NEXT − 128 to NEXT + 127. However, if this condition is not true, we must use

```
        CMP     AX,25
        JNE     NEXT
        JMP     LOOP2
NEXT    ...
```

The assembler will tell the programmer if the former version cannot be used, so most of the work is handled for the programmer.

The 8086/88 has indirect addressing for unconditional branch instructions. In fact, the JMP instruction has a number of forms: short ones using displacements for branches to nearby instructions, direct ones with 16-bit addresses for branches within the current segment, direct ones with two 16-bit addresses for branches to another segment (one address is the new segment address), and two versions of an indirect branch—one for a branch in the current segment and one for a branch to another segment. The two versions of an indirect branch can be written in the form

```
JMP          TABLE[BX]
```

or similar forms. If this is a table of branch addresses within the current segment, the action is to add the content of BX to TABLE, fetch the 16-bit word at that address, and store it in IP (the Instruction Pointer). Note that the index BX should be doubled, because each table entry takes 2 bytes. If, on the other hand, the addresses in the table are to other segments, each entry takes 4 bytes, 2 for the new value of IP and 2 for the new values of CS, the code-segment register. In this case, the index register, if used, must be quadrupled. The assembler can tell which form to generate in machine language based on information that the user must give when the table is defined. This will be discussed in Chapter 6.

2.10 CHAPTER SUMMARY AND PROBLEMS

Information is stored in the memory as words of a number, N, of bits. Information is represented by patterns of these bits. The natural binary coding scheme is a way of representing integers. In this scheme, the weights of the bits are 1, 2, 4, 8, . . . , starting from the rightmost end and moving to the left. In the sign/magnitude representation of signed numbers, the leftmost bit simply represents the sign, 0 being positive and 1 being negative. Character information is also represented as patterns of bits. The ASCII 8-bit code is the most commonly used representation, but the EBCDIC code is also used on many IBM computers. Some characters are printing characters, others are control characters. The collating sequence is the numerical ordering of the characters according to the code. Hexadecimal and octal representations are used as an easy way to write binary patterns.

Memory consists of a large number of cells, each of which can hold one word. Each cell has a unique numeric address. Many modern systems can address any 8-bit byte in memory. Symbolic addresses are the names of cells used in programming languages.

The CPU may contain of a number of registers that can store data. The CPU can perform various arithmetic operations on data obtained from memory or from these registers. A machine instruction consists of an operation and zero or more operand addresses. Common forms of instructions utilize zero through three addresses, and machines that predominantly use one of these are correspondingly named. Three- and two-address instructions use their addresses to reference memory cells, although in some organizations that have many registers in the CPU, the addresses may refer to some of the registers. An accumulator is a register that accumulates results and is used in the CPU of a one-address machine. A stack is a set of registers, each of which can be used to provide an operand to arithmetic instructions. However, the instructions operate on the top one or two levels of the stack only. Most machines include mixtures of various instruction types for efficiency. Most modern machines either have a set of general registers, any of which can be used as an accumulator, or an accumulator and a set of registers, which can be used to provide operands to avoid slow references to memory.

Instructions are stored in the primary memory. They are packed one or more per word. Fields are allocated for an op-code to represent the operation and for the addresses used by the operation. Instructions are fetched from memory in order of increasing memory address. This is done under the control of the instruction counter, also called a control counter or a program counter. The instruction counter always contains the address of the next instruction to be executed. Branch instructions are used to change the sequential order of execution. A conditional branch tests a condition such as the sign of a register or result to determine whether to branch or not. A number of machines use a condition register, which is set by the result of a prior instruction. In these machines, conditional branches test the content of the condition register. Because different instructions need different numbers of addresses and other information, many computers have variable-length instructions.

Assembly language is a way of representing machine instructions using mnemonics for operations and symbolic addresses for operand addresses. Pseudo instructions allow data to be specified in a simple way, such as decimal and hexadecimal. Directives tell the assembler where to place instructions and data, when to end assembly, etc. An assembler instruction consists of an optional label, an operation, one or more addresses, and an optional comment. Different assemblers use different separators between these fields.

A debugger allows the user to execute a program one step or a group of steps at a time while watching the contents of the registers and memory. At any point, the user can change the values in registers or memory for test purposes.

Index registers can be used to address arrays and to count through loops. An index register contains a displacement to the operand address given in the instruction. Index registers are contained in the CPU. They have addresses distinct from memory addresses. The effective address is the address finally constructed and sent to memory. It is formed by adding the index contents to the operand address. On some machines (IBM 370 and VAX) a set of registers function as both index registers and accumulators, so an additional set of index instructions is not needed. Other machines, such as the CYBER 170, have separate sets of accumulators and index registers, so two sets of instructions are needed. A base register is physically similar to an index register; it is used to provide the base address of an area of memory. The operand address provides an offset or displacement from that base. Segment registers provide additional address bits so that a short effective address can be lengthened to a memory address to allow more memory to be addressed than would be possible with a short address. Indirect addressing is the use of a cell in memory to contain the address of the data. In single-level indirect addressing, the operand address in the instruction refers to the first cell, which contains the address of the second cell containing the data. Multilevel indirect addressing carries this process further. An immediate operand is data that appears in place of the operand address in an instruction. Immediate operands save an additional read of data from memory. They can be used for small constants. Some machines (the IBM 370, for example) modify most addresses with the contents of two index registers. (One is used as a base register.) This allows operand addresses to be 12 bits long only; thus such machines use shorter instructions and pack more instructions per word.

Basic logical operations are AND, OR, and NOT. EXCLUSIVE OR is also provided on many computers. These operations are bit-wise and usually have the same format as the arithmetic instructions. Shifting moves all the bits in a word right or left. The rules for determining the value of bits shifted in at the bottom on a left shift or top on a right shift depend on the instruction. In rotations, the bits shifted out of the other end are shifted in. (On some computers, they rotate through a carry bit position.) Shift and logic instructions can be used to test single bits or groups of bits anywhere in a word.

Problems

2-1 How many bits are needed to represent an address in a memory with (**a**) 4,096 locations, (**b**) 131,072 locations, and (**c**) 1,048,576 locations?

2-2 How many bits are needed to represent all characters on a typical typewriter?

2-3 Using the one-address instructions LOAD and STORE and the zero-address instructions ADD, SUB, MPY, and DIV for a stack machine, write code to calculate

$$(A * (B + C - D)/E + F * G) * (B + C - D)$$

using as few instructions as possible.

2-4 If the instruction DUP (short for duplicate) puts a copy of the top of the stack on the stack, can your answer to Problem 2-3 be shortened?

2-5 Assuming that memory locations A, B, C, D, E, F, G, and Z are all different, and the contents of all except Z should not be changed, write programs for the simple three-, two-, one-, and zero-address machines discussed to perform

$$Z = (A + B - C)/(D * E * F - G)$$

Temporary cells T1, T2, . . . can be used as necessary.

The job of the computer designer is to pick an organization that will permit high-speed calculation at reasonable cost. The speed is partially controlled by the number of memory references needed to perform a calculation, since memory references are usually much slower than arithmetic (except in the smallest computers). The next two questions illustrate this.

2-6 Assume that the cost of executing each instruction in any one of the simple machines used in Problem 2-3 is equal to $p + m * q$, where m is the number of addresses in the instruction and p and q are constants. Thus, if 5 two-address instructions are executed, the cost would be $5p + 10q$. Discuss the desirability of each of the four simple designs in relation to the cost of execution for Problem 2-3. How does the lowest-cost machine depend on the ratio $r = pq$? Display the results graphically by plotting $cost/p$ against r.

2-7 We have noticed that in the case of two- and one-address machines, extra instructions are used to move information to and from temporary storage. In fact, a relation between the number of extra instructions needed in the two cases is known if the restriction that the operands on the right-hand side must not be changed is enforced. Consider an arbitrary calculation of the type in Problem 2-6—that is, only the four operations +, −, *, and / occur; each involves two operands (unary operations do not occur); all symbolic addresses A, B, etc., are different; and their contents may not be changed (except for the left-hand side). Suppose that in the minimum-cost programs (as defined by Problem 2-4) the two-address machine requires E MOVE instructions and that there are N other instructions (this means that there are N operations on the right-hand side). Write expressions for the cost of executing the minimal-cost program for each of the four simple computers in terms of N, E, r, and p. Noting that all of these numbers are positive, show that the two-address machine can never have the lowest cost of all four. Can it ever cost no more for the calculation on the two-address machine than on the one of the other three machines with the lowest cost?

2-8 How many bits are needed to represent an instruction in a computer that has 53 different instructions, all of which are two-address, when the computer has a 65,000-word memory?

2-9 What three steps are taken in the fetch part of instruction execution?

2-10 What changes would be needed in the fetch sequence if the control counter contained the address of the current instruction? What effect would this have on the branch instruction?

2-11 Write a program for a typical stack machine to compute the greatest common divisor of a pair of values in the top of the stack.

2-12 Do you think it preferable that a conditional branch instruction in a stack machine that tests the sign of the top stack level should leave the tested operand in the top of the stack or pop it out? Illustrate with examples.

It is not necessary to have a "rich" instruction set in a computer. Operations can be performed using very simple instructions; the operations will just take longer, as the next two problems illustrate.

2-13 Suppose there is a computer with the three-address instruction

```
SBTST     A,B,T
```

(and no others), which subtracts the contents of location B from location A, returns the result to location A, and then branches to T for the next instruction if the result is 0. Otherwise, it takes the next instruction in sequence. Arithmetic is integer. Write a program to put the absolute value of the content of Y into X. Location Y should not be changed.

2-14 Consider a two-address machine with the two instructions

```
SUB     A,B     (A) − (B) stored as (A)
BZN     A,T     Branch to T if (A) 0 or negative.
```

Indicate how to perform the operations of addition, multiplication, and division using only these two instructions. Assume that integer arithmetic is used.

2-15 Consider a computer with 32,768 words of memory and 15-bit index registers. Assume that index arithmetic is done *modulo* 32,768; that is, if the answer is greater than 32,767, then 32,768 is subtracted from the answer. If the contents of index registers are added to addresses, what should be put in index register 1 so that the effective address of LOAD A(1) is A − 327?

2-16 Suppose you wished to use a small constant in a program, but might want to change the value of this "constant" occasionally. Would you use an immediate operand for this value or not?

2-17 An *access table* is a table of addresses of data. Suppose we have a set of N words stored in various locations in memory, and the addresses of the cells containing these words are in location A, A + 1, A + 2, . . . , A + N − 1. What addressing features would be useful for forming the sum of these N words? Suppose you wanted to sort the information so that the words could be read in increasing numerical order. What information would you move around?

2-18 Show by means of truth tables that the following relations are true:

a (x AND y) AND z = x AND (y AND z)
b (x OR y) OR z = x OR (y OR z)
c x AND (y OR z) = (x AND y) OR (x AND z)
d NOT (x AND y) = (NOT x) OR (NOT y)
e NOT (NOT x) = x

2-19 Special symbols are used for the logical operations, just as the characters +, −, etc., are used for the arithmetic operations. Because many computers are short of characters in their printable character set, we sometimes use the characters + for OR, * for AND, and unary − for NOT. This choice is partly governed by the strong resemblance between the rules for logical and arithmetic manipulation. Thus rule (a) in Problem 2-16 can be written as (x * y) * z = x * (y * z), which is true in arithmetic and logic. Can you give rules that are true when the symbols are interpreted arithmetically but false when interpreted logically, and vice versa?

2-20 In a 4-bit computer, the following sequence counts the number of 1 bits in the word in register R1. R2 is assumed to be a second register. Shifts are assumed to be logical.

```
MOVE    R2, R1         Copy of data to R2.
AND     R1,=1010B      Operand is binary 1010.
SUB     R2, R1
RS      R1, 1          Shift R1 right one place.
ADD     R1, R2         Add R2 to R1.
MOVE    R2, R1
AND     R1,=1100B
SUB     R2, R1
RS      R1, 2
ADD     R1, R2         Result in R1.
```

Examine this to determine the method used, and extend it to 16-bit words.

The following programming problems can be tried on any computer.

2-21 Write a program to count the number of 1 bits in a word by shifting and testing.

2-22 Write a program to perform an n-bit, double-length, circular left shift of a register pair. Assume that n is in another register.

2-23 A *list* is a set of pairs of locations, each pair containing some data and the address of the next pair. Location START contains the memory address of the first element of the list; that is, (START) is the address of the first element, whereas ((START)) is the data in that element. The address of the next element is in address (START) + D, where D is an offset. Thus ((START) + D) is the address of the second element, the address of the third element is (((START) + D) + D), and so on. The last item in the list is indicated by a 0 in the location containing the address of the next pair. Write a program to form the sum of the data items in the list. The data and address lengths can be assumed to be the natural word and address lengths in the computer you are using.

CHAPTER **3**

REPRESENTATION OF INFORMATION

A computer designer chooses methods of representing information in a computer on the basis of an evaluation of cost and speed considerations, and occasionally on the basis of accuracy and programmer convenience. A computer design is then chosen that has operations to handle information in those representations. Normally, just a single representation is used for character data of the type discussed in the previous chapter (although some computers provide both ASCII and EBCDIC representations). However, a single representation for numeric information is inadequate for a wide range of problems, so large general purpose computers frequently have more than one form of number representation. Typically, there are integer and floating-point binary representations, and possibly also representations of strings of decimal characters. Different instructions must be provided for each form of number handled. The IBM 370 and VAX, for example, have three types of addition instructions: integer, floating-point, and decimal string. The CYBER 170 has integer and floating-point instructions only. The PDP-11 has integer arithmetic as standard and floating point as an option. The INTEL 8000 computers, like many small microprocessors, have only integer binary arithmetic, but they have a special instruction to facilitate decimal arithmetic. However, it is always possible to program arithmetic in any representation, so even if a computer does not have floating point, it can be provided by software.

In Chapter 2 we discussed the representation of signed integers in sign/magnitude and of characters in 8-bit bytes. Many computers use a different representation for signed integers. It is also necessary to represent floating-point numbers and fixed-point numbers for scientific work and data processing. This chapter will discuss a number of methods used in these representations, including those in several common computer systems.

3.1 INTEGER AND FIXED-POINT NUMBERS

In the sign/magnitude representation, integers between −127 and +127 were represented in 8 bits. However, a word (in that case, 8 bits) can represent anything we want it to represent. We can just as well think of the binary point as if it is in some other place than at the right-hand end, as it is when we work with integers. If, for example, we put the binary point immediately after the sign bit, we can represent numbers between −1 and +1. Thus the 8-bit sign/magnitude value $b_7b_6b_5b_4b_3b_2b_1b_0$ considered with the binary point on the right, represents the integer

$$(1 - 2b_7)(b_6^*2^6 + b_5^*2^5 + b_4^*2^4 + b_3^*2^3 + b_2^*2^2 + b_1^*2 + b_0)$$

but if the point is immediately before b_6, it represents the value

$$(1 - 2b_7)(b_6^*2^{-1} + b_5^*2^{-2} + b_4^*2^{-3} + b_3^*2^{-4} + b_2^*2^{-5} + b_1^*2^{-6} + b_0 2^{-7})$$

which is a scaling by 2^{-7} of the integer value. That is to say, we can represent the values

$$-\frac{127}{128}, -\frac{126}{128}, \ldots, -\frac{1}{128}, 0, \frac{1}{128}, \ldots, \frac{126}{128}, \frac{127}{128}$$

For this reason, we sometimes call these "fractions," although the correct name is *fixed-point numbers*. A fixed-point number is a number whose point is in a fixed place in relation to the word. Thus an integer is also a fixed-point number.

Addition of two words is independent of whether the binary point is thought (by the user) to be at the right end of both words, at the left end of both words, or in the middle, provided it is in the same position in both words. The result is the same. Therefore, as long as the same convention is used for all values, the computer does not have to distinguish. It is true that if one word has the assumed point in a different position than in the other word, one word must be *shifted* to align it with the other, and this must be programmed by the user in machine-level languages using special instructions for that purpose. In general, however, we work with integers and floating-point numbers rather than fixed-point numbers at the machine level.

3.1.1 Rounding and Range

The *range* is the set of values that can be represented. This is necessarily a finite set. If a word contains N bits, the value of a sign/magnitude fraction lies between $-1 + 2^{-N+1}$ and $1 - 2^{-N+1}$, whereas the *range* of an integer is from $-2^{N-1} + 1$ to $2^{N-1} - 1$. If an arithmetic operation generates a result greater than the range of numbers that can be represented, an *overflow* has occurred.

When values between $-\frac{127}{128}$ and $\frac{127}{128}$ are represented in an 8-bit word, only 255 discrete values can be represented. This is illustrated in Figure 3-1 for 6-bit sign/magnitude fractions whose values lie between $-\frac{31}{32}$ and $\frac{31}{32}$. If a number that is not one of these discrete values is to be represented, only an approximation can be made. For example, if $\frac{2}{3}$ is to be represented in a 3-bit word, then either $\frac{1}{2}$ or $\frac{3}{4}$ must be used instead (see Figure 3-2). As a binary number, $\frac{2}{3}$ is 0.101010 . . . ad infinitum. This can be reduced

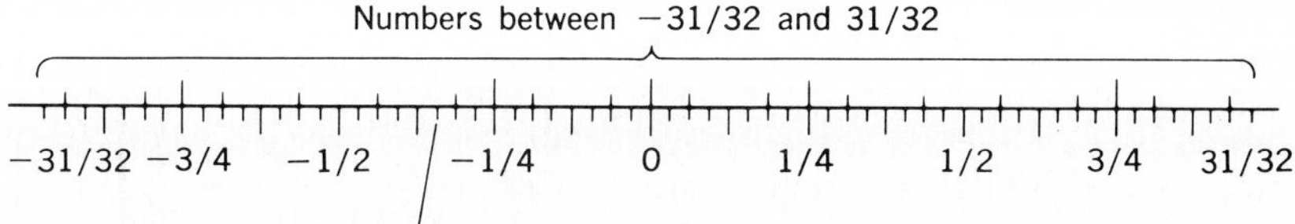

FIGURE 3-1 Six-bit sign/magnitude fraction values

to 2 bits by chopping off, or *truncating,* all bits after the second, so that the approximation is 0.10. However, it is generally better to choose the closest available value, in this case 0.11, since the error is then $-\frac{1}{12}$ rather than $\frac{1}{6}$. Taking the closest value is called *rounding*. By rounding rather than truncating, the *round-off error* can be kept to not more than one-half the distance between two adjacent representable values, or 2^{-N}. It is important to remember that, except for division, integer arithmetic is exact as long as the range is not exceeded (overflow), whereas fractional arithmetic is only exact in those unusual cases in which the numbers represented are exact and the result can also be represented exactly. For example, multiplication of fractions almost always requires a final rounding or truncation to get a representable value.

3.1.2 Shifting Binary Numbers

If we perform a 1-bit logical left shift of the binary value $b_7b_6b_5b_4b_3b_2b_1b_0$ we get the bit pattern $b_6b_5b_4b_3b_2b_1b_00$. Provided that the answer has not overflowed, this is double the original value. For example, 5 is 00000101 binary. If it is shifted left one place, we get 00001010 binary, which is 10 decimal. Similarly, shifting a binary number right one place halves its value. It is equivalent to moving the binary point in the representation. This changes the value by powers of two, just as moving the decimal point in a decimal number changes the value by powers of ten.

However, when a signed number is to be doubled or halved, we may have to handle the Sign bit separately. When a sign/magnitude number is shifted to halve or double it, the bits representing the magnitude are shifted, but the sign is not moved. A right shift of a sign/magnitude number is shown in Figure 3-3. Zeros are shifted into the

FIGURE 3-2 Truncation and rounding

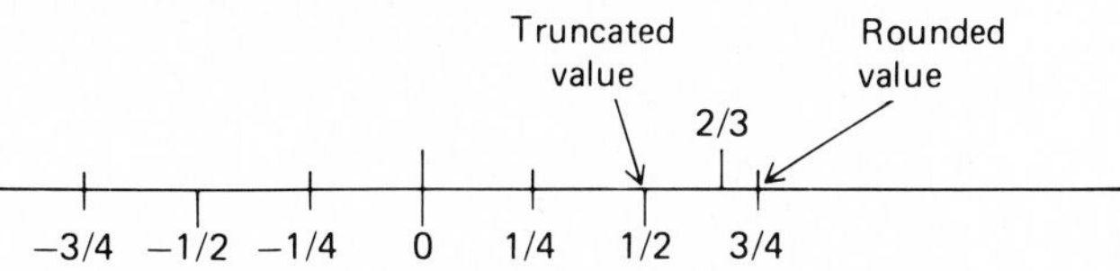

FIGURE 3-3 Right shift in sign/magnitude

left-hand end of the magnitude, and bits shifted off the right-hand end are lost. This may result in loss of accuracy. For example, if −13 is halved, a result of −6 or −7 must be accepted in integer arithmetic. In that case, the sign/magnitude representation 10001101 would change to 10000110, or −6.

When a number is doubled by a left shift it may overflow, and as the result it may exceed the range of the representation. In a sign/magnitude number, digit b_{N-2} prior to the shift must be a 0 or overflow will occur.

3.2 REPRESENTATION OF SIGNED INFORMATION

The sign/magnitude system of negative number representation is familiar in everyday life. A number of computers use this system, but there are two other systems that are important: twos complement and ones complement.

3.2.1 Twos Complement Representation of Numbers

The *twos complement* system arises in the following manner: consider an 8-bit computer in which the left-hand bit is reserved for a Sign bit and the other 7 represent an integer in the usual way. Suppose two positive numbers are subtracted, such as 00000101 from 00001011. Because the result is positive, we can treat the Sign bit as any other bit. In this case we get

$$\begin{array}{r} 00001011 \\ -00000101 \\ \hline 00000110 \end{array}$$

If, however, the result is negative, we must do the subtraction "the other way around" and make the Sign bit of the answer negative.

This is familiar to us in decimal arithmetic, where, if asked to calculate 25 − 43, we form −(43 − 25). Suppose, however, that we did the subtraction without such consideration in 3 decimal digits:

$$\begin{array}{r} 025 \\ -043 \\ \hline 982 \end{array}$$

The leading 9 in the answer is due to the borrow from the second digit, which in turn generates a borrow from the leftmost digit. It is clear to us that 982 is not 25 − 43 = −18, but we can see that it functions like −18 if we add it to another number, such as 64:

$$\begin{array}{r} 982 \\ +064 \\ \hline 046 \end{array}$$

The answer is indeed 64 − 18. What brought about this magic? After the subtraction, the borrow from the second digit indicates that another 100 is needed to perform the subtraction of the first 2 digits. Hence the 9 in the first position of the answer represents −100. When the addition was performed, 82 + 46 generated a carry from the second digit to the leftmost. The value of this carry is +100. When added to the 9 in the first position, it yields a 0 (and a carry that is lost). Thus we could represent negative 2-digit decimal numbers in 3 digits by "representing" a value −100 with a 9 in the first digit. (This is called the *tens complement* representation.) This is the same phenomenon that occurs when we wind a digital counter backwards. If a counter is initially set to 025 and we wind it back 25, it will be reduced to 000. Reducing it one more turns it to 999, which, in a sense, represents −1.

The same idea can be used in binary. Thus, if we subtract 00001011 from 00000101, we get

$$\begin{array}{r} 00000101 \\ -00001011 \\ \hline 11111010 \end{array}$$

The answer represents −(00001011 − 00000101) in the following sense. The value of each bit after the first is as usual, namely 64, 32, 16, 8, 4, 2, and 1. However, the value of the Sign bit is $-2^7 = -128$. That is, it represents a borrow from the position to its right, b_6. Thus the value of this number is

$$1 \times (-2^7) + 1 \times 2^6 + 1 \times 2^5 + 1 \times 2^4 + 1 \times 2^3 + 0 \times 2^2 + 1 \times 2^1 + 0 \times 2^0$$

We see that this is exactly −00000110, or −6. This representation is called the twos complement representation. Note that, unlike the sign/magnitude representation, the Sign bit has a weight in twos complement. In sign/magnitude, the Sign bit represents nothing but the sign; it has no numeric value. In twos complement, the weight of the Sign bit in an integer representation is -2^{N-1}. In all representations, a number is negative only if it has a negative Sign bit.

The twos complement representation has many attractive features. The principal one is that addition of twos complement numbers can be performed without regard for the sign. Whereas to add 45 and −63 in sign/magnitude arithmetic, we must compare signs to decide whether to add or subtract, and possibly to decide in which order to subtract, twos complement numbers are simply added. If the answer is in range, it is correctly represented.

The name "*twos complement*" is derived from the fact that the negative of a fraction can be obtained by subtracting it from 2. Thus, to find the negative of 00100000 (= $\frac{32}{128}$ as a fraction), we write

$$\begin{array}{rr} 2 & 100000000 \\ -\frac{32}{128} & -00100000 \\ \hline & 11100000 \end{array}$$

The result is the twos complement form of $-\frac{32}{128} = -1 + \frac{96}{128}$ if the binary point is assumed to be immediately after the Sign bit. However, as we have said, the binary point is where we want to put it, so this is equally well the twos complement representation of the integer -32 if the binary point is at the right end of the word. A twos complement representation is simply a representation in which the weight of the first bit is negative; otherwise it is identical to an unsigned representation.

Subtraction in Twos Complement Addition is particularly simple for a computer in twos complement. Subtraction also turns out to be a simple modification of addition, making it very simple for a computer. Instead of calculating $A - B$, a computer usually computes $A + (-B)$, so it can use the circuits that are already present to perform addition. Thus the question is "How can we form $-B$?"

The answer is that we simply change each bit in the binary representation of B from a 0 to a 1, or vice versa (this is the NOT operation, and is called *complementing*), and then we add one. This is shown mathematically in the next paragraph. It can be skipped if you are prepared to believe it. (Forming the negative of a number in twos complement is often called "taking the twos complement.")

Suppose we have an integer $b_{N-1} \ldots b_2 b_1 b_0$ whose value is

$$B = -b_{N-1}2^{N-1} + b_{N-2}2^{N-2} + \cdots + b_0 2^0$$

Note that

$$\begin{aligned} 0 &= -2^0 + 1 \\ &= -2^1 + 2^0 + 1 \\ &= -2^2 + 2^1 + 2^0 + 1 \\ &\cdots \\ 0 &= -2^{N-1} + 2^{N-2} + \cdots + 2^0 + 1 \end{aligned}$$

Subtracting the previous equation from this identity, we get

$$-B = -(1 - b_{N-1})2^{N-1} + (1 - b_{N-2})2^{N-2} + \cdots + (1 - b_1)2 + (1 - b_0) + 1$$

This number is the value of the twos complement number $c_{N-1}c_{N-2} \ldots c_1 c_0$ plus 1 in the least significant place. Note that $c_i = 1 - b_i$, so c_i is the complement of b_i.

As an example, the binary value of decimal -6 can be obtained as an 8-bit twos complement integer by using the following steps:

+6 decimal	00000110
Complement	11111001
Add one	00000001
Result	11111010

Subtraction can be performed in a computer by use of a complementing mechanism (which is extremely simple) followed by addition of 1. To form $A - B$, a computer actually forms

$$A + \text{complement of } B + 1$$

if it operates in twos complement. The addition of +1 is performed in the same step as the addition of A and the complement of B. The adder mechanism contains circuits for each digital position that are capable of adding two digits *and* the carry from the position to the right. The +1 is obtained by providing a carry into the rightmost position of the adder. The programmer simply sees a subtract operation.

Yet another way of viewing twos complement is as follows. Since there are 256 combinations of 8 bits, we can represent all integers between −128 and +127 in an 8-bit word. Add 128 to the integer, I, to be represented to get a positive integer in the range 0 to 255. (This positive integer form is frequently used for exponents in floating-point numbers and is called the *characteristic* representation.) If we represent this positive value in N bits and complement the Sign bit, the result is the twos complement form, as can be seen in Table 3-1.

Note that the range of numbers in twos complement is asymmetric, that is, there are more negative values than positive values. This can be annoying, because it means that negating a number can cause overflow. Sign/magnitude does not have this problem (and neither does the next representation we will discuss, ones complement). On the other hand, these other representations have a potential difficulty because there are two representations of 0: +0 and −0. For this reason and the simplicity of the logic, virtually all computers use twos complement for integer arithmetic; the only major exceptions in current computers are the Cyber series computers, which use ones complement, to be discussed in Section 3.2.2.

Extending the Precision of a Twos Complement Number When the precision of a sign/magnitude number is increased, it is only necessary to add zeros. Thus the

TABLE 3-1 TRANSFORMATION FROM DECIMAL TO TWOS COMPLEMENT

Decimal	Decimal +128	Binary integer (characteristic form)	Twos complement	Ones complement	Sign/ magnitude
−128	0	00000000	10000000	—	—
−127	1	00000001	10000001	10000000	11111111
−126	2	00000010	10000010	10000001	11111110
...	...	...	...		
−1	127	01111111	11111111	11111110	10000001
0	128	10000000	00000000	11111111 or 00000000	10000000 or 00000000
1	129	10000001	00000001	00000001	00000001
...	...	...	...		
126	254	11111110	01111110	01111110	01111110
127	255	11111111	01111111	01111111	01111111

6-digit integer −123456 becomes −000123456 in 9 digits, whereas the 3-digit fraction +.123 becomes +.123000 in 6 digits. Similarly, binary zeros are added to the left or right of sign/magnitude binary numbers to extend their precision. However, twos complement causes problems when negative integers have their precision extended. This arises because in twos complement the weight of the Sign bit is -2^{N-1}, which changes as N changes. No problem arises if the number is positive, as the value of the Sign bit is then 0 independent of N. However, consider the 6-bit twos complement representation of −19. It is 101101, standing for −32 + 13. As an 8-bit number it is 11101101, standing for −128 + 109 = −19. Note that two copies of the Sign bit have been added on the left. We call this *sign extension*. The rule is that *when a twos complement integer is made longer, the bits added to the left must all be equal to the Sign bit*.

When a twos complement number is shifted to halve or double it, there is no problem if the number is positive and the answer is in range. However, a special process must be used for negative numbers. Suppose the number is first halved by discarding the right-hand bit (we are assuming it is an integer, although the process is identical for fractions). Now it must be restored to its original length by adding a bit to the left-hand end. Since this is the same as extending its precision, this added bit must be a copy of the Sign bit, that is, sign extension must be used. The net result is that we halve a twos complement number by shifting it right and *duplicating* the Sign bit. This is shown in Figure 3-4.

If overflow on left shifts of twos complement values is to be avoided, the left 2 bits must agree before the shift. This can be seen by noting that if the result of a left shift does not overflow, halving the result by right shifting should return the original value, and that would cause the left 2 digits to agree. If there is to be no loss of accuracy on the right shifts, the rightmost bit must be a 0 before the shift.

Carry Bits in Twos Complement Many small-word-length computers (the VAX, PDP-11, and INTEL 8080 and 8086/88, for example) have a special *Carry bit* that aids in arithmetic on data too long to store in a single word (*multiple-precision arithmetic*). Some computer manuals give very confusing descriptions of the function of this bit, although most utilize it in the following straightforward way.

Addition If two words, considered as unsigned integers, are added, the Carry bit is set to a 1 if the result is larger than can be held in 1 word. For example, if in an 8-bit computer, we add 10110110 to 11000101 and get:

	10110110
+	11000101
1	01111011
(Carry bit)	(Result word)

Thus the sum can be considered as the 9-bit quantity consisting of the carry bit followed by the 8-bit result, so the Carry bit is exactly the *carry* out of the leftmost position.

FIGURE 3-4 Right shift in twos complement

Subtraction If the difference between the two numbers, considered as unsigned integers, is negative, the Carry bit is a 1. In this case, it is a *borrow* from the leftmost position. For example:

	00110101
−	01010011
1	11100010
(Carry bit)	(Result word)

It is as if the result is a 9-bit, twos complement integer consisting of the carry bit followed by the 8-bit result word. Why is this useful? Consider a 16-bit twos complement integer contained in two 8-bit words, as shown in Figure 3-5. If we view this as an integer, the least-significant (right-hand) word is an unsigned integer. If we add two such numbers, we need to add the two least-significant halves first as unsigned integers. (Twos complement arithmetic does this for us.) Next we must add the most significant halves, adding in the carry, if any, from the least-significant-half addition, as shown in Figure 3-6. The carry is precisely the quantity in the Carry bit. In subtraction, we subtract the least significant halves first, then the most-significant halves, subtracting the borrow, if any, from the least-significant-half subtraction, again the quantity in the Carry bit.

FIGURE 3-5 Twos complement 16-bit integer in two bytes

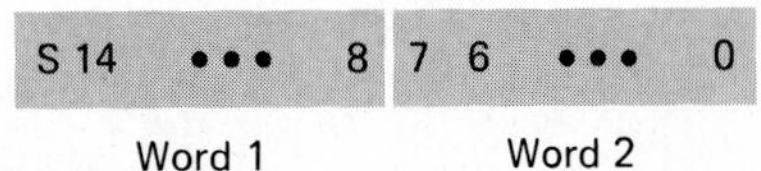

FIGURE 3-6 Double precision addition in twos complement

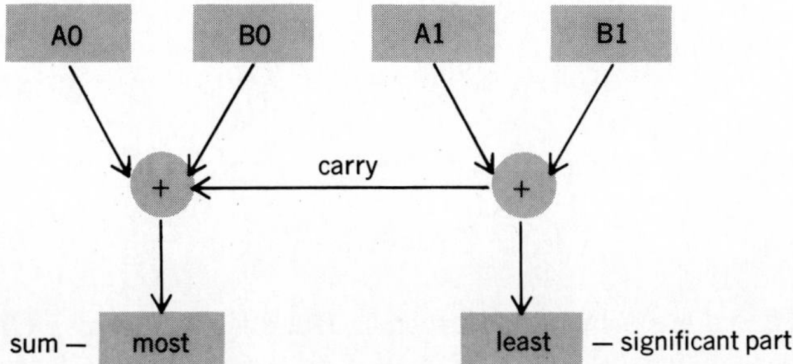

3.2.2 Ones Complement Representation of Numbers

The third scheme for representing negative numbers is *ones complement*. This is derived by requiring that the negative of a number be the bit-wise complement of the number. Thus the negative of $\frac{6}{128}$, or 00000110 in binary, is 11111001. The least significant 1 is not added in after complementing each bit, as is done in twos complement. Because of this, the weight of the sign position is $-(1 - 2^{-N+1})$ rather than -1 as in twos complement, so that the value of the ones complement fraction $b_{N-1}b_{N-2}\ldots b_0$ is

$$-(1 - 2^{-N+1})b_{N-1} + b_{N-2}2^{-1} + \cdots + b_0 2^{-N+1}$$

if the number is considered a fraction, or

$$-(2^{N-1} + 1)b_{N-1} + b_{N-2}2^{N-2} + \cdots + b_0 2^0$$

if the number is considered an integer. The addition rules for ones complement require that the Sign bits be added and that the carry out of the top position (the sign position) must be added to the least significant position. This is called *end-around carry.* It arises when a carry into the sign position, which has a value of $+1$ for fractions, is added to a 1 bit already there, with value $-(1 - 2^{-N+1})$. The result is 2^{-N+1}, which is a 1 in the least significant position. Thus, if $\frac{11}{128}$ is added to $-\frac{6}{128}$ in ones complement, we perform

$$\begin{array}{lr l}
\frac{11}{128} & 00001011 & \\
+\ -\frac{6}{128} & 11111001 & \\
\hline
 & 100000100 & \\
+ & 1 & \text{(End-around carry)} \\
\hline
\frac{5}{128} & 00000101 &
\end{array}$$

This can be written out as

$$\begin{array}{rl}
0 + \frac{0}{2} + \frac{0}{4} + \frac{0}{8} + \frac{1}{16} + \frac{0}{32} + \frac{1}{64} + \frac{1}{128} & (00001011) \\
+\ -(1 - \frac{1}{128}) + \frac{1}{2} + \frac{1}{4} + \frac{1}{8} + \frac{1}{16} + \frac{0}{32} + \frac{0}{64} + \frac{1}{128} & (11111001)
\end{array}$$

Add to get

$$\frac{1}{128} + \frac{0}{2} + \frac{0}{4} + \frac{0}{8} + \frac{0}{16} + \frac{1}{32} + \frac{0}{64} + \frac{0}{128} \quad (00000001 + 00000100)$$

Carry the $\frac{1}{128}$ around to get

$$0 + \frac{0}{2} + \frac{0}{4} + \frac{0}{8} + \frac{0}{16} + \frac{1}{32} + \frac{0}{64} + \frac{1}{128} \quad (00000101)$$

Note that ones complement representation has two zeros: +0 is 000...0 and −0 is 111...1. The representation of 8-bit ones complement numbers is included in Table 3-1.

Extending the Precision of a Ones Complement Number The precision of a ones complement integer is extended in exactly the same way as in twos complement, namely, by sign extension. Consequently, right shifts to halve ones complement numbers must duplicate the sign digit, as shown in Figure 3-4 for twos complement. If a ones complement fraction is to have its precision increased, the bits added to the right end must also be copies of the Sign bit. This is because the weight of the Sign bit is $-(1 - 2^{-N+1})$ and changes as N changes. Consequently, when a ones complement number is left-shifted to double it, copies of the Sign bit must be inserted in the right-hand end. This is just a *left circular shift,* or *left rotate*.

3.3 CONVERSION OF NUMBERS

A number can be converted from one base to another by multiplication or division. We will illustrate this for several cases. In all cases, the rules for doing the conversion can be seen by writing down the representation in each base and manipulating it in a way that depends on whether we are doing the arithmetic by hand, in which case most of us want to work in decimal, or in the machine, which prefers to work in binary.

Consider first the integer N represented by the decimal digits $d_2d_1d_0$. (Note that N cannot exceed 999.) Suppose we wish to find the binary representation of N in 10 bits (which is sufficient for the range of N because 10 bits can represent integers as large as $2^{10} - 1 = 1023$). If the conversion is to be done by hand, we want to use decimal arithmetic. In this case, we *divide by the new base*. We write down the unknown binary representation as $b_9b_8 \ldots b_1b_0$, where the digits b_i are to be determined. We know that the values of the decimal and binary numbers are to be identical, so we must have

$$N = b_9 2^9 + b_8 2^8 + \ldots + b_1 2^1 + b_0$$

Noting that both sides are integers, we divide by 2 to get

$$N/2 = b_9 2^8 + b_8 2^7 + \ldots + b_1 \quad \text{remainder } b_0$$

If we form $N/2$ as an integer with a remainder, the least significant digit, b_0, is that remainder. The remaining 9 bits can be converted by the same mechanism, that is, each succeeding bit is found by a division by the new base.

Example

Convert 44 decimal to binary:

$$\begin{aligned}
\tfrac{44}{2} &= 22 \quad \text{remainder } 0 \quad b_0 \\
\tfrac{22}{2} &= 11 \quad \text{remainder } 0 \quad b_1 \\
\tfrac{11}{2} &= 5 \quad \text{remainder } 1 \quad b_2 \\
\tfrac{5}{2} &= 2 \quad \text{remainder } 1 \quad b_3 \\
\tfrac{2}{2} &= 1 \quad \text{remainder } 0 \quad b_4 \\
\tfrac{1}{2} &= 0 \quad \text{remainder } 1 \quad b_5
\end{aligned}$$

Hence, 44 decimal = 101100 binary = 54 octal = 2C hexadecimal. Note that the digits in the new base are obtained in the reverse order (right to left) when we divide to convert.

The conversions to octal and hexadecimal above were done by grouping the bits. A quicker way is to convert directly from decimal to octal or hexadecimal by dividing by the new base. Thus, to convert 44 decimal to octal, we perform

$$\tfrac{44}{8} = 5 \quad \text{remainder } 4 \quad o_0$$
$$\tfrac{5}{8} = 0 \quad \text{remainder } 5 \quad o_1$$

Hence 44 decimal = 54 octal. To convert to hexadecimal we perform

$$\tfrac{44}{16} = 2 \quad \text{remainder } 12 \quad h_0(=\text{C in hexadecimal})$$
$$\tfrac{2}{16} = 0 \quad \text{remainder } 2 \quad h_1$$

Hence 44 decimal = 2C hexadecimal.

In the above examples we were doing the arithmetic in the old base, that is, decimal. When we wish to do the arithmetic in the new base, we *multiply by the old base*. For example, to convert 3E5 hexadecimal to decimal, we first write down the value of 3E5 as

$$\text{Value} = 3 \times 16^2 + \text{E} \times 16 + 5$$

where the hexadecimal digit E has a decimal value of 14. We can factor this in the following way:

$$\text{Value} = (3 \times 16 + \text{E}) \times 16 + 5$$

We can calculate this by starting with the first digit, 3, multiplying it by the old base, 16, adding the next digit, E (or 14 decimal), multiplying by 16 again, and adding the last digit, 5. This is shown below as a sequence of assignments:

```
Set P ← 3                (Most-significant digit)
Set P ← P × 16 + 14      (14 is decimal for E, the next digit)
Set P ← P × 16 + 5       (5 is the least-significant digit)
```

This scheme works for numbers of any length; each digit is added in turn after a multiplication by the old base.

In the computer the arithmetic is being done in binary, so to convert an external number from decimal to binary we must work in binary using the second scheme above, multiplying by the old base 10. To convert a binary number back to decimal, we use the first scheme above, dividing by the new base, 10.

Example

Convert 473 decimal to octal using octal arithmetic. (Note that all numbers and arithmetic below are octal!)

P ← 4
P ← 4 × 12 + 7 = 57   (Remember that 12 octal is 10 decimal.)
P ← 57 × 12 + 3 = 731

Hence 473 decimal is 731 octal.

Fractions The rule for converting fractions is exactly the opposite of the rule for integers given above. For fractions we either *multiply by the new base* or *divide by the old base*. Thus the decimal fraction 0.3125 can be converted to octal in decimal arithmetic by multiplying by 8. This can be seen by observing that if the octal representation is $0.o_1o_2$ we have

$$o_1/8 + o_2/64 = 0.3125$$

If we multiply by eight we get

$$o_1 + o_2/8 = 2.5$$

Since the only part of the left-hand side that is larger than one is o_1, its value must be the integer part of the right-hand side. Hence $o_1 = 2$, and by subtracting 2 from both sides we get

$$o_2/8 = 0.5$$

Multiplying by 8 again we get $o_2 = 4$. Hence 0.3125 decimal = 0.24 octal. As before, we prefer to use the other rule inside the computer because we work in the new base. To convert 0.635 decimal to an internal binary form, we can write down the value of 0.635 as

$$6 \times 10^{-1} + 3 \times 10^{-2} + 5 \times 10^{-3}$$

It is convenient to reverse the order of the digits to get

$$5 \times 10^{-3} + 3 \times 10^{-2} + 6 \times 10^{-1}$$

This can be factored to get

$$((5/10 + 3)/10 + 6)/10$$

This can be computed in the following steps:

TABLE 3-2 RULES FOR CONVERTING BETWEEN BASES

Value converted	Arithmetic in: New base	Arithmetic in: Old base
Integer	Multiply by new base	Divide by old base
Fraction	Divide by old base	Multiply by new base

Notes: When arithmetic is done in the old base, the new representation is computed a digit at a time. When arithmetic is done in the new base, the digits of the old representation are used one at a time.

When division is used, the digits are used (or generated) in the reverse order.

P ← 0
P ← (P + 5)/10
P ← (P + 3)/10
P ← (P + 6)/10

Note that the digits are converted in the reverse order, just as digits obtained by dividing integers by the new base are obtained in the reverse order. The rules are summarized in Table 3-2.

Although the method above may be the fastest way to convert fractions, it is usually better to convert the number as if it were an integer, in this case getting the binary form of 635. No rounding errors can occur in this step. Finally the integer can be divided by the appropriate power of 10, in this case 10^3. If a table of powers of 10 is available, only one rounding error occurs. Thus, to convert the number 75.678×10^{-6} to binary, we would usually convert 75678 as a binary integer and then divide by 10^{6+3}.

3.4 FLOATING-POINT REPRESENTATION

It is not always convenient to restrict the representable numbers to fixed point. In many problems, numbers that vary in size for 10^{-50} to 10^{50} must be used. For this reason, most scientific computers include floating-point arithmetic. We frequently use decimal floating point to write numbers in "scientific notation." For example,

$$1.05203 \times 10^{16} = 10{,}520{,}300{,}000{,}000{,}000$$

and

$$5.32635 \times 10^{-14} = 0.000{,}000{,}000{,}000{,}053{,}263{,}5$$

The first part of the scientific representation is called the *mantissa,* whereas the second part is called the *exponent* — in this case, a decimal exponent. The mantissa is frequently called the *fractional part,* although this is a misnomer because it is not a general fraction but a decimal fixed-point number. In the first example above, the mantissa is 1.05203 and the exponent is 16. In a binary machine we usually use an exponent base, which is a power of two such as 2, 4, 8, or 16, rather than a decimal base. Part of a word may be used to represent the mantissa in binary and part to represent the exponent as

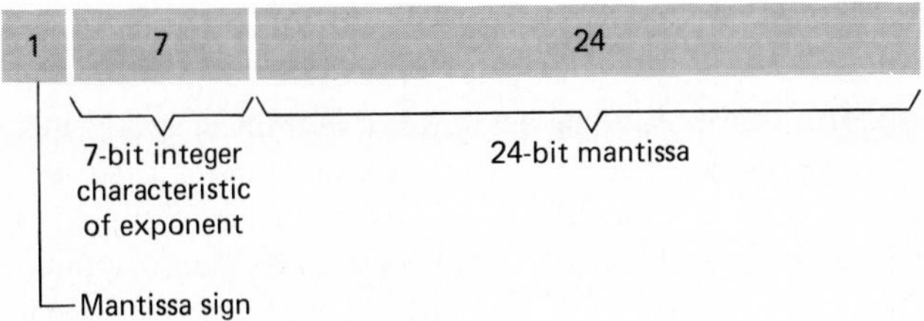

FIGURE 3-7 Floating-point word in the IBM 370

a binary integer. In most machines the mantissa is represented as a value less than 1, although the CYBER 170 uses integer mantissas. Figure 3-7 shows the representation used in the IBM 370. The exponent is a base 16 exponent E between -64 and $+63$. The mantissa is a sign plus 24-bit mantissa F between $-1 + 2^{-24}$. The value of the number represented is $F \times 16^E$.

Many microcomputers do not have a built-in floating-point representation. Instead, floating-point arithmetic has to be programmed. In that case, the programmer can choose the floating-point representation. Usually, 1 word or byte is used to represent the exponent, and the fraction is stored in additional bytes as a signed value using whatever representation is used in the machine for signed information, often twos complement. For example, in the INTEL 8080, 1 byte could be used for the exponent and 3 bytes for the fraction. In the INTEL 8086/88 we might choose to use 2 words (4 bytes) for the fraction.

Note that in floating-point arithmetic, roundoff error in representing a number depends on the exponent. The number 0.00173 could be represented in a decimal machine with a 6-digit mantissa in any of the forms

$$0.000173 \times 10^1$$

$$0.001730 \times 10^0$$

$$0.017300 \times 10^{-1}$$

$$0.173000 \times 10^{-2}$$

If there is roundoff error due to the finite precision, the error in each of these can be limited to

$$0.0000005 \times 10^1$$

$$0.0000005 \times 10^0$$

$$0.0000005 \times 10^{-1}$$

$$0.0000005 \times 10^{-2}$$

respectively. As the exponent is reduced, the size of the error is reduced correspondingly. Thus, in the IBM 370, the error in the mantissa can be limited to 2^{-25} (half of the spacing). However, the actual error is limited by $2^{-25}16^{E}$. Hence it is desirable to make E, as small as possible so as to make the error as small as possible. For each unit that E is reduced in the IBM 370, the mantissa is multiplied by 16 (the base of the exponent). However, the absolute value of the mantissa must be less than 1, so it can only be increased until it is at least $\frac{1}{16}$ (unless it is 0). A floating-point number that is represented in the form with the minimum exponent is called *normalized.* Of the four representations of 0.00173 above, only the last form is normalized.

Normalization in a computer consists of left-shifting the mantissa until the first digit is nonzero while reducing the exponent correspondingly. In a binary machine with a base 2 exponent, the first bit will be nonzero in the normalized form. In the IBM 370 with a base 16 exponent, the first group of 4 bits will contain a 1, that is, the first hexadecimal digit will be nonzero.

Floating-point zero cannot be written in a form with a nonzero leading digit. Instead, most computers use a representation in which the smallest possible exponent indicates a zero, possibly coupled with a zero mantissa.

Arithmetic operations on floating-point numbers can cause overflow if the resulting exponent is too large. An operation can also give a result with an exponent that is too small to be represented. This is called *underflow.* Some computers replace the result of underflow with a formal floating-point 0.

Even if the result of a floating-point operation is not 0, errors that are large relative to the size of the answer can occur. In fixed-point addition, the number of bits and their position relative to the point do not change, so the error is in a known bit position. When two floating-point numbers with opposite signs are added, the result may contain very few significant bits, so that it is seriously contaminated by errors in the original operands. The user may, however, be fooled by printing the answer to high precision. For example, if the two floating-point numbers, $.65284 \times 10^{-3}$ and -0.65252×10^{-3} are added, the result after normalization is 0.32000×10^{-6}. However, it is no longer accurate to 5 digits. If the original numbers had errors as large as 1 in the least significant digit, the result has an error as large as 2 in the second digit. The problems of floating-point numerical errors are complex and not a subject for this text; they are part of numerical analysis.

Although most small microprocessors do not have floating-point arithmetic built into the hardware, recent larger, 32-bit microprocessors do have floating point. Some of them are implementing a proposed standard version of floating point developed by a committee of the Institute of Electrical and Electronic Engineers.[1] This standard for floating-point arithmetic on microprocessors includes a number of additional features designed to help with numerical accuracy and handling of special problems, such as overflow and underflow. Numerical work usually requires two different precisions: single and double. In the standard they are represented in 32 and 64 bits, respectively. The formats are shown in Figure 3-8. The mantissa is in sign/magnitude representation. The characteristic is an integer between 0 and 255 for single precision, or 0 and 2047

[1]"A Proposed Standard for Binary Floating-point Arithmetic," Draft 8.0 for IEEE Task P754, *Computer,* March 1981, pp. 51–62. Also see articles following this one for related discussions.

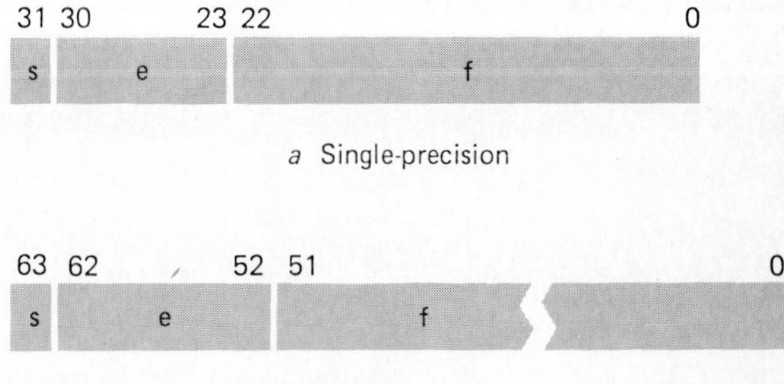

Figure 3-8 IEEE microprocessor floating-point format standards

for double precision. Usually the mantissa is normalized to lie between 1 and 2. This means that the first bit before the binary point is always a 1. Therefore, this bit is not stored, and only the bits after the point are stored. Thus, if the fraction stored in the mantissa bits is f, the mantissa value is $1.f$. This representation is called a *hidden bit* representation. Clearly, 0 cannot be represented this way, so the smallest exponent available, indicated by a characteristic of 0, is used with all 0 bits in the mantissa to indicate a 0. (A characteristic of 0 with a nonzero mantissa is used to represent unnormalized values that are smaller than the smallest normalized number representable. This is called *gradual underflow.* Its justification is not the subject of this text. Articles following the proposal referenced above discuss the topic.) In addition to a range of numerical values, the standard also allows the representation of some special non-numerical values. *Infinity,* meaning a value that has overflowed, can be represented in the proposed standard. It is represented by combining the largest possible characteristic with a zero mantissa. If two large values are multiplied and the result overflows, an answer of infinity is returned. This can be very useful in determining where the program ran into numerical difficulty. A second type of special value called *"Not a Number,"* or NAN, is represented by a maximum characteristic coupled with a nonzero mantissa. These arise in arithmetic when the answer is undetermined. For example, if infinity is divided by infinity, the answer could be anything, so it is set to a NAN. (Infinity and NANs were first provided in CDC computers and are useful in numerical work.)

3.5 PARITY

Usually memory devices have some error-detection equipment, typically a *parity bit*. A parity bit is an additional bit appended to each stored word. It is set so that the total number of bits equal to 1 is even (or odd). This is called an even (or odd) parity scheme. It provides for single-error detection, because an error in any single bit in a word changes the number of 1 bits from even to odd. However, a double error will go undetected. If the probability of a single bit error in a word is independent of all other bit errors and is, say, 1 chance in 10^8 for each memory fetch, the probability of two single bit errors occurring simultaneously is 1 chance in 10^{16}. If the memory cycle time[2] is 100 nanoseconds (10^{-7} seconds), the expected time between undetected memory errors would be 10 seconds without parity and about 32 years with parity.

[2]Cycle time is the length of time for a single memory operation, either reading a word from memory or storing a word into memory.

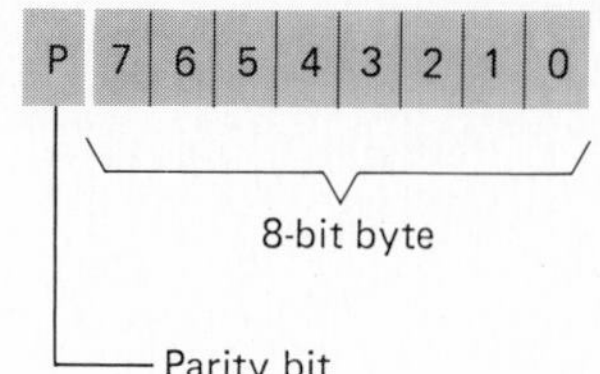

FIGURE 3-9 Eight-bit byte with parity

Error detection by parity is most frequently used in memories and data transmission. In memory devices, a parity bit is often added to each byte stored. The bit is not seen by the user; rather it is checked entirely by the hardware. Thus a byte stored in memory may consist of 9 bits, as shown in Figure 3-9. When the CPU or I/O unit sends a byte to memory for storing, the parity bit is generated and appended. When the same byte is read from memory, its parity is checked. If it is correct, execution continues and the user is unaware of the problem. If there is an error, the operating system takes control and determines the next action, as described in Chapter 8.

Some codes for information transmission include a parity bit as part of the actual data. For example, the ASCII code shown in Table 2-2 can be used with or without parity. If parity is used, the leftmost bit is set to get odd or even parity. In this case the checking can be done by hardware, if it is built into the computer, or by software. For example, the INTEL 8080, which is often used as a controller for communication equipment and terminals, has instructions that test the parity condition bit set by most arithmetic and logical instructions.

Parity makes possible the detection of isolated errors, but multiple errors in the same group of bits can go undetected. If the designer has to use a technology for which the probability of errors is too large, it may be necessary to use automatic error correction schemes. Such schemes are used in some of the high-speed memories in current computers. They require about 8 additional bits to be stored with each 60- to 64-bit word. Thus a word stored in memory consists of the bits of the word and the *error-correcting code* (ecc) bits, as shown in Figure 3-10. These additional bits allow the computer to detect not only the existence of an error, but also to determine exactly what it is in some cases and correct it. As with simple parity, the user is unaware of the existence of the error-correcting code. If there is no error or it can be corrected, execution continues as if nothing has happened. A detailed discussion of these schemes can be found in a number of books.[3] Here we will be content with an illustrative example. Suppose the 5-by-5 array of bits in Figure 3-11 is to be stored. By storing an additional column and row such that the column and row parities are all even, a *single-error correcting, double-error detecting* code is formed. In the example in the figure, the circled bit has been changed from a 0 to a 1, so that the parities of the third column and fourth row are incorrect. This indicates that the circled bit is incorrect. A

[3] See W. W. Peterson, *Error Correcting Codes,* 2d ed, MIT Press, Cambridge, MA, 1972.

FIGURE 3-10 Error-correcting code bits stored with word

ecc bits	Word

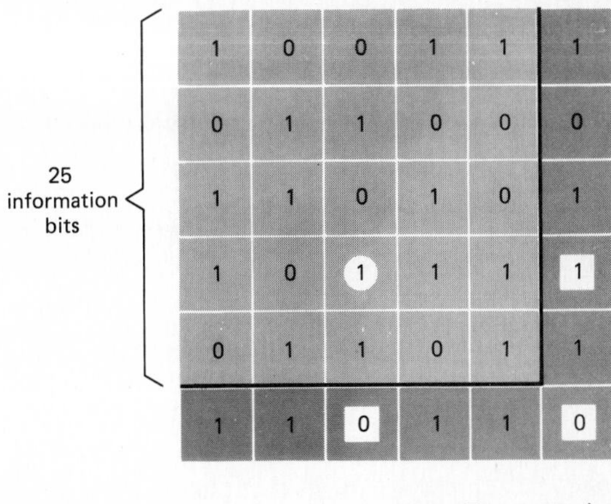

FIGURE 3-11 A simple error-correcting code

double error will always be detected, because there will be parity errors in two rows and/or columns. A triple error could be mistaken for a single error. For example, if the 3 bits in square boxes in Figure 3-11 were wrong, this would be indistinguishable from a single error in the circled bit.

3.6 ARITHMETIC IN COMPUTERS

The arithmetic instructions operate on data in a representation determined by the computer design. Many computers allow more than one type of numerical data to be represented. All computers allow integer arithmetic, usually in a binary representation and most commonly in twos complement; some computers have floating-point arithmetic also. Because scientific calculation often requires a precision greater than that provided in typical computers, there is often provision for double-length arithmetic. This allows 2 words to be considered as a single value of double the number of bits. Multiple-precision arithmetic is a generalization of this, allowing several words to be considered as a single value. Computers that have built-in floating point have instructions that handle arithmetic on such data, as well as the usual integer arithmetic instructions. For example, the IBM 370 has an integer addition instruction written in the form

```
A       R4, X
```

and floating-point addition instructions written in the form

```
AE      FPR4, Y
```

and

```
AD      FPR2, Z
```

AE does a single-precision addition of a 32-bit value, whereas AD does a double-precision, 64-bit addition. The registers used in floating-point arithmetic in the

IBM 370 are a different set from those used for integer arithmetic, hence the different names (which stand for Floating-Point Register 2, etc.).

Almost all computers use different instructions for different types of data, and most use different registers for integer and floating-point data, if they use registers. However, there is one very important type of design in which the data is *tagged* with bits indicating its type. If, for example, the first 2 bits of a data item are used to tag the data with a type indication—perhaps 00 meaning integer, 01 floating point, 10 decimal, etc.—then only one addition instruction has to be provided for the user; it can decide what type of addition to perform on the basis of the data read from memory or registers. This type of organization is not common, and it does have drawbacks, because it can restrict the freedom of high-level language designers who may want to allow operations between data of different types or disallow it in the spirit of strong typing. Other types of instructions may be provided for decimal addition in a computer that provides for decimal data. These instructions usually operate on variable-length strings of data, often represented in 2 BCD nibbles per byte. Some computers permit the direct addition of strings of decimal digits represented in ASCII or EBCDIC.

Integer data can usually be manipulated in shift instructions. The exact form of shift instructions provided depends on the representation used; most computers have *arithmetic shifts* that halve and double the number as well as the logical and rotational shift operations described in the last chapter. (In ones complement representation, a left rotate is also a left arithmetic shift, but a right arithmetic shift is the same as a right arithmetic shift in twos complement, in that it duplicates the sign bit.) A shift instruction may have no addresses and just bring about a shift of 1 bit, or it may have an address that gives the number of shifts to perform. Thus in the IBM 370 we find the instruction

```
SRA     R4, 16
```

which is a Shift Right Arithmetic of register 4 by 16 places. Since the 370 uses twos complement arithmetic for binary integers, this duplicates the Sign bit, as in Figure 3-4. In the INTEL 8080 we find the instructions

```
RRC
```

which is a Rotate Right and set Carry; it rotates the bits in the accumulator one place to the right, copying the bit from position 0 on the right to bit 7 on the left, and also putting a copy of it in the Carry bit. Multiple shifts have to be done by repeating the single shift in such computers.

Whatever computer is used, there are occasions when arithmetic in a precision longer than that provided by the computer must be programmed. Figure 3-6 illustrates the technique used to add double-length integers in twos complement. It requires that the Carry bit be propagated from the least significant addition to the most significant. Short-word-length computers usually have instructions to make this operation straightforward.

Multiplication of multiple-length values requires a sequence of single-length multiplications followed by additions of the partial results. We can illustrate this with decimal arithmetic by assuming that we have hardware to multiply a pair of single-digit numbers (to get a 2-digit result) and must do the rest by addition. Suppose we want to multiply 84 by 79. Below we show the arithmetic. Each multiplication yields a result that is written on a separate line. Then, multiple-precision addition is used to sum the lines of partial results. Trailing zeros are indicated on the partial results to indicate the position of the decimal point (on the right) more clearly.

```
   84
  ×79
 ----------------
   36   4 × 9
  720   8 × 9
  280   4 × 7
 5600   8 × 7
 ----------------
 6636   (Result)
```

Each word in a multiple-length number can be viewed as a single "digit." If the computer has a multiplication operation for single words, it can be used to handle the multiplication of each pair of "digits." If signed information must be handled, the technique depends on the representation chosen. We will discuss handling the sign in twos complement arithmetic in an example below. An alternative is to extract the magnitude of the numbers and multiply those as positive values. The sign can be calculated separately and attached at the end of the calculation in a way depending on the representation.

If the computer uses sign/magnitude or ones complement arithmetic internally, it is often simpler to ignore the sign position in all but the leftmost word of a multiple-precision value and use only the remaining bits in the representation. Thus, if we had a 60-bit computer with ones complement integer representation (such as a Cyber computer), a double-precision number would best be represented as a 119-bit value with the sign and first 59 bits in the first word and the remaining 59 bits in the second word. (In this case, it is best to put a copy of the sign bit from the first word into the second word.) In multiple-precision twos complement arithmetic, the Sign bits of all but the first word can be used as regular, positively weighted bits. We can see this in the example that follows, which shows how to multiply two binary numbers in the twos complement representation and also gives an indication of how to multiply two unsigned binary values in a computer by means of shifts and adds.

Example: Multiplication of Twos Complement Integers Some microcomputers do not have a multiplication operation, so it must be programmed using addition. The technique given below will multiply two 8-bit twos complement values, X and Y, to get a 16-bit answer, Z. (The lengths of the values, 8 and 16, can be replaced by any pair N and $2N$, where N is the word length.) We will first multiply the two values as though they are unsigned integers to get a 16-bit unsigned integer result, P, and then correct that result to take account of the sign. When we view the bit patterns of X and Y as unsigned integers, we are assuming that the weight of the leftmost bit is $+2^7$ instead of -2^7. Hence we are forming

$$P = (X + 2^8x_7)(Y + 2^8y_7)$$

where X and Y are the signed values and x_7 and y_7 are their leftmost (Sign) bits. Consequently, to get the correct answer we must take the product P and form

$$P - 2^8x_7Y - 2^8y_7X + 2^{16}x_7y_7$$

Since the result P is a 16-bit quantity, we can ignore $2^{16}x_7y_7$; it is out of range of a 16-bit representation because it represents a 0 or 1 bit in the seventeenth position. Thus we must subtract X and/or Y from the most significant part of the result, as Y and/or X are negative, to get $P - 2^8x_7Y - 2^8y_7X$. Even though we have ignored out-of-range partial results, we have seen that, in twos complement arithmetic, the answer is correct if it is in range. Since the maximum value of the product of two 8-bit twos complement integers is $(-2^{N-1} \times -2^{N-1}) = 2^{2N-2}$, which is in range, we know that there can be no overflow.

The unsigned integer multiplication can be performed by addition and shifting as follows. Suppose the numbers X and Y are to be multiplied. Assume that they are unsigned integers. Suppose X is represented as $x_7x_6 \ldots x_0$. Its value is

$$x_72^7 + x_62^6 + \cdots + x_0$$

This is multiplied by Y to form

$$x_72^7Y + x_62^6Y + \cdots + x_0Y$$

which can be written as

$$(\cdots((0 + x_7Y)2 + x_6Y)2 + \cdots + x_1Y)2 + x_0Y$$

Thus we start with 0 and add Y if x_7 is a 1. Then the result is shifted left one place to double it. Next we add Y if x_6 is a 1 and shift left. We repeat this process until x_0 has been tested.

To test the bits of Y, Y can be shifted left a bit at a time. During the course of the multiplication, the *partial product,* consisting of the values of X that have been added and shifted so far, is generated. This will be up to 16 bits long, so a 16-bit quantity must be stored and shifted. If we are working in an 8-bit machine, this means working in double precision. However, notice that the partial product is only 8 bits long after the first addition. After the first left shift it will be 9 bits long, and the next add could make it 10 bits long. Thereafter it will increase 1 bit in length for each shift, but not in the subsequent addition. Thus, after three addition steps (two shifts), the partial product will be $8 + 3 = 11$ bits long.

By this time we will have tested the leftmost 3 bits of X to determine whether to add in Y in each of the first three steps. This is best done by shifting X left a bit at a time *logically,* so that the bits are discarded after they have been tested. Thus after three steps, only 5 bits will remain in X. These can occupy the unused 5 bits in a double-

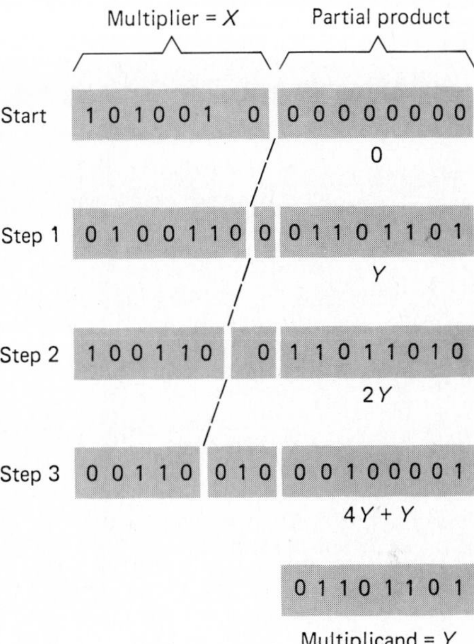

FIGURE 3-12 Multiplication by shift and add

precision data item used to hold the partial product. This is illustrated in Figure 3-12. Step 0 shows the initial state with X in the leftmost part and the partial product set to 0. After the first step, the partial product has been shifted left one place and Y has been added to it because the leftmost bit of X is a 1. The second step causes just a shift, since the next bit of X is a 0. The third step causes another addition after the shift. After eight steps, X will be shifted out completely. The structure of a program to do the multiplication of the unsigned values is shown in Program 3-1. The twos complement value can be found by performing the corrections described above.

Program 3-1 Multiplication of unsigned binary integers

```
Place the multiplier, X, in the left of a double-length
  register, R.
Clear the right half of R.
Use another register, C, for a count.
do for C ← 8 to 1 by −1
  Double R by double-length left shift, saving
    old sign bit in S. (On some computers, the
    Carry bit can be used for this.)
  if S = 1
    then add Y to R in double precision
    endif
  enddo
```

3.6.1 Arithmetic in the INTEL 8080

The 8080 uses twos complement arithmetic and has a Carry bit, CY. It is one of the condition bits, along with the Sign, Zero, and Parity bits. Addition and subtraction set the Carry bit, as described in Section 3.2.1. They also set the other three condition bits. Most arithmetic is 8-bit. For these, the Add with Carry (ADC) instruction and Subtract with Borrow (SBB) instruction are just like the ADD and SUB instructions, except that they also Add/Subtract the Carry/Borrow bit as described in Section 3.2.1 and illustrated in Figure 3-6. For example, suppose registers B and C contain a double-precision (16-bit) integer that is to be added to a similar integer in registers D and E. Let us suppose that the most significant parts are in B and D. The instruction sequence below does the desired addition following the pattern shown in Figure 3-6:

```
MOV     A, C     ;C to Accumulator
ADD     E        ;Sum of least-significant parts
MOV     E, A     ;Return result to E
MOV     A, B     ;B to Accumulator
ADC     D        ;Sum of most-significant parts
MOV     D, A     ;Result now in DE
```

(If a subtraction of DE from BC were to be done, the ADD instructions above would be replaced by SUBs, and the ADC replaced with SBB.) None of the data movement instructions (LDA, STA, or MOV) change the value of the Carry bit, so the Carry added in the ADC instruction is value left in the Carry by the earlier ADD instruction. The ADC and SBB have immediate operand versions, ACI (Add with Carry Immediate) and SBI (Subtract with Borrow Immediate). The Carry bit can be set with the zero-address STC (SeT Carry) instruction and complemented with the zero-address CMC (CompleMent Carry) instruction.

Logical instructions in the 8080 clear the Carry bit but set the remaining three condition bits on the basis of the answer computed in A.

Shift instructions in the 8080 modify the accumulator and the Carry bit. Other condition bits are not changed. There are two types of shift instructions; both are circular. One type rotates the 8 bits of the accumulator A one place, setting the Carry bit, CY, to the bit rotated around the end. The other type rotates the 9-bit quantity consisting of the Carry bit CY followed by the 8 bits of the accumulator on its right. Both types have a left- and a right-shift version. They are

8-Bit Rotates:

```
RRC     ;Rotate Right and set Carry
RLC     ;Rotate Left and set Carry
```

9-Bit Rotates:

```
RAR     ;Rotate All Right
RAL     ;Rotate All Left
```

These instructions do not do halving and doubling directly because of the twos complement representation. To double a number, the Carry bit must first be cleared. This can be done with the instruction ANA A (which ANDs A with itself and sets the Carry bit to 0). Thus, the following pair of instructions doubles A because it shifts a 0 into the right end of A.

```
ANA     A       ;Clear CY
RAL             ;Double A if answer in range
```

To halve a number, the Carry bit must be set equal to the Sign bit. This can be done by using the 8-bit rotate left followed by the 8-bit rotate right. Then the 9-bit rotate right will give the halved result:

```
RLC             ;Sign bit to bit zero
RRC             ;Carry and Sign bit equal
RAR             ;Bits 7 and 6 now equal
```

The 8080 has no floating-point or general decimal arithmetic instructions, but it does have an instruction to make decimal arithmetic fairly easy to program. DAA, Decimal Adjust Accumulator, can be used after an addition to give the effect of a 2-digit decimal addition. It operates in conjunction with an *Auxiliary carry* bit, AC, which is set if there is a carry from bit three to bit four during an addition (or a borrow during subtraction). (The AC bit can be viewed as another condition bit, but it cannot be tested.) The principle of operation of the DAA instruction is as follows.

> Suppose that we have two 2-decimal-digit values, each stored in 8 bits as 2 nibbles per byte, and we add them using standard twos complement arithmetic. If the sums of the corresponding pairs of digits do not exceed 9, the answer is correct viewed as a pair of decimal digits or as a pair of hexadecimal digits. For example, 42 + 37 = 79 in both decimal and hexadecimal. However, if the sum in either position exceeds 9, the answer is incorrect viewed as a decimal summand. Thus, in hexadecimal, 45 + 37 = 7C and 48 + 39 = 81. These examples illustrate the two cases: in one, the sum digit is between 10 (A) and 15 (F) in the result; in the other, there has been a carry into the next position, that is, from bit three to four, or out of bit seven. The result can be corrected in either of these cases by adding 6 to the appropriate digit. Thus 45 + 39 + 06 = 82 hexadecimal, giving us the sum of 45 and 37 in decimal. Similarly, 48 + 37 + 06 = 87 hexadecimal, which is the decimal sum of 48 and 39. If the left digit overflows, the Carry bit CY must be set: 64 + 82 + 60 = 146 hexadecimal; the 46 should be left in the accumulator and the leftmost 1 put in the Carry bit. The DAA instruction does these steps for us: after an addition, DAA adds 06 to the accumulator if the bottom 4 bits are greater than 9 or the auxiliary Carry bit, AC, is on. It then adds 60 if the top 4 bits are greater than 9 or the Carry bit, CY, is on.

In the 8080, the DAA does not work directly after subtraction; instead a number of intermediate steps must be executed. (These are given below. However, the Z80, which is an advanced form of the 8080, has an additional bit, the N bit, which is set to 1 if the prior arithmetic operation was a subtraction. It is used by the DAA instruction so that it also adjusts correctly after a subtraction.)

To do a decimal subtraction in the 8080, we must form the *nines complement* of the subtrahend (Q) and add it to P together with an additional 1 in the least significant digit. This is an exact analogy of twos complement subtraction, which is done by complementing and adding. The nines complement of a decimal number is computed by subtracting the number from 99 . . . 9, where there are as many nines as digits in the number. For 1-byte (2-digit) values, a decimal subtraction can be done with the sequence

```
MVI     A,99H
LXI     H,Q     ;Form nines complement
SUB     M       ;of value in Q.
ADI     1       ;Add least significant 1 to get -Q.
LXI     H,P
ADD     M       ;Add P to it.
DAA             ;Correct result for decimal addition.
```

The 8080 has no multiply or divide instructions, but the method described in the previous section can be coded. The code in Program 3-2 uses the technique shown in Program 3-1 for the multiplication of the unsigned integers and then makes the corrections for twos complement, also described in the previous section. In this program, the double-length register R of Program 3-1 is held in the DE register pair.

The Z80 arithmetic is almost identical to that of the 8080, except for the action of DAA described above and the Parity bit, which is called a Parity/Overflow bit in the Z80. Generally, it is set according to the parity of the result after logical operations, but according to overflow after arithmetic operations.

3.6.2 Arithmetic in the INTEL 8086/88

The 8086/88 uses twos complement arithmetic, which sets the Carry bit, CF, and the Overflow bit, OF, as well as the Sign and Zero bits, SF and ZF. (See Table 2-4.) Arithmetic is 8-bit or 16-bit. In either case, the Add with Carry (ADC) instruction and Subtract with Borrow (SBB) instruction are just like the ADD and SUB instructions, except that they also add/subtract the Carry/Borrow bit as described in Section 3.2.1 and illustrated in Figure 3-6. For example, suppose registers CX and BX contain a double-precision (32-bit) integer that is to be added to a similar integer in registers DX and AX. Lets us suppose that the most significant parts are in B and D. The instruction sequence below does the desired addition following the pattern shown in Figure 3-6:

```
ADD     AX, BX     ;Sum of least significant parts in AX
ADC     DX, CX     ;Sum of most significant parts in DX
```

(If a subtraction of CX, BX from DX, AX were to be done, the ADD instruction above would be replaced by SUBs and the ADC replaced by SBB.) These instructions also work on byte arithmetic in a similar manner.

Program 3-2 Code to multiply contents of registers A and B

```
;Register C is used to hold a count
;Register DE is used to accumulate a double-precision
;product. Register H saves a copy of A, the multiplier.
;
         MVI    C,8      ;Count of number of multiplication steps
         MOV    H,A
         MOV    D,A      ;Multiplier to most significant part of DE
         SUB    A        ;Clear A. It will hold the least
                         ;significant part of the product
                         ;at start of this loop.
LOOP:    ANA    A        ;Zero carry
         RAL             ;Shift double-length partial product
         MOV    E,A
         MOV    A,D
         RAL             ;Finish double-length shift
                         ;Carry bit is next bit of multiplier
         MOV    D,A
         MOV    A,E
         JNC    SKIP     ;Jump if multiplier bit zero
         ADD    B        ;Add multiplicand to E
         JNC    SKIP
         INR    D        ;Increment D if carry
SKIP:    DCR    C        ;Decrement count
         JNZ    LOOP     ;Repeat loop if not zero
;  Double-length positive integer product now in D,A
         MOV    E,A
         MOV    A,H      ;Copy of multiplier A
         RAL             ;Move sign to CY for testing
         JNC    APLUS
         MOV    A,D      ;If A was negative, subtract B
         SUB    B        ;from most significant part
         MOV    D,A
APLUS:   MOV    A,B      ;Move multiplicand B to accumulator
         RAL             ;Sign bit to CY for testing
         JNC    BPLUS
         MOV    A,D      ;If B was negative, subtract A
         SUB    H        ;from most significant part
         MOV    D,A
BPLUS:                   ;Signed product now in DE.
```

The Carry bit can be set with the zero-address STC (SeT Carry) instruction, complemented with the zero-address CMC (CompleMent Carry) instruction, and cleared with the zero-address CLC (CLear Carry) instruction. Logical instructions also clear the Carry bit, except for NOT and the shift operations. (The rules on which condition bits are affected by which operations in the 8086/88 are not easy to describe, so the programmer is advised to check each instruction in the manual if there is doubt.)

Because the 8086/88 is designed to work with 8- or 16-bit operands with equal ease, it has an instruction to convert an 8-bit operand to a 16-bit operand by sign extension (which is necessary in twos complement). CBW, Convert Byte to Word, is a zero-address instruction that fills the AH registers with copies of the sign bit in AL, that is, it converts the 1-byte twos complement value in AL to word-length twos complement value in AH. The CWD (Convert Word to Double) instruction behaves similarly for the register pair DX, AX. It fills DX with copies of the Sign bit of AX to create a double-length representation of the value in AX. These are particularly useful prior to signed division, discussed below. They should also be used when bytes are added to words, as in

```
MOV     AL, BYTE    ;Load AL with byte operand from
                    ;memory.
CBW                 ;Convert to a word operand.
ADD     AX, WORD    ;Add in a word operand from
                    ;memory.
```

There are four types of shift instructions; two are circular and are similar to those in the 8080, and the other two are arithmetic and logical. The rotates act on 8- or 16-bit operands, setting the Carry bit to the bit rotated around the end. RCR and RCL (Rotate through Carry, Right and Left) treat the operand and the CF bit as a 9- or 17-bit quantity that is rotated in the requested direction. In all shift instructions, the number of places shifted is either one or the integer held in the CL register. In assembly language, these instructions can be written in forms such as:

```
RCR     AH, 1       ;Rotate AL through Carry Right 1 bit.
MOV     CL, 4
RCL     DX, CL      ;Rotate DX through Carry Left
                    ;4 places.
```

In the other type of rotate instruction, the 8- or 16-bit operand is rotated. The bit shifted around the end is also copied into the Carry bit. Examples of the instructions are

```
MOV     CL, 7
ROR     BX, CL          ;Rotate BX right 7 places.
ROL     BYTE-ADR, 1     ;Rotate memory byte left 1 place.
```

Halving and doubling can be accomplished with the arithmetic shifts, SAL and SAR (Shift Arithmetic Left and Right, respectively). The right shift does the sign duplication necessary in twos complement. The Carry bit is set to the last bit shifted out. After a single-place left arithmetic shift, the overflow bit indicates whether there was an overflow.

The logical left shift, SHL, is identical to SAL (and is simply a second mnemonic for the same instruction). The logical right shift, SHR, moves bits to the right, inserting zeros on the left end as required.

The INTEL 8086/88 has no built-in floating-point operations, but INTEL does produce a chip, the 8087, that implements the IEEE standard floating point. It can be added to 8086 and 8088 systems. It is called a *coprocessor* and can be connected to an 8086 or 8088 system so that floating point instructions are executed by it while the 8086 or 8088 proceeds with the execution of other instructions.

The 8086/88 has no direct decimal arithmetic instructions, but it does have instructions to make decimal arithmetic fairly easy to program. The instructions DAA and DAS (Decimal Adjust after Addition and Decimal Adjust after Subtraction) can be used to give the effect of a 2-digit decimal addition or subtraction. They operate in conjunction with the *Auxiliary carry* flag, AF, which is set if there is a carry from bit three to bit four during an addition (or a borrow during subtraction). The principle of operation is described in the preceding INTEL 8080 section and will not be repeated here. Its effect is such that if a pair of bytes is added in the AL register, and these bytes each contain 2 decimal digits encoded as BCD nibbles, the DAA will yield the correct decimal answer. The Carry flag CF is set if the answer is greater than 99. After a subtraction, DAS can be used. Thus, to form X + Y − Z in 2-digit decimal arithmetic, where each operand is packed into 1 byte as a pair of nibbles, we can execute

```
MOV     AL, X
ADD     AL, Y
DAA
SUB     AL, Z
DAS
```

Note that DAA and DAS are zero-address instructions.

Decimal arithmetic can also be performed on characters. If two bytes each contain a BCD nibble in the lower 4 bits, those bytes can be added in decimal by using an ADD instruction followed by AAA (ASCII Adjust for Addition). It subtracts 6 from the lower-order nibble in AL and adds 1 to AH if the lower-order nibble exceeds 9 or the Auxiliary carry flag is set. Then it clears the higher-order nibble in AL. Thus the sequence

```
MOV     AH, 0
MOV     AL, X
ADD     AL, Y
AAA
```

leaves a decimal representation of the sum of the single digits X and Y, 1 digit per byte, in AH and AL. AAS (ASCII Adjust after Subtraction) does the same thing for subtract.

Unpacked decimal arithmetic (that is, 1 decimal digit per byte) is also aided by the AAD and AAM instructions (ASCII Adjust for Division and ASCII Adjust for Multiplication). These can be used before a division or after a multiplication of 2 decimal digits as bytes using the DIV and MUL instructions. AAD sets AL to be AL + 10*AH and AH to be 0. If we now divide AX by a value and the quotient is less than 10, it is the correct decimal answer. AAM divides AX by 10 and sets the quotient in AH and the remainder in AL. Thus, if AX contains 93 decimal, AAM sets AH to 9 and AL to 3 to get the decimal representation of AX.

We discussed the unsigned integer MUL and DIV instructions in Chapter 2. The IMUL and IDIV (Integer MULtiply and Integer DIVide) instructions perform twos complement arithmetic. (The name is confusing, because MUL and IMUL are both integer operations, one unsigned and one signed.)

3.7 SUMMARY AND PROBLEMS

A computer frequently has several ways of representing numerical information, including integers and one or more lengths of floating point. Decimally encoded information may also be handled, as well as character data.

The binary point can be assumed to be in any fixed position in a word, so we can use the same arithmetic to handle integer and fixed-point values. The range of a representation is the interval between the most negative and most positive value that can be represented. The precision is the spacing between the representable values. Only a finite number of different values can be represented; when a value that is not one of the representable set must be stored in the computer, it must be truncated or rounded. The error that occurs in this process is called round-off error. Shifting a binary number doubles or halves it, provided that the result is in range and that there is no loss of precision due to bits "falling off" the right end.

Signed numbers can be represented in three ways: sign/magnitude, twos complement, and ones complement. Twos complement is used in many computers because it makes addition and subtraction logically simple. Ones complement representation has similar properties, and it is particularly easy to negate a number in ones complement—each bit is inverted. Extending the precision of twos complement on the left requires that the Sign bit be duplicated. Extending the precision of ones complement numbers on the right or left requires that the Sign bit be duplicated. For this reason, shifting ones and twos complement numbers to halve or double them requires special rules—the propagation of the Sign bit. Machines with twos complement arithmetic frequently provide a Carry bit that allows multiple-length arithmetic to be programmed. Ones complement addition requires an end-around carry.

Conversion between different bases can be done using the following guide:

Integers

Divide by new base

or

Multiply by old base

Fractions

Multiply by new base

or

Divide by old base

When hand methods are used, we want to use decimal arithmetic. To convert from decimal to binary, it is easier to convert to octal or hexadecimal first and then rewrite in binary.

Floating-point values consist of an exponent and a mantissa. The exponent is made as small as possible by normalization. Floating-point underflow occurs when the exponent becomes smaller than the smallest permissible value. Floating-point overflow occurs when the exponent becomes too large. Some representations of floating-point information include representations for numbers that are too large ("infinity") or undetermined (NAN, or Not a Number).

Parity is used to detect errors. All single errors are detected, but double errors can go undetected. If the probability of error is too high, then an error-correcting code should be used. This not only can detect more than one error, it has enough information to correct some multiple errors.

Computers have separate instructions for fixed and floating-point arithmetic, and some have special instructions for decimal arithmetic. Some microcomputers do not have multiplication and division operations, but they can be programmed. Many do not have floating-point instructions, but these can also be programmed in software.

Problems

3-1 How many different integers can be represented in a sign/magnitude number with 6 bits?

3-2 How many different representations of zero are there in an N-bit integer, ones complement representation?

3-3 What is the range of an N-bit ones complement integer?

3-4 How many bits are required to represent all numbers between -1 and $+1$ with an error of not more than 0.0001 decimal in ones complement (fractions)?

3-5 What are the answers to problems 3-2, 3-3, and 3-4 for twos complement and sign/magnitude representations?

3-6 How many representations of zero are there if floating point is used and there is an 8-bit exponent and a sign/magnitude mantissa?

3-7 How many representations of $+1$ and -1 are there in twos complement floating point with a binary base for the exponent and a 25-bit mantissa (including sign)? What about ones complement and sign/magnitude?

3-8 Express $-63, 91$, and -23 decimal in sign/magnitude, twos complement, and ones complement using an 8-bit word.

3-9 Add the four signed binary numbers 100110, 001101, 010101, and 111101 together as (a) sign/magnitude, (b) twos complement, and (c) ones complement numbers.

3-10 What is the 10-bit (double-precision) result if 10010 and 10101 are multiplied in each of the three representations as integers?

3-11 Divide the integer 0001010111 by 01001 to get a 5-bit quotient and remainder in each of the three representations.

3-12 Show that when a ones complement fraction is extended on the right to get increased precision, the correct process is to add copies of the sign bit.

3-13 Prove that the correct rule for doubling a ones complement number is a left circular shift.

3-14 Can you suggest a simple rule for dividing a binary number by 2^n and getting a rounded result?

3-15 How can overflow be detected during shifting operations in each of the representations of integers?

3-16 How can loss of accuracy be detected during right shifts in each of the representations of integers?

3-17 What are the answers to problems 3-15 and 3-16 if fractions are represented?

3-18 In Chapter 2 we saw that instruction addresses could be modified by performing arithmetic on the instructions. Thus we could add 1 to LOAD A to get LOAD A + 1. Why must twos or ones complement arithmetic be used?

Programming Problems

3-19 Write a division program to divide a $2n$-bit unsigned integer by an n-bit unsigned integer to get an n-bit quotient and remainder without using the machine divide instruction (if the machine has one). The integer n should be the length of a single register (8 in the INTEL 8080, and 16 in the INTEL 8086/88.) To divide, put the dividend in a pair of registers. Shift left one place and make a "trial subtraction" of the divisor from the most significant half. If the result is positive, the most significant bit of the quotient is 1. If not, that bit is 0, and the subtraction should not be done. Repeat the process $n - 1$ more times, each time shifting, trial subtracting, and developing 1 more bit of quotient. The remainder is what is left in the most significant part of the pair of registers. You can be clever and assemble the bits of the quotient by inserting them in the least significant bit of the register pair as they are generated. Then the left shift moves them over appropriately.

3-20 Suppose a floating-point value is stored in two words, the first containing the exponent and the second the mantissa. The mantissa is an integer. Write a program to add two such values if the result is in range or to detect whether the result has underflowed or overflowed.

3-21 Suppose you have a floating-point value represented as described in Problem 3-20. Write a code to pack it into 1 word, putting the sign bit on the left, a suitably defined characteristic next, and the mantissa on the right.

3-22 Write a program to multiply two 4-digit decimal numbers, where each digit is stored in byte as 4 zero bits followed by a 4-bit nibble containing the BCD coding of the digit.

CHAPTER **4**

INPUT, OUTPUT, AND SECONDARY STORAGE DEVICES

In this chapter, we shall discuss the input and output that are common to general-purpose systems. However, the principles involved do not differ from those in online computers. This chapter provides a quick survey of historical and current input-output (I/O) equipment. Many readers will be familiar with a number of these devices from earlier computer experience.

The function of a computer system is to process information. We have seen how this is done using the memory and processor units. The computer system must also be able to transmit information between itself and its environment. The information to be processed must be input to the system, and the results must be output back to the external world. The computer may be in one of a variety of environments; these affect the type of input-output communication required. In most familiar systems, the computer communicates primarily with humans, who prepare the problem for solution, provide the initial data, and wish to interpret the answers. In other applications, the input can be directly obtained from a mechanical device. For example, complex experiments in the physical sciences can be measured automatically by the computer. In such a case, the principal inputs to the computer are the electronic outputs taken directly from the various instruments used to monitor the experiment. In other applications, both input and output may be connected directly to mechanical or electrical equipment. For example, an airborne computer may be used to calculate the position of a plane at any moment (by use of inertial guidance devices such as gyroscopes and accelerometers, or by use of navigation beacons), to compare this position with the desired flight path derived by computation, and then to output correction signals to the control mechanisms of the aircraft. Computers for online instrumentation and process-control applications are usually smaller and more specialized than the general-purpose computers that we have been discussing.

The general-purpose computer may need to communicate either directly with the user or with a computer-readable medium. The former is referred to as input-output, whereas the latter is called *secondary storage,* since the information is not yet "out" of its computer representation. It is also possible to connect the output lines from one computer to the input lines of another so that information can be transmitted directly between two computers . In this mode, each computer looks like an input-output device to the other. In a generalized form of this, many computers can be interconnected in a *network* so that any computer can send information to any other. Secondary storage can also be used to transmit information to another computer if the *recording medium* (the physical material on which the information is recorded) can be removed from the unit that wrote it on the first computer and mounted on a similar device on the second computer. This is still an economic way to move large amounts of information relatively slowly, although national and international networks, using satellite relays, for example, are rapidly becoming competitive. The more important use for removable-storage-medium secondary storage devices is for very-long-term storage at low cost—the information can be stored on tape, for example, and the tape can be left on a shelf, using no computer devices other than the relatively inexpensive tape until the information needs to be read again, at which time the tape can be mounted on a tape drive unit. This type of storage device can also be used to *backup* information normally kept on more volatile devices that are subject to occasional failure, such as high-speed disk units. In a back-up of a disk, a copy of the total content of the disk, or of that information that has been changed since the last back-up, is made on a medium such as tape, which is then removed to a safe storage place.

We will classify secondary storage devices as removable media devices, usually used for long-term storage, and nonremovable media devices, more commonly used for shorter-term storage. Nonremovable devices are usually faster than removable devices and often have a higher capacity.

The next four sections describe the characteristics of various devices used for input-output and secondary storage. Chapter 8 discusses the ways in which these devices are connected to computers and controlled by program instructions. In this chapter we will give some typical speed and capacity figures; these should be viewed as the values for units likely to be found in standard systems. Greater values are always possible by means of special engineering designs, and smaller values are obviously possible at a lower cost (although the cost does not reduce linearly as the capacity or speed decrease, so the best price/performance figure is usually obtained for a unit near the "top" end of the spectrum of available units).

4.1 INPUT-OUTPUT DEVICES

Input-output devices are of two basic types: *hard-copy* devices and non-hard-copy devices. The former provide the output on paper or other permanent form and obtain the input by reading it from punched cards or by optically or magnetically sensing special printed information. The latter present the output directly to the user in a non-permanent form, such as the screen of a terminal, or input the information directly from the user as a result of some action of the user, such as the pressing of a key on the terminal keyboard.

4.1.1 Online Terminals

One of the most common I/O devices today is the online terminal. It consists of a keyboard, by means of which the user can enter alphabetic and numeric data, and an output device. The output device may either be a printing device, such as a typewriter-like mechanism, or a cathode-ray-tube (CRT) display. The latter may either be limited to the display of alphanumeric characters, in which case it is called a *video display unit* (VDU), or be capable of displaying graphical information as well. In this section we will consider only VDUs; graphical terminals will be considered in Section 4.1.3. A VDU can display a number of lines of characters, typically 20 to 24 lines of 60 to 80 characters per line, although there are terminals that can display up to about 60 lines of up to about 132 characters each.

A printing terminal is limited to displaying (printing) the information output from the computer in the order in which it is sent. (Mechanical backup of the paper is possible in some terminals, but it is not reliable.) On the other hand, CRT-based units can be used in a variety of modes. In the *scrolling mode,* the latest information output from the computer is written on the bottom line of the terminal after all previous lines have been moved up one line. The top line of the display disappears off the top. This simulates a printing terminal, displaying the last 20 to 60 lines output from the computer. In the screen-addressing mode, characters can be sent to any place on the screen. This mode is used with screen-oriented editors. It allows the computer to selectively modify any part of the display screen. Because highly interactive systems may want to move information around on the screen (for example, to open up space in the middle to allow additional material to be inserted), a large amount of information must be retransmitted from the computer unless the terminal has the ability to perform some elementary data-movement operations. Such terminals are called *smart terminals* and have the ability to selectively erase part of the information currently displayed and to move part of it to other places on the screen under command from the computer. The terminal may also have internal storage for more information than appears on the screen at any one time, so that the user can recall information that was transmitted from the computer to parts of the display that are now "off the screen." Printing terminals usually have about 90 to 100 different printing characters, which can be extended by *overstriking* (for example, to underline the letter "k" the computer outputs the letter "k" followed by a backspace and an underline character). VDUs do not provide overstrike capabilities, because exactly one character must be displayed in each character position. However, some VDUs provide many options for the display of each character. For example, one character can have a different intensity than the other characters, so that it is highlighted; it can be in *reverse video,* which also makes it very visible (dark on light instead of light on dark, or *vice versa*); it can be *blinking;* or it can be underlined.

Input to the keyboard is limited to typing speed (perhaps a peak of ten to fifteen characters a second in very short bursts, with an average close to a maximum of eight even for a very proficient typist). Output speed is determined by the capacity of the line connecting the terminal to the computer in the case of CRT-based terminals, but by the mechanical speed of the terminal in most printing terminals. These mechanical speeds are typically 30 characters per second, but some printing terminals will operate at 120 characters per second. There are a number of standard line speeds. They are measured in *baud*. A baud rate of 300 indicates that 300 bits per second are being transmitted in most common transmission schemes. Although each ASCII character requires only 8 information bits, the standard technique for transmission to terminals uses 2 additional bits to permit information flow to start and stop between characters. This is called *asynchronous* transmission. When it is used, the character speed can be found in characters per second by dividing the baud rate by 10. Standard line speeds for terminal use include 150, 300, 1200, 9600, and 19,200 baud. Typewritelike terminals normally use 300 or 1200 baud lines. Connection via switched phone lines is usually limited to 1200 baud because of the electrical properties of the lines. The majority of *hard-wired* terminals (that is, terminals directly connected by permanent wiring to the computer) use 9600 baud if they are VDU terminals.

Most terminals are connected to the computer by two independent circuits, one connecting the keyboard to the computer for input and the other connecting the computer to the output device for output. (Even when one phone circuit is used, the two independent circuits are present. They are *multiplexed* over one phone line.) The use of two independent circuits is called *full duplex;* it allows simultaneous transmission in both directions. Although in many cases it appears to the user that each character typed on the keyboard is immediately printed or displayed on the output, in fact the keyboard is not connected to the output, but the code for the character is sent to the computer and retransmitted from the computer back to the output part of the terminal. This is called *echoing*. In some systems it is possible to type faster than the computer can generate the response, so that the echo is noticeable. It is also possible to disable the echoing in some systems, and this is used in some screen editors to allow the user to type commands to the editor that do not clutter up the text on the screen. A few systems use *half duplex,* whereby only one transmission line is used for both directions. When the user types a character in half duplex, it is sent simultaneously to the computer and to the output. In such systems the user has to be careful not to type while the computer is transmitting information back to the terminal, because if both occur at the same time the two signals on the transmission line will conflict with each other and information will be lost. Some sort of *protocol* is needed for communications between the terminal and the computer so that each knows when it has permission to transmit and so that each can be guaranteed to get a turn. A third system is called *simplex*. It uses one line that can only be used in one direction. Simplex systems are not used for terminals.

4.1.2 Line and Page Printers

The printing device in terminals is a one-character-at-a-time printer. This limits its speed, because it is difficult to print a single character mechanically in much less than 4 milliseconds because of the time it takes to move a mechanical device. The *line printer* is a device that prints a line at a time. The computer transmits a complete line of information to the printer unit and the line is printed. A printing mechanism exists at every print position across a line, which can vary in width from 80 to 132 characters in common printers. Because of the parallelism present in such a printer, it can achieve speeds of 1000 to 2000 lines per minute by mechanical means. Nonmechanical printing techniques (photographic or xerographic, for example) can achieve even higher speeds (up to 30,000 lines per minute).

Nonmechanical printers are also important, because they are not limited to a small character set. Various types of *laser printers* are available today that can either print at extremely high speeds, using a moderate number of different character fonts, or somewhat more slowly, providing a much larger number of fonts (character styles). In this type of printer, the characters are "drawn" by the computer by means of a computer-controlled laser beam. It can be instructed to draw almost any letter (Roman or Greek), number, mathematical symbol, etc. For example, the print in many books is prepared by such devices today. (The actual pages are printed by conventional offset press means, but the plates are prepared photographically from output produced by a computer-controlled printer.) Another advantage of this type of printer is that it can also be used to produce line drawings. This type of usage will be discussed in the next section.

4.1.3 Plotters and Display Devices

Although printer output is very useful for many purposes, frequently the user needs to present the information graphically to be able to understand its significance. This may be in a form of a very simple graph plotting one variable against another, or it may be a complex pictorial display representing a multidimensional item. For example, three-dimensional pictures are frequently represented by two-dimensional contour maps, where lines represent the paths of constancy in the third dimension (weather maps, for example, in which the contours of constant pressure are drawn to indicate the high-pressure and low pressure regions).

If graphs have to be prepared by hand from numerical computer output, a large amount of output is typically needed, and time-consuming drawing must be done by the human user. Therefore, direct graphical output devices have been developed for computer use. There are both hard-copy–based and CRT-based devices, and both have two basic forms: one allows the user to place a point at any location on the output display (which might be a sheet of paper in a hard-copy plotter or might be the face of a CRT), and the other allows the user to draw a line between any two points. The former can be used to output line drawings or *shaded drawings* (that is, regular pictures as transmitted on TV), whereas the second can only be used for line drawings. The first is called a *raster output* device because it permits a raster to be generated for a conventional TV display (although computer graphics can work at much higher levels of precision than conventional TV). The second is called a *vector ouput* device. Whichever form of device is available, software is available in most computer systems to permit the user to do most common tasks with simple subroutine calls. For example, there are always subroutines that permit lines to be drawn. A vector output device can do this directly, but it has to be decomposed into a sequence of points for a raster device.[1]

Historically, the second form of output was available first. The *incremental plotter* is a popular example of this type of device. It is a device with a moving pen and a large sheet of paper. The pen can be moved by a small increment in any of several directions.

[1]Details of the hardware can be found in W. M. Newman and R. F. Sproull, *Principles of Interactive Computer Graphics,* 2d ed, McGraw-Hill, New York, 1979.

In a typical plotter, the pen can move a distance of 0.005 inch vertically or horizontally or a distance of 0.007 inch in any of the four 45-degree directions. All lines must be made up of these short, straight-line segments. Before any incremental move is made, the pen can be set down on the paper or it can be lifted up to prevent it from leaving a mark. Subroutines in the computer allow the user to request straight lines, standard curves such as circular arcs, or characters. These are converted to a sequence of small increments by the software or, in some cases, by hardware in the plotter device (by using a microcomputer dedicated to this task inside the plotter). The commands given to the actual plotter mechanism to plot a 45-degree right triangle lying on its hypotenuse are shown in Figure 4-1. The software will permit the user to issue a sequence of commands, such as

```
CALL  MOVE(1.0,1.0)     Move pen to A.
CALL  LINE(1.5,1.5)     Draw line to B.
CALL  LINE(1.0,2.0)     Draw line to C.
CALL  LINE(1.0,1.0)     Draw line back to A.
```

to accomplish the same task. Incremental plotters vary greatly in speed, varying from 1 or 2 inches per second to a hundred times that speed. Their size ranges from small units capable of plotting on 11- by 14-inch paper to units that can handle large engineering-drawing–size paper. Many are able to change pens during the course of making a drawing and so can produce multicolored diagrams.

Vector-output CRT devices are normally used for *interactive graphics*. The user can examine a line drawing, rotate it, change it in various ways by changing the data in the computer, and continue to modify it until the result is satisfactory, at which time it can be drawn in hard copy form, or the internal data can be used as input to other programs that can generate, for example, the control information for numerically controlled tools, thus allowing a part to be designed interactively on a computer and then produced directly from the data. A typical vector CRT allows from 512 to 4096 points to be addressed in the horizontal and vertical directions on the screen, and allows lines to be drawn between any two points. Such units often have built-in *character generators,*

FIGURE 4-1 Plotting a triangle

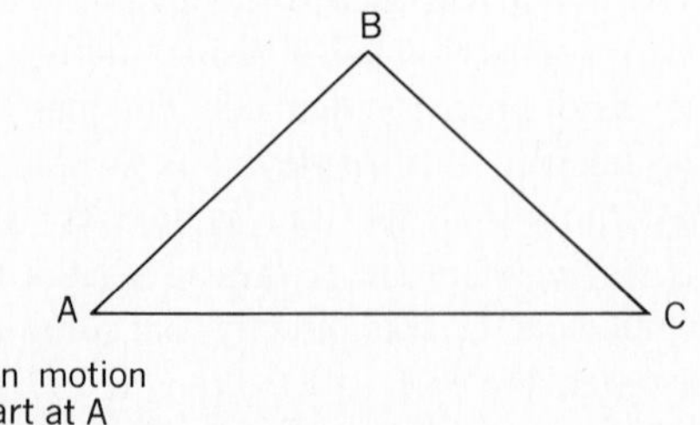

Pen down
Move up, right (100 steps)
Move down, right (100 steps)
Move left (200 steps)
Pen up

which display characters directly. If not, they can be drawn using a sequence of short vectors, although this takes many computer commands. *The storage tube* CRT display is a device that stores the image displayed until it is subsequently erased under computer control. This is useful for some applications, but if the image needs to be moved or modified frequently (if, for example, it must be rotated) the *refresh* display must be used. This is closer in spirit to the TV display. The image is redrawn thirty times a second (approximately) so that changes are seen almost as soon as they are made. This requires that a computer regenerate the commands to the display at that frequency. Because this would consume most of the capacity of the computer, it is usually done by a dedicated microcomputer in the display device.

An important additional feature available with CRT displays is a pointing device. This may be a *light pen,* which is a photoelectric device that can be pointed at the screen, generating a signal when the screen underneath it is illuminated. This signal is processed using an interrupt, to be discussed in Chapter 8. It tells the program what was being displayed at the light pen position. With suitable software, the program can determine which part of the image on the screen is under the light pen, or the (X, Y) coordinates of the light pen. A number of other related devices are in use, including a *tablet,* which is a flat tablet with a pen whose position can be electronically determined, so that the user can input line drawings directly, and a *mouse,* which is a small object that fits under the palm of one hand and can be moved around on a flat surface. The movement can be detected by the computer, and that movement can be used to move a cursor around the screen.

CRT output devices can be coupled to computer-controlled cameras so that microfilm or microfiche can be generated directly by the computer. In addition to the commands to plot lines and characters, there are commands to advance the film or position the microfiche negative. These devices can be used for alpha-numeric output as well as graphics. They have the advantage over paper hard copy of being physically much smaller, and the size of the output is also much reduced. (Some very large computers used in massive numerical calculations produce so much output on 30,000-line-per-minute printers that a forklift must be used to move the printed output away from the printer, since about an 8-inch stack of 11- by 14-inch paper is produced every minute. Output on microfiche can be carried away by hand.)

Raster graphic output devices are more recent. The image is constructed in the computer as a *bit map* of the picture. In the simplest display, each point in the image can be black or white, and 1 bit is used for each point. If a 1000- by 1000-point picture is to be generated, 1 million bits are needed. First all are set to the *background* state, which may be black or white. Then bits are changed to create the desired image. For example, if a line is to be drawn, a sequence of connected points is changed. When all of the desired bits have been changed, the image is sent to the display device. If this is a CRT display, it is normally refreshed 30 times a second, so any changes are almost immediately reflected in the displayed image. CRT displays permit more than two *gray levels,* that is, intensities of light, so more than one bit may be used in each position. If a color CRT display is used, then several bits may be used for each of the three primary colors (blue, green, and red). Refresh, bit-mapped CRT displays range from 512-by-512 points to 4096-by-4096 points. Each display point is called a *pixel.* The number of bits per pixel ranges from 1 to about 12. The smaller number is used in modern *work-station* terminals, which provide line-drawing graphics in addition to the usual alphanumeric terminal characteristics, whereas the larger number is needed in computer graphic terminals, which are used in image processing and CAD (Computer-Aided Design).

4.1.4 Networks

A network is a collection of interconnected computers. To the operating system on an individual computer, the network can be viewed as an I/O device. Information is placed onto the network much as information is sent to any other I/O unit. Part of the information is the address of the computer that is to receive the information. At higher levels, the user is unaware of the nature of the network and may see the network as simply providing an extension to the system actually being used. For example, the user may be able to access files of information stored on other computers just by using a name that includes the name of the other computer in addition to the name of the file, or the user may be able to send messages, such as electronic mail, to users of other systems in exactly the same way that mail is sent to a user of the same system. The software techniques are very similar to those to be discussed for simple I/O devices in Chapter 8.

The next two types of I/O discussed are almost obsolete. Punched cards are still used in some business applications in which a small amount of information is to be received by mail from a large number of sources (for example, identifying information returned with bill payment), and punched paper tape is occasionally used for low-speed recording of data from experiments. We discuss them here because they have an important historical contribution, and understanding paper tape makes the understanding of magnetic tape much simpler.

4.1.5 Punched Cards

The most common form of punched card is a rectangle of heavy card stock (usually about $7\frac{1}{2}$ by $3\frac{3}{4}$ inches) that can be punched with a hole in any one of 960 positions on a 12- by 80-position rectangular array. Other sizes of cards—with 51 or 90 columns instead of the 80 columns mentioned above—are in use, but the 80-column card is the most common. Punched cards were used for machine control in the weaving industry long before they were used in data processing. The first major application of punched cards to data occurred during the late 1800s, when Herman Hollerith adapted them for use with the 1890 census. Because of his work, the cards are sometimes called *Hollerith cards,* and one way in which alphabetic information is encoded as punched holes is called the *Hollerith card code.* This code is a means of representing the decimal digits, the 26 upper-case letters, and a few special characters such as the comma and period. One column is used to represent each character, so that up to 80 characters can be punched in one card. As shown in Figure 4-2, the card rows are labeled 12, 11, 0, 1, 2, 3, 4, 5, 6, 7, 8, and 9. A blank character or space is represented by a lack of holes, the numeric digits are represented by a punch in the corresponding row, and the letters

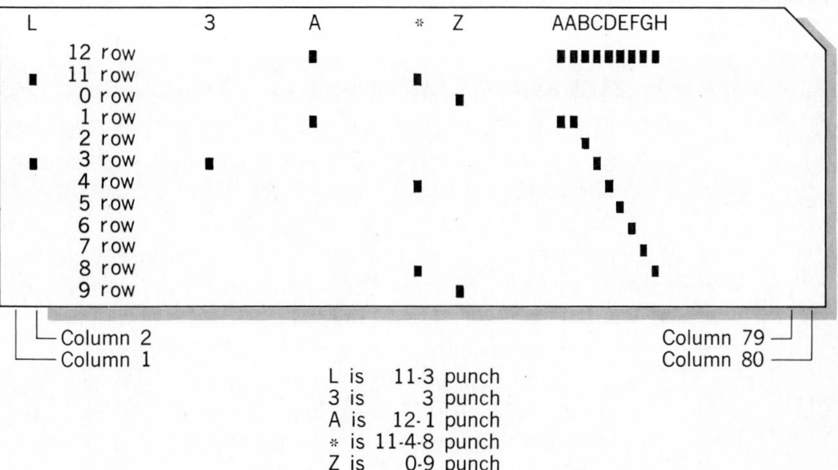

FIGURE 4-2 Hollerith punched cards

are represented by double punches. A through I are presented by a 12-row punch together with a digit punch from 0 through 9, respectively; J through R by an 11-row punch with a digit 1 through 9, respectively; and S through Z with a 0-row punch with the digit 2 through 9; respectively. Other characters are represented by other combinations of punched holes. This code is also known as the BCD card code. A more recent card code, called EBCDIC for Extended BCD Interchange Code, has extended this to a larger set of characters including the lower-case characters and more special characters.

When a card written in this format is read into the machine, it is converted into a string of eighty characters in memory. If the BCD code is used, 6 bits are sufficient to encode the forty-eight characters available, and so machines using this code often used the 6-bit BCD code for internal character representation. Most of these earlier machines used word lengths that were a multiple of 6 and packed several characters into 1 word. For example, the earliest series of IBM scientific computers, of which the IBM 7094 computer was one of the last, used a 36-bit word, packing six characters in each word. The EBCDIC code requires 8 bits and is used in the current IBM computers. On these, a card is read into 80 consecutive bytes of storage.

Each column of the punched card can contain up to 12 punches, for a total of 2^{12} different combinations. However, if 6- or 8-bit codes are used, far fewer combinations are used. In some older systems the *binary card* used all of the combinations. This is a card that can be punched in any position, so that each column contains 12 bits of information and is mapped directly into 12 bits of memory.

Cards can be read at speeds in the range of 1000 to 2000 per minute and punched at speeds of 200 to 400 per minute. Because card reading and punching are prone to error, a card reader usually has two *read stations* through which the card passes. It is read twice and the information is compared to check for errors. Similarly, a card punch often also has a read station that reads the information punched to check for errors.

4.1.6 Punched Paper Tape

Punched paper tape is very similar to punched cards in that it consists of a heavy paper stock in which information is represented by the presence or absence of punched holes. It differs from punched cards in that paper tape is in continuous strips of arbitrary lengths, whereas cards are of a fixed size. Tape was commonly used in three different widths containing five, seven, or eight information-hole positions across the width of the tape. Each of these positions is called a *channel*. Today, only eight-channel paper tape is used, and even that is used rarely, because it has been replaced with low-cost magnetic tape recorders. Eight-channel paper tape is 1 inch wide. It is shown in Figure 4-3. Notice that in addition to the eight information positions or channels, there is a ninth position that is always punched with a *sprocket hole*. This is present to locate the position where information (holes or no holes) should appear in the other channels across the tape. Without these holes, a series of characters consisting of no punched holes would lead to a strip of completely blank tape. It would then be impossible to tell how many characters there were in such a string except by measuring the length of the tape, a procedure that would be very prone to error. (The sprocket hole is also used to mesh with a sprocket gear on the slower mechanical tape readers.) Since paper tape is very prone to error, it is common to use one of the information channels as a parity bit for the other seven channels. If the ASCII code is used, as it commonly is, one bit is available for parity. (If the ASCII code is used, a hole corresponds to a binary one and channel eight contains the most significant bit. If even parity is used, blank tape corresponds to the null character—see Table 2-2. Having all eight holes punched corresponds to the Rub Out or Delete character. It got this name because it was used to "erase" a character punched on the tape by punching all holes.)

Paper tape can be read at speeds of 1000 to 2000 characters per second and punched at about one-third of that speed. The slowest devices operate at only ten characters per second—the speed of the early teletype keyboards and printers used in the newspaper industry that formed the basis for the early computer terminals and slow input-output devices.

FIGURE 4-3 Paper tape

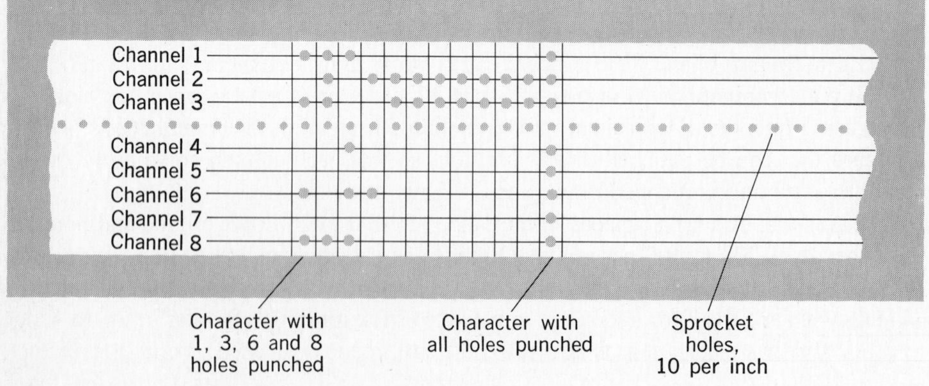

4.1.7 Document Readers and Other I/O Devices

The applications of punched cards in business are rapidly being taken over by direct document-reading systems. These are input devices that can read data printed in one of a number of fonts. A phone company bill, for example, will contain a printed slip to be returned with the payment rather than the punched card that was previously used. A document reader can read the customer account number from the printed slip when it is returned, so that the payment can be credited to the correct account. (The company knows the font used to print the slip because it was printed by the company's own computer.) This type of reader is called an *optical document reader,* because it is using optical methods to obtain the data. The check sent in with the bill contains the bank clearing number and the customer's bank account number encoded on the left of the bottom edge in magnetic ink. A special font is used for these characters that is relatively easy to read magnetically with low error. The device used to read this is called a *magnetic ink character reader* (MICR). Other special input systems are used for special purposes. For example, many *point-of-sale* (POS) terminals have some sort of optical reader for determining the inventory number of the item being sold, both to update the stock-on-hand data and to determine the price by consulting a table in the computer. The data may be printed in a fairly standard font or in a code of thin and thick bars (such as zeros and ones) that is used on virtually all items now sold in grocery stores. This form of coding (which is also easy to read and relatively error free) has been used for other, more computer-related purposes. For example, at least one manufacturer has distributed software for microcomputers and calculators in this form.

Other forms of graphic input have been the subject of research. Attempts at handwritten character recognition have been successful when the recognition is done *online,* that is, the computer "watches" the character as it is drawn so that it has not only the shape to work with, but also the order in which it was drawn. *Computer vision* is an attempt to use the computer to take a raster scan of an image (via a TV camera) and determine the content of the picture. This yields results if the number of objects that might appear in the picture is severely limited. Such work is of great importance to *robotics,* as it will enable a robot arm to "watch" what it is doing and adjust for minor changes in the position of the objects it is working on. At the moment, either such sensing is not done (the part to be manipulated by a robot must be in a known position) or limited sensory information is obtained by pressure sensors (that is, by "touch") or by optical or audio sensing of distances.

Acoustic output is commonly available for computers through the use of voice synthesizers. These devices can generate combinations of the various sounds that constitute human speech. The computer sends codes to the synthesizer to tell it which combinations to use to get the required output. Voice input is possible, but currently the number of words that can be recognized by a system is very limited (in the hundreds), and systems usually have to be trained to recognize a particular voice.

4.2 LONG-TERM STORAGE

Large amounts of information are retained in computer centers for long periods of time. Some problems involve the use of extremely large amounts of data that must be periodically updated in a predictable manner. Problems in this class include commercial jobs, such as the record keeping associated with the maintenance of customer accounts, and scientific jobs, such as the comparison of data gathered from a particular physics experiment with similar data gathered from many previous experiments. Both of these jobs have the characteristic that the amounts of data involved are larger than can be reasonably kept online. The size of files of data is often measured in megabytes, or MB. One megabyte is 1 million bytes of information. Files of several hundred MB are common in these sorts of applications, but they can be much larger. (For example, a file containing nothing but the social security number and a twenty-character name of everybody in the United States would occupy approximately 6000 MB, or 6 gigabytes.) These characteristics dictate the need for a storage device that has virtually unlimited total capacity, although it only need be accessible in a serial fashion (that is, in sequential order, one unit of information at a time). Since the electronics associated with storage devices are the expensive part of the device, a desirable form of storage is one in which the information is stored on a simple medium that can be removed, kept on a shelf, and replaced. There are a number of devices that have this capability, which is typically based on magnetic recording technology. These devices include magnetic tapes and disks. This section will discuss the nature of this type of hardware.

4.2.1 Magnetic Tape

Magnetic-tape storage was derived directly from audiotape principles. The storage medium is a long strip of tape with a fixed width. The most common tape systems use a ½-inch tape width. The length of the tape depends only on the size of the reel used. Tape drives can usually accommodate up to 10½-inch reels, which contain 2400 feet of tape. The tape itself is about 1/1000 to 1/500 of an inch thick and consists of a backing of flexible material, such as Mylar, with a coating of a magnetic material (an iron oxide). Information is stored on the tape by magnetizing the oxide coating in one directon or the other, which is similar in function to the presence or absence of a hole in paper tape. A *track* on the tape is a narrow strip along the tape in which the magnetically coded information is stored (see Figure 4-4). It is similar to a channel on paper tape. Since a track is less than 1/20 of an inch wide, several tracks can be placed across the tape. Half-inch tape usually has nine tracks, although there are still some seven-track tape units around for compatibility with earlier systems. Nine-track tape

FIGURE 4-4 Magnetic tape

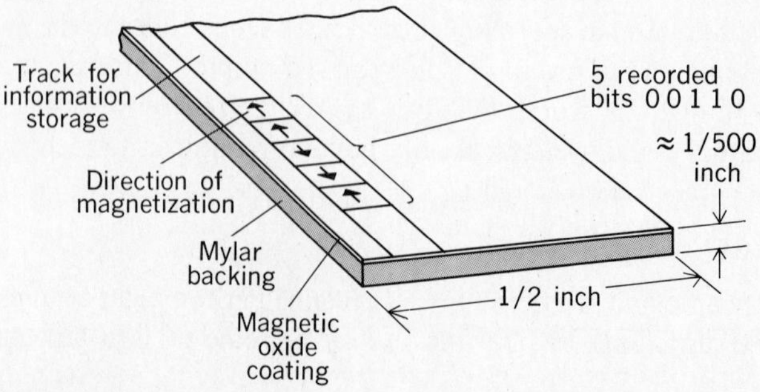

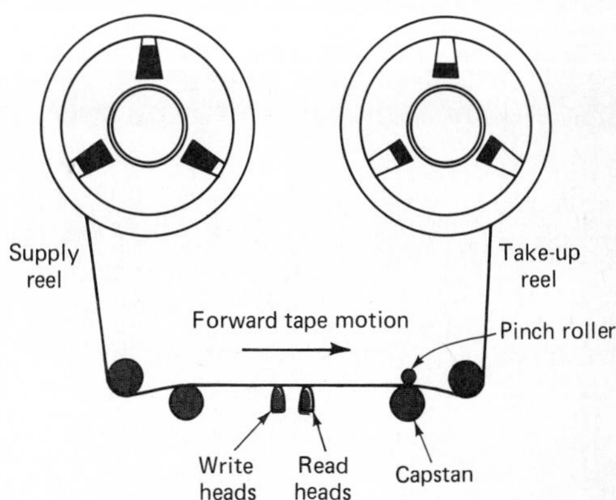

FIGURE 4-5 A tape drive

can store 9 bits in each *character position* on tape, and this is usually used to store one 8-bit character plus a parity bit. To read or write on tape, the reel of tape must be mounted on a tape drive, which is a mechanism with two drive reels, *read heads, write heads,* and a *capstan* (a rotating wheel against which the tape can be pressed by a *pinch roller*), which pulls the tape across the heads at an approximately constant speed (see Figure 4-5). When the tape is written, it is pulled across the heads by the capstan, and amplifiers drive electric current through the write heads to magnetize the tape according to the information to be stored. The information on a tape is read by pulling the tape across the read heads with the capstan. The magnetism in the tape causes small voltages to be induced in the read heads, and these are sensed by the read amplifiers. (During a write operation, the read heads are also used to read back the information written to check its parity; this makes early detection of write errors possible, so that the block can be rewritten in case of error while the information is still available in primary memory.)

In practice, the bits of information are packed very densely along the length of the tape; standard *densities* include 200, 556, 800, 1600, and 6250 bits per inch (bpi) in each track. The lowest densities are not frequently used any longer, neither is seven-track tape, since most computers use 8-bit characters plus parity. (Since the tape has seven or nine tracks, each with the same density, this means that the same number of characters can be stored per inch on the tape as the number of bits stored per inch in each track.) Since the tape is moved at speeds in the neighborhood of 120 inches per second, it is out of the question to start or stop the tape between each character on tape. Therefore, the information is usually written on the tape in continuous *records* or *blocks,* with gaps between the blocks for starting and stopping tape motion. These gaps are called *interrecord gaps* or *interblock gaps* and range in length from 0.75 inches for densities up to 800 bpi to 0.6 inches for 1600-bpi and 0.3 inches for 6250-bpi tape densities. The length of the recorded blocks is either fixed by the computer system or allowed to vary under program control.

We recall that paper tape has a sprocket hole in order to allow the tape reader to know where a character is punched on tape. In a similar manner it is necessary for the computer to know where a set of bits (a character) is written on the magnetic tape. This is not done with a sprocket hole (it is difficult to punch 6250 holes per inch!) but in some systems the equivalent—a *timing track*—is used. A timing track is a tape track that contains a magnetic signal in every bit position. The tape reader can use this track to tell when a character is in position under the read head, and then it can read the actual information bits. The alternative is to demand that every character written on tape contain at least one magnetic signal, so that the logical OR of all the signal tracks is guaranteed to contain a signal in every character position, or to use a form of recording in which every track contains a magnetic signal in every character position. The former can be done by using odd parity, whereas the latter is possible if certain types of recording modes are used. Modern high-density recording techniques use the latter scheme, but a discussion of the detail is beyond the scope of this text.

The important difference between magnetic tape with timing tracks and that without is that the former must be *formatted* before use by writing the timing track all the way along the tape and leaving it there permanently. This makes it possible to return to the same point on the tape by counting the timing bits. If, however, a timing track is not used, the tape drive must provide its own timing information during the writing of new information via an electronic clock. Since it is not possible to guarantee that the tape moves at exactly the same speed on successive write operations, a written block of a given number of characters may differ in length from one write operation to another. The effect of this is shown in Figure 4-6. In the top diagram the tape has been written with two blocks of 20,000 characters each at 1600 bpi (about 12.5 inches each). In the second diagram, the first block has been rewritten with the tape moving 10 percent faster. Consequently, 1.25 inches of the next block have been overwritten. The bottom diagram shows the effect of rewriting the first block with the tape moving 10 percent

FIGURE 4-6 Effects of nonconstant tape speeds

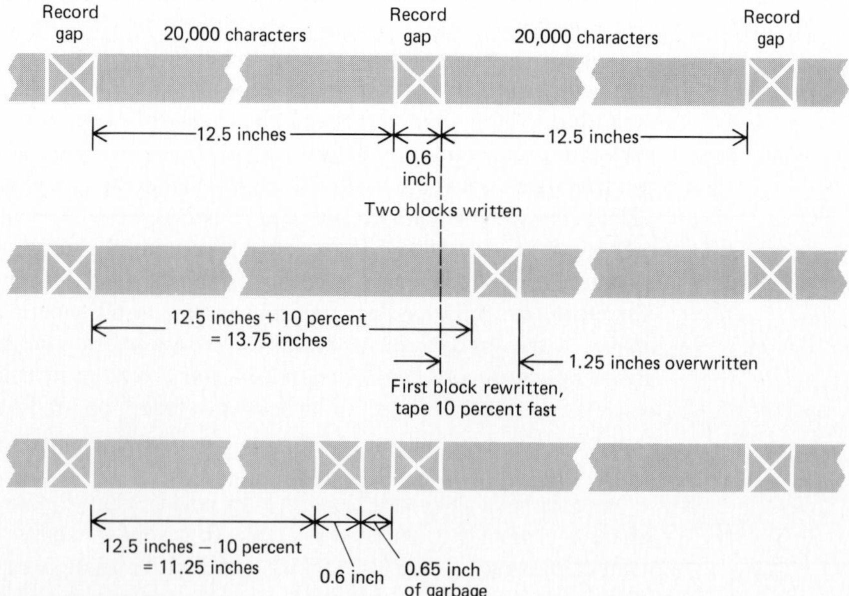

slower. This time, about 0.65 inches of the previous block remains between the new interblock gap and the old. If the user were to attempt to read the second block, errors would occur in either case.

Tape that uses timing tracks can be rewritten at any point, whereas tape without can only be written in a sequential manner—once any block is written, all subsequent blocks previously written on the tape are effectively lost. However, most tape units do not use timing tracks, because a much higher density of information is possible without them.

Because the probability of error is not infinitesimal when high-density recording is used (dust particles can be several times the size of the area in which 1 bit is recorded), a block on tape is recorded with some sort of *longitudinal* check. This can be as simple as another parity bit. (Figure 3-11 indicates how this provides for single-error detection.) When the probability of error is even higher, additional *cyclic redundancy check* (CRC) or error correction bits can be written at the end of a block to permit the correction of even more errors. Tape without timing tracks can be written with blocks of information of virtually any length. However, in most applications, all blocks are of the same length to ease the programming tasks.

Basic tape operations include writing and reading blocks of information. In addition, tape-handling operations are necessary to enable the program to reach the particular block needed. After a tape block has been written, it is necessary to *backspace* the tape to the beginning of the block if it has to be reread (although some tapes allow a block to be read in the reverse direction). Sometimes it is necessary to *forward space* one or more blocks to reach something further down the tape. Because these tape-handling operations are nonproductive (no information is being transferred between the tape and the computer, so a program may just be waiting for the tape movement and the information transfer to finish before it can proceed), it is usual to organize tape so as to minimize these movement operations by using tape for *sequential files* only. In this use, a complete file consisting of a sequence of blocks is written. When the information is needed again, it is read sequentially from the beginning to the end of the file. To get to the start of the tape after it has been written, a *rewind* operation is provided.

Magnetic tape is only sequentially accessible, that is, it is more like a scroll than a book. A scroll is read by unwinding it from one end; to reach a particular paragraph in the middle it is necessary to roll through all of the previous paragraphs. In the same way, there are no operations with which to access an arbitrary block on the tape; instead it is necessary to skip over all preceding blocks one at a time.

The terminology connected with magnetic tapes is based on business data processing, where tape was first used extensively. The individual unit of information written on a tape is the character, usually 1 byte. To the program, characters are grouped into units called *fields,* such as the name field and the address field. A number of related fields are grouped into a *record,* for example, the record of one employee. A group of related records is called a *file*. For example, a file could contain all the employee records or all the customer records.

Historically, the word "record" was also used to mean a recorded block on tape; it frequently contained just one record of information. Today, several records are usually packed into a single block for magnetic recording purposes (although very long records could occupy several blocks). The packing is done to reduce the amount of tape used (and hence to increase the effective transfer rate). For example, if a density of 1600 bpi is used and eighty-character records are to be written, writing one record in each block will use 0.65 inches of tape—0.60 for the record gap and 0.05 for the block. This is an effective density of only 123 characters per inch. If four records are packed in each block, the effective density increases to 400 characters per inch (320 characters in 0.8 inches), still only a quarter of the maximum possible. The number of records packed into each block is called the *blocking factor*. On a tape, a sequential group of blocks can form a *physical file*. The end of a physical file is indicated by an *end-of-file mark,* which is a short block containing a special mark. A write-end-of-file operation is available to write this mark. If an end-of-file mark is read during a normal tape read, an end-of-file indicator is set. This can be tested by the program. Tape-handling operations also include forward and backward spacing to the next end-of-file mark. A physical file can be used to store a logical file—the use of tape files is up to the program. If a logical file is relatively small, so that several can be stored on one tape, it is common to store each logical file in a physical file. However, some logical files are very long, requiring many reels of tape. In that case, each reel may be broken into one or more physical files for ease of access.

A common analogy to draw for files, records, and characters on a tape is that of a book. The paragraphs in a book are similar to the records, whereas the file is the whole book. The blocks on tape are similar to the pages of a book. This analogy does not take into account the groupings of paragraphs into sections and chapters; these must be handled in the program by using multiple physical files and/or *header* information stored at the start of each block or file to indicate its use.

When a file of information on magnetic tape is to be updated (that is, some of the information is to be changed), it is necessary to read the original from one tape and make an updated copy on another tape. Because it is not possible to store the complete content of a tape in primary memory, there must be a second drive. The update information has to be available from another source and should first be ordered according to the order on the tape to be updated. Then the blocks can be read from the old tape and the information can be modified as necessary and written on the new tape. Thus the minimum number of tape drives necessary if it is not possible to copy the contents of a complete tape into other memory is two. If the amount of update information is so large as to also require its storage on a tape, at least three tapes are needed. If other forms of storage (such as disk, to be discussed later) are not available, four tapes are really needed to perform operations such as sorting through use of *merging*. Today, most systems have disk units that are large enough to hold the contents of several tapes, so that sorting and update operations can be done on disks. Tapes are used mainly for archival storage of large amounts of data and for *back-up* to guard against loss of information on disk units.

A 2400-foot reel of tape can hold between 30 and 100 million characters if it uses a large blocking factor. An unlimited number can be stored on shelves. Since a reel of tape is inexpensive (about $10), it provides a low-cost, long-term storage medium at about 10^{-5} cents per byte, compared with around 10^{-1} to 1 cent per byte for primary memory. However, it is considerably slower. Mounting a tape on a drive takes on the order of a minute, plus the time to find the tape and carry it from a storage room.

Moving across blocks takes about as long as reading a block, which can be in the range of a few thousand characters per second to the order of a million characters per second. Moving from one end to the other by a rewind takes from 1 to 2 minutes. The time required to start or stop the tape in the record gap is in the range of 1 to 20 milliseconds.

4.2.2 Disk File Units

A *disk file unit,* also called a *direct access storage device,* resembles a phonograph record and its playback mechanism. Physically, a single-disk platter is a circular sheet of metal about 10 to 20 inches in diameter and 1⁄16 to 1⁄4 inch thick. It is coated on one or both surfaces with a magnetic material, so that the thickness of the disk is for mechanical strength only. Information is recorded on the disk surface magnetically, just as information is recorded on magnetic tape. The difference between the recording on a phonograph record and that on a disk platter (in addition to the method used for storing information, which is by undulations in the grooves in a phonograph record) is that whereas a phonograph contains one continuous groove, or track, in a spiral, a disk surface contains many tracks arranged in concentric circles. The read-write head (the same head is used for both) is mounted on a movable arm that can be positioned over any one of the tracks; there may be from 100 to 1000 tracks on a surface. A diagram of a single-disk platter is shown in Figure 4-7.

A disk unit usually contains many platters, although there are some single-platter disk file units on the market. The early forms of disk files units used a single read-write head on a movable arm that not only could be positioned in and out from one concentric track to another, as shown in Figure 4-7, but also could be moved from one platter to another. Modern, multiplatter disk file units have a read-write head for every side of every platter, as shown in Figure 4-8, so that it is only necessary to move the heads in and out across a platter to access every track. On some disk file units, the set of platters (or single platter), called a *disk pack,* can be removed from the unit and replaced with

FIGURE 4-7 Disk unit

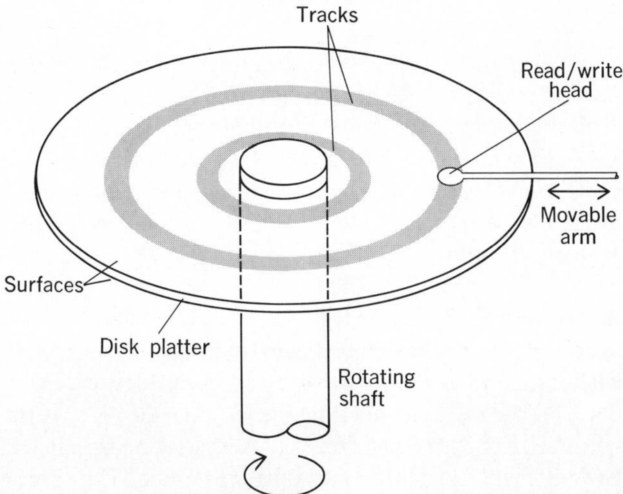

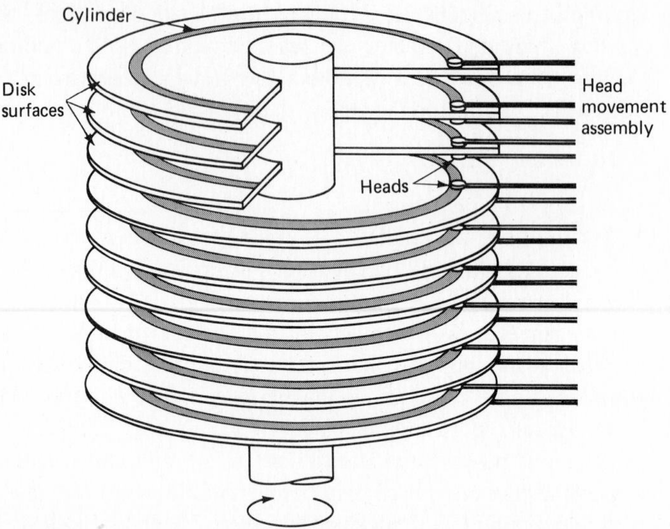

FIGURE 4-8 Multiple-surface disk file unit (cutaway view)

another pack, thus providing relatively inexpensive long-term storage. In another design, the disk platters *and* the read-write heads and access arm are packaged in a sealed, removable cartridge. Units with removable media are discussed in this section.

Disks are rather similar to magnetic tapes in that it can take a long time to move from the track currently under the head to another track relative to the time it takes to read a single block of information. However, both times are considerably faster than corresponding times for tape. Typical head movement times range from 2 to 100 milliseconds for disk units. The data rate from large disks ranges from 100KB (kilobytes) per second to about 1MB per second. The capacity of large disks is about four times larger than that of tapes. Currently, large disk packs hold around 300MB.

The method of recording on disks is almost always in a fixed-block mode. Each track is divided into a number of sectors long enough to record one block. Typically, there are between 20 and 40 sectors in each track and each sector contains exactly the same amount of information (which means that the actual density in bits per inch is higher towards the center of the disk). The disk contains *sector marks,* which are marks that can be read by the disk to determine the start of each sector. Of these, one is a special mark called an *index mark,* which indicates the beginning of a track. The index mark is usually a permanent mark on the disk, such as a hole. Sector marks may be permanent, in which case the disk is said to have *hard sectoring,* although most large disks use magnetically recorded sector marks, called *soft sectoring*. The sectors on a track are numbered starting from the one following the index mark. After the heads have been positioned over a particular track by moving the head assembly, using what is called a *seek* operation, the disk waits for the desired sector to rotate under the head by counting the sector marks from the last time the index mark was read. Then the data can be read or written. When the data is written, an internal electronic clock in the disk drive determines the rate at which bits are written. The very small speed variations are handled by leaving enough space between the end of one sector and the start of another. The data is written in such a way that when it is read back, the timing information can be determined from the data itself. The information is usually recorded with at least a parity bit to detect errors, and on high-density drives an error-correcting code is used so that a modest number of errors can be corrected. Because the positioning of the heads to a particular track in a seek operation is mechanical, it is also open to error. This is checked by also recording additional information at the start of each block, called a *header*. This consists of about 50 bits of information that essentially contain the address of that block. This information must be placed on the disk before it is first used in what is called a *formatting* operation. At this point, the block size is chosen by choosing the number of sectors per track (unless the disk is hard-sectored). Most users are not aware of the headers or any of the checking that goes on. If, after a seek and an attempted read or write, the wrong header is read, the seek is repeated automatically. If errors are detected by the error-correcting code and they can be corrected, there is no noticeable effect. If they cannot be corrected but are detected, the read can be reattempted, by hardware if the *disk controller,* which is the etectronic device that controls the disk drive, has enough intelligence, or by the operating system software otherwise.

While the heads remain in any one position, the computer has access to one track on each surface. If we visualize this set of tracks on the disk shown in Figure 4-8, we see that they lie on the surface of a *cylinder.* For this reason, disks are often addressed by the *cylinder address,* the *surface address* and the *sector address.* The first refers to the position of the heads, the next-to-the-disk surface being used, and the last to the sector around the track. When several blocks of information are to be transmitted between the computer and a disk, it is faster if they are on the same cylinder, so that no head movement is involved. If they are on the same cylinder, it is faster if they have consecutive sector addresses, so that there is no wait to skip over unwanted sectors.

The smallest type of disk is the relatively new *floppy disk.* It is so named because the disk is a thin sheet of flexible material like mylar, similar to a heavy magnetic tape. The two common sizes are 5¼ inches and 8 inches in diameter. There are also a number of small "floppies" in the range of 3 to 4 inches. Floppies hold from 100KB to on the order of 1MB (although new recording techniques promise to increase that to on the order of 10MB in the near future). They are normally much slower than the older *hard disks* discussed above, because the rotation speed is slower and the mechanical head positioning is done with a low-cost simple incremental motor arrangement. Their main feature is their small size and their low cost—the drive units cost between $300 and $1000, whereas the disks themselves are $2 to $5 each. (Note that although the price seems remarkably low, the cost per byte of higher-density storage media such as large disk packs is even less. A 300MB disk pack costs in the neighborhood of $1000, which is about 3×10^{-4} cents per byte, whereas a 300KB floppy at $3 is three times as expensive per byte.

4.2.3 Variations of Tapes and Disks

Many devices have been marketed that are in the same class as tapes and disks, that is, they have the characteristics of removability (so that storage is virtually unlimited) and a reasonable speed and capacity for a single loaded storage module. Some are minor variations of the basic idea—the floppy disk is a direct descendant of the hard disk—whereas some add additional mechanical access features that allow larger amounts of storage medium to be available without human intervention. These take the form of packages of disklike or tapelike storage media that can be accessed so that individual pieces of the medium can be placed in the read-write mechanism. With devices of this type, storage capacities of hundreds of gigabytes are possible, with any byte accessible within seconds or minutes. A gigabyte is 1000 million bytes (1 billion in American English, but not in other languages).

One such device is a unit that contains cartridges, each containing a very wide strip of material like magnetic tape. An individual cartridge can be picked up from a large array of these cartridges and the tape wound around a rotating drum. The tape can then be read or written on using conventional read-write heads.

A variation of the magnetic tape unit is called a *streamer tape*. Basically, this is a tape unit that writes extremely long blocks, so it does not stop for a long time. This allows very high densities to be obtained, in part because there are almost no interblock gaps. These tapes cannot usually be written directly by the central computer, because the size of the blocks written is much larger than the size of primary memory. Instead, the information is copied directly from, for example, a disk, cylinder by cylinder. A streamer tape unit may have a sizable *buffer* memory (similar to a primary memory) so that the unevenness between the disk and the tape speeds can be smoothed out, but the tape is written or read essentially at disk speed. This type of tape unit is very useful for making back-up copies of disks.

Another device with similarities to the disk unit is the *optical disk*. Information on such a disk is recorded in a fashion that can be reread optically using a laser to project light at the desired track. Because there are very few mechanical parts in such a device, high densities and speeds are possible. Current optical disks can only be written once, so most of the time they are used in the *read only* mode. They are valuable for storing large, permanent databases or making archival copies of important information. Within a few years we can expect to see optical disks that can be written a few times, relatively slowly.

4.3 MEDIUM-TERM STORAGE DEVICES

By *medium-term storage,* we mean the retention of information for short to medium times (seconds to weeks) between processing, when it is not practical to *unload* the storage medium between uses. Devices in this category are characterized by speeds ranging from those available with long-term storage devices to those approaching that of primary memory, namely, several megabytes per second. The capacities of these devices range from very large (in excess of 1 gigabyte) to quite small (a few megabytes). Typically, there is a trade-off between speed and capacity. These devices are used as extensions of primary memory in problems in which there is insufficient primary memory, for the *on-line* storage of large amounts of data that must be almost immediately accessible at any time, and for the retention of information from one run to another. Typical situations that call for these applications include, in the first case, the sorting of large amounts of data that might normally be kept on magnetic tape but that must first be sorted using faster memory. This is use of secondary memory as *scratch* storage. An airline reservation system is an example of the second type of usage. Since a request for information about any flight or passenger could occur at any time, all data must be on-line at all times. The saving of user programs and data in a time-sharing system is an example of the third type of usage. When a user logs onto a system, it is highly desirable that those files likely to be needed are on-line. If they are not, they must be retrieved from slower memory devices such as magnetic tape.

The needs of the examples given above can be satisfied by some of the long-term storage devices, such as disks, discussed in the previous section, but some problems exist for which the maximum data rate available, or the average access time (to move the heads, for example), is inadequate, so improvements must be sought.

4.3.1 The Nonremovable Disk

The disk was discussed as a device with removable disk packs for long-term storage. If the platters do not have to be removable, it is possible to put more platters in a single unit; to make each platter larger; to increase the speed of rotation; to have more than one head on a single surface, so that either several cylinders can be accessed without head movement (if the heads are over different tracks) or any of several sectors on a given track can be read at any one time (by having several heads over one track); to increase the density of information storage on the platter (because there are fewer problems with dirt contamination); etc. All of these serve to increase the capacity and/or speed of the disk. (In fact, the first disks did not have removable packs.) Such devices can achieve very high transmission speeds (into the megabytes per second) with capacities on single units of in excess of a gigabyte. If the capacity is very high, there will be some access time delays for head movements across the large number of tracks involved, but these can still be very fast through use of very powerful drive systems. If capacity is compromised, the average access time can be reduced by placing one head over every track to get the *fixed-head* disk. This is only possible if the number of tracks is not too large, and such a device has no head movement, so the average access time is half the revolution time, a number that can be as low as a few milliseconds if the disk is small enough to be rotated at a very high speed. This average delay, waiting for the start of the desired sector to appear under the read head, is called the *latency*.

4.3.2 The Drum

The drum was developed before the disk, but it is convenient to think of it as a variant of a disk file with fixed heads. Instead of the information being stored on the surface of a disk, it is stored on the surface of a drum, which may be about 25 centimeters in diameter and up to 50 centimeters long. Because drums are much more compact, they can be rotated at higher speeds than disks, and because the heads are fixed, the tracks can be close together and high information densities in each track are possible. This permits high speeds with moderate capacities. A drum is shown pictorially in Figure 4-9. Drums have to a large extent been replaced by disks because it is clearly possible to provide a much larger recording surface in the same volume using a set of disk platters, and modern disk technology has increased capacities and speeds to the point that the additional speed of a drum is not worth the decreased capacity.

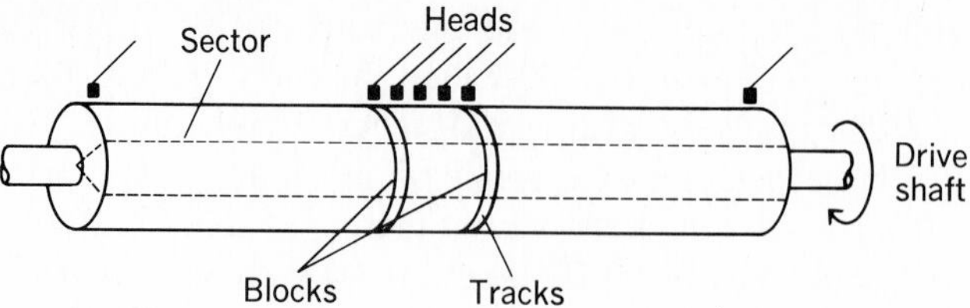

FIGURE 4-9 Drum unit

4.3.3 Bulk Storage Devices

The primary memory of a computer is constructed from many identical elements, each of which can store 1 bit. From about 1956 until the mid-1970s, magnetic cores were the principal form of storage. Since then, large-scale integrated circuits have made it possible to use electronic circuits for high-speed primary storage. These can operate at speeds of 10 to 100 nanoseconds (a nanosecond is 10^{-9} second). By sacrificing some of this speed, or by going back to core memory, it has been possible to build very large memory that is conceptually very similar to primary memory but may be used in the same way as secondary memory, that is, blocks of data are transferred between it and primary memory when needed. Such a device is called a *bulk store*. One organization, used by CDC in their extended core storage unit (ECS), made use of a very wide "word" in the bulk memory, 480 bits. Since it was attached to a Cyber computer, which has a 60-bit memory, 8 words could be read from the bulk memory at a time. This took 800 nanoseconds, and the words could be moved to primary memory, which had an effective rate of 100 nanoseconds per word (achieved by overlapping four 400-nanosecond memories). In the way the bulk store was organized accessing the first word took 3.2 microseconds, but the rest of the block took 100 nanoseconds per word. This type of device is functionally similar to a nonremovable disk or drum, but the latency is greatly reduced.

4.4 SPEED AND CAPACITY COMPARISONS

The speeds and capacities of various types of storage media are compared in Figure 4-10.

4.5 SUMMARY AND PROBLEMS

Input and output provide an interface between the computer and the "outside world," be it human or devices being controlled by a computer. The principal devices for human interface are

	Hard copy	Non–hard copy
Input	Cards Paper tape Optical scanner	Keyboard Light pen Tablet Mouse
Output	Printer Microfilm Microfiche	Alphanumeric CRT Computer graphic CRT Plotter

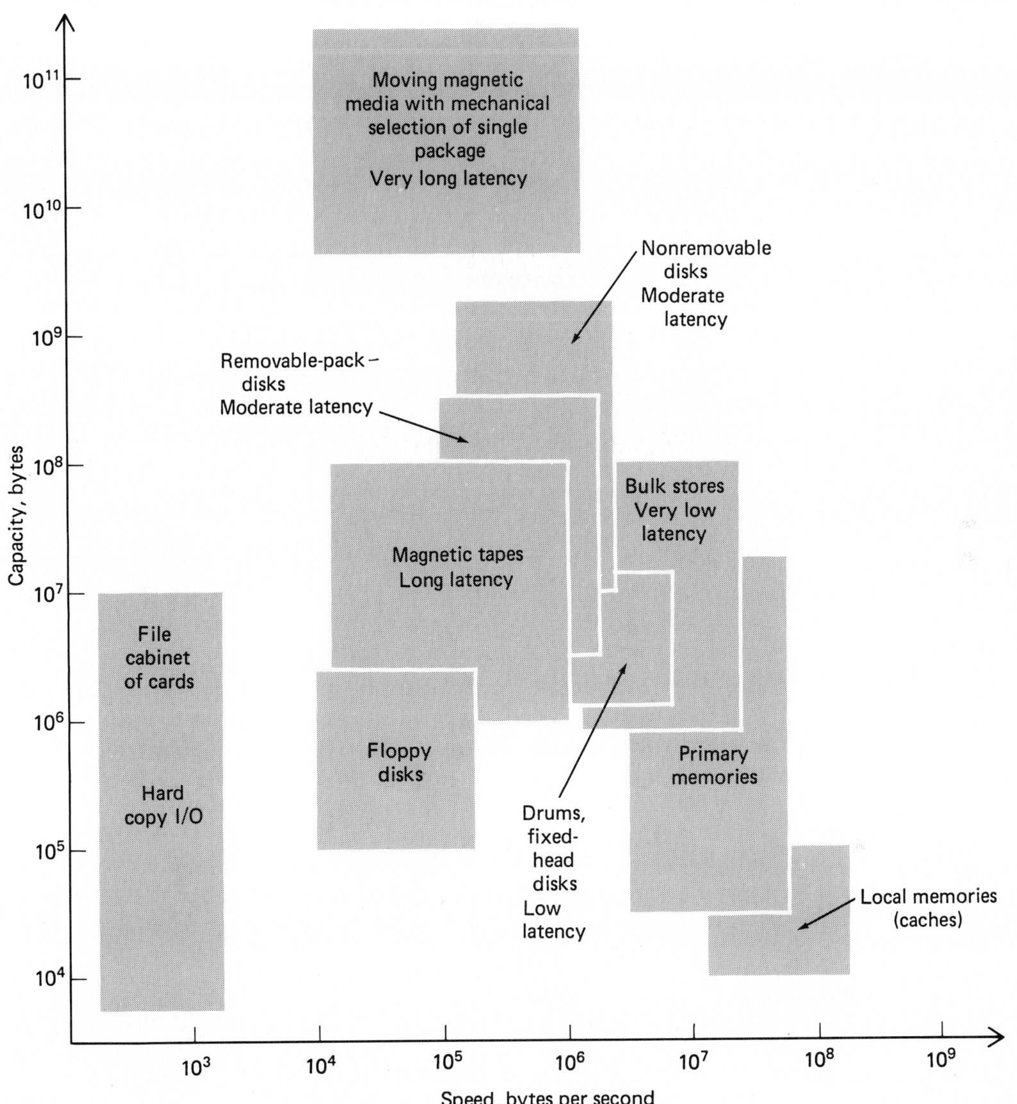

FIGURE 4-10 Current memory speeds and capacities

Most terminals are full duplex—the computer echos each character back to the terminal after it has been sent from the keyboard to the terminal.

The principal long-term storage devices are magnetic tapes, magnetic removable-platter disks, and variants of these. Tapes range in size to reels holding 10^8 characters. Disks range from small floppies holding a few hundred thousand characters up to about 300MB packs. Very-large-capacity devices that can select strips of tape from a large depository of such strips can hold in excess of 200 gigabytes. The principal medium-term storage devices are disks, drum, and bulk stores. These are usually faster than removable-pack disks. The largest nonremovable pack disk unit can store in the region of a gigabyte.

The basic operations on long- and medium-term storage devices are reading and writing of blocks of data. Usually, fixed-length blocks are used for ease of operating system organization or because the block size has to be fixed before the unit can be used. These blocks may not correspond to the logical structure of the data, so several logical records may be packed into one block or one record may extend over several blocks. Additional operations for tapes include forward and backward spacing over records or files, writing end-of-file marks, and rewinding. Other operations for disks include seeking to move the head to the correct track. Many disks have a header, which is information permanently recorded on the front of each block to help check that the correct block has been accessed. Parity bits, and perhaps error-correction code bits, are also written with each block. Information on tape can only be accessed sequentially, whereas disk heads can be moved to any cylinder; hence the average access time for disks is lower than for tapes. Some forms of bulk store function like disk units but provide much lower latency.

Problems

4-1 If all users of a computer system actually read their printed output, and if the average person reads at about 5 words per minute, estimate how many users a single 3000-line-per-minute printer could keep busy full-time if people work 8-hour shifts, 5 days a week (doing nothing but reading), and the printer works for 23 hours a day, 7 days a week (1 hour for maintenance, cleaning, and paper changing, per day, average).

4-2 Suppose a user wishes to examine the relationship between two variables, where one is a function of the other. The user could choose to output numeric values or plot a graph. Suppose that a graph with a *resolution* of 50 points vertically and 100 points horizontally is adequate. How might you use a line printer with at least 120 print positions per line to plot such a graph? How would the number of lines needed for the graph compare with numerical output in some convenient form?

4-3 A plotter accepts commands of the form

```
MOVEP     PEN,X,Y
```

and

```
SETP      PEN, X,Y
```

which move the pen from the current position in a straight line either a distance X and Y in the x and y direction, or to positions X and Y, respectively, with the pen down and making a mark if PEN has the value DOWN, or with the pen up and not marking if PEN has the value UP. Thus the command

```
MOVEP     DOWN,P,=0
```

draws a horizontal line of length given by the value in location P, starting from the current pen position. Write code to do each of the following tasks: (a) Draw a 20 by 20 square whose center is at the current pen position and which will return the pen to the same position as at the start. (b) Draw the capital letter L of height 7 and width 5, with the lower left-hand corner in the current pen position, such that the pen is left a distance 6 to the right of the original pen position. (c) Do the same for the letter H. (d) Use the code just written to draw a square centered at U,V, with the string HL printed just to the right of the center of both vertical sides.

4-4 Paper tape is 1 inch wide and has ten characters per inch. If the thickness of paper tape is double that of 8½- by 11-inch bond typewriter paper, give the approximate relative storage capacity, per pound of paper, of paper tape versus standard typing paper, assuming 1-inch margins.

4-5 Consider a reel of 1600-character-per-inch tape with 0.6-inch interblock gaps. Draw a graph of the average read speed and the average density as a function of block size, assuming that the tape moves at 125 inches per second.

4-6 Suppose that a movable head disk is such that it takes 5 milliseconds to move the head from one track to an adjacent one. Suppose that the rotation time is 30 milliseconds and that there are 23,900 characters on a track. Draw a graph of the average character rate for the transfer of a record of N characters, $0 < N < 200{,}000$, if it assumed that the first 23,900 characters are on track 0, the next 23,900 on track 1, and so on, and that consecutively numbered tracks are adjacent. Also assume that the disk is in a random position with respect to rotation when the transfer is requested, so that we must wait for the start of track 0 to appear under the read head. However, assume that the heads are already over track 0, so that a seek is unnecessary. (The time for a read is taken as the time from when the read is first requested to the transmission of the last character. Assume that the 23,900 characters are distributed evenly around a complete track.)

4-7 Suppose that in the previous problem, which assumed one block per track, you had the chance to specify the formatting of the disk into blocks, with the following options:

Blocks per track	Characters per block
1	23,900
2	11,900
3	7,900
4	5,900
5	4,700
6	3,900

(Essentially, there are 24,000 characters on a track, but 100 are lost for each block.) A clever copy program can start copying when the next block appears under the read head. How does the answer to the previous question change as a function of number of blocks per track?

CHAPTER **5**

SUBPROGRAMS

The hardware in the CPU is capable of executing simple arithmetic and logical instructions, but for ease of programming a number of more complex operations such as input-output commands are needed. In most computers, these extra operations are implemented by means of subprograms. Subprograms are sections of code that perform the desired operations. Subprograms are also called *procedures, subroutines,* or *functions,* depending on the language used and their characteristics. In higher-level languages, a subprogram is *invoked* (that is, set into execution) by *calling* it. In some languages a call statement uses the keyword **call**, whereas in others a subprogram is invoked by simply writing its name. For example, in most languages, the function SQRT would be invoked by executing SQRT(expression). A subprogram such as SORT(A,N) might require a statement of the form **call** SORT(A,N). The CALL instruction is the machine-language equivalent of a subprogram **call** in a higher-level language. The section of code representing a subprogram appears only once in memory, and each time that it is called in another part of the program, a branch is made to the start of the subprogram. The CALL instruction implements this branch. After the subprogram has been executed, the subprogram must return to the instruction following the CALL instruction. This immediately poses the problem of "How does the subprogram know to which location to return?" (There may be many calls on each subprogram, so the *return address* can change. This problem is solved in many different ways on different computers. On early computers, the call was nothing but a simple branch instruction, and an additional instruction had to be executed prior to this branch. Its job was to place the return address in a standard place, such as the accumulator. For example, we could call a subprogram by executing

```
           LOAD      RETURN
           BRANCH    SUB
RETURN     BRANCH    RETURN+1
```

and the subprogram could contain the code

```
SUB        STORE     EXIT
           ...       Body of subprogram
EXIT       BSS       1
```

With this code, a branch instruction is placed in the accumulator by the calling program, and the subprogram, in its first instruction, plants this branch instruction at the end of its code. When the subprogram code has been executed, this planted branch returns to the calling program. Not only is this clumsy, using several instructions to accomplish a simple task, it also modifies the program, a practice that is considered to be poor programming style today because it increases the chance of error and has other effects on efficiency. Today, most computers have a single instruction for branching to a subprogram and a matching instruction for return. We will use the name CALL for this instruction, although it may have other names in particular computers. Typically, the call instruction places a copy of the program counter in a register (sometimes an index register) and branches to the address given as its operand. The return instruction is a branch that gets its address from the same register. If index registers are used, an indexed branch instruction does this. The address specifying the return point is called the *link* address because it provides the link back to the *calling routine*. For example, the IBM 370 computers use the BAL (Branch and Link) instruction.

```
           BAL       R14,SUB
```

branches to location SUB after setting register R14 to the address following the BAL instruction (which is the content of the program counter after the BAL instruction has been fetched from memory). The subprogram starting at location SUB can then return to the calling program by executing the instruction BR R14 (Branch to Register 14), which branches to the address held in R14.

The mechanism described above handles a *single-level* subprogram call without problem. However, in many situations a subprogram itself calls another subprogram. For example, program MAIN calls subprogram X, which in turn calls subprogram Y. If the return link from X to main is placed in a register by the call instruction, and then the return link from Y to X is placed in that same register when X calls Y, the link from X back to MAIN has been overwritten. In computers that use this scheme, the link address must first be saved before the next subprogram is called. Thus, in the IBM 370, the content of register 14 must be saved by subprogram X so it knows how to get back to the calling program after it calls Y. Similarly, if Y calls another subprogram, Z, it must also save the return link.

When there is a sequence of programs each of which calls another, as when MAIN called X called Y called Z in the discussion above, the return links are needed in the reverse order, that is, control first returns from Z to Y, then from Y to X, and finally from X to MAIN. A data structure that organizes information so that it is available in the reverse order in which it was generated is called a *last-in-first-out* (LIFO) queue or stack. It was discussed in Chapter 2. Many modern computers have one or more built-in stacks to assist with subprogram calling. (The VAX and INTEL 8000 series computers do, for example.) The subprogram CALL instruction automatically saves the return address in the stack, and a corresponding RETURN instruction removes an entry from the stack and places it in the program counter. Specifically, when the CALL instruction is executed, the content of the program counter, which by now has been advanced to point to the instruction after the CALL since the CALL has already been fetched from memory, is placed on top of the stack. The RETURN instruction removes the top entry from the stack and places it in the program counter, thus causing the next instruction to be taken from the location following the CALL, so that the RETURN instruction is the last instruction to be executed in a subprogram.

The stack is normally kept in primary memory and addressed via a special register called a *stack pointer*. The stack pointer usually contains the address of the top level of the stack, although in some machines it contains the address of the next free entry. Placing a datum into the stack or removing it from the stack changes the stack pointer appropriately. Since it is either difficult or impossible to calculate how many entries will be placed in a stack during the execution of a program, the programmer must set the stack pointer to some appropriate value prior to the start of a program. In some systems, this initialization is done by the operating system. A stack may run either *forward* or *backward* in memory, meaning that the top of the stack may be in a higher or a lower memory address than the bottom of the stack. Many systems use a backward-running stack. This permits the stack pointer to be initialized to the highest available address in memory. Then, as entries are placed in the stack, it grows down towards the region occupied by the program. It is then the responsibility of the program to be certain that the stack gets no larger. Other systems run the stack forward, so that the program should initialize the stack pointer to the first available location beyond the program and data. If the system has *memory protect* (which detects when a program uses memory not allocated to it by the system) a *stack overflow* will be detected when it attempts to use memory beyond the region allocated to the user. This causes an *interrupt,* to be described in Chapter 8.

Naturally, different machine organizations use different methods, but all have the same basic principle: when the subprogram is written, the programmer does not have to know from where it will be called.

When a subprogram is used, data must be passed from the calling program to the subprogram and results must be returned. CPU registers or memory cells must be used for this. When we are writing programs that call other programs, we have to be told how this data is passed. When we are writing subprograms to be used elsewhere, we have to select a method for passing the data. If a subprogram is to be a well-documented and easy-to-modify section of code, we must use standard techniques that are understood by all users. Since subprograms usually represent self-contained pieces of code, it is quite common to want to assemble them separately as individual units and to retain versions of the programs in binary form suitable for loading with other programs. This places constraints on the type of techniques to be used. These will be discussed in Chapter 6.

5.1 PARAMETERS AND DATA TRANSFER

It is necessary for the subprogram to have access to data in the calling program and to return results to that program. Because subprograms may be used from many different points in the program, it is wise to organize this data carefully to avoid errors and to reduce the complexity of the links between the calling and called programs. Subprograms could exchange data by referring to the same locations. One of the purposes of a subprogram structure is to hide data from other programs, so such sharing of symbols should be discouraged. Another purpose is to make it possible for sections of the code to be assembled separately and to be entered into the library in a translated form. This is particularly true of commonly used subprograms, such as square root, that are coded once and made available to all users. In these circumstances, it is not possible to refer to variables with the same name (except via the external option, to be discussed in Chapter 6), since the program compiled first will have no knowledge of the locations allocated to variables in the program compiled later. Thus, although separately translated subprograms have effectively "hidden" their data from other programs, it is necessary to allow some transmission of data among programs. The techniques used for this include external variables, common storage, and parameters.

Common storage is an area of memory that is used in common by several programs for variable storage. It derives its name from the Fortran COMMON statement, which we examine first. If we write, in Fortran,

```
COMMON   A, B, SUM, X
```

the compiler allocates a block of four locations to hold the variables A, B, SUM, and X, as shown in Figure 5-1. (We assume that each is a single-precision real number or integer that is not dimensioned so it will fit into one location.) Within this block of four locations, the compiler knows that A is the first location, B the second, etc. If a similar

FIGURE 5-1 COMMON storage

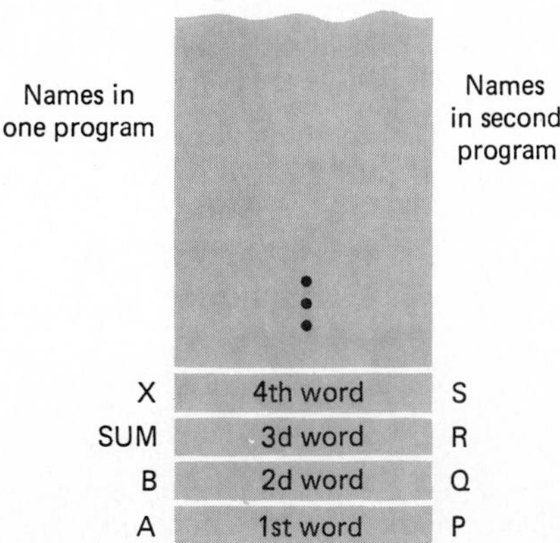

statement is made in another Fortran program, the compiler performs similarly. For example, if the statement

```
COMMON    P,Q,R,S
```

appears in another subprogram, the four variables named are identified with a set of four locations in a COMMON block. P is the first, etc., as shown in Figure 5-1. References to COMMON within an individual program are to specific locations in COMMON. In our example above, the first program refers to the second COMMON location whenever B is referenced, whereas the second program references the second location of COMMON whenever Q is referenced. Consequently, B in the first program is equivalent to Q in the second program. This is one of the drawbacks to the philosophy of COMMON, because it is better to use the same names for a particular variable no matter where it is referenced, a policy that cannot be enforced when COMMON is used. The loader handles COMMON by treating it as another form of relocation (relocation with respect to the COMMON base) or by constructing a table of addresses that refer to COMMON and linking the base address of COMMON into each of these addresses. The information passed to the loader indicates the size of a COMMON block needed. The loader examines the request for COMMON blocks by all programs loaded and allocates a piece of storage whose length is the maximum length of all COMMON blocks requested.

Fortran also allows for *labeled* COMMON. In Fortran, it is written as

```
COMMON/AREA1/A,B,R,Z
```

which says that a COMMON block with name AREA1 contains the four variables A,B,R, and Z. The unnamed COMMON block is called the *blank* COMMON block.

Passing data to subprograms through shared storage such as COMMON can be inefficient and clumsy, as the following simple example illustrates. Consider a square-root subprogram. If we write

```
A ← SQRT(X)
```

in a high-level language, we expect the value of X to be passed to the subprogram and the result returned. In machine language, we could assume that the SQRT subprogram took a value from location IN, formed the square root, and left the result in location OUT. If we did that we would have to code

```
LOAD     X
STORE    IN
CALL     SQRT
LOAD     OUT
STORE    A
```

This seems very tedious, and it would be much more complicated if we wanted to pass an array of data in and out. We would like to pass the parameters and the answers in a simple fashion. The obvious solution in a simple one-address computer for functions with one parameter is to pass the input and output in the accumulator. This reduces the code to

```
LOAD    X
CALL    SQRT
STORE   A
```

Unfortunately, this is not general enough, because most subprograms have more than one parameter. We need a scheme that enables us to pass a set of parameter values. The accumulator is a suitable place for passing the single-output value of a function because its value will be needed in an expression, but it is not suitable for passing sets of input parameters or sets of output values such as one normally returns via parameters in higher-level languages. (We call these *output parameters.*)

What types of parameters can we have? A number of types of information may be passed from the calling program to the called program as parameter data. (We call these *actual parameter values,* or *arguments,* to distinguish them from the *formal* parameters, which are the identifiers used in the definition of a subprogram.) Actual parameter values include

1 A constant (for example, 2. in SQRT(2.))—input only.

2 A variable (for example, X in SQRT(X))—input or output.

3 An array name. This could be used for input or output; the subprogram could use or change any or all of the array elements.

4 The name of another subprogram. This is often restricted to input, but could be used for output.

5 The address of a section of code (a statement label)—input or output.

A subprogram call must indicate a list of the parameters that are to be used. In most high-level languages, the list is written in parentheses following the name of the subprogram. In machine-level language, each of the parameter values must be in memory or some accessible register. In a stack machine the parameters could be placed in the stack, since it is arbitrarily large (at least in principle), but on other machines the parameters will have to be put in memory. They are often placed in locations following the call, or in a block of storage whose address is passed to the subprogram.

In designing parameter lists for particular subprograms, it is tempting to try to minimize the amount of space and time by taking note of special cases, but this is the short route to disaster, as it soon causes problems of incompatibility between different translators and can lead to errors when a fixed rule is not followed. The parameter list organization should be as uniform as possible so that any reader can understand it, and so that all needed information is available. The only item that can be used as a parameter "value" in all of the cases listed above is an address. This can be the address of a constant or a variable, the address of the first element of an array, or the address of a subprogram or section of code.

The use of addresses as parameters is common, but it can cause difficulties. If, for example, a constant is passed as a parameter to a high-level language program, say by writing CALL SUBPROGR(X,1.5), and the code for SUBPROGR stored something into the second parameter, the value of the "constant" 1.5 is changed because its address has been passed. For this reason, some high-level languages such as Pascal require specific declarations if a parameter is to be used for output and attempt to detect such errors. If checking is to be done between subprograms that are compiled or assembled separately, one scheme is to pass a "descriptor" of the parameter along with its value or address. In that case, each type of parameter can use a different format; the format can be determined from the descriptor. We will describe schemes that pass the addresses of the parameters.

If the parameter addresses are placed in memory immediately following the call, the assembly language equivalent of the code

```
array A(10)
...
call SUB(A,B,1.5,X−Y,SIN)
```

is the code

```
A        BSS      10
TEMP     BSS      1
         EXTERNAL SIN
         ...
         LOAD     X
         SUB      Y
         STORE    TEMP
         CALL     SUB
         ADDR     A        Parameter list starts here...
         ADDR     B
         ADDR     =1.5
         ADDR     TEMP
         ADDR     SIN      ... and ends here.
```

where ADDR is a pseudo that causes the address to be loaded into the next location. If this approach is used, the return branch from the subprogram must branch to the location beyond the last parameter. Unless the number of parameters is also passed to the subprogram in some way, this restricts the user to a fixed number of parameters determined at the time the subprogram is written. Partly for this reason, many systems put the parameters in a separate block of storage. If this is done, the CALL and subsequent lines given above could be replaced by

```
         LOAD     =PLIST   Address of parameter list to Acc.
         CALL     SUB
         ...
PLIST    ADDR     A        Parameter list
         ADDR     B
         ADDR     =1.5
         ADDR     TEMP
         ADDR     SIN
```

This code puts the address of the parameter list in the accumulator. If there are index registers or a stack available, the address of the list is best put in one of those, since this makes it easy for the subprogram to access the parameters.

Conventions for parameter passing in many systems vary from language to language; that is, the method used in code produced by one compiler may differ from the method used in code produced by another compiler. This is unfortunate, because it frequently means that it is difficult or impossible for a program written in one language to use a subprogram written in another.

5.1.1 Subprograms and Parameters in the INTEL 8080

The 8080 has a stack that is addressed by the register SP. The stack runs backward in memory. SP always contains the address of the current top entry of the stack, that is, the address of the least significant byte of the top entry, which can also be used to address the whole 16-bit word in that entry. The CALL instruction does exactly as described above, placing the content of the program counter into the stack, whereas the RET instruction does the inverse, moving the top of the stack into the program counter. Hence, the CALL instruction decrements SP by 2 before the data is put into the stack, whereas the RET instruction increments SP by 2 after the data has been removed from the stack.

The CALL and RET instruction each have eight conditional versions corresponding to the eight conditional branches. Each of the four condition flags, Carry, Sign, Zero, and Parity, can be tested. The assembler mnemonics are CC, CNC, CM, CP, CZ, CNZ, CPE, and CPO, for CALL if Carry, No Carry, Minus, Plus, Zero, Not Zero, Parity Even, and Parity Odd, respectively. Replacing the initial C with an R gives the corresponding conditional RETURN instruction (and replacing the initial C with a J yields the corresponding conditional BRANCH instructions).

A few instructions can be used to manipulate SP. It can be initialized by means of the LXI instruction.

```
LXI         SP,MEM
```

places address MEM into SP. It can also be loaded with the content of the HL register using the SPHL instruction, which has no address. It can be incremented or decremented using the INX and DCX instructions. It can be added to HL using the DAD instruction. For example, to move the fifth byte in the stack to the accumulator, we can execute

```
LXI         H,4         ;Fifth byte is four up in stack
DAD         SP          ;Address of fifth byte of stack to HL
MOV         A,M         ;Move byte to A
```

The HL register can also be exchanged with the top of the stack using the XTHL instruction.

Two other instructions can be used to move data in and out of the stack. They are PUSH and POP. They move data from or to a 16-bit register pair. The register pair can

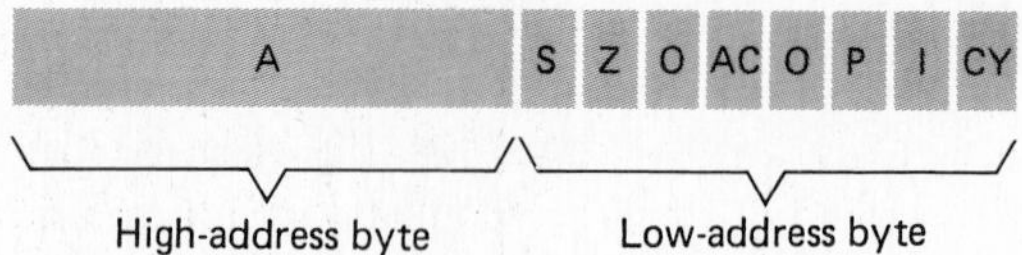

FIGURE 5-2 Program Status Word (PSW) in INTEL 8080 S, Z, AC, P, CY = Sign, Zero, Auxiliary Carry, Parity, and Carry

be specified as B, D, H, or PSW, meaning BC, DE, HL, or the combination of the accumulator and an 8-bit byte containing the 5 status bits (which are the 4 condition bits plus the auxiliary carry). The format of the 8080 PSW is shown in Figure 5-2. Uses for PUSH and POP will be seen in Section 5.3.2.

If very little data is to be passed to an 8080 subprogram, the registers can be used. However, if more data has to be passed than can fit in the registers, or if a more formal scheme is to be used, it is conventional to place the address of each of the parameters in a list and to place the address of the first word of the list in the HL register pair. For example, a subprogram to perform a floating-point addition of two words might require three parameters: the addresses of the two operands and the address of a location for the result. The call to execute A = B + C might appear as

```
         LXI     H,PLIST     ;Address of parameter list
         CALL    FADD
         ...
PLIST:   DW      B           ;First operand address
         DW      C           ;Second operand address
         DW      A           ;Address of result
         ...
A:       DS      8           ;Space for floating-point value A
         ...                 etc.
```

Parameters could also be passed in the stack of the INTEL 8080, but its instruction set does not make it easy to access the stack, so unless there is some other reason to use a stack (as there is if recursion, discussed later, is required) it is simpler not to use the stack.

5.1.2 Subprograms and Parameters in the INTEL 8086/88

The 8086/88 has a stack that is addressed by the register SP together with the segment register SS. The stack runs backward in memory, and SP always contains the address of the current top entry of the stack, that is, the address of the least significant byte of the top entry, which can also be used to address the whole 16-bit word in that entry. The CALL instruction branches to the address given and pushes the return link into the top of the stack. There are two forms of the CALL instructions in machine language: one branches to an address in the same segment (called a NEAR branch) and pushes the content of IP into the stack; the second branches to an address in another segment (a FAR branch) and pushes the current control segment address (the quantity in CS) into the stack first, followed by the contents of IP. There are two RET instructions at the machine level that do the inverse: a NEAR RETurn pops the top of the stack into IP, and a FAR RETurn pops the top two levels of the stack into IP and CS. In assembly language, the programmer uses the instructions CALL and RET. The effect of a CALL is to decrement SP by two or four, depending on whether it is a NEAR or FAR call; the effect of the return is the opposite. Assembler directives indicate which type of CALL and RETurn is involved. The example in Program 2-7 is coded as a FAR procedure to be called by the system. The first statement inside the code segment is

```
START       PROC        FAR
```

which declares START to be the name of a procedure of type FAR. Any CALL to START will assemble as a CALL to another segment (intersegment call). Any return in the procedure START will be assembled as a FAR RETurn. Note that the end of the procedure has to be indicated by the ENDP directive with the name of the procedure in the location field, that is, by

```
START       ENDP
```

The stack pointer can be manipulated in arithmetic instructions, because it is one of the 16-bit registers addressable in the 16-bit manipulation instructions, such as MOV, ADD, and SUB. The value in SP can also be incremented in the RET instruction by an immediate quantity. The instruction

```
            RET         6
```

pops the top one or two words from the stack into IP (and CS in the case of a far return), and then adds the immediate operand, 6 in this example, to SP. The contents of any general 16-bit register, segment register, or word in memory can be pushed into the stack or popped from it with the PUSH and POP instructions. It is also possible to push and pop the state of all of the flags. They are collected in a 16-bit word, as shown in Figure 2-14.

If very little data is to be passed to an 8086/88 subprogram, the registers can be used. However, if more data has to be passed than can fit in the registers, or if a more formal scheme is to be used, either addresses of the arguments can be pushed onto the stack before the call or they can be placed in a list in memory and the address of that list can be passed in a register. Suppose, for example, that a subprogram to perform a floating-point addition of two words requires three parameters: the addresses of the two operands and the address of a location for the result. In this case, the call to execute A = B + C could appear as

```
            (in data segment)
PARMS       DW          first parameter
            DW          second parameter
                        . . .
            DW          last parameter
            (in control segment)
            MOV         BX,OFFSET PARMS;Offset in segment to BX
            CALL        SUBROUTINE
            . . .
```

The address construction "OFFSET PARMS" forms an immediate quantity that is the offset of the address parms within the segment it is defined. Thus, if it is in location 00D4H of the data segment, the MOV instruction above puts 00D4H in the BX register. Chapter 6 will cover more details of the assembler. The block of parameters in PARMS is assumed to be in a data segment whose address is currently in DS, so that the first parameter can be addressed as 0[BX], the second word as 2[BX], etc. The alternative is to push each of the parameters onto the stack prior to the call. In that case, the subroutine should remove them during the return. This can be done with the RET *n* instruction. If, for example, three words are pushed into the stack prior to the call with

```
PUSH     WORD_PARM1
PUSH     WORD_PARM2
PUSH     WORD_PARM3
CALL     SUBROUTINE
```

the subroutine should use an RET 6 instruction that will pop the return link of one or two words and then add 6 to SP, effectively popping the three 2-byte parameter values.

When control is handed over to a program by the system, it is done by a far jump. The CS code-segment register has been set to the start of the code (which is guaranteed to be loaded in an address divisible by 16 so that its rightmost 4 bits are 0) and IP is 0. The SS stack segment register has been set to the start of an area for a stack, and SP has been set to 200H to allow 512 bytes for stack use. The return address to the operating system is given by the segment address in DS with an offset of zero. Referring back to Program 2-7, we see that the instructions initially executed in that code are concerned with setting up the return linkage in the stack. The sequence

```
PUSH     DS
SUB      AX,AX
PUSH     AX
```

puts the return segment address in the stack followed by a zero offset, so that the RET at the end of the code returns to the address in DS. The next two instructions initialize the data segment register DS to the segment used for data, called WKAREA in Program 2-7. Because WKAREA is defined in a SEGMENT directive, the assembler knows that the first instruction in

```
MOV      AX,WKAREA
MOV      DS,AX
```

is to have an immediate operand consisting of the top 16 bits of the 20-bit address WKAREA. (Two moves are necessary to load DS with a segment address because moves to and from a segment register do not have an immediate operand option.)

5.2 PARAMETER-LINKING MECHANISMS

Let us consider the subprogram

```
EXAMPLE: subprogram (A, B, C, D)
  A ← B
  C ← D
  endsubprogram
```

called by

```
call EXAMPLE(P, 1.0, Q, P)
```

The effect of this call may be different in different languages. One interpretation is to perform the operations

```
P ← 1.0
Q ← P
```

which would assign a value of 1.0 to P and Q. The value of P is changed by the first statement, and this affects the result of the second statement. Now consider the call

```
call EXAMPLE(X, 1.0, Q, X-Y)
```

Should this be equivalent to

```
X ← 1.0
Q ←X - Y
```

so that Q would be set to 1.0 − Y? In most languages this is not what happens, because most languages require that the compilers produce code to do the equivalent of

```
TEMP ← X - Y
call EXAMPLE(X, 1.0, Q, TEMP)
```

so that X − Y is evaluated prior to entry and stored in a temporary location, called a *temporary*. The value of the temporary is used by the subprogram, so that changes to variables used in calculating the temporary are not reflected in the temporary during execution of the subprogram. If provision is made for evaluating expressions used as actual parameter values each time they are referenced inside the called subprogram, we say that the parameters are used *by name*. ALGOL 60 parameters are used by name unless the user explicitly declares otherwise. Parameters that are used by name introduce both flexibility and inefficiency into programs. (Call-by-name parameters are not provided in the newer programming languages because of both their inefficiency and the increased probability of programming errors when they are used.) For an example of their use, we consider the following, taken from the Algol report.[1]

```
procedure Innerproduct (A, B, K, P, Y);
  value K;
  integer K, P;
  real Y, A, B;
  begin real S;
    S : = 0;
    for P : = 1 step 1 until K do
        S : = S + A × B;
    Y : = S;
    end Innerproduct
```

The parameters A, B, P and Y are used by name because they are not declared otherwise. K is declared to be a *by-value* parameter, which we will discuss shortly. Consequently, Innerproduct can be used in the inner loop of matrix multiply as follows:

```
Innerproduct (A(I,J),B(J,K),N,J,R)
```

which will calculate the sum of the terms A(I,J) × B(J,K) for J = 1 to N. This works because the parameters A and B are reevaluated each time they are used, and each time they are used a new value has been assigned to J in the procedure (where it is called P).

Parameters that are not passed by name are either passed by value, by result, or by location. If parameters are passed *by location* (also called *by address* and *by reference*) the address of the parameter is passed to the subprogram, and each time the subprogram refers to the parameter, it refers to the cell addressed. If parameters are passed *by value,* the value of the parameter is stored into a cell local to the called subprogram by the subprogram. (This is the action in an Algol 60 parameter that is declared to have type **value**.) Pascal language parameters are automatically of type value unless declared otherwise. In this case, the subprogram manipulates only the value of the variable in the cell local to the subprogram, so a variable provided as an actual parameter value is not changed by this mechanism and cannot be used for output parameters. Call *by result* refers to passing the value back to the calling program at termination of the called subprogram. It is not necessary in call by name and call by location, because the parameter mechanism refers directly to the actual parameter value in the calling program. However, additional instructions are required if a call by value mechanism is used. These extra instructions copy the value from the cell local to the called procedure back to the actual parameter address specified just before the return from the procedure. In the Pascal language, parameters must be declared to be **var** parameters for this to be done.

[1]"Revised Algol Report," *Communications of the Association for Computing Machinery,* January 1963, pp. 1–17.

Most Fortran compilers use call by location, although the standard for Fortran restricts the use of parameters in such a way that the use of value/result has the same effect. Call by location is more efficient than call by value for arrays or other large data structures because of the cost of copying data into local storage in call by value.

Fortunately, there are only a few cases in which results can differ among parameter-calling mechanisms. The principal one is the difference between the value mechanism in Pascal, which cannot be used for output parameters, and all other mechanisms, which can. The two other cases in which the result may depend on the parameter-passing mechanism used are (1) when the same variable is used as an actual parameter value for more than one parameter and (2) when the value of an actual parameter is changed during the course of execution of the subprogram because it is referenced by the subprogram via another mechanism, for example, by direct reference to its name or use of variables in COMMON. (Such changes are called *side effects;* their use is discouraged because codes including them are hard to follow and debug.) Standards in many program languages disallow these cases, but in machine language the programmer is free to try anything!

If an actual parameter is passed by name, it is necessary for the calling program to provide a section of code that will evaluate the actual parameter each time it is used. This piece of code is best made into a parameter subprogram that is part of the calling program. The starting address of the parameter subprogram should be passed to the called program so that it can be called when needed. Since the parameter may be used for output, the parameter subprogram must provide the address of a location containing the parameter each time it is called. Thus, if the parameter is A(I,J), the parameter subprogram should provide the address of the (I,J) element of A. This mechanism is inefficient for parameters for which call by name is not important, which is one reason that ALGOL provides the option of declaring parameters to be by value. An alternative solution is to pass bits with each actual parameter value to indicate the type of information being passed. In that case, simple variables and constants need not be reevaluated each time they are used. However, the bits have to be tested each time.

Indirect addressing provides a simple way to access the values of parameters whose addresses have been passed to subprograms. If an index register is loaded with the address of the start of the parameter list (which could either follow the call or be elsewhere in memory), indexed indirect references to the parameter list can be made by the called subprogram to fetch parameter values directly. In computers with many registers, it is usually preferable to bring the parameter addresses and/or values into the registers, where they can be accessed rapidly. Multiple-level indirect addressing can be used to pass parameter values down through multiple levels of subprogram call. For example, suppose program X calls program Y, passing an argument of Q to parameter-2 of Y. Y now references parameter-2 by an indirect reference to the second location in the parameter list it was passed when called. This is illustrated in Figure 5-3. Now suppose Y calls subprogram Z and wants to pass its parameter-2 as the argument for the fourth parameter of Z. It can pass an indirect reference to its second parameter as parameter-4 for Z. Then, when Z refers to its parameter-4, it references the fourth entry in its parameter list indirectly. That contains an indirect reference to the second entry in the list given to Y, which refers back to Q. This is also shown in Figure 5-3. Note

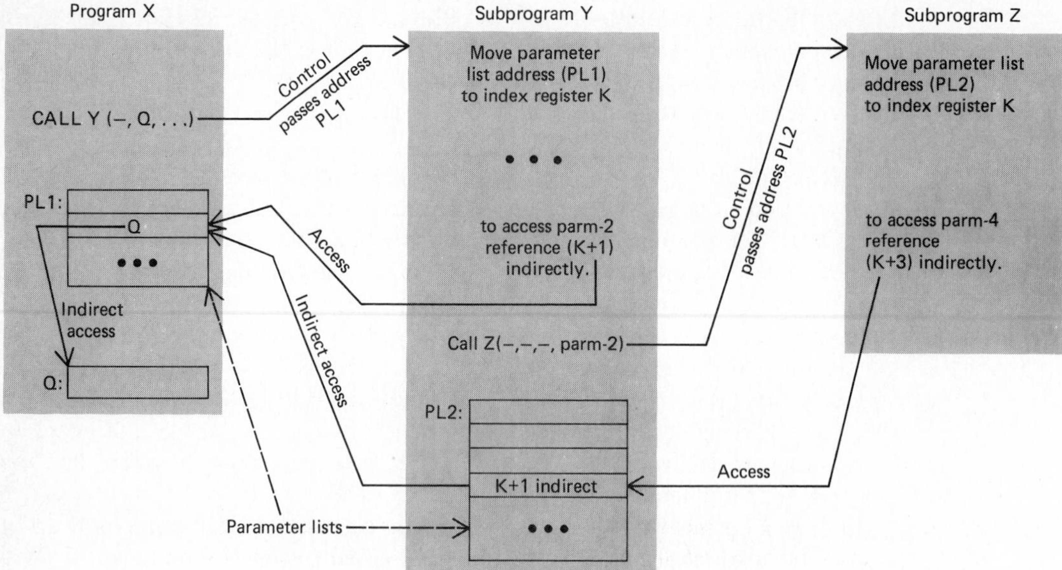

FIGURE 5-3 Use of multilevel indirect addressing for parameter access

that the address X + 1 must be "planted" in the parameter list created by the subprogram Y because, at the time the address is used in subprogram Z, the index register K will contain PL2 rather than PL1. With multiple-level indirect addressing, these references are obtained in a single machine instruction. A carefully designed indirect-addressing scheme can make parameter passing simple; a careless design can make it very difficult. Fortunately, apart from small micros, newer computers are providing designs that make this task simple.

5.3 SUBPROGRAM CONVENTIONS

Subprograms are used as a means of making code written by one person available to others, since subprograms are written in such a form that subsequent users do not have to concern themselves with the inner workings, but only with the macroscopic details. For example, if someone else writes a subprogram for graph manipulation, you can use it as long as you know where the parameters are to be placed. You do not have to know how the subprogram does its job.

By collecting the general-purpose subprograms written by the users of a large system, a substantial program library can be built; it will save future users a lot of effort when they have to write their programs. However, that is not all there is to forming a library. There are substantial problems concerned with making sure that programs in the library are reliable. (Unreliable library programs are worse than no library programs at all, since the average user cannot be expected to be able to determine whether the results from a complex program are correct. However, testing for the level of reliability needed for library programs is beyond the scope of this text.) It is also necessary that the use of library programs be straightforward. If there is a large number of library programs, it is unreasonable to expect a programmer to examine each of them in great detail to see how to use them. If all subprograms use consistent calling sequences, the chance of mistaken use is minimized. Therefore, it is a good idea for the programmer to use the same conventions in a personal library as are used in the general libraries. In addition to the question of where parameters are placed for transmission, there is the question of what is stored as a parameter and what format is used. These conventions should be as consistent as possible, although it is usually impossible to allow enough generality for everybody without introducing too much inefficiency for some uses. Even different compilers are not consistent with each other because of this problem.

In addition to the transmission of parameters, there is the problem of understanding all the effects of a subprogram. The write-up should describe the action of a program in terms of how the output parameters are related to the input parameters and what side effects occur. In general, side effects should be avoided except where there are important questions of efficiency that dictate allowing direct access to a large common data base. For example, in an airline reservation system there will be a large data base shared by many programs. Several subprograms may be used to modify the information, with a consequent need to share access to the data base. Since it may be unwieldy to pass many parameters in every call, it is natural to consider sharing variables via an external mechanism. However, maintainability considerations dictate that actual access to the data base should be restricted to as few programs as possible, and even fewer should change it. The types of access and modification needed should be determined before coding starts, and a very small number of subprograms should be written to provide the required modification and access actions needed. All other programs should call these subprograms.

In machine-level languages, we have to be concerned with the registers in the CPU. These may or may not be changed by a subprogram. Therefore, some conventions must be adopted for their use. Either all subprograms should save a particular register or the programmer must assume that all subprograms change it, since it is out of the question to check every subprogram that is used, not to mention the probability of errors that would be very difficult to locate. Some registers are clearly going to be changed when a subprogram is used. For example, if an index register is used for the return link, it will be changed by the call instruction. For this reason, it is conventional to use the same register for the link in all subprograms. Usually, we expect the subprograms to leave the contents of other index registers unchanged. The same attitude could be taken relative to the accumulator or general registers, but in a computer with few registers, the registers are so important to the subprogram that we usually adopt a convention that they may be changed—in which case we must assume that they are changed by any subprogram we use. In stack machines, we usually expect the contents of the stack before the start of the call sequence to be unchanged. (The call sequence itself may change the stack by placing parameters and a return link on top, but these can be removed by the subprogram.)

When index registers or multiple accumulators must be saved, it is certainly not convenient to avoid their use altogether (otherwise, why have them?). Therefore, the contents of any index registers used in a subprogram must be stored in memory by that subprogram so that their values can be restored before the return to the calling program.

Examination of subprograms in most computers will reveal that the first few instructions are concerned with storing the values of registers that are needed by the subprogram, and that the last few instructions are concerned with restoring those values. The memory locations used to save the contents of registers must not interfere with the execution of any other piece of code; hence they must be separated from other subprograms' temporary storage areas. Therefore, each subprogram must have a region of memory associated with it for temporary storage. On a stack machine, this could be an area in the stack. Thus, on a fifteen-index machine, the start and end of a subprogram could take the form

```
        STX     1,A
        STX     2,A+1
        ...
        STX     15,A+14
        ...
        body of subprogram
        ...
        LDX     1,A
        LDX     2,A+1
        ...
        LDX     15,A+14
        RETURN
A       BSS     15
```

Here, STX and LDX stand for Store Index and Load Index, respectively. Since this sequence of instructions would be very common on a fifteen-index computer, it is likely that the designer will provide two instructions, one of which stores several index registers and the other of which loads them.

5.3.1 Stack Frames

Because stacks provide an automatic storage allocation scheme precisely suited to the last-in-first-out organization needed by subprograms, many computers either provide a stack mechanism directly or have instructions that make stack manipulation easy. An example of the latter is the set of auto-increment and auto-decrement index reference instructions that were a feature of the DEC PDP-11 and have been included in the VAX and other machines. With this feature, some instructions that get an address from an index register have an option to automatically increment the index register by the length of the data in bytes, or to automatically decrement it in similar fashion. If the incrementation is done *after* the address in the index register has been used to get data, and the decrement is done *before,* the index register can be considered to hold the address of the byte immediately below the top level of a stack, if the top of the stack is in the lowest numbered address used by the stack—that is, if it runs backwards in memory. A push can be done using a store with auto-decrement, whereas a pop can be done using a load form with auto-increment. If the stack has to be run in the other direction, the auto-incrementing has to be done before the use of the address, and the auto-decrementing after.

Regardless of the mechanisms provided in the hardware, some sort of stack has to be used to handle the code compiled for most languages. If no stack is provided in the hardware, one must be simulated in the software. During execution of a subprogram, information is placed on the stack for the return link, for saving the process state prior to entry to the subprogram, and for temporary use by the program. (For example, if some parameters are passed by value, storage space for local variables can be taken from the stack.)

The set of information placed onto a stack during a subprogram execution is called a *stack frame*. Each subprogram that is currently *invoked* (that is, has been called and has not yet returned to the caller) has a frame on the stack. When a subprogram is entered, a new stack frame is created for it. When it returns, the corresponding stack frame must be deleted. This suggests that one piece of information worth saving is an indication of how large the stack frame is — in other words, how much must be popped off the stack during the return sequence. If the subprogram in current execution retains the starting and ending address of its stack frame, it knows how far to move the stack pointer back prior to a return. If it should call another program in the meantime, the information about the starting address of the stack frame must be saved by the called program, because it will need to create its own value of this variable; it is equal to the ending value from the previous stack frame, but it must create its own ending value, as only it knows how much space it will need on the stack. Naturally, the value can be saved on the stack. It is very desirable to save the value in a standard place. For example, the first two values placed in the new stack frame during a call sequence could be the return link and the start of the previous stack frame. Then, the second entry in the current frame is a pointer back to the previous frame. This means that it is possible to determine the sequence of calls that have brought execution to the current subprogram by looking back through the stack. This can be very useful in debugging, because the operating system can tell the user which subprograms were invoked in which order when a fatal error occurs. This is called a *traceback*. (It is also common to store a large amount of additional information in a stack frame, including a pointer to the start of the subprogram associated with that frame and a pointer to the next stack frame. If each subprogram includes an ASCII encoding of its name in some *heading* information near its start, the pointer to the subprogram will allow the system to give the names of each subprogram in the traceback. When a serious error occurs and the program loses track of the stack pointer, the pointer to the next stack frame allows the system or other diagnostic routines to start from the bottom of the stack and "trace forward" to find out which subprograms were active. The organization of a typical stack frame is shown in Figure 5-4.

Because subprogram calling and return involve so much manipulation of a stack, some computers have CALL and RETURN instructions that automatically do much of this manipulation. Some keep a separate stack that contains nothing but the return link and a pointer to a stack frame in another stack. The latter is used for saved data, parameters, local variables, etc. The VAX computers and some PRIME computers are in this category.

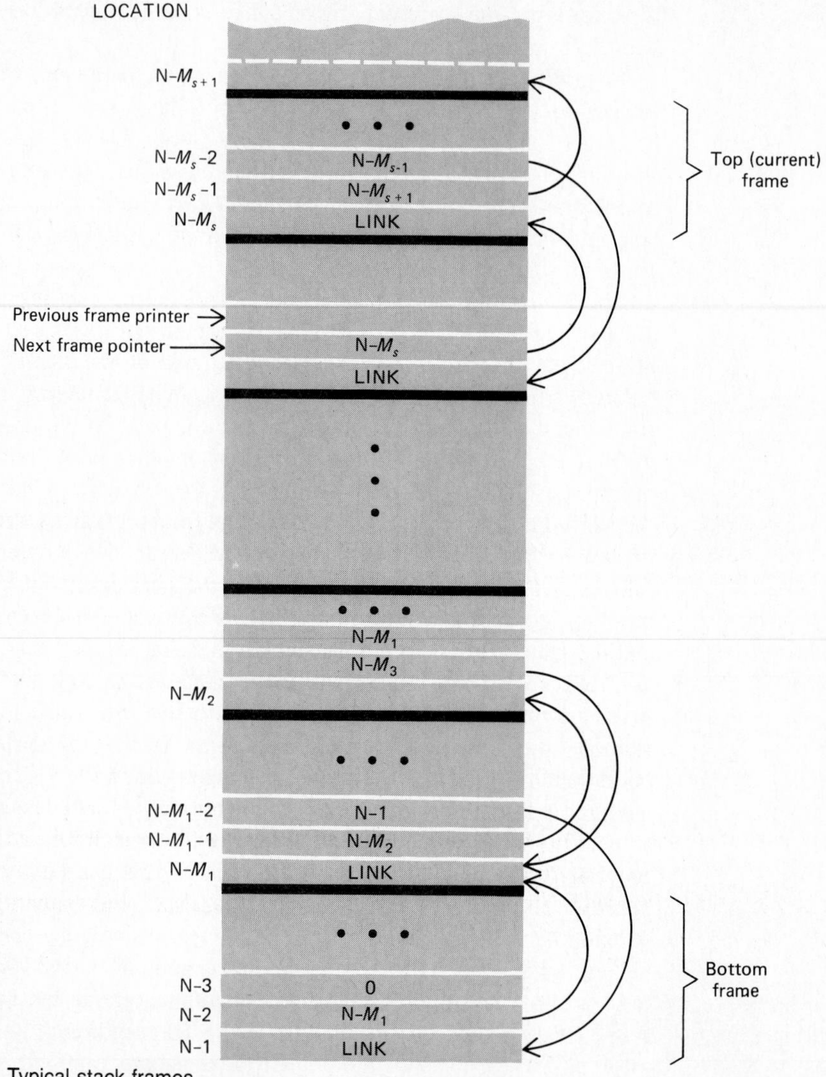

FIGURE 5-4 Typical stack frames

5.3.2 INTEL 8080 and 8086/88 Subprograms

The stack is a natural place to save register contents in either of these computers. The PUSH and POP instructions can be used to store the contents of registers on the stack at the start of the subprogram and to restore the values to the registers at exit. For example, if we wish to save all of the registers in the 8080 at the start of a subprogram, we can begin it with

```
SUB:        PUSH    B
            PUSH    D
            PUSH    H
            PUSH    PSW
```

Each PUSH instruction pushes the content of one register pair into the stack. The same subprogram should be terminated with

```
POP     PSW
POP     H
POP     D
POP     B
RET
```

Note that the contents of the registers must be reloaded in the reverse direction. Code for the 8086/88 is similar; all of the 16-bit registers can be pushed into the stack, including the segment registers. The flags can be pushed into the stack as a 16-bit word with the PUSHF instruction and popped back out with the POPF instruction.

5.4 RECURSION

It is possible that one subprogram will call another. We say that the second subprogram is at a lower level. The second subprogram is *nested* inside the first from the point of view of execution. While the second subprogram is being executed, the first subprogram is still alive, but temporarily dormant. The contents of variables used by the first subprogram must not be changed, so that it can continue when the second subprogram returns. In a large program there can be many levels of subprogram nesting. What if, somewhere in the chain of calls down to lower levels, the same subprogram is called a second time or more? We then say that the program is being used *recursively*. The purpose of recursion is best explained in higher-level languages such as Pascal, Algol, and PL/I, which provide it. We will not discuss its purpose here, but will examine what is involved at the machine level. For the purposes of discussion, we will consider one of the simplest examples of recursion—a calculation that should never actually be done recursively because it is much faster to do it iteratively! This is the factorial. Consider the subprogram definition

```
FACTORIAL: subprogram(N)
  integer N, FACTORIAL
  if N ≤ 1
    then return 1
    else return N*FACTORIAL(N − 1)
    endif
  endsubprogram
```

If this is called by FACTORIAL(1), the value 1 is returned as the answer. If this is called by FACTORIAL(2), the answer is 2∗FACTORIAL(1), or 2. FACTORIAL(3) is 3∗FACTORIAL(2), or 6, and so on.

Consider the calculation of FACTORIAL(2) in terms of the subprogram calls. First, FACTORIAL is called with a parameter N whose value is 2. If this call is from a main program, the return link back to the main program must be stored somewhere. Next, the registers must be saved before they are changed. Now N can be tested. Since it exceeds 1, the value of N − 1 is calculated and passed as a parameter on another call to FACTORIAL. Again, FACTORIAL must store the return link somewhere, save the registers somewhere, and then begin the calculation. This time, the calculation immediately yields the answer 1, and a return can be executed. Just before this return, the registers must be restored. The return link takes control back to FACTORIAL again. Now, 2 times FACTORIAL(1) can be formed, giving the final answer 2, and registers can be restored and a return back to the main program executed. Because the single program, FACTORIAL, can be currently invoked more than once, any storage it uses *must not* be in fixed areas of memory. Each time it is invoked, new storage space must be allocated, naturally from a stack. We should also note that the program FACTORIAL calls FACTORIAL several times with different parameter values. This means that we may need separate storage space for each set of parameters. For this reason, it is also a good idea to pass the parameters on a stack when recursion is used. This is illustrated in Figure 5-5 for the computation of FACTORIAL(3). The state of the stack when FACTORIAL has been called for the third time to compute FACTORIAL(1) is shown.

The basic organization for the start of a recursive program is

1 Save link on the stack.

2 Save working registers on the stack (including the pointer to the previous stack frame).

3 Allocate space on the stack for all variables used temporarily in the subprogram.

4 Before a call is made, place the parameters on the stack and place the start of the next stack frame in the standard location in the current stack frame.

Thus, one form of the factorial program at the machine level is

```
FACTORIAL: Save link on stack
  Save registers on stack
  Get value of N from the bottom of the current stack frame
```

FIGURE 5-5 Stack usage in recursion

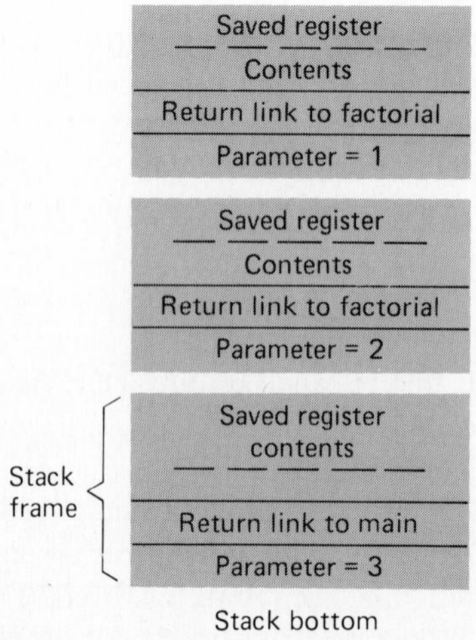

```
If N > 1 BRANCH FACT1
   Set VALUE to 1
   BRANCH FACT2
FACT1: Compute N - 1 and store in stack as start of next stack frame
   Call FACTORIAL
   Set VALUE to N times result of call
      (Note that N must be fetched from the current stack frame.)
FACT2: Restore registers from stack
   Restore link from stack
   Return with VALUE
```

It is abundantly clear that this is not the way to calculate a factorial. However, there are many examples of complex programs for which recursion is not only reasonably efficient, but is the only way to describe the algorithm in a comprehensible fashion.

5.5 REENTRANT PROGRAMS: PURE PROCEDURES

We have defined a process as a code plus its state, that is, the values of all of its variables, registers, program counter, condition flags, etc. A *pure procedure* is a section of code devoid of any of the process state information. If we have that code and combine it with the process state, we can put the process in execution again. A reentrant code is a program organized so that the procedure part is kept separately from the process state. This is significant in timeshared, multiuser systems, because it means that several users can use the *same* copy of a procedure if they happen to be doing the same thing—for example, all editing or all compiling from the same language. The process state for each user can be maintained independently of the other users. A natural way to do this is to provide a separate stack for each user and require that all storage for process state information be obtained from this stack. When a *process switch* occurs, it is only necessary to save the values of the CPU registers for the one user and load those for the next user. One of those registers will contain the stack pointer.

5.6 USE OF SUBPROGRAMS FOR STRUCTURE

Subprograms are an important tool for good program structure. On one hand, they can be used to break a large program into a number of separate, manageable segments; on the other hand, they can be used to restrict direct access of data to a few key subprograms, so that it is easy to determine in what way data can be changed. During program design, the programmer should isolate subtasks and define subprograms to handle those tasks. The tasks should be self-contained relative to the data they need, that is, a small group of subprograms should be allowed to access a particular data structure, and the tasks should be independent in the sense that each subprogram performs a "complete" basic action. For example, in the design of an assembler itself, it is clear that frequent access must be made to the table of symbols used by the program being assembled. Therefore, a small set of subprograms should be written to manipulate this symbol table; no other programs should touch it or be dependent on its internal format. There might be four such subprograms:

1 See whether a particular symbol is present in the table and, if so, return its value.
2 Add a symbol to the table.
3 Modify the information stored with a symbol already in the table.
4 Initialize the table to be empty.

No other subprogram need touch the actual table. Hence, if there is some reason to change the format of the table (perhaps because it is found necessary to include additional information in the table) no code beside these four subprograms need be changed. Therefore, the variable names associated with the table can be declared locally to the four subprograms so that no other program can access it by name. (It is virtually impossible to prevent programs in assembly language from constructing erroneous addresses and hence accessing data they shouldn't, but this is a program error that can be detected, not an oversight or misunderstanding by a programmer.)

An alternative to "hiding" the table in one block of code containing the subprograms is to make it a parameter to each subprogram. This would be wise if the same subprograms could be used to access more than one table with similar formats. For example, in an assembler, the same subprograms might be used to access both the table of mnemonics and the table of symbols. However, it is probably wiser to pass only a single parameter indicating which table is to be used. In this way, the flexibility is retained, but the data is still inaccessible to unauthorized programs.

Once these subprograms have been defined, the design of the main part of the assembler can continue. When the assembler makes reference to the tables, it does not have to be concerned about the way the tables are stored or manipulated. If, during debugging, errors are found in the format of the table, it is known to be the fault of the subprograms that manipulate them. In fact, the subprograms can be debugged independently by writing small *driving programs* to call them with data for different cases. If this is done before the main part of the assembler is written, the main part can be written and checked with no concern for the tables. Preparing the inner subprograms first is known as *bottom-up programming,* because the lower levels of the code are written and checked first. Alternatively, the main part of the assembler can be written first. Short "dummy" subprograms, called *program stubs,* can stand in place of the table manipulation subprograms. These can print each time they are called and/or input data to return to the calling program, allowing precise checking of the main program. (If the program can be debugged interactively, the programmer can function as the subprograms by writing and reading each time a subprogram is called.) This is called *top-down programming*. Both techniques are valuable. Generally, the former should be used for frequently used subprograms whose speed is critical to the speed of the whole problem and whose functions are clearly understood initially. This ensures that the correct parameters are chosen for the subprograms. Top-down programming is generally better if the precise nature of the subprogram cannot be determined until a much more detailed analysis has been completed. Top-down programming also tends to allow easier debugging of the main program, because much more control can be exerted on the data it receives from subprograms. Top-down programming is also a natural partner to *step-wise refinement*. Generally, no one approach or methodology is used exclusively.

In planning a subprogram, the programmer must decide which variables to share among programs and which to put in the parameter list. The decision should rest largely on which parameters change from call to call and which are the same. If a particular actual parameter value is always the same variable, then it is more efficient to share it via COMMON or some other mechanism. There is less writing and less time is spent passing parameters. The only drawback is a slight loss of information for the reader who may not be aware of the additional information passed. If, on the other hand, different executions of a subprogram need to access different variables, it is far more preferable to pass those variables, as via a parameter list.

5.7 CHAPTER SUMMARY AND PROBLEMS

The CALL is an instruction for branching to subprograms. It saves the return link in a register or a stack. The RETURN branches back from the subprogram to the calling program. Parameters, common storage, or shared variables can be used to pass data from a calling program to a called program. Parameters are the least error-prone; other methods can lead to side effects, so they are discouraged. There are several parameter-passing mechanisms. They are by value, by result, by location, and by name. By-value parameters cannot be used for output parameters. By location is the most efficient mechanism, especially if large data structures have to be passed. Indirect addressing can be used to implement parameter passing efficiently.

Subprograms should adhere to rigid conventions to make them easy to use. The conventions include which registers to save, how parameters are passed, and where local storage is obtained. Many modern computers provide a stack, and all local storage, parameter storage, and link information are kept in a frame on the stack. A new frame is pushed onto the stack at each call and is removed at the corresponding return.

A recursive program is one that can call itself. This requires that a stack be used for all local storage. When this is done, it is simple to have reentrant programs, which are ones in which a single copy of the program in memory can be shared by many users.

Subprograms are an important tool in structured-program design and development. They can be used in bottom-up or top-down development. They can be used to "hide" data from programs that should not have access to it, thus reducing the probability of error.

Problems

5-1 Methods for a subprogram to pick up its parameter addresses include indirect addressing, or moving copies of the variables from the calling program storage area to the subprogram storage area. Which method would you use for by-value parameters and which for by-location parameters?

5-2 Some computers do not have character-string operations, but can deal with single characters. Design a storage scheme for character strings in such a machine and a parameter list for a subprogram that compares character strings. The scheme should permit a very simple parameter list with few entries.

5-3 Suppose you have a computer with a modest number of index registers (say, seven) and a "Branch and store program counter in index I" instruction, and addresses of all instructions can be indexed. Discuss what mechanisms you would use to permit all subprograms to be recursive.

5-4 Propose a set of conventions for parameter passing to subprograms such that call by name or call by value can be handled within the subprogram (that is, the decision between by-name and by-value is made by the subprogram).

5-5 How would you organize subprogram conventions to make programs reentrant?

5-6 In Section 5.3.1 it was stated that auto-incrementing and auto-decrementing must be done after and before the use of the address, respectively, if the stack is to run backwards in memory, and that the stack pointer given by the index register then contains the address of the top entry in the stack. Why can we not reverse these (increment before and decrement after) so that the index points to the first empty location in the memory region being used for the stack? (The answer has to do with the use of the stack for data of different lengths.)

CHAPTER **6**

THE OPERATING SYSTEM AND SYSTEM PROGRAMS

System software has many objectives, including maximizing computer resource utilization, making it easier for the user to get a job into the computer, and making it easier for that user to run the job and test it when it is in the computer. In Chapter 2 machine-level languages were discussed. The hardware can execute the machine operations. Additional power is provided at the operating-system level, where the user sees a language enhanced with additional commands. The operating system provides more than one level of support. It provides access for the program in execution to powerful software for a variety of difficult or messy tasks, such as input-output (I/O), which users do not normally program for themselves. We call these facilities the *run-time support*. It also provides the user with a variety of tools for manipulating programs and data, such as editors, compilers, and debuggers. Most important, it provides a command language in which the user can communicate needs to the operating system. Whether these additional levels are provided by hardware or software is of no concern to the ordinary user; the effect is to provide a more powerful system at the higher level.

In this chapter we are going to look at the system-level facilities in more detail than we did earlier. At the top level, the system is in direct control of the computer and executes commands given by the user. At the next level down, various system programs, such as the assembler, are in control. At a still lower level, the user program is in execution, aided by various system programs. The discussion of the command level of the system begun in Section 1.5 will be continued, after which we will examine facilities typically found in the run-time support part of the operating system. Next we will go into more detail on the assembly process covered briefly in Section 2.5, and finally we will look at the loading process, which is an important adjunct to the compilation and assembly process.

6.1 THE SYSTEM COMMAND LEVEL

At the command level, the operating system is in complete control of the hardware and all the user sees directly are those functions provided in the operating system. We have already seen some common commands in Section 1.5.

The ability to create new commands is an important feature of many systems. We have seen one way in which this can be done—by preparing a binary file containing a program that performs the desired command. A second way available in many systems is by the creation of a file containing a list of system commands. Specifying the name of the file as a command causes the lines in the file to be executed as commands. (This is exactly the same as the use of a subprogram in machine language.) The name of the file name may be required to have a particular suffix, such as .CMD. For example, if we created a file whose name was RUNMYPROG.CMD that contained the three commands

```
ASMBL MYPROG
LOAD MYPROG
MYPROG
```

execution of the "command" RUNMYPROG would be equivalent to executing the three commands above and would cause MYPROG to be assembled, loaded, and executed. Unfortunately, we would have to create such a command for every different program we wished to assemble, load, and execute, so systems often allow parameters to files of commands. A typical mechanism uses the identifiers $1, $2, . . . , for the first, second, etc., parameters. Thus if the file RUN.CMD contains the lines

```
ASMBL $1
LOAD $1
$1
```

execution of RUN MYPROG would be equivalent to the three lines given earlier—each instance of $1 in the file RUN.CMD would be replaced by MYPROG, whereas execution of RUN TEST would be equivalent to execution of

```
ASMBL TEST
LOAD TEST
TEST
```

To illustrate the use of more than one parameter, suppose that we wish to have a command that assembles a program with one name, loads it, and then renames the binary file. The file

```
ASMBL $1
LOAD $1
RENAME    $1.EX $2.EX
```

does this if RENAME changes the first name to the second. If this file is called PREPARE.CMD, execution of PREPARE TEST EXAMPLE is equivalent to execution of

```
ASMBL TEST
LOAD TEST
RENAME    TEST.EX    EXAMPLE.EX
```

Some systems permit a file of commands itself to use another file of commands, and more advanced systems even permit a high-level language syntax in files of commands, which allows for conditional execution using "if-then-else" constructs and looping using "while" and similar constructs. Details are very system-dependent and are left for study when examining specific systems.

An important feature in many systems is the ability to specify only part of a file name and thereby perform an action on all files that match that part. A common convention is that the character "?" is a *wild card* that matches any character, whereas the character "*" matches any string of characters, including a null string. If this convention is used, the file name MYPROG.* would match any file that started with MYPROG., so it would match files such as MYPROG.ASM, MYPROG.BIN, MYPROG.OBJ, etc. In such a system,

```
DELETE    MYPROG.*
```

would delete all files starting with MYPROG., whereas PRINT MYPROG.* would print all such files. Similarly, TYPE ??PROG.LST would print any files with six-character primary names whose last four characters were PROG and whose secondary name was LST. Features such as this make it easy to perform a large number of actions with very few key strokes on the terminal, an attribute liked by people who use a computer frequently. The same feature also makes it possible to do considerable damage with very few key strokes. For example, carelessly typing DELETE * might delete every file in such a system, an action that is not desired very often, especially the day before a project is due.

In Section 1.5 we pointed out that the directory of files is itself a file and that, on some systems, the user can have multiple directories. Since a directory is a file, it could be stored in a directory like any other file, so a directory could contain both regular files (programs, data, etc.) and other directories. Figure 6-1 illustrates this. The primary directory contains files PROG.ASM, PROG.OBJ, DATA, and CLASSWORK. The file CLASSWORK is a directory that itself contains files HOMEWORK1, HOMEWORK2, and NOTES. Once we permit this structure, we can allow a subdirectory, such as CLASSWORK in Figure 6-1, to contain further subdirectories, as illustrated in Figure 6-2. The structure pictured is called a *tree* and the top of it is called its *root*. Starting from the root, we can trace a path to the file LECT1 by the sequence:

CLASSWORK/NOTES/WEEK1/LECT1

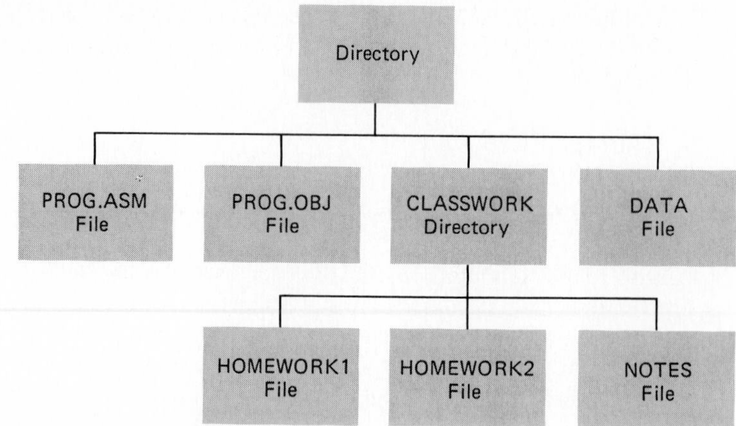

FIGURE 6-1 Directory and subdirectory

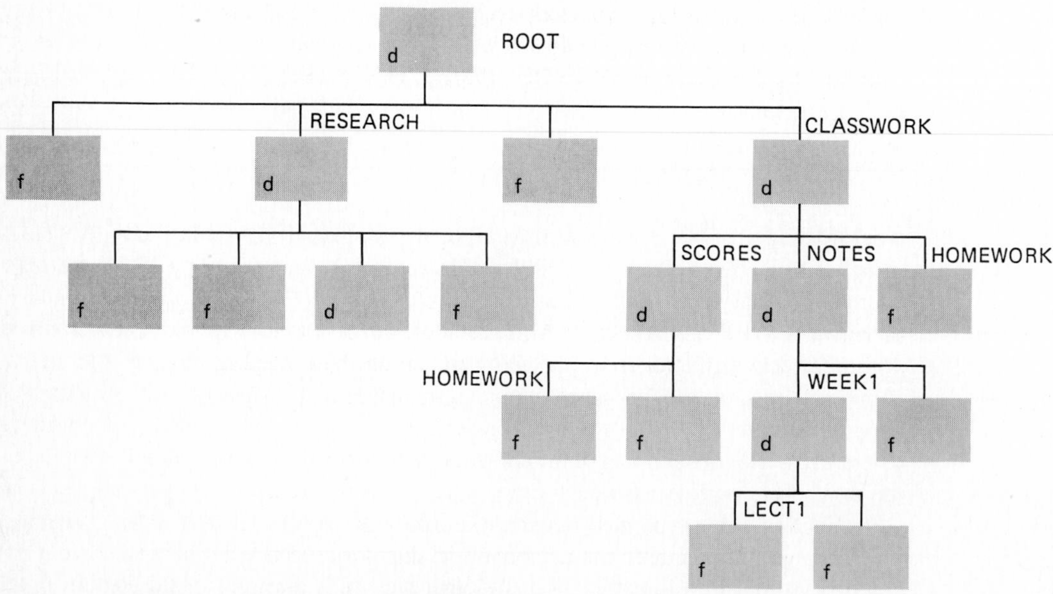

FIGURE 6-2 Tree-structured file system

This would be called the *pathname* if we were currently in the top directory (the root). If our current directory were CLASSWORK, the path would be NOTES/WEEK1/LECT1. From any directory above the desired file we can specify a path down to the file. If, however, we were in the directory RESEARCH, there would be no direct path down to LECT1. In that case, we could start at the top, indicated in some systems by a leading "/" character, as in

/CLASSWORK/NOTES/WEEK1/LECT1

or we could go back up the tree towards the root and then come down. Backing up is indicated by ". ." in some systems, so that the pathname from RESEARCH to WEEK1 would be . ./CLASSWORK/NOTES/WEEK1/ LECT1 in such systems. Similarly, to go from the directory SCORES in Figure 6-2 to LECT1 we can use the pathname . ./. ./NOTES/WEEK1.

Observe that there are two files named HOMEWORK in Figure 6-2. As long as these are in different directories, there is no confusion: no matter what the current directory, the pathnames to the two files are different.

The type of file system structure described above appears in the UNIX system (Western Electric). This system is rapidly becoming available for microcomputers, and some of its features are being adopted in later versions of common microcomputer operating systems, such as DOS. The ideas of I/O redirection and pipes, to be discussed next, are such features.

I/O Redirection Most system commands invoke the execution of programs, be they system-provided programs or user-written programs. Some of these programs work directly with files of data. For example, a COPY command may require two file names as parameters, one to read from and another to write into. Other commands accept input from the keyboard and/or put output on the screen. For example, TYPE reads from a file and puts the output on the screen, whereas an editor reads from a file, writes to a file, accepts input from the keyboard, and types to the screen. Input taken from the keyboard is sometimes called the *standard input* file, whereas output to the screen is sometimes called the *standard output* file. The action of a simple command that gets input from the standard input and puts output on the standard output is diagrammed in Figure 6-3. A program organized to take input from the standard input and transmit it to the standard output is sometimes called a *filter*.

It makes no difference in the program whether input is obtained, a character at a time, from a keyboard or from a file. Similarly, a program writing a stream of characters to a file is not affected by whether that "file" is being saved on disk or being written to a terminal screen. In some cases it is desirable to be able to specify that the output of a program intended for the terminal screen when the program was written should be saved in a file instead. This can be done in some systems by using the notation ">FILENAME" following the command. The ">" character indicates that the standard output from the command is to *redirected* into the file whose name follows. Thus the command

```
TYPE        PROG.ASM > PROG.OLD
```

FIGURE 6-3 Standard input/standard output

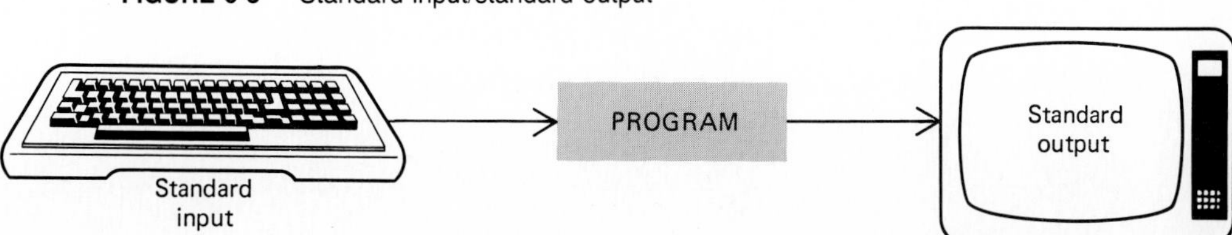

makes a copy of file PROG.ASM in file PROG.OLD. In some cases, the user wants to redirect output to the end of an existing file, that is, to concatenate more output onto existing data. Many systems use the character pair " > >" to accomplish this, as in the command line

```
TYPE        PROG2.ASM>>PROG1.ASM
```

which appends a copy of PROG2.ASM to the end of the file PROG1.ASM. The file PROG2.ASM is not changed in this operation, but the file PROG1.ASM is increased in length.

The example above illustrates *output redirection*. Input redirection is similar; it causes a command to get its input from a file instead of from the standard input. This often is indicated with the "<" character. For example, if the system contains a command SHOW that simply reads from the keyboard and echoes the characters on the screen, the command

```
SHOW        <PROG.ASM
```

has the same effect as TYPE PROG.ASM, since it reads characters from the file PROG.ASM and outputs them to the terminal screen. If such a command exists, then SHOW<PROG.ASM>PROG.OLD has the same effect as COPY PROG.ASM PROG.OLD, and SHOW>DATA can be used to allow a file named DATA to be entered directly from the keyboard. (When a file is read from the keyboard, one of the characters has to be interpreted as an end-of-file character. This is often the control-Z character, although on some systems, control-D is used.) The action of redirection is diagrammed in Figure 6-4.

The availability of redirection allows a single command to be used in several ways, thus preventing the need for several commands, meaning that there are fewer things for the user to have to remember. For example, the SHOW command suggested above can be used to replace TYPE, COPY, and a program for the input of files from the keyboard.

Pipes There are many examples in computing in which data must be processed through a sequence of programs. Suppose, for example, that we have a program SORT that can sort the lines into order on the basis of the collating sequence of characters.

FIGURE 6-4 I/O redirection

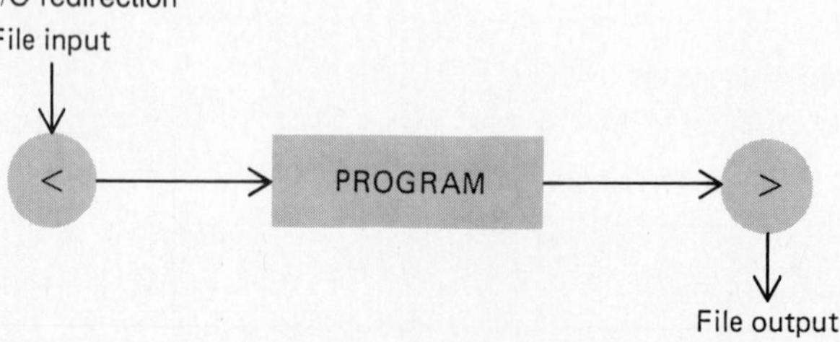

Such a program would print a file of student exam records in alphabetical order if the names were the first entry in each line and the input were redirected from a file using

```
SORT        <STUDENT.REC
```

On the other hand, it would print them in rank order if the exam scores were first in each line. If the names were first in each line and we wanted to print the entries in rank order, we would first have to switch the name and exam score in each line. Suppose that we have another program, SWITCH, that does this for lines from the standard input, putting lines to the standard output. We could use the sequence of commands

```
SWITCH      <STUDENT.REC>TEMP
SORT<TEMP
```

which first creates a new file, TEMP, containing the lines with the exam scores first, and then sorts that file. Here the file TEMP is being used to simply "buffer" the output from SWITCH to the input to SORT. This can be done directly with a *pipe,* which is a way of indicating that the output from one command is to be fed as the input to another command. It is often written as

```
COMMAND1 | COMMAND 2
```

which indicates that the output of COMMAND1 is to be made the input of COMMAND2. Using the pipe mechanism, the above sorting example can be written as

```
SWITCH<STUDENT.REC | SORT
```

The action of a pipe is diagrammed in Figure 6-5.

Batch and Background *Batch* jobs are programs not run in the interactive mode. In earlier systems, they were submitted on punched cards or tape and left with the computer center for later execution. Today such jobs are normally prepared via a terminal with an editor and submitted for execution when time is available. In a large time-sharing system, such jobs are queued and a few are executed at a time. When any one finishes, another is taken from the queue. In smaller systems, the user may place a job in *background* execution directly, so that its execution is time-shared with other jobs and with continued interactive work by the user at the terminal. In single-user microcomputer systems with no time-sharing, batch jobs are simply run when the system is not otherwise in use. All of these modes of operation are similar in that the

FIGURE 6-5 Pipe

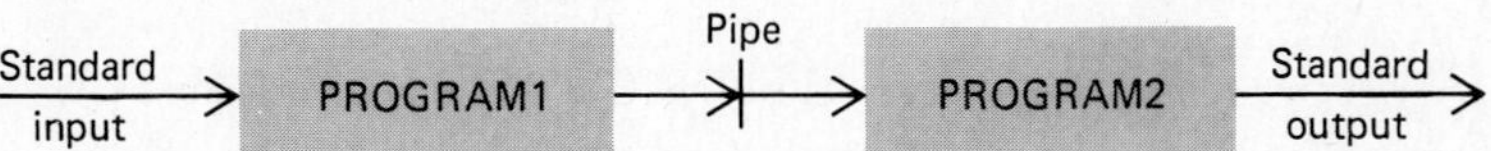

user prepares a file of commands and then requests that the file be executed as a batch or background job.

CP/M and DOS The CP/M and DOS operating systems share many common features. In particular, both permit file names to be specified using "?" and "*" characters as described above. The commands that permit this option depend on the system, so the appropriate reference manuals should be consulted. In both systems, these wild card characters can be used in the DIR command. For example, when a name is given as a parameter to DIR, it lists only those file names that match, if any. Thus

```
DIR        B:M?PROG.*
```

lists any files on drive B whose primary names have six characters and that are specified as above except for the second character. Thus file names MYPROG.ASM, MEPROG.ABC, MXPROG.XYZ, and MYPROG.BAK would be listed if they existed on drive B. Similarly, the wild cards can be used in the ERA[ASE] commands in both systems.

6.1.1 The Command Level in CP/M

CP/M permits a file of commands to be created and filed with a suffix SUB. It can then be executed using the SUBMIT command. Thus if the file TEST.SUB contains a sequence of CP/M commands, the command SUBMIT TEST will cause those commands to be executed in sequence. The file can contain parameters indicated by \$1, \$2, etc. For example, suppose the file PREPARE.SUB contains

```
ASM      $1
LOAD     $1
REN      $2.COM=$1.COM
ERA      $1.PRN
ERA      $1.HEX
```

This file can be executed by typing "SUBMIT PREPARE parm1 parm2". The values of parm1 and parm2 are substituted for \$1 and \$2, and the resulting file is executed. In this example, SUBMIT PREPARE MYPROG JOB would have the same effect as executing the commands

```
ASMBL    MYPROG
LOAD     MYPROG
REN      JOB.COM=MYPROG.COM
ERA      MYPROG.PRN
ERA      MYPROG.HEX
```

which would create a file JOB.COM that corresponds to MYPROG.ASM but is ready to execute. Other files that were created would be deleted.

6.1.2 The Command Level in IBM DOS

The discussion of DOS in Section 1.5 referred to DOS Version 1. The more recent version, DOS 2.0,[1] has a number of facilities in addition to all of the facilities available in Version 1. In this section we will give further details of DOS and refer to some of the facilities in Version 2.0.

New commands can be defined as lists of existing commands by means of batch files (suffix .BAT). These commands can be invoked by simply entering the name without the .BAT suffix as a command. Parameters may be passed to the file of commands by naming them %1, %2, . . . , %9. For example, to create a command to move a file from disk A to disk B, we could define the file MOVE.BAT as

```
COPY A:%1 B:%2
ERASE A:%1
```

Executing MOVE PROG.ASM OLDPROG would be equivalent to executing

```
COPY A:PROG.ASM B:OLDPROG
ERASE A:PROG.ASM
```

This batch feature is in DOS Version 1. Version 2.0 also permits looping, branching, and conditional execution of commands in batch files. The beginning user does not need to use these features, and, since the way in which such structures are specified varies considerably from one operating system to another, they are best understood by reading the manual at the time they are needed. The important fact to keep in mind is that the command language is simply another programming language, and as such, programs can be written in it. These programs use files as their primary operands; the operations are file operations, such as copy, erase, translate, etc.; loops are needed to handle each member of a set of files; and commands are conditionally executed on the basis of the existence of files or the outcome of operations. Thus IF statements can test whether a file exists in a directory or whether the result of a translation was successful.

Version 2.0 of DOS allows a general, tree-structured directory as illustrated in Figure 6-2. Path names are much as described earlier, except that the character "\" is used to separate names. Thus the pathname \WORK\FRIDAY\HAPPYHOUR describes a file starting from the root and going down through WORK, through FRIDAY, and on into HAPPYHOUR. Each disk drive has its own root directory, so this one will be on the default drive. A path name can be preceded by a disk drive name. For example, B:\PLAY\SAIL describes a file SAIL in the directory PLAY in the root on drive B. If an initial \ is not specified, the search starts from the current directory on the current (default) drive. The user can change the current directory with the CHDIR command, which can be shortened to CD. For example,

```
CD          PLAY\SAIL
```

[1]Disk Operating System, IBM Personal Computer, Computer Language Series, Document Number 6936752, IBM Corporation, Boca Raton, FL, 1983.

changes the current directory on the default drive to directory SAIL in directory PLAY in the old current directory. (Of course, if such a file does not exist, or if it is not a directory, the CD command fails.) A current directory exists on each drive, so changing drives causes a change to the current directory on the new current drive. New directories can be created with the MKDIR command, written

```
MKDIR    NEWNAME
```

which creates a directory, called NEWNAME in this example, in the current directory. For example, suppose we have a file named PROG.ASM in the current directory and we wish to put a copy of it in a new directory named SAVE "under" the current one with the same name. This could be done with

```
MKDIR    SAVE
COPY     PROG.ASM SAVE\PROG.ASM
```

Directories can be deleted with the RMDIR command (Remove Directory). Before it can be used, the directory must be empty. This can be done by changing to that directory, removing all files with an "ERASE *.*", backing up to the next higher directory with a "CD . ." command (as in the general discussion above, ". ." is the name of the directory above the current one), and removing the directory just emptied. Thus, if the current directory contains a subdirectory called SAVE, the user can execute

```
CD       SAVE
ERASE    *.*
CD       ..
RMDIR    SAVE
```

If the directory SAVE itself contains subdirectories, this code will not work, because ERASE will not remove directories. They will have to be removed with an RMDIR first.

When the user enters a command that is not known to the system, the system searches for a file with suffix .BAT and the same primary name as the command. The first file searched is the current directory on the default drive. If it is not found there, an error is reported unless the user specifies alternative search paths. This can be done with the PATH command. It is written in form

```
PATH     path1;path2;path3;...;pathm
```

It specifies a sequence of paths that must be the path names of directories. Each of the directories is searched in turn until the command name is found or there are no more directories to search. If a file corresponding to the command name is found with a suffix .BAT, that file is executed as a sequence of commands.

Version 2.0 of DOS provides I/O redirection and pipes exactly as described in Section 6.1.

6.2 RUN-TIME SUPPORT

This section examines the part of the operating system that helps the user program during execution. At the machine level we have direct access to the hardware via the instruction set of the computer. In Chapter 2 we examined arithmetic, logical, and control instructions. A computer also has instructions for I/O and other specialized control operations that will be studied in later chapters. The typical programmer does not use these instructions directly, because they are very complex and their use depends on the detailed knowledge of the particular hardware being controlled. For example, the type of instructions used to control one type of disk drive might be very different from the type of instructions used to control another type of disk drive. The operating system attempts to make the differences *transparent* to the ordinary user by providing *device-independent I/O*. This is done by providing access to a set of programs that perform standard functions for various forms of equipment. For terminals, the user needs to be able to read and write characters and lines of characters. For disk files, the user needs to be able to manipulate files of data. Each file could be a string of characters, called an *ASCII file* if the ASCII character encoding is used, or it could be a string of machine words (or bytes) of binary information, called a *binary file*. For printers, punched-card readers, magnetic tapes, and other devices of this sort, the user needs to be able to transmit characters and/or *records* (lines) between primary memory and the device.

Access to the functions provided by the operating system is often obtained via the subprogram CALL instruction or a special instruction that branches directly to the operating system in a similar manner. When the instruction is used to invoke an operating system function, the user can view it as an instruction that performs the required function directly. The operand address of the CALL instruction or an argument is used to indicate which function is required. For example, there may be functions GETCHR and PUTCHR that get characters from the terminal keyboard and put characters onto the terminal screen. CALL GETCHR might read the next character typed on the keyboard and put it in the accumulator of a one-address machine. CALL PUTCHR might send the character in the accumulator to the terminal. In such a system, execution of the code

```
CALL        GETCHR
CALL        PUTCHR
```

would read one character into the accumulator and then display it on the terminal, which is called *echoing* the character.

Similar functions might be available to input and output lines of characters. These lines of characters have to be stored in memory, so parameters have to be specified that tell the system code where to put the characters read and where to find the characters printed. We must consult the system reference manual to find out which parameter must be put where. In a typical system for a one-address machine, the address of a set of data might be placed in the accumulator prior to execution of the CALL. For example, there might be a GETLINE function that reads a complete line from the terminal to a region of memory starting at the address held in the accumulator, so that

```
          LOAD     =BUFFER
          CALL     GETLINE    READ a line to BUFFER
          ...
BUFFER    BSS      128        Space for a line of characters
```

reads one line to BUFFER, BUFFER+1, . . . , BUFFER+N−1. The number of characters read has to be given somewhere. This type of detail is very system-dependent. Some systems put the count of the number of characters in some register or at the start of the character string. Others terminate the string with a special character called *end of string*.

Transmission of information between memory and disk files is more complex. The physical nature of disk file units was discussed in Chapter 4. At the system level, the user sees a disk file unit not as a single device but as a set of files with user-created names. In a typical system, a named file can be *opened* for use, after which data can be read or written from or to it, and then it can be *closed,* meaning that it is no longer in use. To open a file, the file name must first be given. This is done with a CALL OPEN instruction. This causes the system to locate the file in the directory. Since there is usually a fairly large amount of information associated with a file, the information is kept in a block of memory called a *file control block* (FCB). The system reference manual must be consulted to determine the information to be stored in the file control block. Typically, it contains the name of the file, information about its actual location on disk, and data concerning its status (read only/ write only, length, amount read so far, etc). Most of the information is of no concern to the user, who only has to put the name of the file to be opened in the appropriate place in the block, put the address of the file control block in a place where it can be found by the system, and execute the CALL instruction. The CALL OPEN command causes the system to fill in the rest of the information. For example, if the format of the file control block is

```
byte0      length of name
byte1      Name in ASCII
...        (max length of
byte16     16 characters)
byte17     Operating system
...        uses next 47
byte63     bytes. Do not use.
```

and the address of the file control block is to be placed in the accumulator before executing the CALL instruction, the code

```
          LOAD     =FCBI
          CALL     OPEN
          ...
FCBI      BYTE     5
          CHARS    'FILE3'
          ORG      FCBI+64
```

will open the file FILE1 for subsequent use. It may be necessary to specify the mode of use of the file in the file control block before the OPEN call. This information is very system-dependent, and in some cases is device-dependent, so details are omitted in this general discussion.

Most systems view a file as a set of *records*. Usually, each record has a fixed length. In some systems, a record corresponds to a line of information (for example, from the card reader or to the printer). In such systems, *line images* are transmitted between primary memory and files. Because most modern systems deal with interactive terminals in which lines of information can have arbitrary length, newer systems view files as long strings of information that may be broken into records for convenience in handling, but in which records have no other significance. A text file is broken into lines by virtue of end-of-line characters present in the file.

For an ASCII terminal, an end of line requires two characters, a *carriage return,* which moves the cursor back to the beginning of the current line, and a *line feed,* which moves the cursor down to the next line. Many systems require the user to type only one of these, usually the carriage return. The other is supplied automatically by the system. In some systems, only one of these characters is stored in a text file to indicate the end of a line; other systems store both.

After a file has been opened, data can be read from it or written into it. The data may be transmitted a character at a time, or more likely a record at a time. When a record is transmitted, the primary memory address of the first byte must be made known to the system as well as the address of the file control block for the file involved. These two values might be put in registers, or the memory address for the first byte to be transmitted might be stored in the file control block. The records transmitted usually have fixed length, in which case no length information is needed, or they might have variable length, in which case a length indication is needed. When arbitrary binary information can be transmitted, it is not possible to use an end-of-string character to indicate the end of the record, because that character might appear as a binary pattern in the file; therefore, the length has to be given as an integer, either at the front of the data, in a register, or in the file control block.

Files may be *sequential,* that is, they can be read or written only in sequential order from the beginning to the end, or they may be *random-access,* which means that any record can be read or written. In the latter case, the system will have to be told the position of the record to be read or written.

Finally, the file must be closed using a CALL CLOSE with an indication of the file control block. Once this has been done, it is not possible to use the file again without reopening it. Closing a file not only permits the space for the file control block to be reused, it also tells the system to complete any updates on the file storage medium and to update the directory entry as necessary. Failure to close a file before terminating a program may cause loss of information, because the new contents of the file may not be recorded properly.

Systems usually permit a number of files to be opened at any one time. New files can be created. In some systems this is done by opening a file that previously did not exist. In other systems a separate function must be used. Systems also permit files to be deleted or renamed. Many of the operations on files can result in errors or other unusual conditions. These are detected by the system and a *return code* is provided to the user to indicate the condition. For example, if a file must be created before it can be opened, an attempt to open a nonexistent file will raise an error condition. In some systems the return code is put in the accumulator by the CALL instruction—perhaps a zero value after a CALL will indicate no error, whereas a nonzero value will give the number of the error or other condition. To illustrate, the following code is used in an attempt to open a file named FILE1. If it does not exist, the return code in the accumulator will be assumed to be nonzero, so the file will be created and then opened.

```
REDO2     LOAD      =FCB2       File control block address to Acc
          CALL      OPEN
          BZ        FCB2OK      Branch if successful open
          LOAD      =FCB2
          CALL      CREATE      Create a new file
          BRANCH    REDO2
FCB2OK    ...                   File now open
FCB2      BYTE      5
          CHARS     'FILE1'
          ORG       FCB2+64
```

This code assumes that creation of a file does not open it. In many systems, creation automatically opens the file.

A condition that can arise in a sequential read operation is an *end of file*. This means that there is no more data to be read, so an appropriate return code must be set. Using CALL instructions and tests on the return codes, it is fairly simple to write programs to perform complicated I/O. For example, suppose we want to read a line from the terminal containing the name of a file, read a second line containing the name of a new file, and make a copy of the first file into the new file, providing that the first file already exists and the second does not. An informal outline of a code for this is

Get first line.
Check that it does not exceed sixteen characters.
Store it in name field of FCB1.
Open FCB1.
Report error "file does not exist" if open fails and quit.
Read second line.
Check that it does not exceed sixteen characters.
Store it in name field of FCB2.
Create FCB2.
Report error "file already exists" if create fails and quit.
Put same memory buffer address for data in FCB1 and FCB2.
Open FCB2.
Read first record using FCB1.
do while return code = 0.
   Write record using FCB2.
   Read record using FCB1.
   enddo.

This code can be translated directly into machine-level language using run-time support programs.

6.2.1 Run-Time Support in CP/M for the INTEL 8080

When the system is loaded, it occupies certain areas of primary memory. These areas are dependent on the size of primary memory and may change in future versions of the system. The use of memory is shown in Figure 6-6. The major area of which the user must be aware is the boot area, which goes from location BOOT to BOOT+OFFH. There must be no code loaded in these locations. In release 2 of the CP/M system, BOOT is location 0, so the user is advised to begin all programs with

```
BOOT:       EQU       0
            ORG       BOOT+100H
```

which defines BOOT and begins assembling code beyond the boot area. *High memory* (the region with the largest memory addresses) is used for the command processor (CMD in Figure 6-6), the basic I/O system (BIOS), and the basic disk operating system (BDOS). As long as the program is not too long to fit into available space, it will not affect these areas.

The operating system CP/M includes the type of facilities discussed in the main section. They are described in the *CP/M 2 Interface Guide.*[2] To use any of the facilities, the program must execute a CALL SYSTEM instruction—the same instruction is used for all facilities. SYSTEM is location BOOT+5; this should also be defined in an EQU statement after the EQU statement defining BOOT. When a CALL SYSTEM is executed, the system feature requested is specified by a numeric code put in register C before the CALL is executed. For example, to read and write single characters to the console (terminal), codes one and two are used, respectively. The sequence

[2]*CP/M 2 Interface Guide,* Digital Research, Pacific Grove, CA, 1979.

FIGURE 6-6 Memory allocation in CP/M

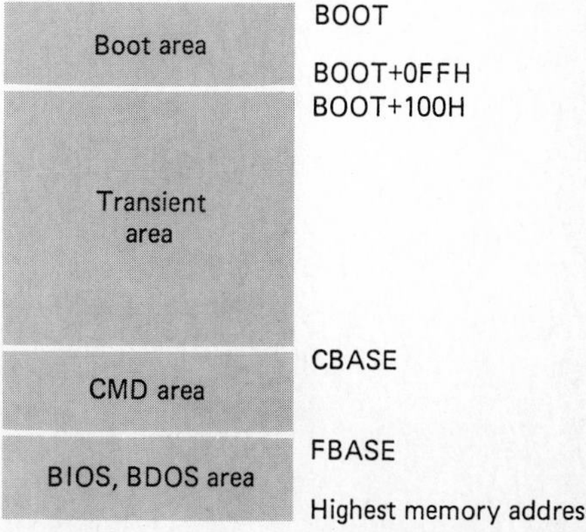

```
CONIN:    EQU     1
          ...
          MVI     C,CONIN    ;Code for Read character
          CALL    SYSTEM
```

puts the ASCII code of the next character typed on the console keyboard into the accumulator. Note that this changes the accumulator and the C register. Program readability is improved if symbols with some mnemonic content are equated to the numeric codes. In the above example, we have used CONIN for CONsole INput. *A system CALL may change any of the registers.* Therefore, when using system facilities, no information should be left in registers. If the contents of registers before the CALL are important, they should be saved in memory before the CALL and recovered from memory. The sequence

```
CONOUT:   EQU     2
          ...
          MVI     C,CONOUT   ;Character output code to C
          CALL    SYSTEM
```

sends the character whose ASCII code is in the E register to the console (terminal screen). For example, the code sequence below inputs and echos each character typed until the # character is typed:

```
LOOP:     MVI     C,CONIN
          CALL    SYSTEM     ;Input next character
          CPI     '#'        ;Check for # character
          JZ      DONE       ;Quit loop if found
          MVI     C,CONOUT
          MOV     E,A        ;Move input character to E for
                             ;output
          CALL    SYSTEM     ;Output character just read
          JMP:    LOOP
DONE:     ...
```

(Note the use of a one-character string in the CPI, or Compare Immediate, instruction.) In fact, this code causes each character to be echoed *twice* on the console screen, because characters typed by the user are automatically echoed by the CP/M system.

The code in Program 6-1 reads a sequence of characters and converts each upper-case character using Caesar's code. Caesar's code changes each character by replacing it with one *N* later in the alphabet, using *wraparound* at the end of the alphabet—that is, the letter after Z is A. The code stops on the first character that is not an upper-case letter. The symbols CONIN, CONOUT, and N are assumed to be defined in some other part of the code. If this code is executed and the sequence ABCXYZ+ is typed with a value for N of 5, the console will echo

```
AFBGCHXCYDZE+
```

Program 6-1 Caesar's code for the INTEL 8080

```
LOOP:    MVI    C, CONIN
         CALL   SYSTEM     ;Input character
         CPI    'A'
         JM     DONE       ;Input before 'A'
         CPI    'Z'+1
         JP     DONE       ;Input after 'Z'
         ADI    N          ;Translate code
         CPI    'Z'+1      ;Check to see whether
         JM     NORAP      ;wraparound is needed
         SBI    26         ;Perform wraparound
NORAP:   MOV    E,A
         MVI    C,CONOUT
         CALL   SYSTEM     ;Output translated character
         JMP    LOOP       ;Repeat loop
DONE:    ...
```

(Each original input character is echoed by the system, followed by the translated character printed by our program.)

Similar functions are available for other I/O devices, such as card or paper-tape readers and printers, that may be attached to the system.

Complete lines can be printed on the console using a system CALL. Code 9 prints the character string whose first character is addressed by the DE register pair. Thus

```
PRINT:   EQU    9
         MVI    C,PRINT
         LXI    D,MSG      ;Address of message to DE
         CALL   SYSTEM
         ...
MSG:     DB     'CHARACTER STRING ENDING IN $'
```

prints the message "CHARACTER STRING ENDING IN" on the console. The end of the string is indicated by a $ character, which is not printed. Input of a complete line can be effected using code 0AH (10 decimal). In this case, the *buffer* address is in DE. The buffer will receive the characters as they are typed. Input continues until a carriage return has been typed. The user is told the number of characters typed: an integer count between 1 and 255 (the maximum length of an input string) is stored in a byte at the head of the string. The user must indicate the maximum string length to be permitted in a byte ahead of that, as shown in Figure 6-7. This is illustrated in the code below,

FIGURE 6-7 Input buffer for console line in CP/M and DOS

BUF	BUF+1	BUF+2	BUF+3		BUF+N+1
Maximum length	LENGTH N	CHAR 1	CHAR 2	• • •	CHAR N

which reads a line of up to 80 characters into the positions BUF+2, BUF+3, . . . , BUF+M+1, where M is the number of characters actually input ($M \leq 80$).

```
BUFLEN:     EQU     80
LINE$IN:    EQU     0AH
            MVI     C,LINE$IN
            LXI     D,BUF
            CALL    SYSTEM
            ...
BUF:        DB      BUFLEN      ;Maximum length of input string
LENGTH:     DS      1           ;Actual length of string
STRING:     DS      BUFLEN
```

Note that the buffer area has to be 2 bytes longer than the maximum string length permitted, as the first byte contains the maximum length (80) and the second contains the actual length. If the above code is executed and the line ABCDE is typed, the contents of locations BUF+1 (=LENGTH) and BUF+2 through BUF+6 (also named STRING through STRING+4) will be 5, A, B, C, D, and E, respectively.

The string input function just discussed recognizes the standard terminal control functions—that is, the line being typed may be edited in a minimal way using the rubout/delete, control-U, and control-H (=backspace) keys, as described in Chapter 1. A call with code 0AH allows the user to type and correct a line. Only when the carriage return is typed is control returned to the using program with the corrected line in the buffer. The use of line input and output is illustrated in Program 6-2, which reads a line and then prints it.

Files in CP/M consist of 128-byte records. The records have no significance to users of the assembler, editor, etc., and lines are separated by carriage returns (ASCII 0DH) and line feeds (ASCII 0AH). Files are controlled by a file control block of 36 bytes, of which 14 must be set by the program when a file control block is created. These bytes are

FCB	Drive: 0=default, 1 to 16 = A to P
FCB+1 to FCB+8	Primary name
FCB+9 to FCB+11	Secondary name
FCB+12	Extent—set to zero
FCB+32	Current record—set to zero

When such a block has been created, a file can be opened with the sequence

```
OPEN:       EQU     0FH
            MVI     C,OPEN
            LXI     D,FCB
            CALL    SYSTEM
```

Note that the address of the file control block is placed in the DE register pair. If this sequence is successful in opening the file (in other words, if it is present on the selected

Program 6-2 8080 CP/M code to read a console line and print it

```
BUFLEN:   EQU   80
LINE$IN:  EQU   0AH        ;Code for Line Input
PRINT:    EQU   9          ;Code for Line Output
CR:       EQU   0DH        ;Code for Carriage Return
LF:       EQU   0AH        ;Code for Line Feed
          MVI   C,LINE$IN
          LXI   D,BUF
          CALL  SYSTEM     ;Input line to BUF buffer
          LXI   D,MESSAGE
          MVI   C,PRINT    ;Print CR/LF
          CALL  SYSTEM
          LHLD  LENGTH     ;Load L with length
          MVI   H,0        ;HL now contains length
          LXI   D,STRING
          DAD   D          ;HL now contains byte beyond
                           ;string end. Note that DE
                           ;contains start of string
          MVI   M,'$'      ;Move string end character
          MVI   C,PRINT
          CALL  SYSTEM     ;Print line
          ...
MESSAGE:  DB    CR,LF,'$'  ;String for CR/LF
BUF:      DB    BUFLEN     ;Maximum length of input string
LENGTH:   DS    1          ;Actual length of string
STRING:   DS    BUFLEN
```

drive), the accumulator will have a positive *return code*. Otherwise the accumulator will be set to −1. Therefore, we may want to follow this code with the sequence

```
          ANA   A          ;Set condition bits
          JP    OPENOK     ;Branch if open successful
          ...              ;Handle difficulty
```

to see if the open was successful or not. If a file does not exist, it must be *created* rather than opened. This is done in much the same way, but code 16H is used rather than 0FH. Thus, if we want to either open or create the file whose control block is in FCB2 and we don't know whether it exists or not, we can use the code.

```
OPEN:     EQU   0FH
CREATE:   EQU   16H
          MVI   C,OPEN     ;First, try to open it.
          LXI   D,FCB2
          CALL  SYSTEM
```

```
          ANA     A
          JP      OPENOK
          MVI     C,CREATE  ;If it is not present,
          LXI     D,FCB2    ;create it.
          CALL    SYSTEM
OPENOK:                     ;Now it is ready for use.
```

The return code from a create will be −1 if the create fails for lack of disk space, so a good program should also check that possibility.

Once a file has been opened or created, it is ready to use. It can be closed in a similar way, using the code of 10H. A close is necessary only if the file has been written on since it has been opened. Reading and writing of records are done through a buffer area of 128 bytes starting at a location called the DMA address. This address is "remembered" by the system. It is set using a system call with code 1AH, passing the DMA address via register pair DE. Thus, to set the buffer to start in location 200H (and to extend, therefore, to 27FH), we execute

```
STDMA:    EQU     1AH
          MVI     C,STDMA
          LXI     D,200H
          CALL    SYSTEM
```

While a file is open, it can be read or written sequentially. The next 128-byte record is transferred between disk and primary memory with

```
          MVI     C,<code>
          LXI     D,FCB
          CALL    SYSTEM
```

where <code> is READ (=14H) or WRITE (=15H). If these operations are successful, the return code in the accumulator is zero; otherwise it is nonzero. An unsuccessful read means that the end of the file has been reached and there is no more data. An unsuccessful write means that the disk is full and there is no more space.

There are also options to read and write *random* records in files. This does not mean that the system flips a coin to decide what to read for us, but that the records can be read or written in any order by specifying the number of the record. Details on this can be found in the *CP/M 2 Interface Guide* cited in footnote 2.

A user program is loaded by the system. Assuming the user has specified an origin in the transient program area starting at BOOT+100H, the user program is loaded there when the user types the primary name of the binary file (.COM) as a command. When the system loads a program, it also prepares a default file control block (DFCB) at location BOOT+05CH and a default DMA address, BOOT+80H. When the command line is entered, the characters following the command name are scanned by CP/M and copied into the DMA area for use by the program. The byte at location DMA contains the number of characters, N (including any blanks after the command), whereas bytes DMA+1 to DMA+N contain the characters themselves. CP/M also checks the characters following the command to see whether they contain one or two file names. If they do contain a file name or names, the first name is placed in the default control block so that it is ready to use without further change. If a second is present, the first 16 bytes of a file control block are constructed for it in bytes 16 to 31 of the default file control block (locations BOOT+06CH to BOOT+07BH). These must be moved to another file control block before either block is used, and byte 32 (the current record) of the second file control block must be set to 0.

To illustrate some of the features covered in this section, Program 6-3 gives a short code that copies one file to another, assuming that the first exists and the second does not. The program prints error messages and returns to the system via a reboot if there is a failure.

Program 6-3 Copy a file in CP/M for the INTEL 8080

```
BOOT:     EQU   0
SYSTEM:   EQU   BOOT+5
FCB1:     EQU   BOOT+5CH
OPEN:     EQU   0FH
CLOSE:    EQU   10H
READ:     EQU   14H
WRITE:    EQU   15H
CREATE:   EQU   16H
PRINT:    EQU   9
          ORG   BOOT+100H
START:    MVI   C,16        ;Count for moving FCB2 name
          LXI   H,FCB1+16   ;FCB2 name start
          LXI   D,FCB2
LOOP1:    MOV   A,M
          STAX  D           ;Move one character of FCB2
          INX   D           ;name
          INX   H           ;Increment addresses
          DCR   C           ;Decrement count
          JNZ   LOOP1       ;Repeat until 16 characters moved
          SUB   A           ;Zero Accumulator
          STA   FCB2+32     ;Set current record number to 0
          LXI   D,FCB1
          MVI   C,OPEN
          CALL  SYSTEM      ;Try to open file1
          ANA   A           ;Set condition flags
          JM    ERR1        ;Open failed
          LXI   D,FCB2
          MVI   C,OPEN
          CALL  SYSTEM      ;Try to open file2, it should fail
          ANA   A           ;Set condition flags
          JP    ERR2        ;Error if file2 already exists
```

```
        LXI     D,FCB2
        MVI     C,CREATE
        CALL    SYSTEM      ;Create file2
        ANA     A           ;Set condition flags
        JM      ERR3        ;Create failed—no file space
LOOP2:  MVI     C,READ
        LXI     D,FCB1
        CALL    SYSTEM      ;Read next record of file1
        ANA     A
        JNZ     DONE        ;Exit loop on end of file
        LXI     D,FCB2
        MVI     C,WRITE
        CALL    SYSTEM      ;Write record to file
        ANA     A
        JM      ERR4        ;Error if no disk space left
        JMP     LOOP2       ;Repeat loop
DONE:   LXI     D,FCB2
        MVI     C,CLOSE
        CALL    SYSTEM      ;Close file2
        JMP     BOOT        ;Return to system
ERR1:   LXI     D,ERM1
        MVI     C,PRINT
        CALL    SYSTEM      ;Print error message
        JMP     BOOT        ;and return to system
ERR2:   LXI     D,ERM2
        JMP     ERROR
ERR3:   LXI     D,ERM3
        JMP     ERROR
ERR4:   LXI     D,ERM4
ERROR:  MVI     C,PRINT
        CALL    SYSTEM      ;Print error message,
        JMP     DONE        ;then close file2.
ERM1:   DB      'CAN"T OPEN FILE 1$'
ERM2:   DB      'FILE 2 ALREADY EXISTS$'
ERM3:   DB      'NO SPACE FOR FILE 2$'
ERM4:   DB      'DISK FULL BEFORE COPY COMPLETED$'
FCB2:   DS      35          ;Space for second file control
        END     START       ;block
```

6.2.2 Run-Time Support in IBM PC DOS

The PC DOS and the CP/M run-time support systems provide equivalent facilities in a very similar manner. In the PC, the user program is loaded into an appropriate number of segments and a certain amount of free memory space is allocated to the program.

(This amount may be increased or decreased by calls on the system.) The operating system occupies other areas of memory, and some areas of memory may be unallocated so that they can be used for programs whose loading will be requested by the executing user program.

To use any of the run-time support facilities, the program can execute an INT 21 instruction. (This is an *interrupt* instruction, to be described in Chapter 8. For now, we can view it as a form of call instruction.) The same instruction is used for all facilities—the particular facility requested is indicated by a parameter in register AH. For example, to read and write single characters to the console (terminal), codes 1 and 2 are used, respectively. The sequence

```
CONIN    EQU   1
         MOV   AH,CONIN   ;Code for Read character
         INT   21         ;Character now in AL
```

puts the ASCII code of the next character typed on the console keyboard into register AL. Program readability is improved if symbols with some mnemonic content are equated to the numeric codes. In the above example, we have used CONIN for CONsole INput. The sequence

```
CONOUT   EQU   2
         MOV   AH,CONOUT  ;Character output code
         INT   21
```

sends the character whose ASCII code is in the DL register to the console (terminal screen). For example, the code sequence below inputs and echos each character typed until the # character is typed:

```
LOOP:    MOV   AH,CONIN
         INT   21         ;Input next character
         CMP   AL,'#'     ;Check for # character
         JZ    DONE       ;Quit loop if found
         MOV   AH,CONOUT
         MOV   DL,AL      ;Move input character to DL for
                          ;output
         INT   21         ;Output character just read
         JMP   LOOP
DONE:    ...
```

In fact, this code causes each character to be echoed *twice* on the console screen because characters typed by the user are automatically echoed by the DOS system.

Program 6-4 is an IBM PC version of the 8080 CP/M code given in Program 6-1. It reads a sequence of characters and converts each upper-case character using Caesar's code. The code stops on the first character that is not an upper-case letter. The symbols CONIN, CONOUT, and N are assumed to be defined in some other part of the code.

Program 6-4 Caesar's code for the IBM PC

```
LOOP:    MOV    AH,CONIN
         INT    21          ;Input character
         CMP    AL,'A'
         JL     DONE        ;Jump on Less: Input before 'A'
         CMP    AL,'Z'+1
         JNL    DONE        ;Input after 'Z'
         ADD    AL,N        ;Translate code
         CMP    AL,'Z'+1    ;Check to see whether
         JL     NORAP       ;wraparound is needed
         SUB    AL,26       ;Perform wraparound
NORAP:   MOV    DL,AL
         MOV    AH,CONOUT
         INT    21          ;Output translated character
         JMP    LOOP        ;Repeat loop
DONE:    ...
```

If this code is executed and the sequence ABCXYZ+ is typed with a value for N of 5, the console will echo

```
AFBGCHXCYDZE+
```

(Each original input character is echoed by the system; the translated character is printed by our program immediately after it.)

Similar functions are available for other I/O devices, such as communication lines (codes 3 and 4 for input and output) and printers (code 5), that may be attached to the system.

Complete lines can be printed on the console using code 9. It prints the character string whose first character is addressed by the DX register (with segment address in DS). Thus

```
PRINT    EQU    9
         MOV    AH,PRINT
         MOV    DS,MSG      ;Address of message to DE
         INT    21
         ...
         (next line in data segment)
MSG      DB           'CHARACTER STRING ENDING IN $'
```

prints the message "CHARACTER STRING ENDING IN" on the console. The end of the string is indicated with a $ character, which is not printed. A complete line can be input using code 0AH (decimal 10). In this case, the *buffer* address is in DS:DX. The buffer will receive the characters as they are typed. Input continues until the ENTER key is pressed. An integer count between 1 and 255 (the maximum length of an input string) is stored in the second byte of the buffer. The user must indicate that maximum string length to be permitted in the first byte of the buffer. The string is stored, one character per byte, starting in the third byte of the buffer, as shown in Figure 6-7. This is illustrated in the code below, which reads a line of up to eighty characters into the positions BUF+2, BUF+3, . . . , BUF+M+1, where M is the number of characters actually input ($M \leq 80$).

```
BUFLEN   EQU   80
LINEIN   EQU   10
         MOV   AH,LINEIN
         MOV   DX,OFFSET BUF ;BUF is assumed to be in the
                             ;data segment held in DS.
         INT   21
         ...
BUF      DB    BUFLEN        ;Maximum length of input string
LENGTH   DB    1 DUP(?)      ;Actual length of string
STRING   DB    BUFLEN DUP(?)
```

Note that the buffer area has to be 2 bytes longer than the maximum string length permitted, as the first byte contains the maximum length (80) and the second contains the actual length. If the above code is executed and the line ABCDE is typed, the contents of locations BUF+1 (=LENGTH) and BUF+2 through BUF+6 (also named STRING through STRING+4) will be 5, A, B, C, D, and E, respectively.

The string input function, code 0AH, recognizes the standard terminal control functions—that is, the line being typed may be edited using the function, rubout, escape, and insert keys, as described in Sections 1.5. A call with code 0AH allows the user to type and correct a line. Only when the ENTER key is pressed is control returned to the using program with the corrected line in the buffer. The use of line input and output is illustrated in Program 6-5. This is an IBM PC version of Program 6-2, which reads a line and then prints it.

Files in DOS consist of a collection of records. The default size of a record is 128 bytes, although this can be changed by the user. The records have no significance to users of the assembler, editor, etc., since the lines of text used by these programs use as many bytes as necessary. Files are controlled by a file control block of 37 bytes, of which 21 should be set by the program when a file control block is created. These bytes are

FCB	Drive: 0 = default, 1 or 2 = drive A or B.
FCB+1 to FCB+8	File name.
FCB+9 to FCB+11	Name extension.
FCB+12 to FCB+13	Current block number—set to 0.
FCB+14 to FCB+15	Logical record size—default is 128 decimal.
FCB+16 to FCB+31	Set by system. Bytes 16 to 19 contain file size. Bytes 20 to 21 contain date of last change.

Program 6-5 IBM PC code to read a console line and print it

```
BUFLEN    EQU    80               ;Max length of line
LINE$IN   EQU    0AH              ;Code for Line Input
PRINT     EQU    9                ;Code for Line Output
CR        EQU    0DH              ;Code for Carriage Return
LF        EQU    0AH              ;Code for Line Feed
          MOV    AH,LINE$IN
          MOV    DX,BUF
          INT    21               ;Read line to BUF buffer
          MOV    DX,MESSAGE
          MVI    AH,PRINT         ;Print CR/LF
          INT    21
          MOV    BL,LENGTH        ;Load BL with length
          SUB    BH,BH            ;BX now contains length
          MOV    BUF+3[BX],'$'    ;Move string terminator
                                  ;to end of string
          MOV    AH,PRINT
          INT    21               ;Print line
          ...
          (Following material is in data segment.)
MESSAGE   DB     CR,LF,'$'        ;String for CR/LF
BUF       DB     BUFLEN           ;Maximum length of input
                                  ;string
LENGTH    DB     1 DUP(?)         ;Actual length of string
STRING    DB     BUFLEN DUP(?)
```

FCB+32	Current relative record # in block—set to 0.
FCB+33 to FCB+36	Current relative record # in file—set to 0.

When such a block has been created, a file can be opened with the sequence

```
OPEN      EQU    0FH
          MOV    AH,OPEN
          MOV    DX,OFFSET FCB   ;FCB is assumed to be
                                 ;in current data area.
          INT    21
```

This sequence opens the file whose name is given in the file control block (FCB), provided that it can be found in the current directory on the referenced drive. Note that the address of the FCB is placed in the DX register. The segment register DS must currently contain the segment address in which the FCB is declared. The OPEN command sets certain information in the FCB. In particular, it sets the logical record size to 128 bytes. If the user wishes to use other sizes, locations FCB+14 to FCB+15 must be changed after the open sequence. The open sequence also changes the drive number (in FCB+0) to the actual drive number when 0 is specified for the default drive. If the open sequence is successful in opening the file (in other words, if the file is present on the selected drive), register AL has a 0 *return code*. Otherwise, AL is set to −1, that is, to 0FFH. Therefore, we may want to follow this code with the sequence

```
TEST    AL,0       ;Set condition bits
JP      OPENOK     ;Branch if open successful
...                ;Handle difficulty
```

to see whether the open was successful or not. If a file does not exist, it must be created rather than opened. This is done in much the same way, but code 16H is used rather than 0FH. This opens a file if it exists and discards its current contents. If the file doesn't exist, it looks for free disk space and creates a file of that name. If there is no space for the file to be created, AL is set to 0FFH; otherwise, it is set to 0. If we wish either to open an existing file and save its contents or to create a new one, we can use the following code, which assumes that the control block in FCB2 contains the name of the file:

```
OPEN      EQU     0FH
CREATE    EQU     16H
          MOV     AH,OPEN
          MOV     DX,FCB2
          INT     21          ;Try to open file
          TEST    AL,0
          JZ      OPENOK      ;Jump if we were successful
          MOV     AH,CREATE   ;If it is not present,
          MOV     DX,FCB2     ;try to create it
          INT     21
          TEST    AL,0
          JP      OPENOK
          ...                 ;Handle difficulty (lack of space)
OPENOK:                       ;Now it is ready for use
```

Once a file has been opened or created, it is ready to use. It can be closed in a similar way, using the code 10H. A close is necessary only if the file has been written on since it has been opened. Reading and writing of records are done through a buffer area of an appropriate number of bytes — 128, if the user does not change the number in the FCB. The buffer starts at a location called the DTA address (Data Transfer Address). This address is "remembered" by the system. It is set using a system call with code 1AH, passing the DTA address via register pair DS:DX. Thus, to set the buffer to start in location FCB2 in the current data segment, we execute

```
STDTA     EQU     1AH
          MOV     AH,STDTA
          MOV     DX,FCB2
          INT     21
```

While a file is open, it can be read or written sequentially. The next logical record is transferred between disk and primary memory with

```
MOV     AH,<code>
MOV     DX,FCB
INT     21
```

where <code> is READ (=14H) or WRITE (=15H). If these operations are successful, the return code in AL is zero; otherwise it is nonzero, indicating that all of the data have been read or that there is insufficient disk space for a write.

Many additional options are provided by DOS. For example, the current directory can be changed, other programs can be loaded and executed, and records can be read or written on the disk in any order rather than just sequentially. Information on these functions can be found in the document referenced at the start of this section.

A user program is loaded by the system. When the system loads a program, it also prepares a default file control block (DFCB) in the Program Segment Prefix. This is an area of 100 hexadecimal locations at the low end of memory occupied by the program. When control is passed to the program, the DS and ES segment registers both contain the segment address of this prefix area (that is, the prefix starts in location DS:0). The 16 bytes from location 5CH to 6BH in the prefix contain the first 16 bytes of an FCB, and the next 20 bytes can be used for the same FCB, if desired. (Earlier we said that an FCB was 37 bytes long. The last byte is not used unless the logical record size is less than 64 bytes. Otherwise, 36 bytes is sufficient.) A default DTA area is also provided in the Program Segment Prefix. It is 128 bytes long, occupying bytes 80H to 0FFH of the Prefix.

When the command line that invokes execution of a user program is entered, the user has the option of following the command name with a sequence of characters. These are scanned by DOS and copied into the DTA area for use by the program. The byte at location DTA (80H in the Prefix) contains the number of characters, N (including any blanks after the command), whereas bytes DTA+1 to DTA+N contain the characters themselves. Note that if input or output redirection is used, any characters following the first < or > character are not copied into the DTA area. DOS also checks the characters copied into the DTA area to see whether they contain one or two file names. If they do contain a file name or names, the first name is placed in the default control block so that it is ready to use without further change. If a second file name is present, the first 16 bytes of a file control block are constructed for it in bytes 6CH to 7BH of the Program Segment Prefix (these correspond to bytes 10H to 1FH of the default file control block). These bytes for a second file control block must be moved to another file control block before either block is used, and bytes 32 through 35 of the default file control block must be set to 0 before it is used.

6.3 THE TWO-PASS ASSEMBLER

To translate the source assembly language, the assembler must replace each mnemonic operation with its equivalent binary code and replace each symbolic address with its numerical equivalent. For example, if the assembler reads the code segment

```
        ORG     100
        LOAD    A
LOOP    STORE   B
        ADD     C
        BMI     LOOP
        STOP
A       WORD    17
B       WORD    23
C       WORD    0
```

it must replace the operation mnemonics LOAD, STORE, ADD, BMI, and STOP with whatever binary equivalent they have on the computer for which the code is being assembled, and it must replace the symbols A, B, C, and LOOP with the addresses of the locations assigned to the three data items and the STORE B instruction. When a symbol is placed in the location field, the symbol is defined. Each symbol must appear in a location field once so that it is defined. It should not appear a second time, because it would then be doubly defined.

If this code is to be loaded starting at location 100, and the operation codes for LOAD, STORE, ADD, BMI, and STOP are 52, 53, 48, 32, and 03, respectively, then the assembler should translate the program to the form shown in Table 6-1. (The numeric form is given in decimal to aid the reader.) The operation mnemonics can be converted easily if the assembler keeps a table of all mnemonic instruction names and their corresponding binary operation codes. When a mnemonic is read, the table can be consulted and the equivalent binary code found. To do the same for symbolic addresses, it is necessary to construct an equivalent table. The operation codes are known ahead of time, but the relation between the symbols that a programmer uses and addresses of their locations in memory cannot be known until the program has been coded and read by the machine. In this example, the assembler cannot know that the symbol LOOP is associated with location 101 until the program is read. Thus there are two distinct actions to be taken for all programmer-defined symbols. The first is to set up a table of all symbols and assign them numeric values; the second is to take those values and substitute them for the symbols. These two phases are usually associated with two scans, or *passes,* over the source code. On the first pass, a *symbol table* is constructed in memory, giving the equivalent address for each symbol. For the example above, the symbol table would be as shown in Table 6-2 after the first pass. On the

TABLE 6-1 ASSEMBLED FORM OF CODE

Location	Content	Input form		
100	52105		LOAD	A
101	53106	LOOP	STORE	B
102	48107		ADD	C
103	32101		BMI	LOOP
104	03000		STOP	
105	17			
106	23			
107	0			

TABLE 6-2 SYMBOL TABLE

Symbol	Value
LOOP	101
A	105
B	106
C	107

second pass, the substitution is made to translate the code into binary. By this time the value of all symbols must be known. Note that the two passes of the assembler take place before the user program is ready to be loaded into memory and executed, that is, the translation is done at *assembly time,* which is the time when the assembler is in control. After the translation process has been completed, the user program can be put into execution. Execution is done at *run time,* or *execution time.*

The first pass requires rules for determining which location is to be assigned to each distinct symbol. The basic principle used involves counting the memory space used by instructions as they are read. If each instruction is to be assembled into the location following that of the previous instruction, this count indicates its address. The count is kept by the assembler and is called the *location counter.* Initially, the location counter is set to 0. It is modified by each instruction or pseudo that allocates space or each directive that changes the place at which subsequent code and data are to be loaded.

Some assemblers have several location counters. One use for this feature is to separate code and data into different sections in memory (this is good programming practice) while placing the data definitions close to their point of use in instructions. Directives allow the programmer to switch from one location counter to another. The programmer can think of these as representing different parts of the code; each part has its own location counter. When a switch is made to another location counter, it is as if a different part is being written. The assembler assembles the code from each part (called a *control section* in some assemblers, a *block* in others) in such a way that the codes from the various parts occupy consecutive locations in memory. Yet another use of this feature is for segmented-memory designs, such as the INTEL 8086/88. In assemblers for these machines, the different segments are associated with different location counters.

Assemblers for simple computers with relatively straightforward hardware do not need many complicated features. However, many computers have complex instruction sets and addressing modes. They are designed by engineers who are trying to achieve an efficient organization. However, if the potential efficiency of the machine is to be realized, the assembler must provide the programmer with a great amount of assistance to make the programming task manageable. If the computer uses base addressing or segmentation, if it has registers of different sizes, if it cannot address all parts of memory from certain instructions, or if it has a multiplicity of options for some instructions, it is preferable that the assembler have features to handle some of the problems automatically. The 8086/88 is a good (or bad?) example of a computer with these complex features. In assemblers for such machines, symbols may have a number of attributes in addition to the "value" (equivalent machine address) that is present in any assembler. For example, it may need to know which segment is associated with the equivalent address (or whether it is not an address, but simply a numeric value such as the length of a buffer). It may need to know the type of data associated with the symbol (if it refers to a data value) and so on. The assembler may determine how to assemble the instruction from this information. For example, in the IBM PC assembler, a single MOV mnemonic is used to indicate a range of instructions, including byte or word operands, immediate data, and indirect addressing. The type of the address determines which instruction to assemble. The programmer may also have to provide additional information to an assembler so that it can make decisions. For example, the assembler for the IBM 370 decides which base register to use with an address by inspecting the information provided to the assembler in directives about the contents of various base registers. Since features such as these are very dependent on the computer and assembler being used, they should be studied when a specific assembler must be used.

The Second Pass On the second scan through the input, the assembler produces the binary object code consisting of the machine-language equivalent of the input and the binary form of the data specified. Where does the assembler place this output? One possibility is to place it directly into memory in the locations requested by the user. This means that execution of the program can begin immediately after translation is complete. Such a scheme is called a *load-and-go* scheme. It suffers from many drawbacks, although it has a very definite advantage of speed over most other schemes. Among the disadvantages are the facts that:

1 A program cannot be loaded into locations occupied by the assembler program. Fancy assemblers on small computers frequently occupy most of the primary memory, ruling out the possibility of direct loading.

2 Each time the program is to be executed, it has to be reassembled. (This is serious if the assembler is slow.)

The first problem can be overcome by placing the object code onto a secondary storage device during the second pass of the assembler. When the assembler has finished its job, the code can then be loaded into memory for execution if the user desires. (If errors have been detected by the assembler, the user may not want the program placed into execution.) This is not strictly a load-and-go system, but it can still retain some of the speed advantages if the secondary storage is reasonably fast. If a copy can also be retained for later use, the next execution will not require reassembly, just a reloading.

An example of an assembly-language program for a typical one-address machine is given below.

```
START   LOAD     A
        ADD      B
        STORE    C
        BRANCH   D
A       WORD     13,15
B       EQU      A+1
C       BSS      2
D       ADD      =10
        STORE    C+1
        HALT
        END      START
```

TABLE 6-3 ASSEMBLED CODE

Location	Instruction	Address or decimal content of cell
0	LOAD	4
1	ADD	5
2	STORE	6
3	BRANCH	8
4	WORD	13
5	WORD	15
8	ADD	11
9	STORE	7
10	HALT	
11	WORD	10

The address field of the END statement on the last line tells the assembler that execution is to commence at the line labeled START. When this program is assembled, the assembler produces the binary equivalent of the code as shown in Table 6-3. For human ease, the operations are left in mnemonic form. Note that the assembler has placed the literal value 10 at the end of the code in location 11. The program stops on the HALT instruction at location 10. In many computer systems, the operating system takes over at this point. If we had omitted the HALT, the computer would have tried to execute the data in the location following the last instruction. This would have caused an immediate error indication if the data had not looked like a valid instruction. If it had looked like a valid instruction, the problem would have been more serious, because the error would not have been noticed immediately, but only when the first location containing a data pattern not equivalent to a legal instruction was encountered. Programmers must be very careful to be certain that their code and data remain distinct so that this type of error does not occur.

Error Detection A typical assembler can do little more than check the syntax of each line and make sure that all symbols are defined exactly once. Hence the errors detected by the assembler can usually be related to a specific input line. If, for example, three addresses are given for a two-address instruction, the assembler can provide an error message, "Too Many Addresses". Usually this is printed on the output listing on the same or the next line, although some assemblers use a shorthand notation such as a single character or an error number. (If just an error number is given, it is convenient if the error numbers are listed again at the end of the program with a more detailed explanation.) Doubly defined symbols cause errors to be listed at the second and subsequent definitions. Undefined symbols usually cause an error listing at each instruction using the symbol.

6.3.1 The CP/M Assembler for the INTEL 8080

This assembler is very straightforward, and most of its features were discussed in Section 2.5.4. In this section we will cover a few additional features.

Address calculations are performed in 16-bit, twos complement arithmetic. The final address must be of the correct size. If it is a word address, as in LDA BUF+4095, the address will be valid, because it is truncated to 16 bits in the arithmetic. However, if it is a byte-length quantity, as in

```
MVI        B,X*(Y+Z)
```

the address expression, X*(Y+Z), must evaluate to a value between 0 and 255 so that it can be represented in 8 bits, because the MVI (MoVe Immediate) requires only 1 byte (8 bits) of immediate address. Address expressions may use the operators

AND	
OR	
NOT	
XOR	Exclusive or
MOD	Remainder of left operand divided by right
SHR	First operand shifted right N places, where N is second operand
SHL	Same as SHR, but left shift

in addition to +, −, *, and /. These operations must be surrounded by spaces in assembly language. The precedence order of evaluation in an expression without parentheses is, from highest to lowest,

```
* / MOD SHL SHR
 − +
NOT
AND
OR XOR
```

In the shift operators, zero bits are shifted into the appropriate end. For example, to move a byte equal to the top 8 bits of address X into the accumulator, we can write

```
MVI        A,X SHR 8
```

The 8 zero bits shifted in on the left make sure that the address fits into 8 bits. On the other hand, to move the bottom 8 bits of the address X into the C register, we must execute

```
MVI        C,X AND 0FFH
```

The constant 0FFH is hexadecimal, and consists of 8 binary ones. The AND operation extracts the 8 least significant bits of X so that the address is valid.

The assembler location counter is represented by the character $. It is replaced by the address of the first byte of the next instruction to be assembled. Thus

```
JMP     $+10
```

causes a transfer to 10 bytes beyond the end of the JMP instruction. Constructions such as this can be used to reduce the number of symbols used, but should be used only for referencing nearby locations; otherwise errors will occur when instructions and/or data are changed.

The symbols for the registers (A, B, etc.) and the names of the mnemonics are predefined in the assembler to have the numerical value corresponding to their register address or operation code. The register addresses are given in Table 6-4. Because the mnemonics are predefined symbols, they can be used in addresses. For example,

```
MVI     C,MOV
```

loads the C register with a byte containing the operation code (01000000) for the MOV instruction with 0 values as the register addresses (which corresponds to a MOV B,B instruction, as the address of register B is 0). Figure 2-11 gives the format of the MOV instruction. There is little point in writing code like this, except in a few special applications that require an instruction to be computed. Unfortunately, because this code is permitted, the assembler does not give an error message when it is encountered.

Because the register names are predefined symbols, they also can be used as address operands. For example, the instruction

```
MVI     7,L
```

moves the integer 5 (which is the address of register L) into A, whose address is 7.

If a particular address field is supposed to contain a register, its address must evaluate to a valid address for that register, as given in Table 6-4. For example,

```
MOV     B+1,A−1
```

is the same as MOV C,M, which is the same as MOV 1,6.

TABLE 6-4 PREDEFINED REGISTER SYMBOL VALUES

Register name	Value
A	7
B	0
C	1
D	2
E	3
H	4
L	5
M	6
SP	6
PSW	6

We saw that the DW pseudo could take the form

```
DW          item1,item2,...,itemn
```

If this is preceded by a symbol, that symbol will be equated with the address of the first byte loaded. Each item is translated into a 16-bit quantity and loaded into 2 consecutive bytes; the least significant byte of the item is stored in the location with the *lower* address. Each item can be one of the following:

A decimal constant, for example 373, −27, or 31D
An octal constant, for example +277O, 135O, or −1111Q
A binary constant, for example, 101B or −111B
A hexadecimal constant, for example 375H or 0FFF
A symbol that is defined somewhere
A character surrounded by quotes
A pair of characters surrounded by quotes
An expression involving any of the above

The 16-bit quantities are normally stored in the right-end-addressing format; that is, the most significant byte is in the higher-numbered address. Characters are an exception to this. The first character of a pair is stored in the lower-addressed byte. If a single character is given in a DW, the second (higher-addressed) byte contains 0.

Errors are indicated in the listing line (.PRN file) by a single character at the start of each erroneous line. The following is a listing of a short section of output from the assembler with a number of errors.

```
 1:
 2: 0100                      ORG  100H
 3: D0100 0C                  DB   2567
 4: E0101 0000                DW   45+*56
 5: P0103 78          PP      MOV  A,B
 6: 0104 78           PP      MOV  A,B
 7: U0105 3E00                MVI  A,GG
 8: V0107 7E                  MOV  45,67
 9: V0108 56                  MOV  4,78
10: R0109 110000              LXI  3,5657
11: 010C 1152B3               LXI  2,4567890
12: 010F                      END
```

The first column is a line number. The second column contains the hexadecimal location into which the first byte will be assembled. It is preceded by a letter indicating any errors detected in that line. For example, line 3 contains an error because the data given in a DB (Define Byte) pseudo is larger than 8 bits. The error code is "D", for Data error. (Using a value larger than 16 bits in a DW or as an address is not an error, as can be seen in line 11. The decimal value 4567890 is 45B352 in hexadecimal. Only the bottom 16 bits of this are retained, B352, and these appear in the instruction in the third column of line 11 in the reverse byte order, 52B3, because of the addressing used. Error flags shown in the second column include:

D (Data error): Incorrect type of data.

E (Expression error): Invalid expression, such as A+*C (appears on line 4).

P (Phase error): Value of symbol is different on second pass than on first pass. This occurs in the example above with the doubly defined symbol PP on lines 5 and 6. When the assembler reaches line 5 on the second pass, it finds that PP has the value corresponding to the line 6 use. (Many assemblers detect the double definition in the first pass and flag the error on the second and subsequent uses.)

R (Register error): Numeric value of address used as register is not one of allowed values (for instance, LXI 3,5657 on line 10 uses register 3, whereas it should use an even-numbered register).

U (Undefined symbol): An example appears in line 7.

V (Value error): Examples of this can be seen in lines 8 and 9. The numeric address for a register is too large.

The CP/M document cited earlier lists other error flag codes and does not list all of those cited here. It is recommended that the user of a system consult the documentation that is provided with the system in use for the meanings of error codes that are not clear.

6.3.2 The Assembler for the IBM PC

The assembler for the PC includes many of the features of the CP/M assembler for the 8080. The current location counter is designated by the $ character. Expressions include those operators mentioned in Section 6.3.1. The PC assembler allows the relational operators EQ, NE, GT, LE, and GE, with the usual meanings. Their precedence is the conventional one for programming languages: they have greater precedence than the logical operators and lower precedence than the arithmetic operators. Further operators will be discussed later.

The IBM PC assembler has to handle segment addressing and is also designed to reduce the number of different instructions that the programmer sees. For this reason, symbols have a significant amount of associated information. A symbol can represent one of three types of information: an *absolute,* such as 17, a *label,* which is the address of an instruction, or a *variable,* which is the address of a piece of data. All of these forms of symbols have 16-bit values. An absolute has no other information associated with it. For example, the pseudo

```
VAL          EQU          25
```

defines VAL to be the absolute 25. For labels and variables, the 16-bit value is called the *offset*. This is the number of bytes from the start of the segment in which the symbol is defined and can be thought of as the location address of the label or variable. Labels and variables also have two additional associated values called *segment* and *type*. The segment value is the first 16 bits of the 20-bit address of the segment in which the label or variable is defined. This number is called the *paragraph* number. (A paragraph is something that starts on a 16-byte boundary and so can be addressed with a 0 offset from a segment register.) The complete address for a label or variable is given by multiplying 16 times the segment plus the offset. The type of a variable indicates the length of the data, whereas the type of a label indicates whether it is expected to be in the same segment or a different one. For example, a variable might have type BYTE (1 byte), WORD (2 bytes), DOUBLEWORD (4 bytes), etc. A label has type NEAR (in the same segment) or FAR (in another segment).

The type information is used to determine the form of an instruction to be assembled. For example, the INC instruction can be used to increment a byte or a word by 1. The instruction INC CH is clearly a byte increment, because the address indicates the byte register CH. However, it is not clear whether the instruction INC MEMCELL1 is a byte or a word instruction until we look at the operand MEMCELL1. The operand must be a variable or the instruction is not valid assembly language, and the type of the variable must be BYTE or WORD. That information is used to determine which instruction to assemble in machine language. The type of the variable is determined from its definition in the obvious way. If we write

```
MEMCELL1 DB     45
MEMCELL2 DW     'AB'
OTHER    DD     4567
```

the variables MEMCELL1, MEMCELL2, and OTHER have types BYTE, WORD, and DOUBLEWORD, respectively. (DD stands for Define Doubleword.)

The type of a label determines the type of jump or call instruction assembled. (Labels can only be used as operands in jump instructions.) If a label is FAR, a far jump is assembled in which both the segment value and the offset are given in the instruction. If the label is NEAR, a near jump is assembled in which only the offset is specified because the label is supposed to be in the current code segment. The type of a label is determined from the way it is defined. Any label appearing in the location field of an instruction is automatically given the type NEAR. A label of type FAR can be created using directives. The directive PROC is used to define the start of a procedure (subprogram). Its location field can be used to define the name of the procedure, which is a label, and its operand field can be used to declare the label to be NEAR or FAR. For example,

```
SUBR1    PROC      FAR
         <body of code>
SUBR1    ENDP
```

defines the sequence of code enclosed in the PROC . . . ENDP (procedure, end-procedure) pair of directives as a procedure named SUBR1. The label SUBR1 has type FAR and thus can be called from another segment. If the FAR is omitted or replaced by the keyword NEAR, the label has type NEAR. The LABEL directive can be used to define a FAR label. For example, in the code

```
LABF        LABEL       FAR
LAB:        ADD         AX,DX
```

the labels LABF and LAB are FAR and NEAR labels for the same location. The LABEL directive defines the symbol in its locations field to have the segment and offset of the current location counter, but to have the type specified in the address field.

The segment value of a label or variable is obtained by the assembler via the SEGMENT directive. This must appear before each segment of code or data. It takes the form

```
NAME        SEGMENT                     options
            code or data
NAME        ENDS
```

This defines NAME as a segment name. It has the segment address associated with it. The assembler now knows that any labels or variables defined inside this segment should be referenced via the segment named. For example,

```
DATA        SEGMENT
VAL1        DW          1,2
VAL2        DB          3,4
DATA        ENDS
```

defines a segment called DATA and defines the variables VAL1 as having type WORD with offset 0 in segment DATA, and VAL2 as having type BYTE with offset 4 in segment DATA. When the assembler assembles a reference to VAL1 or VAL2, it uses these offsets from a segment register. Since these are variables, they can be used only for data references, so either the DS or the ES segment registers must be used. The ASSUME directive can then be used to tell the assembler which segment register contains which segment address. For example,

```
CODE        SEGMENT
            MOV         AX,DATA     ;Move segment address of DATA
            MOV         DS,AX       ;to AX and then to DS
            ASSUME      DS:DATA
            . . .
```

puts the segment address of DATA into the DS segment register and then tells the assembler that DS contains that segment address. Note that it is the responsibility of the programmer to load the segment registers. ASSUME is simply a directive that tells the assembler that it can assume that the named segment register contains the indicated segment address. This allows the assembler to determine which segment register to use, or to determine that the variable or label is not addressable. If the programmer omitted the MOV DS,AX instruction given above, the assembler would still assume, incorrectly, that DS contained the segment address of DATA, causing errors at execution time.

In some cases the programmer needs to get particular attributes of a symbol or to override others. The IBM PC assembler has a number of special operators for this. For example, the instructions

```
        MOV     AX,SEG NAME
        MOV     DX,OFFSET VAR
```

place the segment address of NAME into AX and the offset of VAR into DX. The TYPE operator gives the type information of symbols. For example, if LOOP1 is a label, TYPE LOOP1 is NEAR or FAR, depending on the definition of LOOP1. If LARRAY is a variable, TYPE LARRAY is an integer indicating the type of data given in the definition of LARRAY. Possible values include 1 for bytes, 2 for words, 4 for double words, etc. Variables and labels can be defined to have different types than those that would naturally be assigned. This can be done with the LABEL directive. For example,

```
            ...
REF1        LABEL       BYTE
LARRAY      DW          100 DUP(1)
            ...
```

defines LARRAY to have type WORD. The LABEL directive defines REF1 as having type BYTE, but it has the same segment and offset as LARRAY. LABEL causes the symbol in the location field to be assigned the current segment and offset, but it takes the type from the address field.

The LENGTH and SIZE operators give information about the definition of variables. LENGTH indicates the number of units of the type that were specified in the definition. With LARRAY as defined above, LENGTH LARRAY is 100, indicating that 100 words were specified in the pseudo defining LARRAY. SIZE indicates the total number of bytes in the definition, that is, it is LENGTH*TYPE. Thus SIZE LARRAY is 200 (100 words of 2 bytes each).

The assembler has some conventional directives, such as ORG and END. It is not normally necessary to use ORG, because the system determines where the program will be loaded (this will be discussed in Section 6.4.6). The END directive must be the last line of the program. Its address field can contain the starting address of the program. Also note that procedures must be terminated with an ENDP and segments must be terminated with an ENDS directive.

We have covered only a few of the facilities provided in the assembler. Additional information can be found in the manual.[3] The programmer is advised to get some experience using a limited number of facilities, such as the ones discussed here, before attempting to investigate the full complexity of the assembler.

[3]*IBM Personal Computer Language Series, Macro Assembler, Document Number 6172234,* IBM Corporation, Boca Raton, FL, 1981.

6.4 LOADERS

An assembler or other translator can generate code and leave it in a file on a secondary storage device. The loader is a program that moves it from the secondary storage device to memory for execution. The simplest form of loader is called an *absolute loader.* It simply moves a copy of the code from a file to primary storage, making no changes of significance to the information. The data in the file must be an exact representation of the information to be placed in primary memory. Typically, the only information in the file besides the binary image of the information to be stored in memory is an indication of the addresses in memory that are to be loaded and the number of words to be loaded. The information in the file can be viewed as a set of one or more *logical records,* each of which contains such information. A typical record format contains three fields:

Field 1: First address to be loaded from this record
Field 2: Number of words or bytes to be loaded from this record
Field 3: Information to be loaded from this record

An absolute loader reads records of this form and copies the information into primary memory. If the loader can read more than one record, there must be some indication of how many. This can be specified in a fourth field, or by adopting a convention that the last record has a 0 length indicator in the second field and contains no information to be loaded.

After the program is loaded, it is normally placed into execution. In some systems, execution may be required to start at a known place, such as the first location loaded. In others, the absolute loader gets that information from the file. For example, if the last record contains no information to be loaded, its first field can contain the starting address.

In many operating systems, this type of loader is invoked when, at the command system level, the user enters a command that is the name of the file to be loaded and executed.

6.4.1 Relocating Loader

An absolute loader can be used to load the output of the assembler if it is in an appropriate format. It was stated that the assembler prepares code as though the first instruction is to be loaded into location 0 unless an alternate origin is given in an ORG statement. There are many circumstances in which it is necessary for the system to be able to control the point at which loading starts. If several sections of program are to be placed in memory simultaneously, it is obviously necessary that they not overlap. This situation can occur when one user combines several sections of code to form a larger program or when several programs from different programmers are placed in memory simultaneously. It is desirable to be able to load any segment of code into any place in memory and to be able to make the decision concerning the point at which to start loading after assembly. In this way, code can be assembled once and not reassembled unless its function has to be changed or errors have to be removed. This flexibility is a necessary condition for the availability of libraries of precompiled or preassembled programs.

It is also desirable to leave the determination of the *load point* until the last minute so that the system can take account of the current environment when loading another program. In fact, programming encourages lazy habits in many ways. As a general rule, it is better to leave as many decisions as possible until the last minute to retain maximum flexibility. The time at which values are assigned to quantities such as the load point of a code section is called the *binding time*. By making this as late as possible, the greatest possible amount of flexibility is left for the system or programmer to use.

Now we are at a seeming impasse. The assembler prepares code as if it is to be loaded starting at location 0, but we want to be able to load it anywhere. The solution is to require the assembler to tell the loader what must be changed if the program is moved. Consider the assembly-language code

```
          LOAD      A
          ADD       B
          BRANCH    C
A         BSS       1
B         EQU       9900
C         STORE     A
```

for a one-address machine that places one instruction per word. If this is loaded starting at location 0, the values of the symbols used are

A = 3
B = 9900
C = 4

On the other hand, if this is loaded starting at location 2300, the values of the symbols used are

A = 2303
B = 9900
C = 2304

Thus some of the operand addresses in the code must be changed by addition of the starting address 2300. The assembler can tell which addresses are to be changed if it knows which symbols change. It can tell which symbols change by the way they are defined. Those that are defined *absolutely* in directives such as EQU do not change. The ones that do change are those defined in such a way that their value depends on the counting mechanism used to assign successive instructions, blocks of storage, or data—that is, those whose value depends on the location counter. Symbols and addresses that change when the program moves are called *relocatable* symbols and addresses. A relocatable assembler keeps track of all symbols used by the programmer. As each new one is defined, the assembler can record not only the value of the symbol, but also whether or not it is relocatable.

The absolute loader described at the start of this section makes no change to the code as it is loaded. When we want to relocate code in memory we must use a *relocating loader*. This type of loader modifies the operand addresses as it loads the program. The assembler must indicate whether or not each operand address in each instruction is relocatable so that the relocating loader knows which operand addresses to change. One way to do this is to use an additional bit in the input to the loader for each operand address position of every word to be loaded. If, for example, we have a machine with one-address instructions and one instruction per word, one bit is passed from the assembler to the loader for each word generated. This bit tells the loader whether or not to add the starting address to the word. The code given in the example above would assemble to the equivalent of

```
0       LOAD      3R
1       ADD       9900
2       BRANCH    4R
4       STORE     3R
```

where we have indicated relocatable addresses by a trailing R. If this program is loaded starting at location 4108 we get

```
4108    LOAD      4111
4109    ADD       9900
4110    BRANCH    4112
4112    STORE     4111
```

The programmer should realize that the use of relocatable addresses may restrict the use of arithmetic expressions in address fields. The scheme just described permits single positive relocation only, that is, the relocation amount can be added once or not at all. Therefore, it would not be possible to write an address such as 100-XVAR, where XVAR is relocatable, since it requires negative relocation. Similarly, an address such as A + B is not allowed if both A and B are relocatable, because A + B requires double relocation. Addresses such as A − B, where A and B are both relocatable, are valid because they need no relocation.

6.4.2 Linking Loader

The assembler can put the *relocatable object code* in secondary storage as the translation proceeds. When assembly is over, the object can be left on secondary storage devices semipermanently for later use and/or loaded immediately. When it is loaded, the user frequently wishes simultaneously to load the object code from several different assemblies or from assemblies and compilations. For that reason, the format acceptable to the relocating loader is normally generated by all translators in the system.

With this technique, a number of separately assembled programs can be loaded in primary memory without interference. The loader loads each one in turn, noting where it starts and how long it is. Usually, the loader loads each program into consecutive areas in memory, starting at location 0 and working up.

When one program is written, the programmer has no knowledge of the location in memory of other programs that may be used by the first program or of the locations of variables in the other code. Therefore, the programmer needs a way of referring to code and variables in separately assembled programs whose locations will not be known until *load time,* which is normally long after assembly time. At the assembler level, these locations will be referenced symbolically, but the value of the symbols will not be defined in the same section of code. We say that the symbols are *external* to that section of code. Many assemblers require that the symbols be declared external by means of a directive such as

```
EXTRNL    S1,S2,SYMBX
```

which declares the list of symbols in the address field to be external.

A symbol that is external to a segment of code must be defined elsewhere. If it is symbol predefined in the system (such as the name of one of the system programs), it is not necessary for the programmer to define it. However, if it is the name of a variable or instruction in another section of user code, the programmer must define it. The point of definition must be declared by the programmer. Most assemblers provide a pseudo such as ENTRY for this purpose. The statement

```
ENTRY    A,B
```

tells the assembler that the symbols A and B are to be made known to other programs for reference by them as external. They are called *entry points* in the current program. They are also known as *global* symbols, or *public* symbols. If symbols A and B are declared as entry points, they must be defined somewhere in the current program as addresses. The ENTRY pseudo can usually be placed anywhere in the section of code containing the definitions of any symbols it uses. It is best to place it very near the front, because it is valuable documentary information. A simple illustration of the use of external symbols and entry points is given below. The two sections of code are assumed to be separately assembled but then loaded together.

Code Segment No. 1

```
          ENTRY     RETURN,A
          EXTRNL    TEST,B
START     LOAD      A
          BRANCH    TEST
RETURN    STOP
A         DATA      15
          END       START
```

Code Segment No. 2 (to be assembled separately)

```
          ENTRY     TEST,B
          EXTRNL    RETURN,A
TEST      ADD       B
          BRANCH    RETURN
B         DATA      13
          END
```

When a segment of code is being assembled, the assembler does not know what value to assign to an external symbol because that value is declared in another segment of code, and will not be completely determined until that other segment of code is loaded. Thus, in the above example, the first code segment cannot know what addresses correspond to symbols TEST and B at assembly time, whereas the second cannot know about A and RETURN. Therefore, the job of assigning a value to an external symbol has to be left to some form of loader, called a *linking loader* or *linkage editor.*

A linking loader or linkage editor is essentially another assembler that accepts partially assembled programs and completes the assembly for the symbolic addresses that were not completely defined during assembly because they are external. These symbols are assembled using a 0 value as their address. The positions of all the address fields that use each external symbol are recorded, and that information is passed to the linking loader. These positions are specified relative to the start of the code segment being assembled so that, when the loader knows where the code is loaded, it knows which external operand addresses need to be filled in. Thus the linking loader has a list of external symbols, and for each external symbol it has a list of the places the symbol is used. The assembler also passes a list of all entry-point symbols defined in each code segment, together with their equivalent addresses in the segment.

The linkage editor reads all code segments and allocates space in memory for each on the basis of the length of the segment. Memory is usually allocated sequentially, just as in the assembly process. As segments are allocated to memory, the memory address of their entry points can be computed. These are kept in a table called a *memory map,* which is very similar to the assembler symbol table; it has an entry for each code segment, giving its location and length (and its name, if a name is required by the system), and an entry for each entry point, giving its name and corresponding address. When the linkage editor has finished reading all code segments, it is ready to do the equivalent of the second pass of the assembler: it examines each external symbol to see if it is in the memory map. If it is, the corresponding address is placed in the assembled code in the locations specified by the assembler output; if it is not, there is an *unsatisfied external reference,* namely, an external symbol that is not yet defined.

It should be noted that a linking loader does not allow address calculation involving external symbols. For example, an address of the form SYMB + 4 is invalid, because SYMB is an external symbol. Some linking loaders and assemblers permit limited address calculation by adding the value of the external symbol to the address field at linking time, but the options are still restricted. In such a system, addresses of the form X + 4 are valid. However, it is often desirable to use addresses of the form FINISH − START + 1, where START and FINISH are the first and last addresses of a block of cells. This construction gives the length of the block, but the construction is not valid unless both symbols are declared in the segment in which it is used. As a general rule, not more than one relocatable or external address in any assembly-language program should appear in any expression, except when the difference of two addresses defined in the current program segment is used.

A linkage editor also handles the allocation of memory to COMMON storage and related usage. Each segment generated by an assembler or compiler is passed on to the linkage editor with an indication of its type of usage. Code is assigned to non-overlapping regions of memory by the linkage editor, but COMMON variable areas are allocated in the same segment of memory for all programs that request them.

The output of a linker can remain in relocatable binary form for later loading. Indeed, it can continue to contain unsatisfied external references, so that it can be linked to additional code later. At some point it must be converted to absolute binary ready to execute. If the linking and loading are done in one step by a single program, we call that program a linking loader; if the linking is done by a separate program, that program is called a linkage editor.

6.4.3 Program Libraries

The objective of a computer system is to make the production of software as painless as possible. After a user has prepared a number of programs, they can often be used as part of a subsequent program. This can be handled by loading those programs needed from a file system. If the system has only an absolute loader, the source for each of the programs must be combined prior to assembly (or compilation) so that all programs can be translated at the same time and loaded together. If a linking loader or linkage editor is available, the object (that is, the assembled relocatable binary form) can be combined and loaded at the same time. If a large number of programs is involved, the user may be required to list a great many programs for loading. A *library* is a collection of programs that can be searched by a linking loader for requested programs. When a library of programs is given to the loader, it does not load them all. Instead, it first loads all of the user-supplied programs and then searches the library to find programs with names that match unsatisfied external references.

Systems usually allow any number of libraries to be specified. A linking loader searches each in turn to try to satisfy all the external references. Computer centers usually make the commonly used programs available in an installation library. In a typical large-computer-system environment, a user may have access to one or more private libraries, a group library, and finally the installation library. For example, a group of users in, say, chemistry may have their own library of chemical analysis programs as well as the public library on the computer. The chemists would instruct the computer to search the chemistry library first. Programs common to everybody, such as SQRT, are kept in the public library. If programs with the same name are in more than one library, the loader selects the one from the first library in which it is found. This points out a very important principle: the user does not have to know the name of every program in the libraries consulted. If the job submitted contains an external symbol that is defined in another part of the same job, the loader does not look for it in a library at all. If the job refers to a program in the user's personal library, the loader will find it there and not check further. Thus the programmer need not avoid using the names of library programs in a section of code if those library programs are not wanted. The definition in the user code will be taken first. This also allows the user to define substitute versions of library programs to be loaded in place of the system versions in a particular job.

6.4.4 Initial Program Load

We have discussed the way in which programs are loaded into memory for execution by another program, the loader. How does the loader get into memory in the first place? The basic hardware is capable of executing sequences of instructions drawn from the computer memory. It is the job of the user and the system to get a user program into the memory and begin execution at the correct point. The I/O section of the computer is capable of reading data into memory, so this is the hardware that must be used to load a program. Internally, a program, numbers, and other data are represented by words (or groups of words) of binary digits; the input instructions of a machine are capable of reading an external representation of these bits into memory. Therefore, if the program to be executed is specified in its binary form exactly as it should appear inside the memory of the computer, input instructions can be used to load it. Unfortunately, this begs the question, since these input instructions must themselves be loaded into memory before they can be executed. How does the first input instruction get into the computer? An *initial load sequence,* also known as an *initial program load* (IPL) or a *bootstrap sequence,* is employed.

An initial load sequence is brought into action by pressing a button on the computer or possibly by turning on the power. This button initiates a single short segment of code that is prewired into the computer and contains a program to start the loading process. Very few programmers need be concerned with this process, since it is built in by the manufacturer and is not usually changed. The initial load sequence is the start of a complex loading process that is used to bring system programs into the computer that will, in turn, load the user programs and assist in their execution. Most of the time, these additional system programs are resident in the computer; the initial program load has to be used only after some catastrophic stoppage of the computer, such as power off, or major hardware or system software error. We will briefly follow the sequence of events that take place after the IPL button is pressed.

Because the IPL sequence must be permanently stored in memory (or worse still, entered by hand), it is kept very short. On some computers it is a single word; on others it is several. Usually the IPL reads a single record from a device such as a disk. If this can be done with a single instruction, the IPL button can force the computer into the state in which it would be if such an instruction had just been fetched from memory and was about to be executed. Suppose that the instruction supplied by the IPL button indicates that the contents of a particular disk block should be read into locations 0 through $K-1$, where the disk block is K words long. (Typical disk blocks are 128 to 2048 bytes long.) If the IPL button also forces the control counter to 0, the computer will execute the input instruction, filling K locations, starting at 0, and then execute the contents of location 0 for the next instruction. Since this has just been filled by the input instruction, control of the computer is now in the hands of the code in the block just read. This code can now be used to load additional code from disk (or other storage device) into memory. This process is called "bootstrapping" because the program is pulling itself in "by its bootstraps." It is also called *booting* the system, and the act of restarting the computer by this means is called a *reboot*. The initial block read in the booting operation is called the *boot block*. It can be read from any I/O unit available to the computer via an appropriate IPL sequence, but disk is normally used if it is available.

The code in the boot block can be used to load parts of the operating system and to pass control to that system so that it can communicate with the user to determine what is needed next. This brings the user into contact with the computer at the command level.

An alternative technique used on some microcomputers is to keep part of the operating system in *read-only memory* (ROM). This information cannot be changed, because a read-only memory cannot be written into. The part of the operating system kept in ROM can include a loader to read additional data from disk, although in some small microcomputers the whole system and a language interpreter, often for BASIC, are kept in ROM.

6.4.5 Loading in CP/M for the INTEL 8080

Systems for the INTEL 8080 are typical of those for small microcomputers and support an absolute loader only. The user must combine all programs needed at the assembly level and assemble them as one unit. The result is an absolute binary object in a hexadecimal representation. In the operating system CP/M, the object is placed in a file <name>.HEX, where <name> is the file name given to the assembler for assembly. The load, LOAD, takes this file and processes it into a core image stored on disk under the file name <name>.COM. Libraries have to be included at the source level using the R command in the editor or by concatenating files using PIP. This means that the user has to be careful of symbol name conflicts between library programs and user-written code.

Because there is no linking, the user has to provide the addresses of the system programs and data areas used in the lower-system-level operations. These should be defined in EQU statements so that changes in future versions of the operating system will require minimal changes in programs. If each program starts with

```
BOOT:      EQU     0
SYSTEM:    EQU     BOOT+5
DFCB:      EQU     BOOT+5CH
DDMA:      EQU     BOOT+80H
```

only the BOOT equivalence will have to be changed if the boot area is moved.

Primary memory is divided into four areas in CP/M, as shown in Figure 6-6: the boot area from BOOT to BOOT + 0FH, the command-processor area from CBASE to FBASE − 1, the disk-operating system from FBASE to the top of memory, and the *transient-program area* from BOOT + 100H to CBASE − 1. The latter transient-program area is used by the system to load and execute subsystems, such as the editor. It is also available for user programs. Generally, these programs can overwrite the command processor area and use memory up to FBASE − 1, since the command processor (the upper system level) is not used during execution of a user program. The address corresponding to FBASE can be found at location SYSTEM + 1. Thus the amount of memory available to the user can be calculated in HL by executing

```
        LHLD    SYSTEM+1
        LXI     D,-100H
        DAD     D
```

The 3 bytes starting at SYSTEM actually contain the instruction JMP FBASE. This allows the location of FBASE to change as the system is updated, without the need to redefine the address FBASE in a user code.

6.4.6 LINK: The IBM PC Linkage Editor

The IBM PC operating system permits separately assembled or compiled programs to be linked together to form an executable program ready for loading. Variables, labels, or absolute symbols can be linked together. They must be declared PUBLIC in the program in which they are declared, and as external in any other programs in which they are referenced. The external directive takes the form

```
        EXTRN   symbol:type,...
```

where symbol is the variable, label, or absolute to be declared external, and type is ABS, NEAR, FAR, BYTE, WORD, or one of the other variable types. The PUBLIC directive takes the form

```
        PUBLIC  symbol,...
```

where every symbol listed must be declared somewhere in that program. For example, if we define a procedure SUBR1 in one program and reference in another, we will have to include the following directives:

```
        EXTRN   SUBR1:FAR
CSEQ    SEGMENT
START   PROC
        ...     Calling program
        CALL    SUBR1
        ...
START   ENDP
CSEG    ENDS
        END     START

SUBSEG  SEGMENT
SUBR1   PROC    FAR
        PUBLIC  SUBR1
        ...
```

```
        RET
SUBR1   ENDP
SUBSEG  ENDS
        END
```

Segment names are passed on to the linker along with some information about the type of the segment. This information can be specified in the SEGMENT directive. When it is not specified, default values are taken. The most important of these is the *combination-type* information. This indicates the way in which segments of the same name may be combined at link time. The default is that there is no combination, and all segments are distinct. If the combination type PUBLIC is declared, segments of the same name are concatenated. If the type COMMON is declared, segments of the same name start at the same location, thus implementing Fortran COMMON. If type STACK is declared, the linkage editor assigns the segment to an area allocated for a run-time stack. At least one segment must be declared to be STACK in the input to LINK. Examples of this can be seen in Program 2-7.

6.5 CHAPTER SUMMARY AND PROBLEMS

The purpose of the operating system is to improve resource utilization and to make it easier to use the computer. The system provides computer capabilities at a number of levels above machine-language level. They include run-time support, which helps with I/O operations and other messy machine details; program and data manipulation, with translators, editors, and debuggers; and command interpretation.

New commands can be defined as files of commands. Parameters can be placed in the files of commands and values substituted for those parameters when the command file is executed. The file names passed to commands can include wild cards, which permit a file name to be only partially specified. The details depend on the particular command.

Some systems allow a directory to include other directories as files and are called multiple-level file systems. Such systems have the concept of the current directory. It can be changed by a command.

Many commands are organized to take input from the standard input (the keyboard) and send output to the standard ouput (the terminal screen). Such a program is called a filter. I/O redirection permits input to be taken from a named file rather than the standard input, or output to be sent to a named file instead of to the standard output. A pipe allows the output of one program to be directed as input to another program.

Batch and background processing are similar and refer to jobs being run non-interactively. Background jobs are run while the user is working interactively on another job; batch jobs are run as time and space become available.

Run-time support programs allow the user to read characters from the terminal and send characters to the screen. It also permits data to be moved between primary memory and files. The principal operations on files are open, close, read, and write. Files are referenced by name, using a file control block to store the information about the file.

The assembler uses two passes: the first to generate a symbol table that lists each symbol used and its equivalent numeric address, and the second to translate the statements to binary. It uses a location counter to count through the program to determine the locations occupied by each instruction. Some assemblers have multiple location counters to allow code to be assembled in different blocks or segments. A load-and-go assembler generates absolute binary code directly into memory and executes it immediately. Other assemblers leave the binary form on secondary storage devices for later loading. An assembler detects syntax errors and errors due to double definition or nondefinition of symbols. These errors are indicated on the listing.

An absolute loader reads a binary program from secondary storage to primary storage, making essentially no changes to it. Relocation transforms a binary program that was prepared for loading in one set of locations so that it can be loaded into another set. Relocatable addresses are those operand addresses that change when the program is moved. Absolute addresses do not change. Relocatable binary code is code that contains information to tell the loader which addresses are relocatable. Relocatable symbols are symbols whose value changes when the program moves. Address expressions may be restricted in their use of relocatable symbols so that the final result can be modified when the program is loaded.

When several programs are assembled separately but loaded together, a linking technique must be used. A linkage editor is like another assembly that just binds together references between programs. An entry point to a program is a symbol in that program that is accessible from another program assembled separately. An external symbol to a program is a symbol referenced in that program but defined in another program. Entry points and external symbols must be declared. A linking loader is a combination of a linker and a relocating loader.

The IPL sequence gets the machine started when nothing is running. It loads a small amount of code into fixed locations in memory. This is called booting. It is used to load the operating system.

Problems

6-1 What is the purpose of the boot sequence—what cannot be done without it?

6-2 What techniques could you use to implement a one-pass load-and-go assembler? What restrictions would you enforce on address fields?

6-3 Using a relocatable assembler, what would be the result of assembling those of the following code segments that can be assembled? Assume one instruction per word. Indicate relocatable addresses.

a

```
            LOAD    B
    B       ADD     ONE
    ONE     STORE   B
            HALT
            END
```

b

```
    D       LOAD    TEN
            ADD     FOUR
```

```
            BRANCH    D
    TEN     WORD      10
    FOUR    WORD      4
    D       STORE     E
            HALT
    E       BSS       1
            END
```

c

```
    N       EQU       10
            LOAD      TEN
            STORE     D
            ADD       FOUR
            STORE     E
            HALT
    E       BSS       N
    TEN     ADDR      N
    D       BSS       1
    FOUR    WORD      3
            END
```

d

```
    B       BRANCH    A
            BSS       2+B
    A       LOAD      C
            HALT
            END
```

6-4 Which symbols are relocatable and which are absolute in the following section of code?

```
    A       MPY       C
            ADD       100
    B       EQU       A+10
    E       SUB       D
            BRANCH    F
    G       BSS       3
    F       ADD       G
    D       EQU       E-A
    C       EQU       7
    H       EQU       C+11
            MPY       H
            ADD       G+1
    I       EQU       C+F
```

6-5 Indicate what information the assembler would have to pass to a linking loader that is to be used to handle the result of assembling the program segments below:

a

```
            EXTRNL    SQRT,TEN
    START   LOAD      TEN
            ADD       TEN+2
```

```
            CALL      SQRT
            STORE     A+3
            SUB       TEN+1
            CALL      SQRT
            BRANCH    B
    A       BSS       7
    B       STORE     A+1
            END
```

b

```
            EXTRNL    X,Y,Z,SIN,SQRT
            ENTRY     SUB1,SUB2
    SUB2    LOAD      Y
            CALL      SQRT
            CALL      SIN
    SUB1    ADD       Z
            CALL      SQRT
            CALL      SIN
            ADD       X
            CALL      SIN
            CALL      SIN
            STORE     X
            HALT
            END
```

6-6 Suppose that a linking loader processes the following three programs. Assume one 1-address instruction per word. The programs have the following characteristics:

Program 1

Entry points: 0

External identifier use:

READ used at 2

SQRT used at 7, 19

PRINT used at 25

Length: 32 words

Program 2

Entry points: 1

Names and values: SQRT with value 1

External identifier use: TYPE used at 56

Length: 64

Program 3

Entry points: 3

Names and values: PRINT 17, TYPE 21, READ 45

Length: 100

Assuming that these programs are loaded, starting at location 0, in the order given and immediately following one another, give the memory map and locations modified by the linker. *Note:* The value of an entry point is its address relative to location 0 of that program. In which programs could the symbols SQRT, READ, PRINT, and TYPE be declared external?

6-7 Which of the following instruction addresses are invalid if relocatable code is to be generated and the loader is capable of single positive relocation by any one value? Give the reason.

```
        EXTRNL  A,E
B       LOAD    D
        ADD     B+4
        STORE   A-B
C       LOAD    B
        SUB     C-B
        STORE   3*E-2*A
        STORE   3*C-2*F
        STORE   C-A
        STORE   C*A
D       BSS     3
F       BSS     2
        END
```

Programming Problems

When preparing a program that depends on specific codes or other information, that information should be made parametric or placed in a table so that the program can be changed very easily should the codes or other information change. The following programming exercises illustrate this and provide practice in using assembly language. These can be programmed for most computers.

6-8 Suppose a string of N bytes contains $2N$ decimal digits. Write a code to convert the string into a string of $2N$ ASCII-encoded bytes containing those digits.

6-9 Suppose the last nibble (4-bit group) of the string in Problem 6-8 indicates the sign—10 for positive and 11 for negative values. Perform the conversion so that an ASCII-encoded sign is placed in the first byte of the resulting string.

6-10 Write a program to *translate* a string of N bytes into another string of N bytes, where a 256-byte *translation table* is used to specify the character correspondence. A translation table specifies, in the nth entry, the byte to be substituted for the byte whose value as an unsigned binary integer is n.

6-11 Suppose that the translation table in Problem 6-10 is *one-to-one,* that is, each 8-bit code is translated to a unique code. Write code to generate the *inverse table,* that is, one which when used in the code for Problem 6-10 will convert the output back to its original form.

6-12 Write a code to convert a string of N bytes into a string of $2N$ hexadecimal digits using ASCII encoding.

6-13 Write a code to convert a string of N bytes into a string of $4N$ ASCII characters. Each group of four should contain a space followed by a 3-digit octal representation of the byte.

6-14 Write a code to convert an 8-bit byte into a 3-digit decimal value in ASCII.

Programming Problems for CP/M and 8080 or the IBM PC

6-15 Write a program to input characters from the console (code 1 with a system call) until a carriage return is entered. Interpret the backspace character as an instruction to delete the last character and control-U as an instruction to delete the whole line typed thus far (in the same way that the line input function handles these characters). Also interpret control-A followed by a decimal digit as an instruction to duplicate the last character the number of times indicated by the digit. When the carriage return is entered, output the resulting line to the terminal using the print-line function, code 9.

6-16 Write a program that will read a file from disk, assuming that it contains text with lines terminated with a carriage return and line-feed character pair. Print each line, one at a time, on the console (using the print-line function, code 9) and then wait for any character to be entered from the console (code-1 function). Stop when the last record has been read from the file.

6-17 Write a program that will copy one file to another, but that will not copy any record whose first byte is binary 0.

6-18 A popular program for a system with pipes is the "TEE" program. The TEE program accepts a file name as an argument and reads characters from the standard input, placing them on the standard output and also storing them in the named file. This can be used to simultaneously watch the output of a program on the screen and make a copy in a file. Thus

```
PROG        |TEE FILENAME
```

executes the command PROG and pipes its output as input to the TEE program. This is both output to the screen and copied to the file. Write a TEE program if you are using a system with a pipe facility.

CHAPTER 7

CONDITIONAL ASSEMBLY AND MACROS

It is important to subdivide a program into a number of modules, each of which is relatively self-contained and small enough to be easily understood. This can be done by commenting and exercising a great deal of discipline in the programming process, but the use of subprograms (discussed in Chapter 5) and macros (to be discussed in this chapter) not only aids the programmer in achieving the goal, it helps enforce some of the objectives. Macros provide a technique for naming a section of code and invoking that code by giving its name. In this respect, they are similar to subprograms. They differ from subprograms in that the name is replaced by the named code where the macro is used, rather than causing a branch to a section of code. This replacement is done before or during the assembly process, as a result of which a macro that is used more than once takes more memory space than a subprogram of which only one copy is loaded. Although macros are usually faster, since there is no overhead for a branch to the subprogram, this is usually not an important factor; the choice between a macro and a subprogram is normally made on the basis of other factors, which will be discussed.

Conditional assembly refers to mechanisms that permit the optional assembly of sections of code only if certain conditions are met. This feature is important when one program is written for execution on several systems or under different conditions at different times. Conditional assembly allows only those parts that are needed to be assembled. This permits the user to have one version of a code for several purposes and makes maintenance, updating, and documentation much easier. Conditional assembly also lets the user specify repetitive constructs, such as tables, very easily and naturally at assembly time. When conditional assembly is coupled with macros, we get a very powerful tool for generating large codes efficiently.

7.1 CONDITIONAL ASSEMBLY

It is impossible to discuss all possible variations on the general theme of conditional assembly, so in this section we shall content ourselves with a discussion of the general ideas. A conditional assembly, as the name implies, is a method in which the assembly code can be suppressed if certain conditions are met. This can be used in code outside of macros, although it tends to find its greatest use inside macro definitions. It can be used to allow one piece of code to take care of several variants of the same basic problem. The essential feature of conditional assembly is the ability to test for given conditions on symbols, such as whether they are defined and whether expressions involving them are zero or positive. A typical conditional assembly pseudo has the form

```
IF     condition
{to be assembled if condition is true}
...
ENDIF
```

where "condition" is a logical expression involving symbols and/or constants. If the condition is not met, the block of code between the IF and the line containing ENDIF is not assembled. This is very similar to an **if** statement in a high-level language, but the decision is made before run time instead of at run time, so that the code actually loaded into memory reflects the result of the decision and cannot be changed without reassembly. Many conditional assemblers also allow an ELSE statement so that alternates can be selected.

In some cases, a similar effect can be achieved using conditional branches at execution time. For example, suppose the symbol N is to be equated to a table size for use in an assembler and we wish to program a loop to examine each table entry. Suppose, also, that the table may have size 0. We could use code of the form

```
        LOAD    =N        Value of symbol N to Accumulator
        BLE     SKIP      Branch around if N ≤ 0
        LXI     X,N       Load index X with immediate
                          value N
LOOP    ...               Code for body of loop
        BCT     X,LOOP    Decrement index, branch if
                          nonzero
SKIP    NOP               End of code to look at table
                          entries
```

Alternatively, we could replace the first two lines and the last to get

```
        IF      N>0
        LXI     X,N
LOOP     ...
         BCT      X,LOOP
        ENDIF
```

The latter form saves two instructions at execution time and does not assemble the loop if N is not greater than 0.

In other cases, conditional assembly provides facilities that cannot be matched easily by run-time code. An example of this is the use of conditionals to generate the appropriate entry in a table according to keywords. Suppose, for example, that we are writing a program for plotting "graphs" on an output terminal like a typewriter, and that this program is to be added to the program library of a number of computer installations. Some of those installations may have one type of terminal unit, others another. There are some minor character code differences between units, although they mostly use the same character set. We should use a final character code table to convert from the internal representation used by the program to an external code for the particular device. If we use an 8-bit internal form, the table will be a list of 256 different values. For example, it could have the form

```
TABLE     BYTE     40       Code for 0
          BYTE     31       Code for 1
          BYTE     32       Code for 2
          ...
          BYTE     127      Code for 255
```

so that the internal form for, say, 2 can be looked up by referencing TABLE+2 to get the external form 32. Suppose, for example, that the internal code 65 (decimal) is to be converted to 173 for teletypes, but to 45 for whiz-bang terminals. This means that we want one entry in the table for a teletype, another for a whiz-bang. We can use a globally known symbol whose value is "TTY" if we are assembling for a teletype, or "WBTRM" if we are assembling for a whiz-bang. This variable can be set by changing a line at the start of the assembly to the appropriate value. (If string variables are not allowed as values of symbols, an integer can be used equally well.) The sixty-sixth entry in the table could be coded in the form

```
IF        TYPE='TTY'
  BYTE      173
  ELSE
  IF        TYPE='WBTRM'
  BYTE      45
  ELSE
  MSG       INCORRECT TYPE
  ENDIF
ENDIF
```

This set of lines generates one line to be assembled. The line is BYTE 173 if TYPE is 'TTY', BYTE 45 if TYPE is 'WBTRM', or MSG INCORRECT TYPE if TYPE is anything else. If the mnemonic MSG is unknown to the assembler, it will cause an error message during assembly, indicating the error in the value of TYPE.

A conditional assembler is a programming language that can be used to generate assembly language. Its operands are the assembly-time values of symbols. Usually we think of these as corresponding to memory addresses and constants, but it is convenient to permit these values to change during assembly in some cases. The SET directive is used for this purpose. The SET directive is related to EQU in that it assigns a value to a symbol. However, it is done in the sense of assignment, and a symbol may be assigned a value in one SET statement and then have this value changed by a later SET statement. For example,

```
MEMSZ    SET    300
MEMSZ    SET    MEMSZ/3
REG1     BSS    MEMSZ
MEMSZ    SET    MEMSZ*2
REG2     BSS    MEMSZ
```

achieves the same effect as the code

```
REG1     BSS    100
REG2     BSS    200
```

First it sets the symbol MEMSZ to a value of 300. Then that value is changed to 100 and a block of 100 locations is allocated to REG1. Finally, MEMSZ is changed to 200, and 200 locations are allocated to REG2.

It is important to understand that SET is a directive and is handled by the assembler at assembly time when the statement is processed. It does not generate any code and has no effect at execution time. For examples, in code of the form

```
XX       SET    20
         code to execute the following loop 15 times
           (part of the body of a program loop)
XX       SET XX + 1
           (rest of body of program loop)
           end of loop
YY       SET    XX
```

the value of the symbol YY is 21 because the assembler reads the code sequentially from top to bottom, though the body of the loop around the XX SET XX + 1 pseudo is executed fifteen times after it has been assembled.

Advanced conditional assemblers also allow looping constructs. For example, we could have the construct

```
A        SET      1
         WHILE    A<4
         WORD A
A        SET      A + 1
         ENDWHILE
```

which would expand to the equivalent of

```
WORD 1
WORD 2
WORD 3
```

Here we see one of the uses of SET symbols. More examples of conditional assembly will be presented in subsequent sections.

7.2 MACROS

Frequently, the same or a similar piece of code must be used in many different parts of the program. There are obvious advantages to providing tools such that the same piece of code does not have to be written out each time it is used. One obvious approach is to write the program once and to provide a mechanism for creating a copy whenever needed. This approach is called using a *macro*. For example, suppose we wish to exchange the contents of locations P and Q at several places in the code for a one-address machine. We may want to write the sequence

```
LOAD     P
STORE    TEMP
LOAD     Q
STORE    P
LOAD     TEMP
STORE    Q
```

in several places. If, instead, we could define a "name" for this group of instructions and just write that name, we could save a considerable amount of writing time. In many assemblers this can be done with a sequence of the form

```
SWAPPQ   MACRO                     Swap the values of P and Q
         LOAD     P
         STORE    TEMP
         LOAD     Q
         STORE    P
         LOAD     TEMP
         STORE    Q
         MEND     SWAPPQ    End of definition of SWAPPQ
```

The definition starts with the pseudo MACRO, containing the name of the macro in its location field. Then the body of the definition appears, followed by the pseudo MEND. (The repetition of the name of the macro in the MEND pseudo is not usually required but is optional in many macro assemblers and helps to make the code more readable.) After this definition has been given, the programmer can write SWAPPQ as the mnemonic and have it replaced by the body of the definition.

The basic function of macros appears to be simply to save the programmer the job of rewriting. However, if the name of the macro is chosen so that is has significance to the reader, the macro also helps in the documentation process. The principle of a macro facility is that a *definition* of an input form can be written so that each time the input form is used, it is replaced by its definition. Elaborate facilities allow for substitution of actual parameter values for *formal parameters* (similar to the arguments of a subprogram). Macro facilities are used not only in assemblers but in all forms of text processing. A macro processor should be viewed as a translator that inputs one string of characters and outputs another.[1] If it is part of an assembler, the string it outputs is fed straight into the assembler. The *macro processing* is actually done prior to the assembly, so we can now distinguish three phases of program processing: macro expansion time, assembly time, and execution time. Normally, macro expansion is done in the same step as assembly, so that the user is unaware of the difference, but it is not logically necessary that they be handled in the same step.

In assembly language, the macro definition is usually accomplished with the pseudos MACRO and MEND. The first appears in front of the definition, whereas the latter follows it. In effect, a macro definition defines a new instruction to the assembler; this is called a *macro instruction*. The name of the macro instruction is placed in the location field of the MACRO pseudos (or, in some assemblers, in the operation field of the following line). Thus the XYZ can be defined by

```
XYZ        MACRO
             LINE 1
             LINE 2
             ...
             LINE N
           MEND        XYZ
```

where LINE1 to LINE N are *any* lines except for lines containing MEND. It is not necessary to the macro expander that these lines be valid instructions; only the assembler is sensitive to that qualification. Each time XYZ appears in the instruction field, the N lines given will replace it. In the following sections we will discuss some of the additional features that are added to macros.

7.2.1 Parameters in Macros

Since the macro substitution is done before assembly, it is possible to change the symbols in the code that makes up the macro definition. Our earlier example gave code to swap the contents of locations P and Q. Clearly a macro that permitted the contents of any two locations to be swapped would be much more useful. If we replace the earlier definition with

```
SWAP       MACRO     P,Q          Swap the values of P and Q
           LOAD      P
```

[1]General-purpose macro processors are described in a number of books and articles. Further reading can be found in P. J. Brown, *Macro Processors,* John Wiley & Sons, New York, 1974; W. Waite, "A Language Independent Macro Processor," *Communications of the Association for Computing Machinery,* July 1967, pp. 433–440; B. Leavenworth, "Syntax Macros," ibid., November 1966, pp. 790–792; and C. Strachey, "A General Purpose Macro Processor," *Computer Journal,* October 1965, pp. 225–241.

```
STORE    TEMP
LOAD     Q
STORE    P
LOAD     TEMP
STORE    Q
MEND     SWAP
```

we define the symbols P and Q to be parameters in the macro definition. Symbols are declared to be parameters by placing them after the macro pseudo. (In some macro assemblers, parameters are distinguished from other symbols by use of a special initial character. For example, in the IBM 370 macro assembler, macro parameter symbols must start with the & character.) If the macro SWAP, defined above, is used by writing SWAP X,Y we get the expansion

```
LOAD     X
STORE    TEMP
LOAD     Y
STORE    X
LOAD     TEMP
STORE    Y
```

Parameters can be used in any place in a macro definition. For example, suppose that we need a piece of code to increment a cell by N (with N an integer) frequently. We want a shorthand notation for

```
LOAD     A
ADD      =N
STORE    A
```

We can define a macro with two parameters, A and N, as follows

```
INCR     MACRO    A,N
           LOAD     A
           ADD      =N
           STORE    A
         MEND     INCR
```

This is used by writing INCR followed by the two actual parameter values (arguments) desired. For example,

```
INCR     XCOUNT,3
```

expands to

```
LOAD     XCOUNT
ADD      =3
STORE    XCOUNT
```

It is important to realize that the arguments to macros are nothing but character strings, in this case XCOUNT and 3. If we had written

```
        INCR      TEMP+2,W/2
```

we would get the expansion

```
        LOAD      TEMP+2
        ADD       =W/2
        STORE     TEMP+2
```

as the result of expanding the macro call. This result is then processed by the assembler whether or not it is valid assembly language. (Most assemblers do not allow expressions in literals.)

Because arguments are treated as character strings during expansion, formal parameters may appear anywhere in the definition (they are not limited to the address field). For example,

```
CNFUSE    MACRO     A,B,C,D
A         B         C         D
          MEND      CNFUSE
```

can be used by writing

```
          CNFUSE LAB,OP,ADR,COMMENT
```

which will expand to

```
LAB       OP        ADR       COMMENT
```

If a macro defines a symbol in the location field, there should not be more than one instance of that particular symbol in a location field; otherwise we will have multiple definition of the symbol. Sometimes it is necessary to use a symbol in a location field inside a macro definition so that the generated code can include a branch. For example,

```
ABS       MACRO                 Set the accumulator positive
            BPL       Y
            CHSIGN              Change sign of accumulator
Y           NOP
          MEND      ABS
```

Unfortunately, if this macro is used more than once, the label Y will be doubly defined. This can be overcome by making Y a formal parameter and giving it a new name every time the macro is used. However, this is unnecessary in many macro processors, as they provide a mechanism for generating unique program labels in each macro expansion. Not untypical of this process is the technique used in the IBM 370 assembler, which has a *system variable* SYSNDX whose value is a 4-digit decimal string starting at 0001 and increasing by 1 for each macro use (expansion). Since a decimal number is not a valid address, a mechanism for *concatenating* such a string with another name is provided. The period character is used to indicate this in the 370 assembler. For example, if A and B are macro parameters whose actual values are P1 and Q4, A.B is replaced with P1Q4. (Note that if we wrote AB, the macro processor would view this as the symbol AB, not as A followed by B.) Using such a mechanism, the example above could be coded as

```
ABS         MACRO                     Set accumulator positive
              BPL      Y.SYSNDX
              CHSIGN                  Change sign of accumulator
Y.SYSNDX      NOP
            MEND       ABS
```

If this is called by

```
            LOAD       A
            ABS
            ADD        B
            ABS
```

and if these are the first macros to be expanded, the expansion is

```
            LOAD       A
            BPL        Y0001
            CHSIGN
Y0001       NOP
            ADD        B
            BPL        Y0002
            CHSIGN
Y0002       NOP
```

A different symbol is generated in each of the two location fields because the system variable SYSNDX has been increased by 1 between the two expansions. If more than one location field symbol is needed in the same expansion, different characters can be concatenated in front of SYSNDX. For example:

```
MX          MACRO      A,B,C          Max of A and B to C
              LOAD       A
              SUB        B
              BPL        X.SYSNDX
              LOAD       B            B larger
              BRANCH     Y.SYSNDX
X.SYSNDX    LOAD         A            A larger
Y.SYSNDX    STORE        C
            MEND       MAX
```

If this is used as, say, the thirty-fourth macro expansion, the two generated names will be X0034 and Y0034. Other macro assemblers permit the programmer to declare symbols to be local to the macro definition.

Macro assemblers differ in details, but all include definition pseudos such as MACRO and MEND and a means of actual parameter substitution. The parameters are specified in the address field of the macro call, separated by various characters. These separation characters are called *break* characters and may be restricted to commas (in some assemblers) or may include other characters, such as the parentheses and other punctuation. At definition time, each dummy parameter is indicated by a valid symbol; at expansion time, all occurrences of the symbol are replaced by the character-string argument specified in the macro call.

Keyword Parameters Complex macro definition can involve a number of parameters, many of which do not need to be specified on every use of the macro. Consider, for example, a macro to do a three-address addition on a register machine such as the IBM 370. It could take the form

```
ADD3      MACRO    A,B,C,R
            LOAD      R,A      Load register R with A.
            ADD       R,B      Add B to register R.
            STORE     R,C      Store result in C.
          MEND     ADD3
```

The arguments are the three addresses for the operands and the name of the register to be used as an accumulator. This might be called with ADD3 X,Y,Z,R0 if register R0 is to be used. We might decide that we want to use R0 most of the time and would rather not specify it. *Keyword parameters* allow just that. If we replace the first line of the definition of ADD3 above with the statement

```
ADD3      MACRO    A=,B=,C=,R=R0
```

the arguments can be specified by name. For example, we could call the macro by writing

```
ADD3      B=Y,C=Z,A=X,R=R0
```

The arguments are substituted according to their names. Note that the arguments no longer have to be in the order specified in the definition. The great advantage of keyword parameters is that they do not even have to be specified. If we omit an argument, the *default value,* the value following the "=" in the definition, is substituted in its place. For example, if we write ADD 3 A=X,B=Y,C=Z with the above definition, R is set to R0 as desired. Some macro processors allow keyword and *positional* parameters (the type we have been using up to now) to be mixed. In that case, the positional parameters should appear first. Perhaps the most convenient definition for the above example is to make the first line ADD3 MACRO A,B,C,R=R0.

Then we can write ADD3 X,Y,Z to use R0 as the register, or ADD3 X,Y,Z,R=R5 to change it to R5.

Conditional assembly can be used in this type of macro to achieve greater flexibility. For example, suppose we would like to be able to use a register name for the parameter C, and in that case get a shorter code. We would like ADD3 P,Q,R3 to generate

```
LOAD    R3,P
ADD     R3,Q
```

thus generating and leaving the result in R3. If a test can be made to see whether a symbol is the name of a register (which is usually possible in macro assemblers for register machines), we can write something like

```
ADD3    MACRO    A,B,C,R=R0
        IF       C is register
          LOAD   C,A           Load register C with A.
          ADD    C,B           Add B to register C.
        ELSE
          LOAD   R,A           Load register R with A.
          ADD    R,B           Add B to register R.
          STORE  R,C           Store result in C.
        ENDIF
        MEND     ADD3
```

7.2.2 Nested Calls

In many cases it is convenient to define one macro in terms of previously defined macros. We refer to this as a nested call, as one macro calls another. If the macro expansion is viewed as a character-string operation, it is easy to understand the steps involved. Consider the two macro definitions

```
COPY       MACRO    FROM,TO,COUNT
             LDX      1,COUNT      Load index 1 with COUNT.
L.SYSNDX     LOAD     FROM-1(1)    Copy one element
             STORE    TO-1(1)      from FROM to TO.
             BCT      1,L.SYSNDX   Decrement index 1 and
           MEND     COPY.          repeat loop if nonzero.
```

and

```
SWITCH     MACRO    BUF1,BUF2,SPARE,LENGTH
             COPY     BUF1,SPARE,LENGTH
             COPY     BUF2,BUF1,LENGTH
             COPY     SPARE,BUF2,LENGTH
           MEND     SWITCH
```

When the macro SWITCH is called, say by SWITCH A,B,C,L, it first expands to

```
        COPY    A,C,L
        COPY    B,A,L
        COPY    C,B,L
```

and then each COPY is expanded using the first definition to get

```
        LDX       1,L          Load index 1 with L.
L0001     LOAD    A-1(1)       Copy one element
          STORE   C-1(1)       from A to C.
          BCT     1,L0001      Decrement index 1 and
                               repeat loop if nonzero.
        ...
```

When arguments are handed from one macro to another, it is sometimes desirable to pass a sequence of symbols separated by commas as a single argument. Unfortunately, the commas indicate the separation of arguments. A convention of placing a special character around a list of arguments to make them into a single argument is used. Many macro assemblers use parentheses for this, although some use quotes. Thus the argument list A,(B,C,D),(E,F) consists of three arguments. The first is A, the second is B,C,D, and the third E,F. When the argument is passed into the macro, the outer parenthese are stripped off to leave the list that is substituted as a string for the dummy parameter. For example, we could define

```
CALL    MACRO    SUB,PARMLST
          JSR      SUB
          WORD     PARMLST
        MEND     CALL
```

If this is used by writing

```
        CALL     SOLVE,(A,B,N,OUT)
```

we get the expansion

```
        JSR      SOLVE
        WORD     A,B,N,OUT
```

This feature can be used to get some fairly elaborate facilities in assembly language. Let us suppose that SIN and COS are the addresses of two subprograms that form the sine and cosine of the accumulator, leaving the result in the accumulator. Consider the definitions.

```
COS     MACRO    A,B
          A        B
        CALL       COS
        MEND     COS
```

```
SIN     MACRO    A,B
          A        B
          CALL     SIN
        MEND     SIN

ACC     MACRO                 Null macro definition!
        MEND     ACC
```

The macro call SIN ACC simply expands as CALL SIN. However, we can also write COS SIN,ACC, which expands first to

```
SIN      ACC
CALL     COS
```

and then to

```
CALL     SIN
CALL     COS
```

The macro call SIN SIN,(SIN,(COS,ACC)) expands to

```
CALL     COS
CALL     SIN
CALL     SIN
CALL     SIN
```

The IBM 370 macro assembler uses an alternative approach to lists as arguments. It treats them as arrays of arguments and allows the user to specify the *I*th element of a list. Other macro assemblers allow expansions to be repeated with an argument substitution for each member of a list.

7.2.3 Nested Definition

When a macro definition occurs inside another macro definition (a *nested definition*), it is possible to define macros by writing macro calls. For example:

```
DEFINE    MACRO      NAME
  NAME      MACRO      PARMS
              CALL       NAME
              WORD         PARMS
            MEND       NAME
          MEND       DEFINE
```

If this is used by writing DEFINE SOLVE, the expansion is

```
SOLVE      MACRO      PARMS
             CALL       SOLVE
             WORD       PARMS
           MEND       SOLVE
```

which defines a call sequence for a subprogram SOLVE.

7.2.4 Recursive Macros

In nested calls, a macro expansion generates a call on another macro. If it generates a call on itself, we have a recursive use of macros. To avoid an infinite loop, conditional assembly must also be used to terminate the recursion at some point. We will illustrate this with an example. Consider a macro that is to construct a table of powers of two. We would like to be able to write

```
           POWER2   16
```

and get the expansion

```
           WORD     1
           WORD     2
           WORD     4
           WORD     8
           WORD     16
```

A recursive macro definition that does this is

```
POWER2     MACRO      N
             IF           N ≠ 0
               POWER2  N/2          (Expressions are integral.)
               WORD  N
             ENDIF
           MEND        POWER2
```

The conditional IF is assumed to test parameter N to see if it is not 0; if it is not 0, POWER2 is called recursively with N equal to half its earlier value. This arithmetic is assumed to be integral, so that the final division of 1 by 2 yields 0. If N is 0 in the IF statement, the next two lines are skipped, and no expansion takes place. Hence POWER2 is called with N to equal 16, 8, 4, 2, 1, and 0. (Actually, the arguments are 16, 16/2, 16/2/2, . . . , and 16/2/2/2/2/2, since the substitution is a string operation.)

This macro can also be handled iteratively if there is a looping facility. The following definition uses the SET pseudo to count through a loop.

```
POWER2     MACRO      N
M            SET        1
             WHILE      M≤N
             WORD       M
```

```
M           SET       2*M
            ENDWHILE
          MEND      POWER
```

7.2.5 Redefinition of Macros

Some macro assemblers allow macros to be redefined. This can be an effective tool in a number of situations. One of the most common situations occurs when the programmer wishes the first use of a macro to cause an expansion different to other uses. This often happens when it is necessary to define some data that is to be used by all expansions, or when some code is to be generated once if a macro is used one or more times, but not generated if the macro is not used at all. Frequently, programmers prepare a large set of macros for handling common tasks and automatically include the complete set in every program they write if the program needs one or more of them. (Indeed, many systems make this simple by providing an "include" statement that automatically copies the contents of a named file into the code prior to assembly or compilation.)

We will illustrate this with an example. Suppose that we wish to write macros PUSH and POP, which will move the contents of the accumulator of a simple one-address machine with indexing to a stack to be simulated in memory. We would like the first use of PUSH or POP to allocate some space in memory for the stack, say 100 locations. We could code PUSH in the following way:

```
PUSH      MACRO
          ALLOC
          PUSH1
ALLOC     MACRO
          MEND      ALLOC
          MEND      PUSH
ALLOC     MACRO
          BRANCH    *+100
STACK     BSS       100
          MEND      ALLOC
PUSH1     MACRO
          Code to move accumulator to stack
          MEND      PUSH1
```

The first use of PUSH allocates a block of 100 locations and then redefines the macro ALLOC to be a null macro. POP can be defined in the same way, so that the first use of PUSH or POP redefines ALLOC.

7.3 CONDITIONAL ASSEMBLY AND MACROS IN CP/M AND DOS

The format of conditional assembly directives and macros in the CP/M assembler for the 8080 and the IBM PC assembler for the 8086/88 are very similar, so we can discuss them at the same time. In this section we will describe the features of conditional assembly and macros common to both systems.

First, it should be noted that the macro features are not in the smallest assemblers for either machine. The standard CP/M assembler for the 8080, ASM, provides only minimal conditional assembly features using the directives IF and ENDIF. If additional conditional assembly directives or macro capabilities are needed, one of the several macro assemblers available for the 8080 must be used. Some CP/M systems have a macro assembler called MAC that is *upward-compatible* from ASM, that is, code that will assemble under ASM will also assemble under MAC in an identical manner.[2] It has additional conditional assembly features and a macro facility. For conditional assembly, an ELSE directive is added. The small assembler for IBM PCs with 64K of memory does not support macros, but it does have the conditional assembly directives. It does not include the looping constructs. The macro assembler MASM runs on machines with 96K of memory and includes all features found in ASM plus looping constructs and macros. Everything we have said about the use of ASM so far applies to MASM, and the latter can be used in place of ASM if the machine has sufficient memory.

The general format of a conditional assembly section is

```
IF              expression
code section 1
ELSE
code section 2
ENDIF
```

which causes code section 1 to be assembled if the expression satisfies a condition that depends on the system, or code section 2 to be assembled otherwise. If the code section 2 is empty, the ELSE can be omitted. In MAC, the expression must have its least significant bit equal to 1 for code section 1 to be assembled. In MASM, the expression must be nonzero. The expression can be any of the usual address expressions discussed in Section 6.3.1 or Section 6.3.2, respectively. It can include relational operators such as GT (meaning Greater Than) between expressions, as in 2*A GT B. The logical operators can be used to combine conditions or invert them. MASM also provides additional forms of the IF statement. IFE, for example, assembles code section 1 if the expression *is* 0. MASM also permits symbols and arguments to macros to be tested to see whether they have been defined, whether they are null strings, or whether they are equal to other strings. The MASM conditional IF directives are

```
IF        expression   true if expression not 0
IFE       expression   true if expression is 0
IF1                    true if pass 1
IF2                    true if pass 2
IFDEF     symbol       true if symbol defined
IFNDEF    symbol       true if symbol not defined
IFB       <arg>        true if argument is null (blank)
```

[2] CP/M MAC Macro Assembler: Language Manual and Applications Guide, Digital Research, Pacific Grove, CA, 1977.

```
IFNB        <arg>          true if argument not null
IFIDN       <str1>,<str2>      true if string1 = string2
IFDIF       <str1>,<str2>      true if string1 < >string2
```

The angle brackets, "<" and ">", must be present to delimit the argument or string. Not all of the facilities are available in CP/M MAC, but it does allow the operator NULL to be used to test whether a symbol is null. The value of NULL Q is true (1) if Q is a null string.

Repetition is possible using the directive pairs REPT/ENDM, IRPC/ENDM, and IRP/ENDM. Each of these pairs causes a block of code to be assembled several times. The address field of the REPT pseudo indicates the number of times that the code between it and its matching ENDM is to be assembled. For example, to generate a table of powers of 2 from 1 to 128 we can code the following for MAC:

```
Q       SET     1
        REPT    8
        DB      Q       ;Assemble byte for next power
Q       SET     2*Q     ;Double Q
        ENDM
```

The code the MASM is essentially the same, except that the SET directive is represented by the "=" character, so the code would be:

```
Q       =       1
        REPT    8
        DB      Q       ;Assemble byte for next power
Q       =       2*Q     ;Double Q
        ENDM
```

The IRPC pseudo, standing for Indefinite RePeat over Character, has two address fields. The first is a symbol whose value is set to each character in the string in the second field in turn. The code between the IRPC and its matching ENDM is assembled the same number of times as the number of characters in the second address field. Thus the code

```
        IRPC    R,987654
        DB      R
        ENDM
```

causes the code

```
        DB      9
        DB      8
        DB      7
        DB      6
        DB      5
        DB      4
```

to be assembled. IRP is similar to IRPC, but it replaces its first parameter with character strings from a list given as the value of the second parameter. A list is constructed by separating the elements with commas and surrounding it with the characters < and >. For example, IRP XD,<P2,A+2,RK> will cause the code between it and its matching ENDM to be repeated three times, with XD taking the values P2, A+2, and RK on successive expansions. Thus

```
        IRP     SYM,<X1,Y1,Z1>
SYM     DW      1
        ENDM
```

expands to

```
X1      DW      1
Y1      DW      1
Z1      DW      1
```

The pseudo EXITM can be used inside any of the repetitive blocks (and in the macro block discussed below). It causes the current block to be terminated immediately.

The macro pseudos are MACRO and ENDM. The code

```
NAME    MACRO   P1,P2
        code for definition
        ENDM
```

defines a macro with two parameters. Any occurrences of P1 and/or P2 in the definition as symbols are replaced by the character strings provided when the macro NAME is used. A simple macro to call a subprogram with a parameter following the CALL can be defined as

```
CALLP   MACRO   SUB,PARM
        CALL    SUB         ;Subprogram name
        DW      PARM        ;Subprogram parameter
        ENDM
```

With this definition, CALLP SIN,X expands to

```
        CALL    SIN
        DW      X
```

A comma-separated list of arguments can be passed as an argument by surrounding it with the < and > characters. For example, with the definition above, CALLP WRITE,<P,Q,R> expands to

```
        CALL    WRITE
        DW      P,Q,R
```

Nested calls of macros are allowed, and macros can be redefined.

If the value of a parameter is to be concatenated with another alphanumeric character, the two must be joined using the & character. For example, if the macro

```
TWO      MACRO   N
TWO&N    DW      1 SHL N
         ENDM
```

is used in the form TWO 3, we get the expansion

```
TWO3     DW      1 SHL 3
```

whose address field evaluates to 8 (1 shifted left three places).

If we wanted to generate a table of powers of 2 of the form

```
TWO0     DW      1
TWO1     DW      2
         ...
TWO7     DW      128
```

we might be temped to try

```
S        SET     0
         REPT    8
         TWO     S
S        SET     S+1
         ENDM
```

using the macro just defined. However, this will generate the same symbol TWOS at the start of each of the eight lines generated in the loop, because the character string S is passed to the macro. We want to *force evaluation* of S to get an equivalent numeric character string representing its value before it is passed to the macro. This is done by preceding it with the character %. If the third line of the code immediately above is changed to TWO %S we get the desired expansion, because the string argument passed in to the macro for expansion is not S but a character string containing the decimal representation of S. We could turn this into a macro to generate a table of powers of 2 of any size by surrounding the code with MACRO and ENDM. Thus, if we define

```
TABLE    MACRO   N
S        SET     0
         REPT    N
         TWO     %S
S        SET     S+1
         ENDM
         ENDM
```

the line TABLE 8 expands as before. (In MASM, the SET directive must be replaced with "=".)

Notice that the above macro uses the symbol S and changes its value. If we were to use this macro, we would have to be careful not to use the symbol S elsewhere unless we first set its value to whatever was needed. This problem can be avoided by making S a *local symbol*. In MAC and MASM, symbols can be declared to be local to a particular expansion. The directive LOCAL declares each symbol given in its address field to be local to the macro. Each time the macro is expanded, a different character string is generated to replace the symbol. The replacements take the form ??0001, ??0002, etc., in MAC, and the form ..0001, ..0002, etc., in MASM. Thus we can add the line LOCAL S to the definition of TABLE given above immediately after the MACRO pseudo so that the S used in the macro will not be related to the symbol S used elsewhere.

The use of LOCAL and the % operator is also illustrated in the following example, which causes

```
          VAL       <P1,,P2,P3,,,P4>
```

to expand to

```
P1        EQU       1
P2        EQU       3
P3        EQU       4
P4        EQU       7
```

where each argument value in the list is equated to consecutive integers, omitting null arguments. The macro definitions needed are

```
GEQU      MACRO     NAME,NUM
          IF        NOT NULL NAME      ;This is the MAC version
          IFNB      <NAME>   ;This is the MASM version
NAME      EQU       NUM
          ENDIF
          ENDM

VAL       MACRO     LL
          LOCAL     P,Q
Q         SET       1                  ;This should be = for MASM
          IRP       P,<LL>
          GEQU      P,%Q
Q         SET       Q+1                ;This should be = for MASM
          ENDM
          ENDM
```

The user may wonder why the fifth line of macro VAL, namely GEQU, is not replaced with the body of the macro GEQU directly, thus avoiding the definition of a second macro. The reason GEQU is needed is that the conversion of an argument to a numeric string using the % operator occurs only when the argument is passed to another macro. Thus, if we had replaced GEQU with the line P EQU %Q, the expansion would have included %Q as the character string.

7.4 SUMMARY AND PROBLEMS

Conditional assembly allows sections of code to be skipped by the assembler or assembled several times in a loop that is executed at or before assembly time. The conditional and looping pseudos form a programming language that is executed by the assembler.

A macro is a block of code that can be substituted for its name. A call of a macro causes the substitution to occur before assembly; a call of a subroutine causes a branch to the subprogram at execution time. Macros and subprograms help divide code into self-contained modules that are easy to understand.

Macro processing is a character-string operation. The result is fed to the assembler for assembly. The result may be invalid assembly language, but the macro processor does not care. Actual parameter values (arguments) to macros are character strings separated by special characters, usually commas. If commas or blanks are needed inside an argument string, the string must be surrounded by some parenthesizing characters, often (and). Macro processors provide ways for concatenating arguments with other strings and for generating internal symbols. Some macro processors allow keyword parameters. These are useful when there are many parameters. Default values can then be specified when the macro is defined. Nested macro calls allow one macro to use another as part of its definition. Nested macro definitions allow a macro to define another macro so that each time the outer macro is expanded a new macro is defined.

Problems

7-1 What is assembled by the following code? (Give the answer in assembly language without conditional operations.)

```
S       SET         0
        WHILE       S<6
          IF         S<3
            BYTE    S
          ELSE
            BYTE    6-S
          ENDIF
S         SET       S+1
        ENDWHILE
```

7-2 Suppose that a conditional assembler has IF/ELSE/ENDIF and WHILE/ENDWHILE pseudos that can test logical expressions constructed in the manner of most high-level languages. Write code that will generate a table of increasing powers of 2 except for those values divisible by 8.

7-3 What is generated by the following macro input?

```
TEST      MACRO     X,Y,Z
            CALL    TEST
            WORD    X
            WORD    Y
            WORD    Z
          MEND
          TEST      P+Q,34.5,RR
```

7-4 Suppose that the following definitions have been made:

```
P         MACRO     X,Y,Z
            LEFT    2
            X       Y,Z,Z
          MEND
Q         MACRO     X,Y,Z
            LEFT    1
            X       Y
          MEND
          MACRO     X,Y,Z
            LOAD    A
            X       Y,Z,Z
          MEND
```

What is the result of expanding the following?

```
a         R         ADD,A,1
b         R         Q,STORE,B
c         R         P,Q,STORE
d         R         P,P,P
```

7-5 Design macros for a typical computer that could be used to start and end counting loops, that is, those loops that can be expressed in higher-level language constructs as

do for I ← L **to** M **by** N
. . .
enddo

Assume the existence of suitable instructions, a SET pseudo that can change the numeric value of symbols, and a conversion function C(SYMB) such that if SYMB has the value 15, XX.C(SYMB) becomes the string XX15, where XX could be any string of characters. You may assume that L, M, and N are known numerically at macro expansion time.

MAC and MASM Problems

In each of these problems, the MAC directive SET should be replaced by the MASM directive = to answer the question for MASM. Note that some of these questions use assembly language for the 8080 or 8086/88. This will be rejected by the assembly process for the other machine, but the macro expansion will still take place correctly, since macro expansion is a string-processing operation.

7-6 What does the following code generate?

```
Q       SET     1
R       SET     1
        REPT    8
          DW    R
S         SET   R
R         SET   Q+R
Q         SET   S
          ENDM
```

7-7 What does the following code generate for N = 1, 7, and 17?

```
S       SET     N
        MVI     B,0
        REPT    7
          IF    S AND 1
            MOV   A,C
            ADD   B
            MOV   B,A
          ENDIF
S         SET   S SHR 1
          IF    S GT 0
            MOV   A,C
            RLC
            MOV   C,A
          ENDIF
        ENDM
```

7-8 Write a macro such that LS N expands to N copies of RLC.

7-9 Write a macro such that TAB WHTQR expands to character in the *n*th line is the *n*th

```
W1      DS      1
H2      DS      2
T3      DS      3
Q4      DS      4
R5      DS      5
```

(The number of lines is the number of characters in the argument values passed, and the first character in the *n*th line is the *n*th character.)

CHAPTER **8**

CONTROL OF INPUT-OUTPUT AND CONCURRENT PROCESSES

Input-output devices are very much slower than the central computer, and many schemes are used to avoid a slowing down of the computer while it is controlling input and output. These schemes utilize both complex hardware control units and system programs, so that the user is able to view any I/O device as if it were connected to the computer in a very simple way. In this chapter we will first look at the computer control of very simple I/O devices to see how an effective speed can be maintained. More complex devices introduce only a few additional features, such as the positioning of magnetic tape or disk heads, but the basic principles are the same as those used in the simplest device. Because I/O units usually operate concurrently with CPU processing, we will also look at concurrent processing and the use of the interrupt mechanism to control interactions among concurrent processes.

8.1 DIRECT CONTROL OF INPUT AND OUTPUT BY THE CPU

Early computers and modern low-cost computers use the same control unit that sequences the CPU to control the I/O units, whereas large systems use separate control units, leaving the CPU free to continue the processing of data during an I/O transfer. We will start by considering the simplest scheme so that we can trace the way in which hardware has evolved to meet the demands for greater speed and efficiency.

An I/O device is a combination of electrical and electromechanical components that must be activated in a certain sequence in order to transmit data. The activation of each component is controlled by *control signals* sent to the I/O unit along connecting wires. At the same time, the computer can determine the current state of the I/O unit by means of *sense signals,* which are electrical signals sent back to the computer from the I/O unit. The control signals might specify, for example, "start tape moving," "stop tape," or "rewind tape," while the sense signals might mean "data ready," "tape stopped," or "unit busy." In the simplest of all systems, it is possible for the CPU to send each of the control signals directly to the I/O unit under program control and to test any of the sense signals with conditional branch instructions. First, we will consider a paper-tape reader, not because it is an important device, but because it is simple and illustrates all the principal features of I/O devices.

An eight-channel paper-tape reader contains nine sensing devices, one for each channel and one for the sprocket hole (see Figure 4.3). After a character of 8 bits has been read from the current position of the tape in the reader, the tape must be moved forward. A capstan similar to that on a magnetic tape is often used. A *pinch roller,* or *clutch,* is used to press the paper against the revolving capstan to move it. After it has moved to the next character, a signal can be sensed from the sprocket-hole sensor. This can be tested as a sense signal by the computer to determine that the next character is available to be read. Such a signal is typically named *data ready.* Suppose that we assume that the character currently under the tape read head has already been transmitted to the computer. The sequence of steps necessary to read the next character is as follows:

1 Start tape moving (control signal).
2 Wait until sprocket hole is sensed (sense signal).
3 Stop tape moving (control signal).
4 Transmit character to computer (control signal).

In a simple computer, the first and third lines will be the machine instructions START TAPE and STOP TAPE, whereas the fourth line above will be implemented by a machine instruction READ TAPE that reads the data into the accumulator (or similar register). The third line will be implemented by a conditional branch that tests the "data ready" signal. The machine-level program is

```
        START TAPE
X       BRANCH to X if not Data Ready
        STOP TAPE
        READ TAPE
```

This has to be executed each time that a character has to be read. Unfortunately, it takes up to 100 milliseconds to execute because the tape first has to be moved to the next position. While that is happening, the CPU is executing the conditional branch instruction up to 100,000 times—not a very productive endeavor!

The wait cannot be avoided as long as the CPU is completely controlling the tape reader. It is necessary to introduce additional hardware to control at least part of the tape-reader function so that two processes can execute simultaneously. This hardware forms an additional processor, although it can be very simple. For example, it need do no more than automatically advance the tape to the next character position as soon as a character has been read by the READ TAPE operation. This reduces the program to

```
X       BRANCH to X if not Data Ready
        READ TAPE
```

The READ TAPE operation not only transfers data to the CPU, it also starts the tape moving to the next position. The tape is controlled by a *tape-reader controller* that transmits the data to the CPU when requested and sends control signals to the tape reader to start the tape moving when the data is read and to stop the tape moving when the sprocket hole is sensed. (The "start tape" signal may simply be the inverse of the "stop tape" signal.) It also passes the Data Ready sense signal on to the CPU. While the tape controller is moving the tape, the CPU can continue to execute other code. The CPU will only have to wait if it wants to read a character before the tape has moved to the next character.

8.1.1 Addressing I/O Units

Even the most simple I/O systems have some sort of I/O unit controller, such as the tape controller described above. Since there is usually more than one I/O unit attached to a computer, there has to be a way to indicate which unit is to be used. There are two principal ways in which this is done with direct I/O. The first uses one or more special I/O instructions whose operand address indicates the I/O unit, sometimes called the *port* address. I/O in most INTEL 8000–based systems uses this method. The instructions

```
OUT        address
```

and

```
IN         address
```

transmit the byte of data in the accumulator to the addressed port, and vice versa. The address is a 1-byte quantity, so 256 different ports can be addressed. Usually, at least two ports will be associated with a given device — one for sense and control lines and one for data. For example, port 0 in an INTEL 8080–based system might be the console keyboard data port, and port 1 might contain the Data Ready signal. (The use of port numbers in 8080–based systems is up to the designer of the system and thus depends on the brand of microcomputer in use.) With such an arrangement, the code to read the next keystroke would consist of a loop to read port 1 and test the Data Ready bit until it is a one, followed by a read of port 0, using the code

```
X       IN      1
        ANI     1       ;Test bit 0 (Data Ready bit)
        JZ      X       ;Branch if not ready
        IN      0       ;Data to accumulator
```

The second addressing scheme used is called *memory-mapped* I/O. In this scheme, a set of memory addresses is not used for regular primary memory locations, but instead refers to registers in I/O control units (ports). For example, if the range of memory addresses was from 0 to 65,535 ($2^{16} - 1$), addresses 61,440 to 65,535 (F000 hex to FFFF hex) might be assigned to I/O ports. In this scheme, memory address 61,440 might be the console keyboard data register and 61,441 might be the control register containing the sense and control signals. Instructions to store into and load from those memory addresses can then be used as output and input instructions. A basic loop to read a character from the console keyboard is essentially the same as above except that the IN instructions are replaced by LOAD or MOVE instructions. This type of scheme is used in the PDP-11 and VAX computers.

8.1.2 I/O Buffering and Interrupts

Although the simple controller described earlier can operate in parallel with the CPU, it does not make the job of efficiently utilizing the CPU and the input device easy. For example, if we have a task that is going to read and compute with 1000 characters, taking 10 milliseconds to read each character and a total of 10 seconds to do the computing, it should be possible to keep both the reader and the CPU fully occupied for 10 seconds at the same time, assuming that some computing can be done even before the first character has been read. However, this would require that the input instructions be spaced evenly (in time) throughout the program, so that after exactly 10 milliseconds of computing another READ instruction would be executed. A moment's thought will convince the reader that this is not feasible in most code!

Since there is no way, in general, of knowing exactly at what point in the execution of the computing process the next input character will be available to be READ, it is necessary to provide a signal from the input device to tell the CPU that the character is available. In fact, we already have one: the Data Ready signal. However, it is not reasonable to include an instruction to test this signal after every CPU instruction used for computing (because of the consequent waste of time), so this test must be done automatically and in parallel with the computing. If the Data Ready signal is **true** and if we want to read the next character, we would like the computing process to be interrupted at the end of its next instruction so that we can input a character. To be precise, we would like to have two CPU processes—one that performs the computing on the data and the other that reads characters from the input—and automatically switch between the two processes. When the next character is ready to be input, we would like to *interrupt* the computing process so that the CPU can execute a process to read the next character. Once that character has been read (and the paper-tape movement started automatically), control can return to the computing process.

Typical computers can interrupt on a number of signals from I/O units, such as Data Ready and Error Condition, and on other signals to be discussed in Section 8.2. To handle an interrupt, the CPU has to switch from one process to another when the interrupt occurs. When the interrupt processing is finished, a special instruction, Return from Interrupt, returns control to the program that was executing before the interrupt.

More details on interrupt processing will be given in Section 8.2. In this section we will look at the use of interrupts for I/O processing.

If the program is to achieve better *overlap* of I/O and computation, it is necessary to allow a large number of characters to be read into the computer ahead of the time that they are needed by the CPU process. Then the CPU can get them as soon as they are needed while the reader is reading further characters, so the CPU process will have to wait only if it needs a large number of characters in rapid succession.

Because an interrupt signal can be used to switch processes when a character is ready to be read, we can keep the tape reader busy reading characters as fast as it can by interrupting the CPU for the small amount of time it takes for it to switch processes, read a character, and switch back. However, what do we do with those characters until the program is ready to use them? We must put them somewhere in memory so that the computing process can use them when they are needed. Memory cells used for this purpose are called *buffers*. A set of cells can be allocated as buffers. As each character is read by the input process, it can be stored in the next available buffer location. A *pointer* variable can be used to keep track of the next available location. It retains the address of that location and is called the *buffer input pointer*. If the buffers are in consecutively addressed memory locations, the pointer has only to be incremented after each character has been read. When the CPU process needs a character, it "reads" one from a buffer. This is normally done by calling a subprogram (which has a name like GET-CHARACTER). This subprogram keeps track of the next character to be read from the buffer in another pointer variable, the *buffer output pointer*.

Clearly, we cannot allocate sufficient buffers to handle an arbitrary number of characters, so at some time the input process will run out of buffers and the buffer input pointer will be pointing to the location beyond the set of buffers. However, as the CPU processes characters, the buffer location from which they are obtained becomes free and should be reused. This suggests the use of a *circular* arrangement of buffers, as shown in Figure 8-1. Here the buffers have addresses B to B+N−1, and location B logically follows B+N−1. As the interrupt-driven input process reads characters, it

FIGURE 8-1 Circular arrangement of 12 buffers

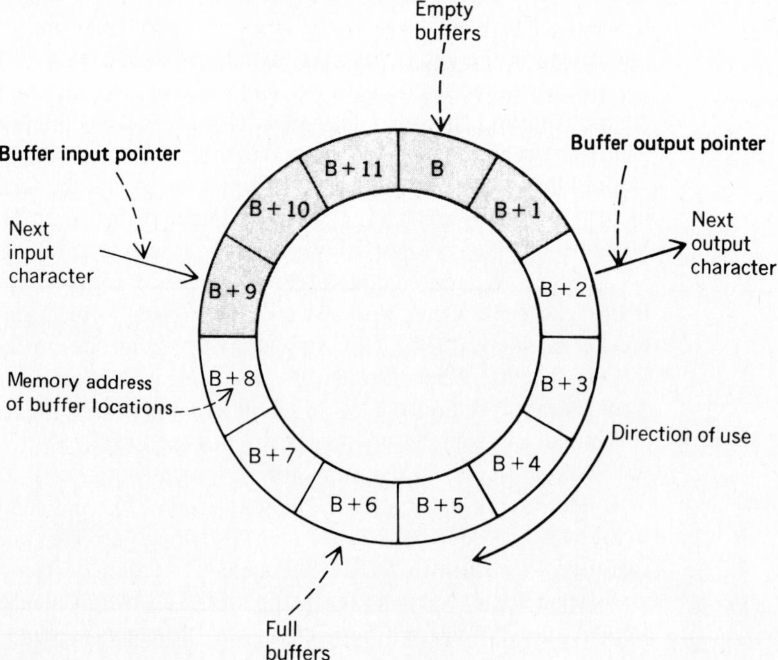

fills the buffer locations sequentially, using location B after B+N−1. The subprogram that provides the characters to the CPU process uses the same order.

Unfortunately, this mechanism will run into trouble when all buffers are full, since there will be no place to store additional characters. Therefore, the input process must test to see if there is space left. If there is, the next character can be read, but if not, no read must be executed. This means that the tape will stop over the current character and no further interrupts will occur. When the CPU process removes a character from the next buffer, it should restart the input process if the buffer was previously full so that the current character in the tape reader can be input and the tape motion restarted.

If the CPU process consumes characters too quickly, all buffers will eventually be emptied and the CPU process will have to wait on the tape reader. This means that the subprogram called by the CPU process must check to see if all buffers are empty. If so, it must wait. The wait can be accomplished by a loop that keeps checking to see if all buffers are empty. Eventually the tape will advance to the next character; the Data Ready signal will cause an interrupt of the loop to the input process, which will read the next character and return to the loop. Since not all buffers are empty at this point, the loop will terminate and the next character can be passed to the CPU process. (Of course, the CPU is wasting cycles in this loop. In a multiuser system, a job for another user would be executed instead. This will be discussed in the Section 8.2 and also in Chapter 10.)

8.1.3 Direct Memory Access I/O

The I/O mechanism described in the previous section transfers characters, one at a time, between the I/O device and the CPU under CPU control. It is possible to add hardware to the I/O processor so that it can transfer the data directly into memory. In such an organization, an instruction can be given to an I/O unit to transmit a character from the unit to a specified memory location. The unit can then execute the instruction by waiting for the data to be available, moving it to memory by means of a *direct memory access* (DMA) operation, and finally interrupting the CPU process to indicate that the character is available in memory. The difference between this mode of operation and that described in the previous subsection is that the READ operation does not cause an immediate copy of data but waits until the data is ready, and the data is not passed through a CPU register but sent directly to memory. The CPU can continue while the I/O unit waits for the data to be ready. In itself, this has no great advantage, but it permits the next extension of I/O processor capability.

The purpose of the input-processing program described in the previous subsection was to fill a set of memory cells with consecutive characters from tape. If a character-at-a-time READ instruction is used, the CPU must be interrupted for each character. Since, in direct memory access, the I/O processor is given a memory address and transmits a character of data from the unit to the specified memory address, there is no need to interrupt the computing process to move a character. Simple additional hardware can be added to transmit a number of characters into consecutive locations. Instructions of the form "Read N characters from the unit to memory locations B to B+N−1" can then be executed. While this block of characters is read, the CPU process can continue execution uninterrupted.

Since the CPU process and the input of the block of characters proceed asynchronously, the CPU process must not attempt to access characters from the block of cells in memory involved in the transfer until the transfer has been completed. Hence an interrupt signal should be issued when the block transfer has been completed. Each block of memory cells is called a single buffer in this case, and the typical software organization employs several buffers so that one can be in the process of being filled by the I/O processor while another is being read by the CPU processor. Logically, the mechanism is the same as for single-cell buffers if we view the block as a single unit of information. This type of organization is always used for devices that are naturally block-oriented—for example, magnetic tapes and disks.

8.2 INTERRUPTS AND TRAPS

We have seen the need for interruption of the CPU process to switch to an I/O process. From time to time a number of unusual conditions arise that require a process switch from the current CPU process. These conditions can arise from three different sources:

1 An invalid condition caused by the currently executing process. For example, the result of an arithmetic operation can exceed the range of representation (overflow), or, because of either machine or human error, the bit pattern in the next word to be used as an instruction may not represent any of the allowed instructions. (This is called an *illegal instruction*.)

2 A condition arising in another simultaneously executing process associated with the same job. For example, an I/O unit may have encountered a parity error.

3 A condition caused by a source not associated with the current job. For example, an interval timer may have indicated the expiration of a certain length of time, or I/O being performed as part of another job may have completed a transfer of data, so that the unit is ready to receive other instructions.

Any of these conditions can cause the current CPU process to stop and another to start by means of an automatic branch to another location. This action is called a *trap* if it is caused by the current CPU process (type 1) or an *interrupt* if it is caused by another process (types 2 and 3). The code brought into execution for a trap or interrupt permits the condition to be handled appropriately and the interrupted (or trapped) process, or another, to then be restarted. The existence of a trap mechanism makes the user's programming task simpler (for example, it is not necessary to follow every arithmetic instruction with a Branch if Overflow instruction to determine whether an overflow has occurred), and the existence of the interrupt mechanism permits switching between users in a multiuser system and the simple overlap of I/O and calculation.

8.2.1 Traps

A trap occurs because of a condition in the current CPU process; something must be done to correct it if execution is to continue. System programs provide opportunities for the user program to specify what is to happen after a trap. For example, after an underflow trap, the user may want the result to be set to floating-point 0 and execution to continue; after an overflow trap, the user may want a special section of code to be executed; and after an illegal instruction trap, the user may want execution to be terminated. The user program gives this information to the system through calls to appropriate system subprograms. (Some high-level languages have built-in statements for traps. For example, the ON statement in PL/1 allows structures such as ON OVERFLOW GO TO PROG1 that cause a branch to the specified section of code when an overflow occurs. At the machine-language level, these are handled by system calls.) After the trap handler has taken care of the condition causing the trap, it will return to the user program and execution will be continued if this is possible and has been requested by the user.

A number of different types of conditions can cause traps. The principle ones are summarized below.

Arithmetic Conditions These interrupts are due to unusual arithmetic conditions, such as overflow, underflow, and attempted divide by 0. Although the user could handle them with conditional branch instructions, it is preferable to have the hardware monitor the conditions continuously. This procedure is more efficient in terms of execution time, because it means that no additional instructions have to be executed unless the condition occurs.

The system program should allow the user to specify the action to be taken for each of these types of traps separately. If no specification is given, the *system default* action is taken, which normally simply aborts the job.

Illegal Instruction A trap on illegal instruction is normally *fatal,* that is, it terminates execution of the user process because the presence of a program error can be assumed. Information concerning the error and the state of the user process (contents of registers and memory) is output for the user and the next job is initiated.

Protection Most computer systems have more than one process in memory at a given time. (For example, in most systems there is one for the CPU and one or more for I/O devices, each of which have to be controlled.) Therefore, most systems provide some level of protection. *Memory protection* refers to the capability of the computer to mark those areas of memory that are available to a particular process and to detect erroneous reference to other areas. An area of memory not available to the running process is called a *protected region* of memory. An attempt by a user process to write into protected memory is clearly a program error and causes a trap. Normally this is fatal, as for illegal instruction traps. There may also be protection on the various I/O devices to prevent a user from accessing a device not assigned to the process.

Machine Errors Ideally, the computer never makes errors, but in practice, two sorts of hardware errors must be accepted. Catastrophic errors occur when an electronic fault is so serious that it stops a major subsystem from functioning. Such errors are immediately evident and relatively easy for the service technician to fix. They also occur relatively infrequently. More frequent in occurrence are errors that are intermittent and that may not recur if the operation is repeated. These errors do not occur very often, perhaps every few hours. The underlying problem may be transitory, such as a sudden "noise spike" on the power supply that causes a temporary loss of data in a register, or a speck of dust on tape. However, some errors are automatically detected by hardware in the machine. The design philosophy should be to provide a machine with error detection such that the probability of undetected errors is so low that the time between them will be many months. When an error is detected, a trap occurs so that the system program can decide what to do. It may try to repeat the action to see whether it can be performed without error a second time. If a repeat is successful, control can be returned to the user process, which will never be aware of the problem. If the error occurs repeatedly, the user process will have to be aborted with a suitably apologetic message.

8.2.2 Interrupts

Traps occur as the direct result of actions in the current CPU process; consequently, they are synchronized with that process. Interrupts arise from another source. They could be caused by another process, by an external signal such as the pressing of a key on a keyboard or operator console, or by a piece of hardware being controlled by the computer. For example, an error on a tape unit may require a CPU-controlled action. These conditions are not synchronized with the process running on the CPU, so they *must* interrupt that process to handle the condition. The asynchronous conditions that cause the interrupts are called *interrupt conditions*. When an interrupt condition arises, the CPU branches to the kernel just as in a trap so that the operating system can determine what to do. The operating system will attempt to take care of the problem causing the interrupt and will ultimately return to the process that was interrupted. In many computer systems, no distinction is made between a trap and an interrupt, and the mechanisms that handle them are identical. In this case, the single mechanism is usually called an interrupt.

Some of the interrupt conditions that can arise are as follows.

Timer Interrupts It is desirable to time the program in execution for several reasons. Three of these are:

1 To charge the user for the computer time.

2 To detect infinite loops that would not otherwise stop.

3 To allocate quanta of time to each of several programs in a timesharing environment.

The latter two reasons require that an interrupt be caused after a certain length of time has elapsed. There are two types of clocks commonly available, the *real-time clock* and the *interval timer*. The latter is a device that can be set to a given length of time (such as 5 milliseconds) and counted down to 0. When 0 is reached, an interrupt condition is raised. The frequency of the count (number of counts per second) is referred to as the *resolution* of the timer. A real-time clock is a register that is incremented on a regular basis, so that in principle it contains the time of day, day of the year, and year. Some systems allow an interrupt when the real-time clock reaches a value specified in another register. Typically, a real-time clock is incremented about every 1/60 to 1 second, whereas an interval timer is decremented many times per millisecond.

I/O Conditions When necessary, I/O events, such as completion of the read of a tape block, can interrupt the CPU execution sequence. The interrupt may be used just to initiate another read, or it may also be used to tell the operating system that a process waiting for the input of data can be restarted when CPU time is available. Errors on I/O units cause interrupts so that the system can request that the operation be repeated.

Synchronization In any system that has multiple processors running, there is a need to synchronize the processors from time to time. Synchronizing I/O operations with the CPU is one example. Interrupts can be used as a means of one processor signaling another.

8.2.3 Interrupt Hardware and Processing

We will use the term "interrupt" to refer to both interrupt and trap mechanisms. The mechanism has to accomplish a number of tasks, including:

1 Ignoring interrupts from devices of no current interest.

2 Identifying the cause of the interrupt and starting a process on the CPU to handle the problem.

3 Restarting the interrupted process at a later time.

4 Adjudicating when more than one interrupt occurs at the same time or when interrupts occur so closely in time that one cannot be handled before the next occurs.

5 Protecting itself against program errors in user programs.

As with most computer mechanisms, some of the actions can be handled by software or built in to hardware to achieve greater speed. Consequently, there are many different implementations of interrupt schemes in computers. We will discuss the types of features found in many common systems.

Arming and Disarming Interrupts The hardware can be set to ignore certain interrupt conditions. This is handled by providing 1 bit of storage for each interrupt condition that may be ignored. This bit is sometimes called an *interrupt mask bit*. When it is 0, the corresponding interrupt signal is ignored; when it is 1, the interrupt signal causes an interrupt. The action of setting the interrupt mask bit to a 1 is sometimes called *arming* the interrupt, and the action of setting it to a 0 is called *disarming* the interrupt. Some signals cannot be ignored, because something has to happen. For example, illegal instruction traps cannot be ignored, because there is no other action for the CPU to take. In many computer systems, a status register is associated with each I/O device. This status register contains the mask bits associated with the interrupt signals that can arise from the device, so the bits can be set or reset by writing into the status register. The program status work (PSW) is the corresponding register for the CPU, and it may have the corresponding mask bits for CPU interrupt conditions.

Identifying Causes and Initiating Processes There are two principal types of mechanisms used to identify the cause of an interrupt, the first of which is based on software and the second on hardware. The first is usually used in systems in which the interrupt causes a branch to a single fixed location, such as location 0. It is then up to the program to test the various interrupt bits to see which one is on. To make this a reasonable process, the interrupt signals are grouped into one or more registers, which can be read. The software can then read each of the registers in turn to test the interrupt signals and determine which one caused the interrupt. In the second type of system, each different interrupt signal causes a branch to a different location. The code starting at each of the locations is the code for handling the interrupt causing the branch to that location. The locations could be permanently assigned to each interrupt (for example, if the interrupts were assigned unique integer names 0, 1, 2, . . . , the ith interrupt signal could cause a branch to location $8i$), or each interrupt could have an associated register in which the interrupt branch address is stored. This address could be set by the operating system.

In many systems, a combination of these two schemes is often used—the interrupt signals are grouped into a number of sets. A separate branch address is associated with each set, so the program knows which of a small set of interrupts was responsible by virtue of the branch address used. The final determination can then be made by software testing of the signals in the set. (This testing can also be avoided by providing hardware that generates the address of the particular interrupt so that is can be read directly by the program.)

The initiation of a new process on the basis of the particular interrupt is almost always done by software. When an interrupt occurs, the current CPU process is stopped and a kernel process is initiated. This process determines which interrupt is to be serviced, and from that it can decide which process needs to be started by consulting tables maintained by the operating system. It can then load the registers appropriately and start the desired process.

Restarting the Interrupted Process The interrupted process state must be saved in its entirety if the process is to be restarted later. The content of the program counter must be saved by the hardware at the time of the interrupt. In most modern machines the address is saved in a stack, much as in a subroutine call. (Some machines maintain one stack just for this purpose so that the user stack is not changed in any way.) Before the contents of any registers are changed, they must also be saved. This can be done by software, although some machines have a single instruction by which all the CPU registers are in stored memory. Once the contents of the registers have been saved in an area of memory reserved by the operating system for the process state, the process can be kept waiting until it is time to restart it by reloading the registers.

Some machines have more than one set of registers, and an interrupt causes a switch to another set. This permits interrupt conditions to be handled very quickly and the original process to be restarted by switching back to the first set of registers.

Multiple Interrupts A condition that might cause an interrupt to occur raises a sense signal (for example, Data Ready). This signal is usually *latched* (that is, stored) into a bit of a register, perhaps the status register for the device causing the interrupt. Hence, even if the sense signal returns to 0, the state of the bit in the register continues to record the fact that an interrupt signal occurred. When one of these interrupt bits is on, an interrupt occurs; if several are turned on at the same time, one of them will cause an interrupt. The interrupt causes another process to be started in the CPU, and it may be necessary for that process to handle the condition causing the interrupt before other interrupts are permitted. To enable this process to execute some instructions without being interrupted, the occurrence of the interrupt causes the *interrupt disable* flag to be set. While this is on, no interrupts are permitted. When the code called into execution by the interrupt has completed its mission, or is prepared to be interrupted, it "reenables" interrupts by turning the interrupt disable flag off. This is frequently done by the Return from Interrupt instruction, which reloads processor registers from specified memory or stack locations at the same time it reenables interrupts, thus restarting a process.

The foregoing type of scheme is found in older computers and in some of the simpler microcomputers. It services the interrupts in the order of arrival and completes the service of one before another is serviced. If several arrive at the same time, or if several arrive while interrupts are disabled, the choice of which one to be serviced must be made by software (or perhaps enforced by the hardware if it branches to different locations for different interrupts). Some devices need to be serviced quickly if time or even information is not to be lost. For example, after the completion of a disk block transfer, there is a small amount of time before the next block on the cylinder comes under the read/write heads, and if another disk read/write operation can be issued in that interval, no disk revolutions will be lost. In a real-time environment in which a computer is gathering data from external sources, such as the temperature or pressure in an oil refinery, it may be necessary to read a data value before it has changed. Therefore, some interrupts need to be given priority over others. It is possible to encode a priority in the software such that if several interrupts arise at the same time, the highest-priority one will receive service first, but we would also like to permit higher-priority interrupt signals to interrupt processes servicing lower-priority signals, but not vice versa. This is handled by a *priority-interrupt* mechanism. Each interrupt condition is assigned a priority level. When an interrupt occurs, its priority level is copied into the interrupt priority register (which may be part of the processor status word) providing the value already present is smaller. The priority of a user program is 0, so it can always be interrupted, but once an interrupt occurs,the new process can be interrupted only by higher-priority conditions. In this scheme, a Return from Interrupt instruction reenables the process that was previously in execution, restoring its interrupt priority level along with the rest of the process status. A stack mechanism has to be used to store the status of each of the interrupted processes. The interrupted process of the highest priority will automatically be on top of the stack and will thus be the one put back into execution on the next Return from Interrupt instruction.

Protection of the Interrupting Mechanisms The code that handles the interrupt is a key part of the *kernel* of the operating system. It must be in the computer with the user program, and at least part of it must be in primary memory. Obviously, its purpose will be defeated if the user program can change it, whether by accident or malicious intent. To prevent this from happening, the kernel is kept in a protected region of memory. When the user program is in execution, it is not allowed access to the protected area of memory. Because the contents of the status registers (interrupt, mask, status bits, etc.) are critical to the functioning of the system, the user program may not change them. Therefore, all instructions that can change them are also protected. These are called *privileged instructions*. Execution of privileged instructions and access to protected memory are only permitted when the kernel program is in control. When a user program is in execution the CPU is in *user mode*. When an interrupt occurs, the mode, which is indicated in a bit that is usually part of the processor status word, is changed to *kernel mode,* or *supervisor mode*. This permits the process started by the interrupt to run in a mode that permits use of privileged instructions and access to other areas of memory. Some computers have more than two modes, with each successively higher-level mode providing access to additional hardware facilities.

8.2.4 Concurrent Process Synchronization

When two or more processes are part of the same job, it is necessary to arrange some synchronization between them. We have seen an example of this that occurs when the input of characters from a tape reader is overlapped with CPU processing of the user program. The input process fills buffers as the characters are read while the user process removes characters from the buffers as they are consumed. If the buffers are empty the user process must wait, whereas if the buffers are full the input process must wait. This can be done by maintaining a count of the number of buffers in use. When it is 0, no further characters can be provided to the user process; when it is N, the maximum number of buffers available, no more can be input. Not only do both processes test the count variable, the input process must cause it to be incremented as characters are read and the user process must cause it to be decremented as it uses characters. Since one of these processes may interrupt the other, we can run into a synchronization problem. The user process must cause the action

$$\text{count} \leftarrow \text{count} - 1$$

which causes the machine-level actions

```
LOAD     COUNT
SUB      =1
STORE    COUNT
```

Similarly, the input process will activate the code

```
LOAD     COUNT
ADD      =1
STORE    COUNT
```

If the input process interrupts the user process between the LOAD and the STORE instructions, the value of COUNT will be in error. For example, the following sequence of actions could happen in real time, where the user-process instructions are denoted by U and the input process instruction by I:

```
U    LOAD    COUNT    Accumulator=M
     (Interrupt by input process, CPU registers saved.)
I    LOAD    COUNT    Accumulator=M
I    ADD     =1       Accumulator=M+1
I    STORE   COUNT    COUNT=M+1
     (Return from interrupt, CPU registers restored.
     Accumulator now contains M.)
U    SUB     =1       Accumulator=M-1
U    STORE   COUNT    COUNT=M-1
```

We see that the incrementation of COUNT by the input process has been lost because the user process moved the value of COUNT into the accumulator just before it was interrupted. This type of problem occurs whenever two or more processes can modify the same variable. It is necessary to prevent one process from modifying the variable while the other is implementing it. In effect, this means that one process must not interrupt the other while the modification is taking place. This means that the user process must either be able to enter the interrupt disabled state or start another process to carry out the variable modification in the interrupt disabled mode. The former would be unwise, because if a user process were able to disable interrupts, it would be impossible for the system to regain control after other interrupts. Therefore the operating system has subprograms that are invoked by means of *system calls*. These are similar to subprogram calls but cause a trap to the system and disable further interrupts (or disable ones of no-higher priority). A system call can be used by the user process to activate a subprogram to remove the next character from the buffer, and it can update the COUNT variable, with the assurance that it will not be interrupted by the input process that uses the same variable.

The difficulty with the scheme proposed above is that it could result in a considerable amount of code being executed under high-priority interrupt status, thus disabling other interrupts. If the objective is to be able to service interrupts as fast as possible, it is best to have as much code as possible at as low a priority as possible. For example, most of the code for the system subprogram that gets a character from the buffers for use by the current CPU process can be run at a very low priority and can be interrupted by I/O devices. All that is necessary is to prevent the code that modifies COUNT in the two sections of programs above from interrupting each other. This can be done by providing *synchronization primitives* in the system, which cause one section of code to wait for the completion of another. The simplest form of these are the P and V operations, which work on variables called *semaphores* by Dijkstra.[1] A binary semaphore is a flag variable, S, on which the two operations P(S) and V(S) can be performed. They are sometimes called *lock* and *unlock*. The function of P(S) is to cause a process to wait if the semaphore is 0, but to allow it to proceed if the semaphore is 1 and set it to 0. One can think of this as a railroad signal that stops a train if it is red (0), but allows it to proceed if it is green (1) and promptly changes to red as the train passes, keeping

[1]E. W. Dijkstra, "Cooperating Sequential Processes," in Genuys F. (ed.), *Programming Languages*, Academic Press, New York, 1968.

other trains from entering conflicting sections of track. The action P(S) can be written as follows:

```
If S = 0 then wait (and keep testing S)
  else S←0 endif
```

If this code is executed immediately before the sections of code that modify the variable COUNT, then it is impossible for both processes to be modifying COUNT in an overlapped manner. Suppose that the semaphore S is initially set to 1. The first process to execute P(S) is allowed to proceed, setting S to 0. This blocks the second process when it executes P(S), causing it to wait for the first to complete its modification of COUNT. The first process signals this by performing V(S), which simply resets S to 1. It is important that the P(S) operation be *indivisible*—that is, nothing should be allowed to interrupt from the time it reads S from memory to test it and the time it sets it to 0; otherwise the other P(S) operations could read an S value of 1 before the first P(S) operation had time to set it to 0. Therefore, this code must be executed at top priority or the hardware must provide a single, uninterruptable instruction for it. In fact, many computers have such an operation. In the IBM 370 it is the Test and Set instruction. It reads a byte from memory, tests it to set a condition code, and sets it to 11111111 in a single memory cycle. This pattern corresponds to the value 0 for a semaphore, so that the equivalent of P(S) is coded as

```
X        TS          S
         BRANCH to X if S was 11111111
```

It does not matter whether an interrupt occurs between the TS and the BRANCH instructions with this mechanism. Using a binary semaphore, the code that inputs characters into the buffers takes the form

```
if COUNT<N
  then
    read_character_into_next_buffer
    P(S)
    COUNT ← COUNT + 1
    V(S)
  else
    not_reading_mark ← true
  endif
```

where the procedure read_character_into_next_buffer inputs a character from the reader, puts it in a buffer, updates the input buffer pointer, and sets the not_reading_mark to **false**. The system program that passes the next character to the user process takes the form

```
wait until COUNT ≠ 0 (this is discussed below)
remove character from buffer and update output pointer
P(S)
COUNT ← COUNT−1
V(S)
if not_reading_mark
  then read_character_into_next_buffer
  endif
```

In a single-user system, the wait can consist of a loop testing COUNT as discussed earlier. This will be interrupted by the input process as long as it has a higher priority, so that eventually COUNT will be increased. In a multiuser system, the wait should permit another process to be put into execution and leave this one waiting for later processing when COUNT is updated.

Counting semaphores provide a direct way to handle the buffer problem. A counting semaphore is similar to a binary semaphore in that it causes the process to wait if it is 0, but it can take on any nonnegative value. The P and V operations on a counting semaphore C can be described as

```
P(C):  if C=0 then wait
       else C ← C−1 endif

V(C):  C ← C+1
```

These operations must also be indivisible. If we use a semaphore variable COUNT to indicate the number of characters available in the buffers and FREE to indicate the number of unused buffers, the input process must not continue if FREE is 0, and no characters can be passed to the user process if COUNT is 0. Hence the code invoked by an input interrupt can take the form

```
P(FREE)
read_character_into_next_buffer
V(COUNT)
```

and the code invoked by a system call to get the next character for a user process can take the form

```
P(COUNT)
remove character from buffer and update output pointer
V(FREE)
```

The P and V operations are usually implemented by software in the inner part of the operating system, the kernel. If the P operations cause a wait, the kernel will select another process that is not blocked by a 0 semaphore value.

8.2.5 Interrupts in the 8080

The INTEL 8080 has an extremely simple, single-level interrupt structure based on three instructions

RST	N	Restart at location 8N, N < 8
DI		Disable interrupts
EI		Enable interrupts

All three are 1-byte instructions. RST is like a CALL in that it pushes the content of the program counter into the stack. It can select one of eight addresses because its 3-bit address, N, can take values from 0 to 7 only. (This restriction permits it to fit into 1 byte.) There are no traps in the 8080—overflows and similar conditions set condition bits that must be tested; all bit patterns are legal instructions, so there is no illegal instruction; and there is no protection of memory or I/O in the 8080 chip. The interrupt mechanism in the INTEL 8080 is largely external to the chip and determined by the design of the I/O and memory systems provided by the microcomputer manufacturer. A single sense signal, Interrupt, tells the 8080 microprocessor that an interrupt should occur at the end of the current instruction unless interrupts are disabled. At that time, the computer disables interrupts, requests the next instruction from the memory (which is external to the chip), but does *not* increment the program counter. The 8080 uses a data bus (described in the next chapter) to connect the processor to memory and I/O units. Normally, when the processor requests data from memory, it is the job of the memory control unit to take the address from the address bus (which is also connected to the processor) and to read the corresponding memory data onto the data bus. Thus a normal instruction fetch consists of sending the content of the program counter on the address bus, incrementing the program counter, and getting the next instruction from the data bus after it has been read from memory. In an interrupt sequence, it is the job of the hardware control external to the chip to provide a suitable instruction on the data bus to implement the interrupt. Usually this is the RST instruction. For example, suppose the designer would like interrupts by the console keyboard to interrupt to location 8. In that case, hardware would have to be built into the console control unit to issue the interrupt signal, and, when the 8080 chip indicated that it was about to start the interrupt sequence (a control signal coming from the 8080 chip), the console control unit would have to force the bit pattern for the instruction RST 1 onto the data bus. The next instruction would then come from location 8 with interrupt disabled.

Other I/O control units could be designed to perform similar operations for their interrupts. If more than one interrupt occurs at the same time, the hardware must decide which one to accept. If it is necessary to arm or disarm interrupts, the necessary hardware must be placed in the control units and set by means of OUT instructions to appropriate ports. If more than eight interrupt signals are used, some will have to share the same interrupt start addresses, in which case it will be up to the software to query the status registers in the I/O units to determine the cause of the interrupt.

After the RST instruction has been issued, a section of code is running with interrupt disabled. This code can handle the cause of the interrupt and then return to the original process by first restoring the contents of any registers changed during the interrupt processing (their values should have been pushed onto the stack at the start of the interrupt), then executing the sequence

```
EI
RET
```

It is possible that an interrupt could occur before the RETurn is executed, but this does not matter, as the return from the next interrupt will bring control back to this RET.

The details of programming for interrupts in the 8080 depend on the design of the I/O system, so the reader should consult manuals for particular systems.

8.3 CHANNELS

An I/O unit controller that moves blocks of consecutive characters between the I/O unit and memory has to have a number of registers to save addresses, character counts, etc., plus hardware to handle interrupt signals and access to memory. In many designs, this hardware is shared among several I/O units by placing it in a device called a *channel*. Each I/O device has a controller that handles the simple operations such as character-at-a-time movement. The controllers for several I/O devices are connected to a channel that is in turn connected to the computer. A system may have several channels, as shown in Figure 8-2. Each channel has a unique address, and each I/O unit on a channel has an address. Thus the second unit on channel B would have address B2. (Addresses are normally numeric, consisting of a channel number followed by a unit number.) When a channel receives an instruction from the computer, it first *selects* the unit and then begins the operation. If the operation is a block transfer of data, the memory address of the data and byte count are set in appropriate registers in the channel and control signals are sent to the I/O controller to cause the transfer of characters. These

FIGURE 8-2 Multiple units on channels

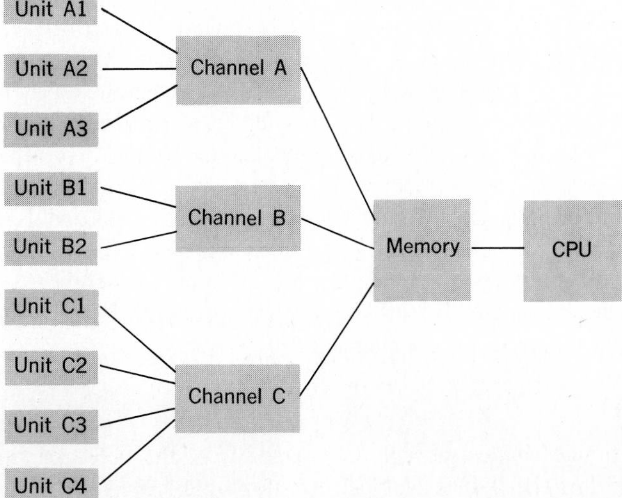

are passed between the channel and the memory using direct memory access, so that the CPU program is unaware of the channel operation.

Usually, a channel is kept busy by the data coming from a high-speed unit such as a large disk, so it can do nothing else at the same time. However, some operations such as "skip to an end-of-file mark" on tape, or a "seek" on a disk require no channel action after the I/O unit has started the operation. In that case, the channel is free to perform other operations, so that several non-data-transfer operations can be executing at the same time as one data-transfer operation on a single channel.

Slow I/O units, such as terminals and hard-copy devices (printers and card readers, etc.), do not take much time in a channel. In that case, the channel may permit a number of devices to be transferring data at the same time. A channel that can do this is called a *multiplex channel*. In this case, the channel must be able to retain the memory address and counts for each device operating at the same time. To the user, a multiplex channel looks like a set of individual channels. The maximum number is limited by the maximum data rate at which the channel can move information to and from memory and the speed of the I/O units in operation.

A channel allows the simultaneous transfer of data between I/O units and primary memory while the CPU is executing another process. Each operating channel and the CPU are competing for the use of memory, so the number of units that can be in operation is limited by the speed (bandwidth) of the memory. It is not possible to saturate the memory (that is, use all of the memory cycles) with I/O transfers in most systems, as the speed of most devices is much lower than that of primary memory. However, some very fast devices, such as bulk stores or large drums, can use an appreciable number of the available memory cycles. In that case the speed of the CPU can be noticeably diminished, because it may have to wait for an I/O direct-memory-access reference to finish before it can get to the memory.

When a block-mode I/O unit, such as magnetic tape or disk, is running, the data must be provided to it or taken from it at a rate sufficient to keep up with the speed of the unit. When a channel has data from such an I/O unit to ship to memory (on a read) or needs to get data from memory for an I/O unit (or a write), it must get access to the memory fairly quickly; otherwise other data will have arrived from the unit (read) or it will be too late to send the data to the unit (write). If more than one fast I/O unit is operating at the same time, one unit could prevent the others from getting data rapidly enough to keep up with their transfer rates. In that case, we would get an *overrun* condition. It is an error, and requires that the operation be repeated. Some I/O controllers contain a large, random-access memory buffer to allow a large number of characters to be read while waiting for memory access. This avoids the problem of overruns. This technique has also been used in combination I/O controllers that control both tapes and disks and permit transfers directly from one to another. In reality, such controllers are small processors capable of controlling several I/O devices in real time, and so are themselves a form of a channel.

8.3.1 Channel Computers

A simple channel accepts commands from the CPU for single I/O operations and performs the details of block transfers, notifying the CPU via interrupts when the operation has been completed or an error condition has arisen. The CPU is still responsible for providing the sequence of I/O operations. In many cases, a sequence of several I/O operations has to be performed to complete a desired action. For example, a disk seek followed by several reads is needed to read a full track, whereas a series of magnetic tape reads until an end-of-file mark is encountered is needed to read a file from tape. It is possible to provide additional capabilities in the channel to execute sequences of I/O instructions called *channel programs*. A programmable channel has its own program counter and can be told by the CPU to begin execution of a program at a designated point in memory. Such a channel is a processor of the same form as CPU. It fetches instructions from memory and executes them sequentially. These instructions can perform a sequence of I/O operations independently of the CPU so that, for example, a disk can be instructed to seek to a particular cylinder and to transfer a sequence of blocks of data.

In such an organization there has to be communication between the channel and the CPU. Although this could be achieved by setting values into agreed memory locations, the usual organization permits the CPU to be the controlling processor; it can stop a channel at any time and start it again at a program location specified by the CPU program. The channel program communicates information back to the CPU by means of interrupt signals. It is permitted to interrupt the CPU on the completion of specified instructions so that the CPU can execute a process to determine what the channel should do next. A typical set of instructions for a channel includes instructions such as

SELECT-UNIT	N	Connect the channel to unit number N
CONTROL-OP	X	Send control signal X to the connected unit
READ-RECORD	M	Read the next record to address M
WRITE-RECORD	M	Write the next record from address M
STOP	The channel program terminates and interrupts the CPU	

Error conditions may also stop the channel and cause interrupts of the CPU. In addition, the CPU can usually interrogate a channel to find out its status—for example, to find out the content of its program counter and whether or not it is busy.

These instructions permit only a *straight-line code* to be executed by the channel; some channels can also execute a small set of counting and conditional branch instructions, so that program loops can be executed. (The use of microprocessors in channels permits a fairly wide range of such operations, so that a channel may have nearly as much power as the CPU for integer arithmetic.) Channels with conditional branch instructions can also test for error conditions and take some of the corrective actions described in the next section.

8.4 SOFTWARE FOR INPUT-OUTPUT

Because the control of I/O equipment is so complex from a programming point of view, it is necessary to adopt a set of conventions concerning the way in which this equipment is used and to provide most of the direct control by system subroutines. This section will discuss some of the methods used to create an efficient and flexible operating system for the user.

The first principle followed in the design of I/O systems is that of *device independence*. This means that it should be possible to write a program that is independent of the particular type of I/O device available on the machine being used to the extent that the program is portable from machine to machine. That is clearly not possible if the types of devices are radically different—for example, there is no way to make a printer look like a magnetic tape unit for input operations! However, if the program needs a device on which a file of data can be written and later reread, it should be possible to write the program so that it will work on any device with such capabilities. Similarly, if the program wishes to read a line of data from a user input device such as a terminal, the program should not have to be concerned with the type of terminal being used. A second principle that is followed is one of trying to relieve the user of the program burdens of error handling and organization of buffers for efficiency of operation. When errors occur on I/O units, there are a number of standard techniques for trying to recover from the error. These techniques can be embedded in the system programs that control the I/O devices, so that in most cases the user is unaware that errors have occurred. We saw that the use of buffers is necessary to provide overlap of CPU and I/O processing, and that control and synchronization of the simultaneous processes are fairly complex. Therefore, these functions are hidden as much as possible from the typical programmer and are carried out automatically inside system programs.

8.4.1 Device-Independent Input-Output

Input and output are usually concerned with files of information. Each file consists of a set of records. For example, on a terminal keyboard or a card reader, the file of data can be considered as a set of lines, in which case each record is a line. (The file could also be considered as a stream of characters in which the end-of-line character is just another character. In this case, the records are single characters.) Different I/O devices permit information to be accessed in different ways. For example, a file from a card reader can only be read sequentially, one record after the other, starting from the first. No backspace operations are possible. A magnetic tape unit with its *write protection* on (write protection prevents writing on a tape that might contain important information) can also only be read sequentially, but backspace operations are possible. Forward spacing is possible on both devices. As concerns operations that are possible on both devices, the card reader and the magnetic tape unit are similar in that both work with sequential files. The idea behind device-independent I/O is that the form of I/O operations should depend on the organization of the information files rather than on the specific I/O device, so that the user is able to write programs to deal with sequential files for any device that can support sequential files, with the details of the particular I/O device buried in the system kernel (in a program called the *device driver*).

Individual records in a file must be identified in some way. In a sequential file, the only identification for each record is its relative position in the file. Types of file organization include:

Sequential: A record can be reached only by reading or skipping over each record prior to it. In some cases backspaces are also permitted.

Direct access: The ith record can be accessed by number. (This is sometimes called *indexed.*)

Key: Each record contains a unique *key* that identifies it, and the record can be referenced by specifying the value of its key.

Virtually all devices support sequential files; other types of file organization must be stored on devices such as disks and drums.

File Directories It is clear how a sequential file is accessed on magnetic tape. Once the tape is positioned at the start of the file, access to the next block is accomplished by a read or write operation. However, it is not clear how to find the desired file when there is more than one file. In the simplest scheme, we simply have to know that we want the ith file on the tape, skipping over the first $i - 1$ files to get there. However, a file on a disk could start anywhere, and it is not practical to remember a file by the (large) address of its first block on disk. Instead, we prefer to name files and to have the system keep a record of where they are on the storage medium. For a tape, this is sometimes called a *table of contents*. It usually appears as the first file on the tape and contains the names and relative positions of all other files on that tape. (Tapes with an initial block or file containing information describing the contents of the tape are said to be *labeled*. An operating system can check to see whether a labeled tape contains files with the desired names, thus checking to see whether the correct tape has been mounted. Such checking is not possible if the user asks simply for the ith file on the tape.) Similarly, a disk usually contains a directory of its contents by file names. The directory gives the actual disk address of the first record of the file corresponding to each file name. The system subprograms OPEN and CLOSE allow the user to specify a file name to indicate that the file named is to be accessed (OPEN) or that it is no longer needed (CLOSE). The OPEN operation permits the system to locate the file in the directory and position the tape for access or note the disk address to be used. If buffers are to be associated with the file, they are allocated at the same time. The CLOSE operation then releases these buffers for use for other purposes.

Disk Space Allocation There are a number of schemes for storing a sequential file on disk. In the simplest scheme, successive blocks are stored under increasing physical address numbers. This means that when space for a file is first allocated on a disk (which is done in many systems when an OPEN or CREATE is issued for a nonexistent file) a given number of blocks must be allocated before it is known how long the file is. This is not convenient, as a result of which many systems allocate space on disk for each block of a file only as it is needed. This means that adjacent blocks in a file may not be in adjacent blocks on the disk. Therefore, it is necessary to know where each block of a file is stored on disk. This can be done in a number of ways. In one method, the disk address of the next block is stored at the end of the previous block. This type of file can only be accessed sequentially. In another method, an *index* of the disk addresses of each block is also kept on disk. In this case the directory normally contains the disk address of the index, which in turn contains the disk addresses of the blocks of the file. This permits both sequential and direct access. In another organization, an index of the keys in each record with the corresponding disk block address is maintained. This permits all three types of organization.

As disk space is needed for a file being written, the system has to find free blocks. This can be done by keeping a list of all free blocks (see Problem 8-7) or by keeping a *bit map* consisting of a bit for each block on disk, with a value of 1 indicating that the corresponding block is free and a value of 0 indicating that it is not. Space is returned to the free list when the user executes a system operation to remove a file (sometimes called remove or erase).

8.4.2. Buffering

The size of a single buffer is determined by the size of a block on the I/O unit. To reduce the time (and space) wasted in interblock gaps, the block size should be as long as possible. Typically, block sizes are in the 512- to 4096-byte range. Because of this, it is undesirable to use too many buffers for each I/O device because of the primary memory space taken. On the other hand, if there are too few buffers, the probability that the computation process will have to wait is increased. Figure 8-3 shows three buffers being loaded by a reading process and used by a computation process. That figure shows the reader waiting at one point because all buffers are full, but shortly thereafter the computation process is waiting because it was able to process all available information more rapidly than new formation could be read. A fourth buffer would have prevented the wait in this example. Two buffers are adequate only if the computation process and the read process have uniform speeds. The more nonuniform they become, the more buffers are needed to prevent waits.

Buffering can be handled by the programmer directly. Memory in the user program area can be set aside for buffers, and each request to the operating system can specify the place in primary memory that is to be involved in the data transfer. In such an organization, the user can issue READ and WRITE requests to the system, usually by a subprogram call, and these begin the transfer between the named file and the primary memory region. Thus the instruction

```
READ      F1,BUF
```

initiates the read of a block of data between file F1 and memory, starting at BUF. WRITE behaves similarly. However, the data has not necessarily been transferred when control is returned to the user program, so if the data is to be used, the program must issue a WAIT request to the system to cause the user program to wait until the specified transfer has been completed. Thus

```
WAIT      F1
```

waits until the last operation on file F1 has been completed. Using a single buffer (which allows for no overlap of operation), a sequence for reading a file from one source and writing it to another would be

```
READ      F1,BUFFER
WAIT      F1
WRITE     F2,BUFFER
```

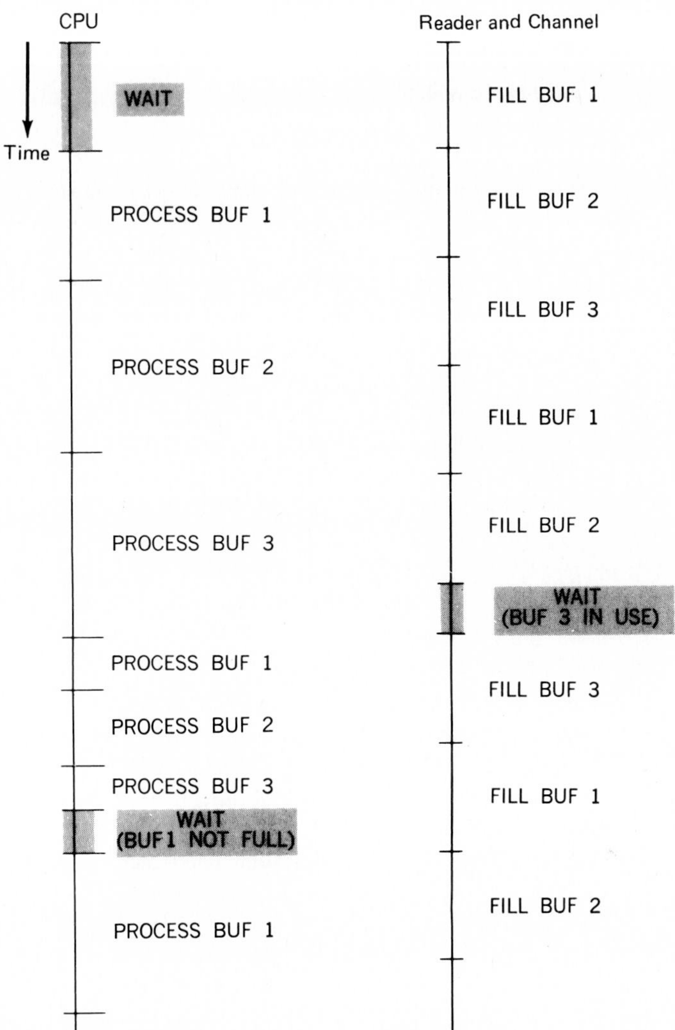

FIGURE 8-3 Use of three buffers

```
WAIT     F2
READ     F1,BUFFER
...
```

However, if two buffers were used, the program

```
READ     F1,BUFFER1
WAIT     F1
READ     F1,BUFFER2
WRITE    F2,BUFFER1
WAIT     F1
```

```
WAIT      F2
READ      F1,BUFFER1
WRITE     F2,BUFFER2
...
```

could be used. Although there are as many WAIT requests, those after the first will not cause a wait if the speed of reading and writing are equal. If the system is such that a second READ or WRITE automatically causes a wait for the previous one on the same file to finish, most of the WAIT instructions can be omitted to get

```
READ      F1,BUFFER1
READ      F1,BUFFER2
WRITE     F2,BUFFER1
WAIT      F2
READ      F1,BUFFER1
WRITE     F2,BUFFER2
WAIT      F1
...
```

because a return from a READ to one buffer guarantees that the previous READ to the other buffer has been completed so that a WRITE can be started on the other buffer.

In many cases the user does not want to be concerned with buffering, so it is handled directly by the system. In this organization, the user issues commands, often called GET and PUT, to read and write logical records of information to a named file. When a file is opened, the user specifies how many buffers are to be provided (if there is any option) and the system allocates space inside its area of primary memory for two or more buffers. During a PUT operation, the system copies the information from the logical record specified by the user into a block-sized buffer in the system area. If more than one logical record is packed into a block, the packing is accomplished as the records are copied. When enough records have been read to fill a block, it is written to the output device. Conversely, during a GET operation a block is read from an I/O device to a buffer and logical records are unpacked from the buffers and copied to the user area of memory.

When the file is opened for reading sequentially, the system attempts to keep the buffers full at all times; each time a buffer is emptied by a user program, the next block is read. Similarly, when a file is opened for writing sequentially, the system attempts to keep the buffers empty by writing buffers to the file as soon as they are filled. It is not easy to decide on strategies for automatic direct-access file buffering, so it is generally better for the user program to do its own buffering.

8.4.3 Error Handling

A number of errors can occur during I/O operations. Some errors are caused by attempts to execute invalid operations on I/O units, such as a backspace operation on a printer. These are due to software errors, and since the I/O units are normally controlled by system programs, it can be assumed that these errors should almost never happen; if they do happen, it is time to call in the system programmers to find the fault. An attempt to perform an invalid operation on an I/O unit may either cause nothing to happen or put the unit in a state in which it fails to respond to further commands. In the latter case, the operator will quickly notice the problem. In the former case, the error will only be noticed through its effect on the programs in execution, if any.

The most common types of errors are data errors. If these are not detected by the system, the onus is on the user program to perform some sort of consistency check on its results to check for errors. However, many data errors are detected by a parity scheme or similar schemes in hardware. The computer designer attempts to make the probability of undetected error so low that the typical user does not have to question the results of a computation. When an error is detected, there is the problem of what to do about it. In the case of I/O transfers, it is often possible to repeat the operation.

In a typical operating system, a read error from a secondary storage device such as magnetic tape or disk causes an interrupt, and the system responds by repeating the read operation. If the error is due to a small dust particle or a marginal magnetic recording level, it is likely that the second read will be successful. If the second read fails, it can be repeated several more times. In practice, the read will be repeated a maximum of about five times (a number that can sometimes be changed by a user program). If it fails every time, there is little that can be done except to inform the user that the block of data cannot be read and abort the job unless the user requests an alternate action.

A write error on secondary storage can be detected if the information is read immediately after writing. If an error is detected, the write can be attempted several more times until it is successful or there are too many failures. In the latter case, there are several possibilities, depending on the nature of the storage medium. If it is magnetic tape, it is possible to leave a blank section of tape and try recording on a later part of the tape. This often works, because even though the surface of a magnetic tape may have become damaged locally, the remainder of the tape may be usable. For this reason, some tape drives permit a section of "blank tape" to be recorded. This looks like an extra-long record gap and permits bad spots on the tape to be skipped in the writing process. (If the tape becomes significantly damaged, it is not a good idea to use it, because particles from the tape will damage the recording heads of the tape unit. Regular tape maintenance includes cleaning the tape and verifying that it is possible to write information on its whole length.) A write error on a disk file that cannot be corrected by repeated writing has to be overcome at a higher software level. The software has to be organized so that a different location on the disk is used in place of the one that is unwritable. Systems that allocate disk space as it is needed can accomplish this by removing blocks that are apparently unwritable from the list of free blocks.

8.5 CHAPTER SUMMARY AND PROBLEMS

An I/O device is controlled by control signals, and the computer can determine its status by testing sense signals. In the simplest systems, these signals can be set and tested by the CPU directly, but most I/O units are controlled by special controllers. I/O units have addresses. In some computer designs, separate I/O instructions are provided whose operand address is that of the I/O unit. In other designs, I/O units have addresses that correspond to regular primary memory addresses; thus any CPU instruction can refer to an I/O unit by referencing that memory address.

The I/O controller can be executing one process while the CPU is executing another. The I/O unit informs the CPU process when it has completed an operation by means of an interrupt signal so that the CPU can issue the next I/O operation. Memory is used to buffer information between the time it is input and the time it is used in computation, or between the time it is generated by the CPU and the time it is output, so that the user and I/O processes do not have to wait for each other. A set of buffers is used to hold several blocks of information (a block is the amount of information transferred in a single operation). I/O can go directly into the CPU or directly into memory using direct memory access (DMA).

Interrupt signals arise in other processes and temporarily stop the execution of the current CPU process so that another can be started. This permits multiple processes to be active on the CPU. Trap signals occur when the current CPU process encounters a condition that cannot be handled, such as illegal instruction. Most interrupts can be disarmed so that they can be ignored by the CPU. When one is armed and the corresponding signal arises, the CPU is interrupted. The process invoked by the interrupt must determine the source of the interrupt and start the appropriate process running. All further interrupts may be disabled until the current interrupt has been handled, or only interrupts of lower priority may be disabled. The interrupt service program in the kernel may have to determine priorities in the case of multiple interrupts, or the priority may be determined by hardware.

Simultaneous processes must be synchronized when they need access to common data. Semaphores can be used for this purpose. Binary semaphores take two values and act like railroad signals. Counting semaphores keep track of the number of units of a resource (such as buffers) available for use. The P and V operations on semaphores must be indivisible. The Test and Set instruction available in some computers can be used to implement binary semaphores.

Channels range from simple devices that share control hardware among a number of I/O units to complex processors capable of executing significant programs.

Most operating systems handle I/O operations in a device-independent manner. The way in which a device is handled is then determined by the structure of the file rather than by the type of I/O device. Any device capable of handling a particular type of file can be referenced by the same user software; the differences in devices are handled within the kernel by the device driver. The principal types of files are sequential, direct access, and keyed. Directories of the names of files are kept with the files so that the system can reference files by name. Automatic buffer allocation is simple to implement for sequential files. Errors are also handled by the system, where possible. In many cases, repeated reads or writes resolve the situation. If a write cannot be performed without error on a tape or disk, a section of blank tape can be skipped, or a disk block can be made unavailable and a different one used. If an operation cannot be performed without error, the user will have to decide whether to abort the job or take some other action.

Problems

8-1 Describe the organization of interrupt-driven output similar to the input described in Section 8.1.

8-2 Suppose you have a computer system that implements binary semaphores. Show how to implement counting semaphores using the binary semaphore operations and regular instructions.

8-3 Suppose that you have a computer with a CPU and a channel. Suppose the channel has the capability of executing any program that can be executed by the CPU, but that the only communication between the two is via primary memory. Assume that each has a Test and Set instruction. The normal situation is that the CPU is executing a user program while the channel is sitting in a program loop waiting for something to do. Describe how you would implement a CPU operation (by subprogram) that would start the channel executing an I/O program, remembering that the CPU might request it to start another program before it had started the first, which should result in the CPU being forced to wait until the channel has finished its first I/O program.

8-4 Suppose that there are six records on tape and that some computation is to be done on each record. Two buffers, B1 and B2, each capable of holding one record, are available. Suppose the instructions available are

```
READ       Bi          i = 1 or 2
COMPUTE    Bi
WAIT                   Wait until reader finished last transfer
```

where the READ instructions read the next block into B1 or B2, waiting until the previous READ has been completed, while the COMPUTE instructions perform the computation on the designated buffer. One way of performing the computation is to repeat the sequence

```
READ          B1
WAIT
COMPUTE       B1
```

six times, but this is slow because of unnecessary waits. Write a program that will not entail any unnecessary waits. If the compute time is exactly equal to the read time for each block, how much faster is the double-buffered program than the single-buffered program given above?

8-5 Suppose that we wish to copy one file (F1) to another (F2) via primary memory. The instructions available are

```
READ     F1,Bi
WRITE    F2,Bi
WAIT     Fj
```

where Bi ($i = 1, 2, \ldots$) represents buffers in memory and $j = 1$ or 2. Each operation waits for the previous instruction on the same file to finish before control can continue to the next instruction. Write a program using two buffers, B1 and B2, to transmit six blocks from F1 to F2 as rapidly as possible. Write a second program using three buffers and a minimum of instructions to do the same thing.

8-6 Consider a process that involves reading blocks of a fixed size B from tape, processing each to produce another block of the same size, and then writing the result to another tape. The average calculation time for any one of any thirty consecutive blocks is precisely the time T taken to read or write one block, including the time for interblock gaps. Assume that it is executing on a two-channel computer and that there is no interference between the CPU and any of the channels over memory use. In theory, it is possible to keep both tapes spinning and the CPU busy. If the maximum calculation time for any single block is $2T$ and the minimum is $T/2$, how many buffers of size B are needed to keep the tapes spinning?

8-7 Consider a system in which blocks of disk space are allocated by a system program. Suppose that these are kept on a *free list* in which each free block in the list has the address of the next free block recorded in it, except for the last, which has an *end-of-list* indicator. (We call the address of the next block a *pointer* to the next block, and we call the list a *linked list*.) Each time a block is used, it is removed from the beginning of the list and the system records the next available free block. Suppose the system passes the address of the free block to the requesting program, and the program uses it for the next block in a file being written. Suppose also that this file chains its blocks using similar pointers to get from one block to the next. What would happen if there were a system crash between the time the block was allocated to the requesting program and the time the pointer in that block was updated, assuming that the requesting program puts a pointer to the new block from the preceding block in the file *before* the new block pointer is updated? What happens if the pointer from the preceding block is not changed until *after* the pointer in the new block is updated?

8-8 Frequently, systems that use large disk files must recognize bad tracks by keeping a record of which tracks cannot be used because of defects. How can this be done if a bit map is used to record free blocks?

8-9 Suppose a linked-list system of disk allocation is used, as described in Problem 8-7. The system tends to lose track of some of the physical blocks when system crashes occur, because the blocks are no longer on either the free list or the list of a particular file. Assuming that the system has a master list of the start of all files, how can a disk-check program be organized to find all lost blocks?

8-10 If the scheme described in Problem 8-7 were used for disk allocation, a machine error could result in an incorrect pointer address to the next disk block being stored in the preceding block. If the incorrect pointer were to address a block in another file, it would then appear that two files shared some blocks. This could cause a great amount of trouble. Assuming that there are some free bits in all blocks, how could a disk-check program determine that such an error has occurred? How could this be done if there were no spare bits in the disk blocks?

CHAPTER **9**

THE HARDWARE LEVEL

We have been looking at the computer at the machine level, at which level the programmer is aware of some of the internal registers and data paths and sees a machine whose primitive operations are the machine instructions such as LOAD and ADD. Internally, at the hardware level, there are registers and data paths that are invisible to the assembly-language programmer, and machine instructions are composed of sequences of even simpler primitives that move data from one register to another. In most cases, the assembly-language programmer need not be concerned about this finer level of detail, just as the higher-level language programmer need not be concerned about the detail of machine-level languages. However, there are situations in which a knowledge of what is going on at the lower level can assist in the efficient use of a computer. In addition, the availability of low-cost chips that can be interconnected relatively easily has made it possible for many people to custom design small, computer-based systems. (This chapter is not intended to give enough information to enable the reader to do such a design, but rather to introduce the general ideas. Many texts provide enough detail for those who are interested to do such designs.[1]) Furthermore, in some machines, called *microprogrammed* machines, it is possible for the programmer to get at this lower level of detail. A microprogram specifies the sequence of primitive steps that make up each machine instruction. Usually, the programmer does not make changes to the machine instructions, but in some special cases it is useful to be able to implement additional instructions for special purposes.

In this chapter we will look at the way registers are interconnected in typical computers and consider the way in which a common microprocessor, the Z80 (a derivative of the 8080), is connected to memory and I/O units. We will then look at the control

[1]For example, John B. Peatman, *Microcomputer-Based Design,* McGraw-Hill, New York, 1977.

of computers and the use of microprogram control. It is important to realize that the concept of microprogram control has nothing to do with microprocessors. A microprocessor is simply a very small processor, similar in principle to a large processor. Microprogramming refers to a particular way in which the internal workings of a computer at the level below machine language are controlled.

9.1 AN OUTLINE OF COMPUTER DESIGN

This section will discuss some of the ways in which components are interconnected to form a computer. The building blocks used consist of register, adders, memory units, gates, etc. The memory unit and registers were introduced in Chapter 2. These components are interconnected using *data paths*. Physically, a data path consists of a set of wires carrying the electrical output signal of one component to the input of another. *Gates* control the movement of these signals from one component to another. If two registers P and Q are connected as shown in Figure 9-1, the gate G controls the information flow. When G is turned on (*opened*), a copy of the information in register P is placed in register Q. The contents of P are not affected by this copying operation. This process is called a *register transfer*. This description is necessarily a simplified description of the process, which can vary in detail from one hardware implementation to another. The register transfer process takes a finite amount of time, typically in the range of 1 to 500 nanoseconds (1 nanosecond = 1 billionth of a second = 10^{-9} seconds).

During the period in which the gate is open, the content of the register supplying the information (P in Figure 9-1) must not be changed. If it is necessary to move some information into P after the current contents of P have been gated elsewhere, there must be some guarantee that the gate from P has been closed before an input gate to P is opened. This is done by performing the basic register transfer operations in periods of time called *cycles*. One cycle is the time needed to turn on a gate, to allow time for the information to flow to the register being set and for the register being set to change to its new state, and to turn the gate back off again. Most computers have a *clock* that times each of these basic cycles. (This clock is different from the real-time clock and interval timer discussed in Chapter 8. It provides electrical pulses at a very high speed corresponding to the fastest events in the computer, which are usually the register transfers.) The computer is controlled by sequences of gate signals, each occupying one clock cycle. These signals are generated by the control section of the computer.

9.1.1 CPU Data Flow

The programmer is aware of only a few of the registers in the machine (they are usually referred to as the *addressable registers*) and of some of the interconnecting data paths.

FIGURE 9-1 Gated transfer of information

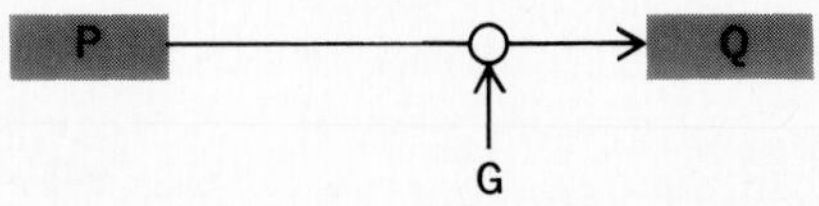

P → Q

G

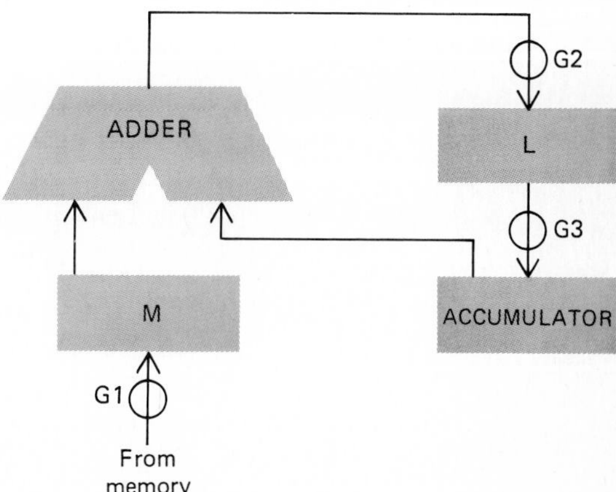

FIGURE 9-2 Data flow for addition

This is because many of the registers are not accessible to the programmer, but are used to implement instructions that affect the addressable registers. For example, a computer with an accumulator can add a value from memory to the value in the accumulator. The data fetched from the memory is usually first gated into a register in the CPU, as shown in Figure 9-2, where we have named the register M. Gate G1 gates the data into M. The data in the M register and the data in the accumulator feed an adder unit whose output can be gated by gate G2 into another register we have named L in Figure 9-2. The output of L can be gated into the accumulator by gate G3. Here we see that three registers have been used to accomplish an addition operation on one register. The two additional registers can, of course, be used to implement a number of other operations, such as subtraction, loading, storing, and shifting. (Shifting of the accumulator, for example, is done by transferring the content of the accumulator to another register, such as L in Figure 9-2, and then gating it back to the accumulator shifted 1 or more bits.) The additional register L, sometimes called a *latch* register, is needed to hold data originating in the accumulator before it is gated back to the accumulator in a modified form. If, for example, we tried to gate the output of the adder in Figure 9-2 directly back to the accumulator, the value of the accumulator would change, in turn changing the output of the adder. If the adder output changed before the gate from the adder to the accumulator closed, the value in the accumulator would change again and would not be the correct result of the addition. (Some types of registers permit data to be gated into them "almost instantaneously," so that all of the additional registers are not necessary; however, in general, gating the output of a register directly back to itself leads to a *race condition* in which the result is not deterministic, but dependent on the speed of the circuits.

High-speed computers have many interconnected registers, as a result of which several register transfer operations can occur in parallel. For example, a double-precision addition in a high-speed computer will usually be implemented using two sets of single-precision registers and adders operating at the same time, whereas in a medium-speed computer it will usually be implemented using the same adder twice—once for the least significant part and once for the most significant part.

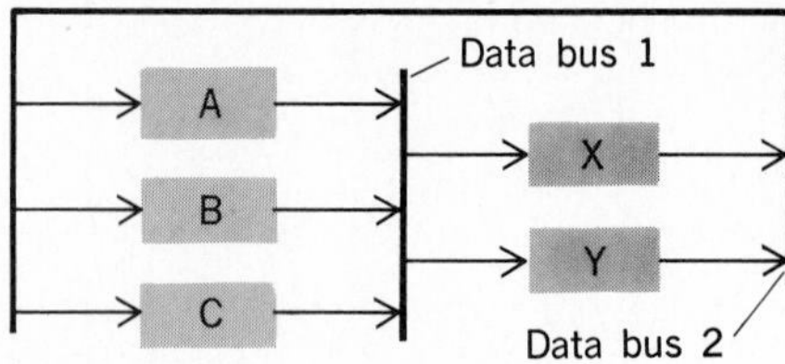

FIGURE 9-3 Data buses (gates are indicated by arrows)

Most small computers are organized internally using one or more *data buses*. These are data paths that can transmit information from more than one register (the *source* registers) to more than one register (the *destination* registers). Figure 9-3 shows five registers interconnected with two buses. Bus 1 can transfer information from either of registers A, B, or C to either of registers X or Y. Bus 2 can transfer information from X or Y to A, B, or C. Because several registers can be the source for a bus, there are gates both onto the bus from the source registers and off the bus to the destination registers. The designer could have connected buses 1 and 2 in Figure 9-3, resulting in just one bus with inputs and outputs to all registers. In that case, only one register transfer operation would have been possible at a time. As shown in Figure 9-3, two transfers could take place at the same time. For example, the content of A could be transferred to X while the content of Y was being transferred to B. It would not be possible to, say, transfer A to X while X was being transferred to B, because a race condition would exist—would the old or the new content of the X register finish up in B? The use of buses usually decreases the number of data paths needed in a computer, but the additional gates that must be used usually slow a register transfer operation (information flows through two gates instead of one).

Another important component in a CPU is the adder (which also performs subtraction, usually by use of twos complement arithmetic). The adder is constructed from a number of circuits (to be described in Section 9.2.1). These circuits are capable of performing a number of other operations, such as the logical operations AND, OR, and NOT, so the unit that performs addition usually has a number of control signals as well as its two data inputs. The control signals specify which logical or arithmetic operation is to be performed on the data input. The unit is called an *arithmetic/logical unit* (ALU). It also has a number of sense signals as output as well as the data output. These signals indicate conditions of the result, such as overflow, zero, and carry out.

Inputs to the ALU can be taken from a pair of registers, a pair of buses, or one of each. A typical design is shown in Figure 9-4. This is the AM 2901 *bit-slice processor* chip. It contains the registers, data paths, and ALU of 4 bits of a computer. Several of them can be used to get an 8-, 16-, or 32-bit computer (or larger, if desired). It does not contain any of the control circuitry—the sequence of gate signals necessary to control this chip must be generated by other components. Figure 9-4 shows four buses, two *internal* and two *external*. The internal buses A and B can each get the content of one of sixteen *scratchpad* registers. (A scratchpad memory is a small set of registers organized like a memory.) In the AM 2901 design, the data from the A and B buses is gated into the A and B registers (there is no other choice). These are latch registers to hold information while other information that may depend on it is gated into the

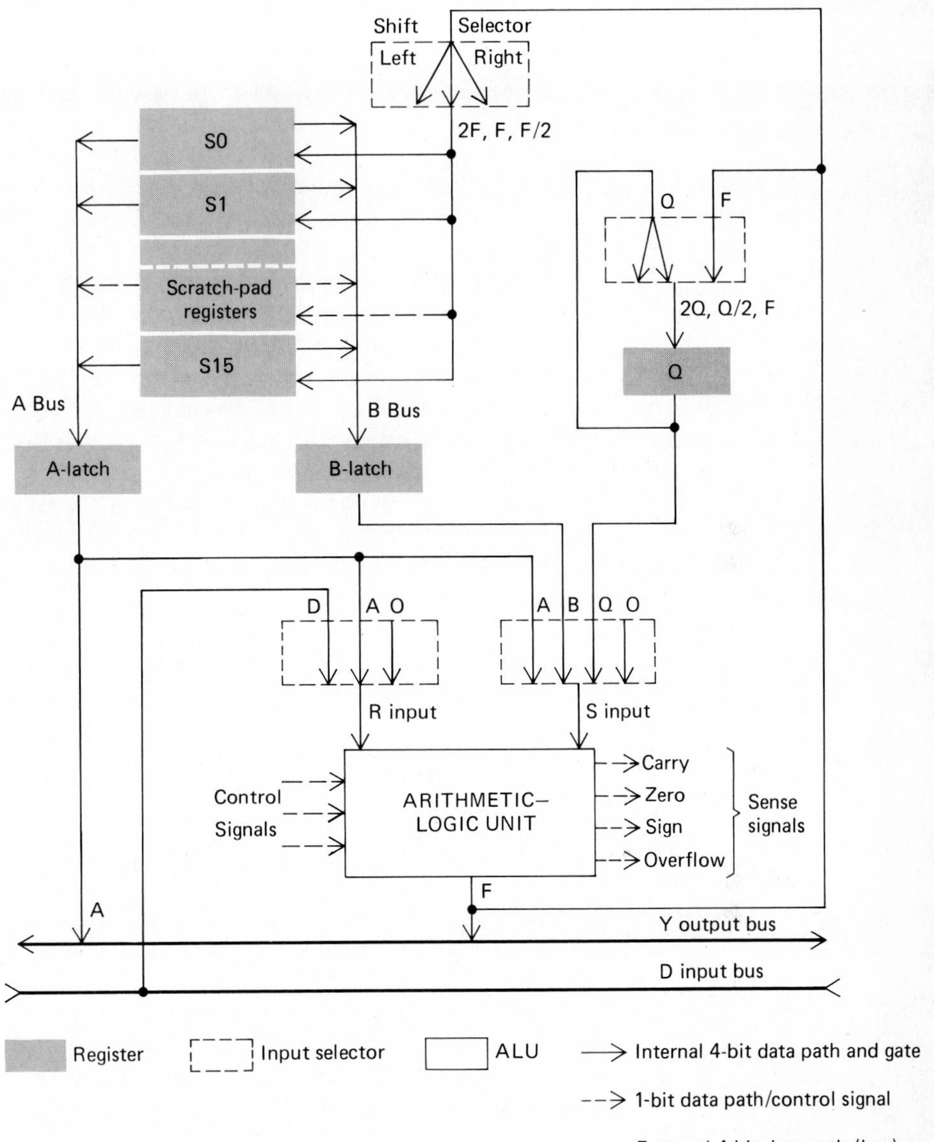

FIGURE 9-4 AM 2901 data flow

scratchpad registers. The inputs to the ALU can be selected from either the A or B registers; from the third internal register; Q, or from the external input bus D. The D bus is used to bring information into the chip from external sources such as memory. The output of the ALU can be either gated back to any of the scatchpad registers directly or shifted left or right 1 bit. It can also be gated to the Q register or to the output external bus Y, which transmits information elsewhere, such as to memory.

The data paths in a unit such as the AM 2901 can be used to perform all the processing necessary to execute an instruction. For example, one of the scratchpad registers can be designated as the program counter. Another can be designated as the accumulator if a one-address organization is to be implemented. Alternatively, a number of them could be designated as general registers addressable by the programmer. Control hardware, to be discussed in Section 9.2, determines the sequence of gate operations necessary to execute each instruction. To execute the next instruction, the content of the program counter must first be sent to memory. Using the AM 2901 hardware, the content of the scratchpad register designated as the program counter is gated to the A register and then onto the Y bus to memory. When the data returns from memory on the D bus, it has to be saved in a register for examination of the operation code. If it indicates an addition of two general registers (whose addresses are specified in the instruction), those addresses have to cause the appropriate gates to be opened from the scratchpad registers to the A and B buses, and the appropriate control signals and gates to be opened to form the sum and to move it back to the destination register in the scratchpad memory. If a designer were constructing a CPU using this chip, it would be possible that some of the scratchpad registers would also be used to hold the instruction fetched from memory to avoid using additional hardware external to the chip.

9.1.2 Memory Data Flow

Data paths from the CPU, usually buses, provide the connection to the memory. Figure 9-5 shows the organization of a primary memory unit for use with a data flow of the type used in the AM 2901. The memory receives control signals that tell it to read or write. Internally, the memory contains a register that takes the address from the bus transmitting it from the CPU and stores it so that the bus is free for other purposes. This is called the *memory address register* (MAR). It is loaded from the bus when a read or write control signal is received. In the case of a read, the memory then uses the address to obtain the corresponding data from the storage medium and gates that data into another latch register called the *memory data register* (MDR). This is then gated onto the data bus for transmission to the CPU. In the case of a write, the memory must receive both the address, gated into the MAR, and the data, gated into the MDR. Then the memory copies the MDR into the memory cell specified by the address in the MAR, during which time the CPU is free to perform other actions.

With the data flow shown in Figures 9-4 and 9-5, a write operation to memory uses the Y bus twice—once to send the address and once to send the data. In many organizations, the inherent delay of these two serial steps is overcome by using one bus as an *address bus* and one as a *data bus,* as shown in Figure 9-6. In this organization, the address bus is only used to specify addresses and the data bus is only used for data. Many microprocessor chips (such as the Z80) use this organization, which will be discussed in Section 9.3. It allows memory writes to be performed more rapidly, but it does not permit the CPU to simultaneously send and receive data. If the chip is being used in a dedicated equipment-control application, the latter operation may be more important, but if the chip is being used in a general-purpose computer, the former is more important.

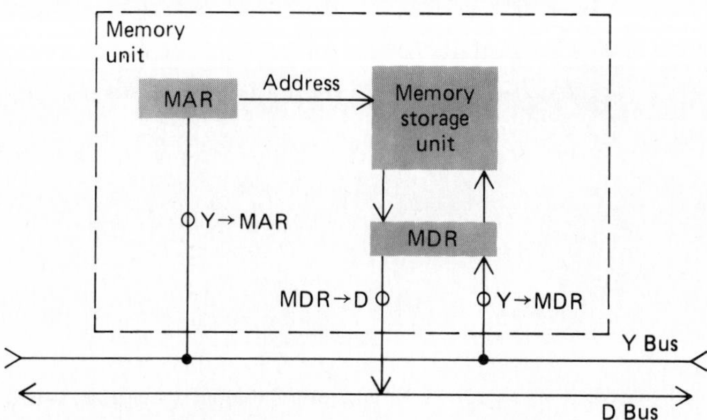

FIGURE 9-5 Primary memory connection

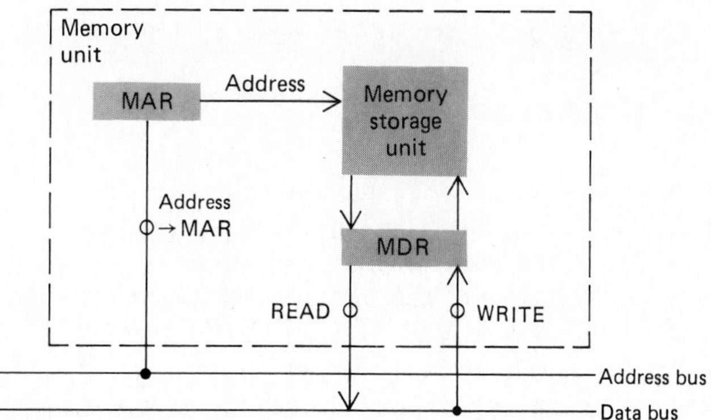

FIGURE 9-6 Separate data and address bus

9.2 CONTROL

This section discusses the way in which data flow can be implemented using logic circuits and how the sequences of gate signals necessary to control the data flow can be generated. This will of necessity be a brief summary.

Signals in the computer are usually transmitted along wires as voltage levels. To make it possible to distinguish between allowed states reliably, only two states are recognized: a high-voltage state, say about +5V, as a binary 1, and a low-voltage state, say about 0V, as a binary 0. (In practice, anything above a voltage such as +2.4V is considered a binary 1 and anything below a voltage such as +0.4V is considered a 0. These values depend on the type of hardware being used.) Logical operations are performed on binary values using circuits that combine them in simple ways. The usual operations are the already familiar AND, OR, and NOT operations. An AND gate is a circuit with two or more inputs and one output. Its output is 1 (high) only if all inputs are high. Conventional block diagrams for each of these three logic elements are shown in Figure 9-7. These elements can be interconnected to perform complex logical tasks. For example, suppose we wish to form the sum of two binary digits x and y. The result

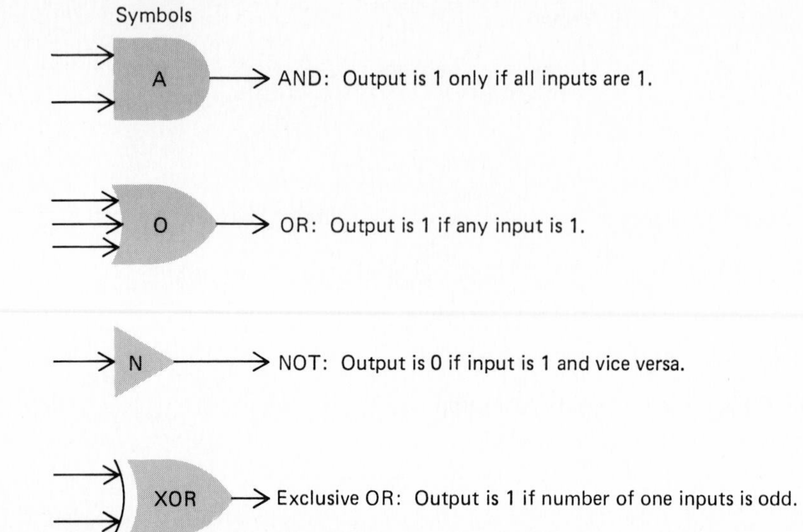
Symbols
A
AND: Output is 1 only if all inputs are 1.
O
OR: Output is 1 if any input is 1.
N
NOT: Output is 0 if input is 1 and vice versa.
XOR
Exclusive OR: Output is 1 if number of one inputs is odd.

FIGURE 9-7 Conventional logic symbols

is shown in Table 9-1. The rightmost digit of the sum is 1 only if x or y (but not both) is 1. This is the exclusive "or" operation. A conventional symbol for it is also shown in Figure 9-7. It is possible to fabricate an exclusive or from ANDs, ORs, and NOTs, as shown in Figure 9-8. This logical circuit uses the fact that the exclusive or of x and y can be written as (x AND(NOT y))OR((NOT x) AND y). This circuit is also known as a *half adder*. The leftmost bit of the sum shown in Table 9-1 is simply x OR y. Using similar ideas, any logical combination of 2 or more bits can be constructed if enough logic elements are used.

Another important circuit that can be constructed from these elements is a *flip-flop*. A flip-flop is a single-bit memory used in the construction of registers. One type of flip-flop, often called a *latch,* is shown in Figure 9-9*a*. It has two inputs, p and q. If both of these are held to 1, the AND element outputs are the same as their second inputs. These are labeled f and g in the diagram. Since the output of one is connected to the input of the other via NOT elements, f and g must satisfy the equations f = NOT g and g = NOT f. These are satisfied by the pair ($f = 0$, $g = 1$) or ($f = 1$, $g = 0$), so that the latch can be in a stable state with the output g at either 0 or 1. If

TABLE 9-1 HALF-ADDER FUNCTION

Input		
x	**y**	**Sum**
0	0	00
0	1	01
1	0	10
1	1	11

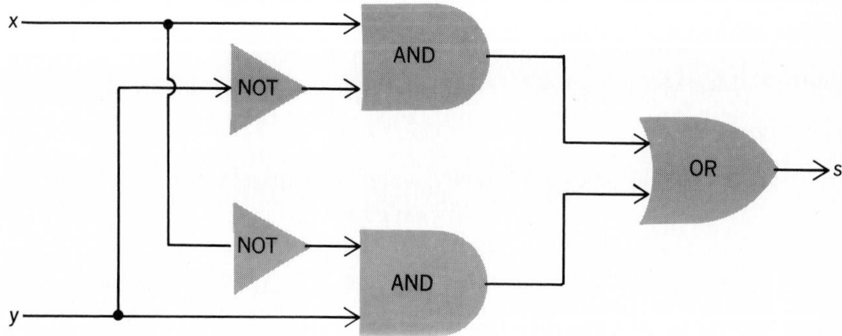

FIGURE 9-8 Exclusive OR (half adder)

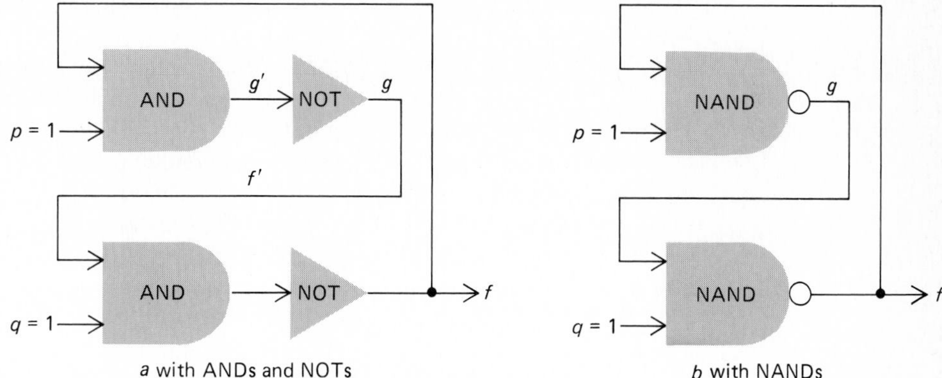

FIGURE 9-9 Flip-flop: (*a*) with ANDs and NOTs, (*b*) with NANDs

the input *p* is set to 0 briefly, *g* goes to 0, causing *f* to go to 1, a stable state even after *p* has returned to 1. If *q* goes to 0 briefly, the reverse occurs, causing *f* to go to 1 and *g* to go to 0, the other stable state. Thus *p* can be used to *clear* the flip-flop, whereas *q* can be used to *set* it. Figure 9-9*b* shows another form of latch using NAND (Not-AND) elements. These are similar to AND elements except that the output is inverted, as if going through a NOT. (It happens that NAND elements are simpler to construct electrically than AND elements.)

A register can be constructed with a set of these flip-flops. It can be cleared to 0 by setting all the *p* lines to 0 and then back to 1. A number can be gated into a register by setting *q* to 0 for those bits that have to be set to 1. (This can be done by combining a gate signal with the bits that have to be gated into the register using NAND elements.) Many other forms of flip-flops are available for use in registers. Arithmetic, such as addition, can be performed by combining logical circuits in straightforward ways, so it is clear that it is possible to build the data flow of any computer (although the detailed design of an efficient, high-speed data flow is a very complex process).

Execution of an instruction requires that a sequence of gate signals be generated. There are two principal ways in which this can be done: by means of logical circuits in which the sequences are "hard-wired" and by means of a sequence of signals stored in a special memory. The latter is called a *microprogram control*.

9.2.1 Hard-Wired Control

The gates have to be opened in a particular sequence. This sequence can be considered as a sequence of indivisible steps. In each step a particular set of gates has to be opened. These gate signals can be generated by assigning a flip-flop to each step and arranging for the output of the flip-flop to be a 1 whenever that step has to be executed. The signals to the gates in the data flow can be controlled by the output of the flip-flops; that is, the gates can be opened when the flip-flop is in a 1 state. A clock signal can be used to set the next flip-flop in sequence to a 1 and the previous to a 0. The clock signals are derived from an *oscillator,* a device that produces a series of electrical pulses at a given frequency, and a counter, a device that counts pulses from the oscillator using logical elements and flip-flops.

At some point the next step has to be determined by the values of data in registers. For example, after the instruction has been *fetched* (which requires a sequence of gate signals to send the content of the program counter to memory as an address, to cause a read from memory to an *instruction register,* and to increment the program counter) the sequence of gates corresponding to the instruction just fetched must be initiated. Consequently, the flip-flop for the next step is set only if the flip-flop for the last previous step is set *and* appropriate conditions are met; for example, the bits in the instruction register represent an ADD instruction.

Many different types of logical elements are used in practical computers, but the principles are those enumerated above. In the early days of computer design, there was a great emphasis on minimizing the number of logical elements in a given piece of hardware. Today, large circuits are fabricated on a single chip of silicon, and the important criteria are the area of silicon needed and the number of external connections to the chip.

9.2.2 Microprogram Control

We saw in the last section that the data flow is controlled by sequences of steps that sometimes depend on values in the data flow being controlled—in other words, by a fixed sequence of gate signals interspersed with tests that determine subsequent steps in the sequence. This has a strong similarity with the sequences of steps in a computer program. A microprogrammed control exploits this similarity by using what is in effect a simpler computer to generate the sequences of gate signals. This simpler computer is called the *microcontrol*. Referring to Figure 9-10, we see that the data flow and memory of a computer can be viewed as a "black box" that is controlled by gate signals sent from the controller. In turn, the controller examines the status of various sense signals transmitted back from the data flow to the controller. When microprogram control is used, the controller consists of a simple device that reads the gate signals from a memory for each step and then tests the sense signals, using conditional branch instructions to determine subsequent actions.

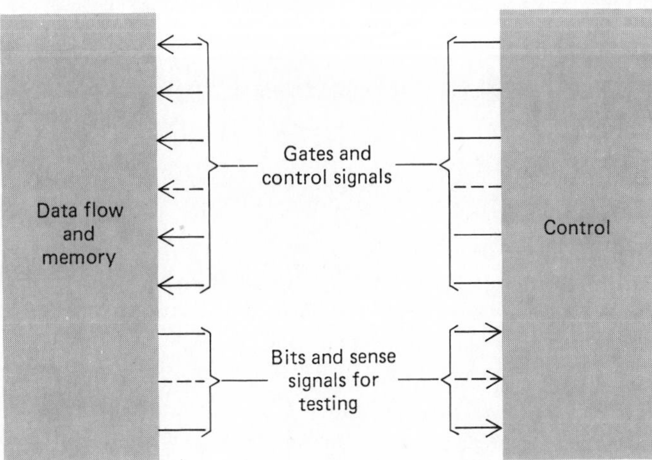

FIGURE 9-10 Data flow and control

How can this be done by microcontrol? Basically, each microstep is represented by a word in the control memory. This word lists the gates that must be opened and/or the tests that must be made for a conditional branch to be successful. In the case of a conditional branch, the word must also specify the branch address. The sequence of microsteps is called the *microprogram*. Each individual step is called a *microinstruction*. As each successive word is read from the micromemory (that is, the control memory), it is used to turn on gate signals. For example, each gate could be controlled by a single bit position in a micromemory word (although we will see that they are usually coded more compactly). Other bits in the word are used to indicate which bits in the data flow should be tested and the branch address to be used if the test is successful.

An organization for a microcontrol is shown in Figure 9-11. It contains a micromemory in which the microprogram is stored. Each microinstruction is stored as a single word in this memory and specifies the gates to be opened in each step. A sequence of words contains the sequence of steps necessary to execute each instruction. Since the instruction set of a computer does not normally change, it is common to store the microprogram in a *read-only memory* (ROM). This is a memory that can be read from but cannot be changed. Its contents are set by the manufacturer or, in some cases, can be changed by special, slow operations. The advantage of using a ROM is that it is usually less expensive and faster for a given number of bits of information. Furthermore, the information cannot be destroyed accidentally. However, some machines store some of the microprogram in read/write memory (called RAM, for *Random-Access Memory*). This allows it to be changed by a programmer so that the instruction set can be modified.

The micro-organization shown in Figure 9-11 shows an MAR with an attached adder for incrementing by 1 (this combination is also called a *counter*). Since the micromachine executes only control instructions and does not read or write data into the control memory, the MAR can serve as a control counter for the micromachine. It can

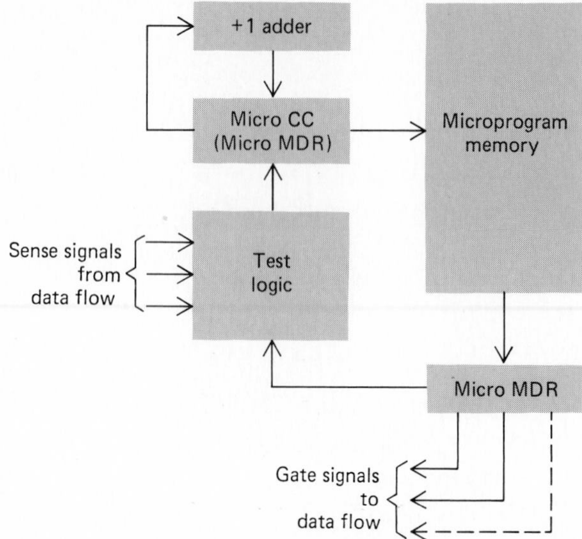

FIGURE 9-11 A microcontrol

always contain the address of the next instruction. Each microinstruction is fetched from memory in turn and decoded from the MDR (which also serves as an instruction register). The decoding determines which gates to open and which bits to test. If conditions tested so indicate, a branch address is gated from the MDR to the MAR in the micromachine.

A large number of gates and control signals is indicated in Figures 9-4 and 9-5, and still more control signals are needed in a complete machine. One could allocate a separate bit for each gate and control signal, but this would result in a very wide word (large number of bits) in the micromemory. This would give maximum flexibility, because any gate could be opened in any step. However, many combinations of gates are invalid. For example, if there are several different gates into a register, no more than one of them can be opened in a single step. Therefore, the gates and control signals are usually arranged into *control groups*. A set of bits is allocated to each control group so that one of the gates in a control group can be selected. For example, if 8 to 15 gates were in the same control group, 4 bits could be used. One combination of the 4 bits would indicate that no gate was to be opened; the other 15 combinations would indicate a particular gate. Even when this is done, micromemories are usually fairly wide—a width of 50 to 100 bits is not uncommon.

Frequently, the microcontrol itself is enhanced to obtain some additional useful functions that improve speed. In particular, a microsubprogram call is very useful. Since there is no place to hold the return address in a ROM, additional registers must be provided. These can be arranged as a stack the top level of which is the program counter. Indeed, chips are available that provide such facilities directly.

Who, we might ask, controls the microcontrol? Do we need a micro-microcontrol to do that, and so on ad infinitum? At some point, hardware control must be used to sequence through the steps of one of the micro-micro- . . . controls. We can see that the micromachine is already very simple, so its control is almost trivial to implement in hardware. Thus we realize that microcontrol can effectively reduce the amount of hardware needed in the control area. It is true that micromemory has to be added, but the cost is usually more than offset by the savings in other circuitry and the increased flexibility for implementing more complex instructions for the user.

Additional advantages accrue to the manufacturer of a microcontrolled computer: they are often easier to check out during the design phase, because the hardware is much simpler and the microprogram can be simulated easily; they are easier to check out during manufacture, because test microprograms can be used to diagnose errors more quickly; and they are easier to maintain in the field for the same reason. Further, subsequent changes (resulting from errors that are discovered in the design after a number of the systems have been installed at customer sites) are easier to repair by replacing the microprogram, which can be done by replacing the ROM, a simple field change.

A number of popular computers use microprogram control. Some of these are summarized in Tanenbaum's *Structured Computer Organization.*[2]

9.3 MICROPROCESSOR SYSTEMS

A microprocessor is simply a processor small enough to fit on a single chip of silicon. The first microprocessors were only 4 bits wide, contained relatively few internal registers, and executed a relatively limited instruction set. A number of additional chips were needed to provide memory, I/O, clock signals, and other facilities. Today there are microprocessors with many wider registers, some "on-board" memory and I/O controllers, and many more instructions. However, even with the more advanced chips, most microprocessors need additional memory and additional I/O controllers. Therefore, a typical microprocessor consists of a number of interconnected chips. Manufacturers have designed *chip sets* of related chips that can easily be interconnected. In this section we will take a brief look at the way in which the Z80 and similar chips can be interconnected; the principles are the same for any set of chips used in microprocessors.

There are a number of different types of circuits (often referred to as "technologies") used for microprocessor chips. These differ in speed, electrical power requirements, the voltage levels corresponding to 0 and 1, etc. The designer will normally use compatible chips so that interconnections can be made directly without the need for special interfaces among different types of chips. We will not consider these questions in this introductory look at microprocessors. Neither will we consider questions of speed and power that are important in an actual design. (The output signal from a chip is capable of driving only so much current into other chips. Furthermore, there are timing restrictions that require that the signals must change by a certain time. Adding connections to the output of a chip can slow down the signal and increase the current drain, so that the number of connections and the length of wire that can be connected are limited, depending on the situation.)

[2]A. S. Tanenbaum, *Structured Computer Organization,* Prentice-Hall, Englewood Cliffs, NJ, 1976.

A complete microprocessor may be contained on a single *board,* which is usually a printed circuit card containing the electrical connections between the chips, or it may require several such cards with connections between them. In either case, there are additional connections to some I/O devices, such as a terminal, and to an electrical power supply. For many chips, a single 5-V power supply is sufficient, so that two of the connections to all chips are the *ground* (0 V) and the 5-V power connections. A third important connection for most chips is the *clock* signal, which keeps everything in synchronization. The clock signal is generated by a circuit and takes the form shown in Figure 9-12*a*. It changes from 0 V (logic 0) to about 5 V (logic 1) and back at a fixed frequency. For the Z80, the required frequency is 2.5 MHz (MegaHertz), which means that it makes the transition from 0 to 1 2.5 million times per second. A clock signal is

FIGURE 9-12 Electrical pulse signals: (*a*) clock pulses, (*b*) single pulse, (*c*) inverted pulse

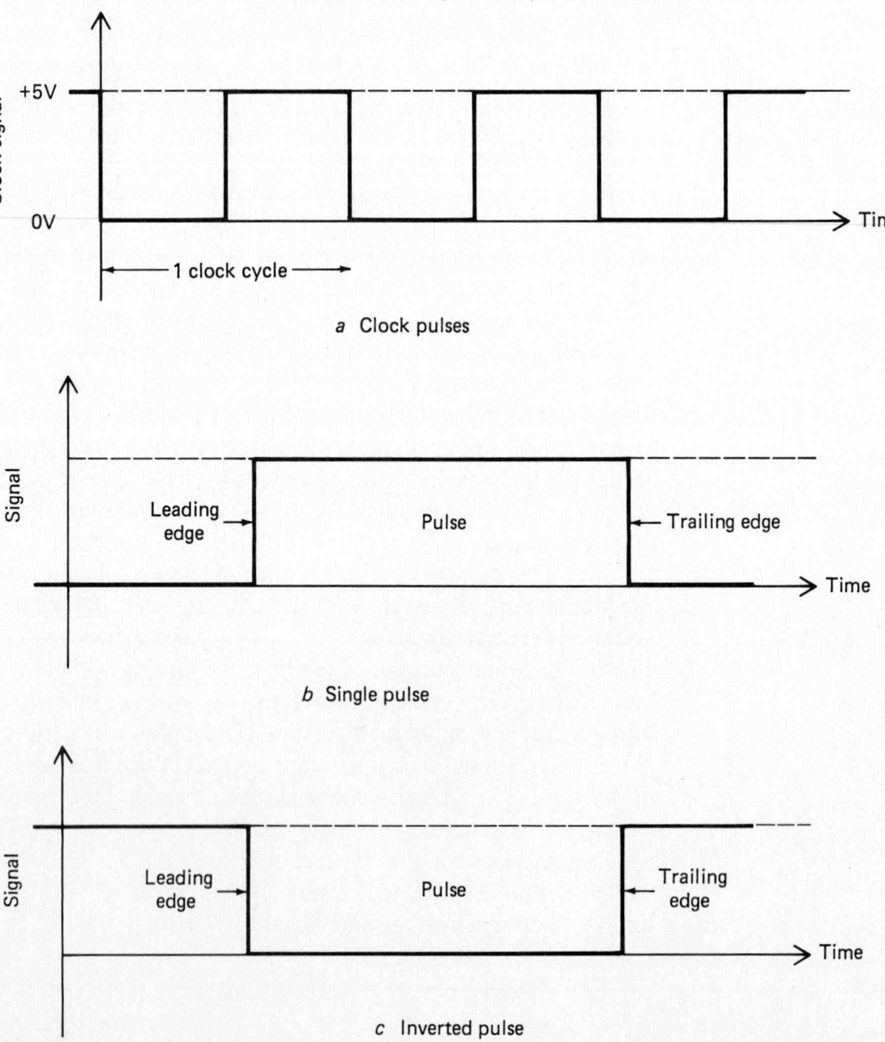

usually *symmetric,* so that the length of time at 0 is the same as the length of time at 1, which is 200 nanoseconds in this case. The clock signal is sent to all chips that need it. Some of these chips generate signals that tell other chips when to take certain actions. These signals take the form shown in Figure 9-12*b*. They are like a single clock *pulse*. Some chips react to the start of a pulse, that is, to the *leading edge* of the pulse. For example, some registers are set by the leading edge of a control-signal pulse. Other circuits respond whenever the pulse is present, so they stop responding at the trailing edge of the pulse. We will see some examples of these circuits in the next two subsections. Many signals are *inverted,* that is, a logical 1 is represented by 0, whereas a logical 0 is represented by a high voltage, as shown in Figure 9-12*c*. Whereas this is of importance to the actual designer, we will not consider it here. Compatible chips will provide an inverted signal if such a signal is needed by another chip.

9.3.1 The Z80 CPU

The Z80 CPU processor chip executes the INTEL 8080 instruction set plus a large number of additional instructions. It has several additional registers (including two index registers); a duplicate set of the arithmetic registers A, B, etc., for fast partial-context switching; and additional interrupt modes. These are shown in Figure 9-13. If we consider only the 8080 subset of instructions, the Z80 is almost identical to the 8080, except for slightly better handling of the DAA instruction following a subtraction (by means of an additional flag bit, N, set after a subtraction) and a redefinition of the Parity bit as a Parity/Overflow bit. However, the Z80 chip is easier to use, because its requirements for clock signals and interconnections are simpler than the requirements of the 8080.

The Z80 chip is packaged in the standard 40-pin configuration called the Dual In-line Package (DIP). The forty leads allow connections to the chip to transmit data to and from memory and I/O devices and to transmit sense and control signals, clock information, and power. For example, pins 7 to 10 and 12 to 15 connect to the 8 bits of the data bus. When the Z80 wishes to write to memory, the data to be written appears on these pins. The corresponding address information appears on pins 30 to 40 and 1 to 5 to specify the 16-bit address where the data is to be written. Two control signals, Memory Request (MREQ) and Write (WR), tell the memory that a write is to take place. MREQ turns on to indicate that a memory operation is to take place. By this time the address is available on the address bus from the CPU. A little later, WR turns on to indicate that the data is on the data bus and should be written into the memory. Then MREQ and WR turn off, indicating that the write process is over (as far as the Z80 is concerned). Similarly,when the Z80 wishes to read data from memory, it places the address on the address bus and turns on MREQ. In this case it also turns on the READ (RD) signal. After a suitable wait, in which time the memory is expected to place the data on the data bus, the Z80 copies the data from the data bus into the CPU and turns off MREQ and RD, indicating the end of the memory read operation. If the Z80 CPU is connected to a memory that obeys the read and write requests described above sufficiently rapidly, and if the appropriate power and clock signals (+5V to pin 11, Ground to pin 29, and the clock to pin 6) are made, the Z80 will execute instructions fetched from memory, once started.

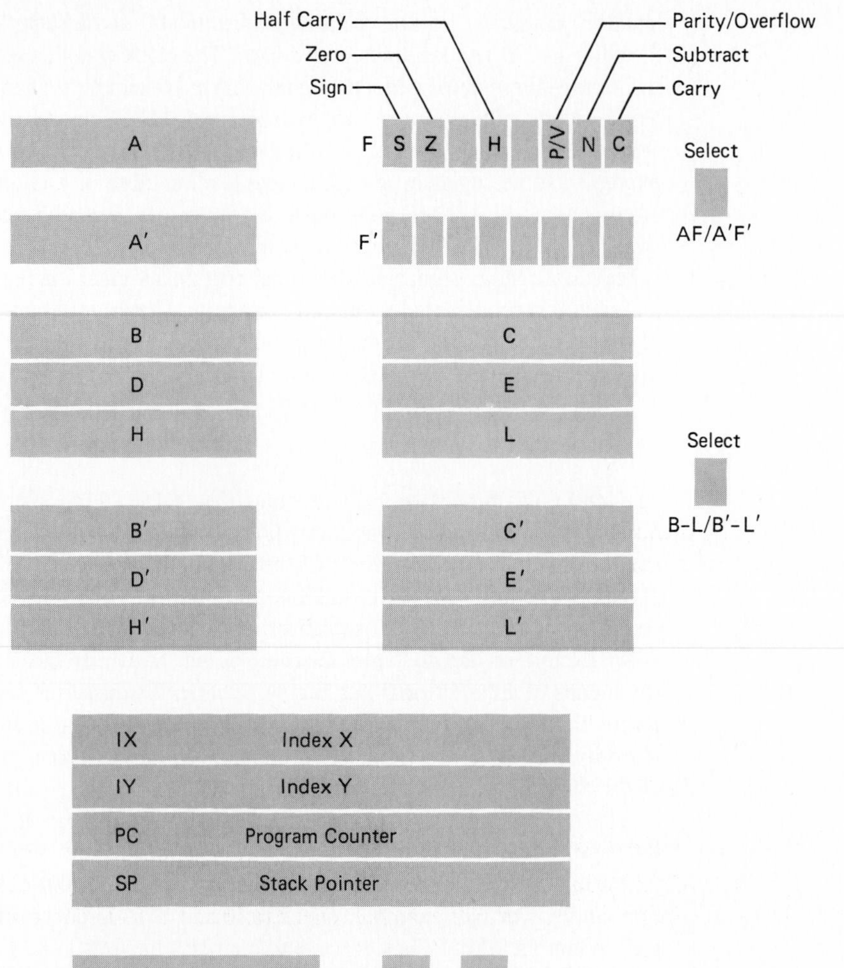

FIGURE 9-13 Z80 registers

A number of other control and sense signals are generated or used by the Z80. One of these is I/O request (IORQ), which indicates that an I/O operation has been requested. When this signal is on, the RD and WR signals indicate whether the operation IN or OUT has been given, and the least significant 8 bits of the address bus contain the I/O port address. The data bus is used to transmit the data between the I/O control unit and the CPU. The Z80 uses a number of basic clock cycles to complete the execution of an instruction. For example, fetching the instruction takes a minimum of four clock cycles (more if it is a multiple-byte instruction). The fetch sequence is called machine cycle 1, and during this time the corresponding control signal M1 is on. It is used in connection with interrupt handling. The Interrupt signal (INT) is sensed by the Z80 at the end of each instruction. When it is on, the Z80 acknowledges its receipt by turning on IOREQ and M1. This is the only situation in which these two signals are on at the same time, so this can be used to indicate that interrupt information should be passed to the CPU from the interrupting device (the one that turned on INT initially). Recall from Chapter 8 that the 8080 expects the 1-byte RST instruction to be provided by the interrupting device. This is done by placing it on the data bus at this time. One of the interrupt modes of the Z80 imitates the 8080 interrupt. A more powerful interrupt mode allows the use of vectored interrupts. For these, the interrupting device must place the least significant 8 bits of a branch address for the interrupt onto the data bus when the interrupt is acknowledged. The interrupt vector register in the Z80 is concatenated with this to get a 16-bit interrupt branch address.

Other signals on the Z80 chip include a WAIT signal, which allows memory or I/O chips to indicate that they need more time to complete an operation, and bus request and acknowledge signals, which can be used to ask the CPU to stop using the Address and Data buses for a while so that Direct Memory Access operations from I/O units can take place. There are also a signal to reset the CPU to an initial state with the program counter set to 0 and a Halt signal that indicates that the CPU has executed a HALT instruction and is waiting to be restarted.

9.3.2 Memory

The amount of memory in a single chip has approximately doubled every 2 years. Currently, chips with 16,000 bits of storage cost very little (under 3 dollars) and 64,000-bit (64K) chips are available at not much more; 256K chips are beginning to appear in computers. Each chip has a set of address lines that can be connected directly to the address bus and a set of data lines that can be similarly connected to the data bus. Some memory chips are available with different widths of information. For example, 16K chips are available as 2K words of 8-bit bytes, as 4K words of 4-bit nibbles, or as 16K "words" of 1 bit each. The designer can select the chip most suitable for the application. The number of connections to the chip clearly depends on its size and configuration. For example, a 16K chip with 8-bit bytes needs eight data lines and eleven address lines to select among its 2048 words.

Additional lines control the operation of the chip. Most chips have a Chip Enable (CE) line that indicates that the chip should respond to its other control signals. These include RD and WR. A memory chip is examining the address on its address lines at all times. If CE is on and RD is received, the chip will execute a memory read cycle, gating the data onto the data bus after the time needed to read it. The CPU chip expects the data to be available within a certain time after the RD signal is issued, and so does not gate data from the bus until that time has elapsed. (The timing constraints involved must be determined from the technical specifications for each chip. The Z80 CPU is described in a technical manual from its manufacturer, Zilog.[3]) If the memory is too slow and cannot deliver the data in time, the designer can include additional circuitry to raise the WAIT signal to the CPU chip for one or more clock cycles. This causes the CPU to wait. Details can be found in the technical manual cited above. The WR signal is used in a similar way. If the chip is enabled and the WR signal is raised, the chip copies the data from the data bus into the location specified on the address bus. Before the CPU raises WR, it gates the address onto the address bus and the data onto the data

[3]Z80-CPU, Z80A-CPU Technical Manual, Zilog Corporation,Cupertino, CA, 1977.

bus and keeps it there for a short period (half a cycle) after the WR signal is turned off. In the time in which the WR signal is on (a full cycle in the case of the Z80), the memory chip must copy the data. If it cannot complete its operation in the time available, the designer must arrange to raise the WAIT signal. (Normally, the designer selects chips that operate in the same speed range as the CPU, so this is not a problem.) ROM chips are similar, except that they do not have a write signal.

A memory chip has only enough address lines to select the between the number of words it contains. For example, if it has 2K words, it has 11 address bits. If the same memory chip is used directly with the Z80 CPU, which has 16 address bits, the bottom 11 would be connected to the memory chip. The MREQ signal from the CPU can be connected directly to the CE control line on the memory chip so that it is enabled when the CPU requests use of the memory. If nothing else is done, we will get memory wraparound: addresses would be treated modulo $2048 = 2^{11}$, so that addresses 2048 to 4095 would be mapped to 0 to 2047, and so on. If we want to use more memory by using additional chips, we want to prevent this wraparound. This can be done by forming a logical combination of the remaining 5 address bits to select the chip only when the appropriate address bits and MREQ are present. Thus, to select a 2K-word chip for addresses 0 to 2047, we must form the logical AND of MEMRQ and the NOTs of A11, A12, . . . , and A15, that is,

```
MEMRQ AND (NOT A11) AND (NOT A12) AND (NOT A13)
          AND (NOT A14) AND (NOT A15)
```

where A11, A12, . . . , and A15 are the most significant 5 bits of the address. This signal is then connected to the CE pin of the chip. If we want to have 16K bytes of memory using eight 2K chips, we must form eight similar signals. There are single chips that do just that, making the designer's job simple. (Some memory chips have multiple CE signals that are logically ANDed internally.) Figure 9-14 shows an interconnection of a Z80-type CPU with typical memory chips for 4K bytes of memory.

9.3.3 I/O

The Z80 CPU uses the same address, data, RD, and WR signals for I/O as are used for memory. The existence of the IOREQ control signal indicates that an I/O operation is to be performed. If this signal occurs during machine cycle 1 (in which M1 is on), an I/O interrupt request is being acknowledged and the I/O unit causing the interrupt is expected to respond. Otherwise, the address on the eight least significant address lines, A0 to A7, contains the I/O port address specified in the IN or OUT instruction, and the RD control signal is on in the case of the IN instruction and off otherwise.

Typical devices use two or more port addresses, one for data and the remainder for control. When data is sent from the CPU to a port by an OUT instruction, that data must be read from the data bus and latched in a register for transmission to the I/O unit or for control of the unit. Similarly, when data is read by the CPU using an IN instruction, it must be available in a register for gating onto the data bus when the RD and IORQ signals are raised. If the device is to use interrupts for synchronization with the CPU, logical circuits must generate the interrupt signals when the device is ready to send or

FIGURE 9-14 A simple microcomputer

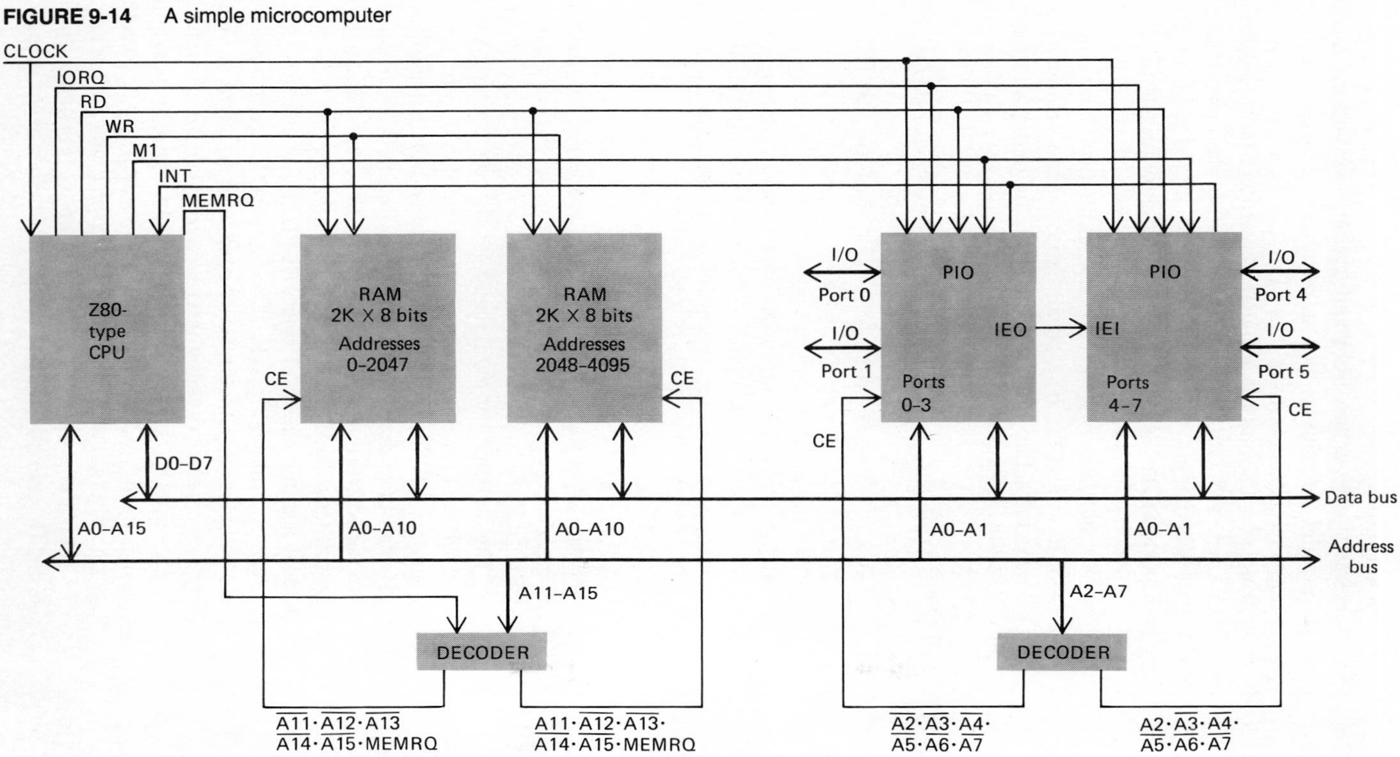

Note: $A11\cdot\overline{A12}\cdot\overline{A13}$ Means A11 AND (NOT A12) AND (NOT A13), etc.

receive data. These functions are performed by chips connected to the buses and control and sense signals. Manufacturers have designed multipurpose chips that can handle a number of standard I/O requirements. We will discuss one such chip, the Z80 PIO (Parallel I/O) chip, which interconnects between the Z80 CPU and I/O devices using eight parallel data lines. The PIO can be used for data input, for data output, or to handle control and sense signals directly. Details can be found in the technical manual.[4] A single PIO can service two devices, or the input and output for one device, as it has two sets of eight data lines for connection to the I/O device. These are called the A and B ports and are selected by a single control line, the B/A select line. Each of these sets of data lines has an associated control port, the C/D port. Another control line, the C/D select, indicates that the current operation is referencing the C or D port rather than the A or B port. If the B/A select line is wired to address line A1 and the C/D select line is wired to address line A0, then the following addressing is obtained:

0	Port A	(Data)
1	Port C	(Control for port A)
2	Port B	(Data)
3	Port D	(Control for port B)

If the other address lines are not used, port addresses are treated modulo 4. As with the memory chips, a Chip Enable control permits the remaining address bits to be decoded to control access to a particular chip. For example, if it is desired that a chip be used to respond to port addresses 28 to 31, the chip's CE signal should be set to

(NOT A7) AND NOT (A6) AND NOT (A5) AND A4 AND A3 AND A2

The same type of address-decoding chips used for memory chip selection can be used to enable I/O chips. Figure 9-14 also shows the interconnection of two PIO chips to the CPU.

The PIO chip has eight data lines for connection to the data bus and has IORQ, M1, and RD control lines. When data is available to be read by the CPU or the chip has completed the transmission of data to an I/O device following an OUT instruction, the PIO can raise the INT sense line so that the CPU enters the interrupt sequence at the next opportunity. The PIO (and other I/O chips designed for use with Z80) are designed to provide a hardware priority interrupt scheme. This is done by means of two additional signals: Interrupt Enable In (IEI), which indicates that the chip is allowed to interrupt, and Interrupt Enable Out (IEO), which passes the previous signal on to the next chip unless this chip wishes to raise an interrupt. Thus, if there are several chips, each is connected to the next in a *daisy chain* of signals. If the first chip wishes to interrupt, it disables the remainder. Otherwise, it passes the interrupt enable signal on to the second, which has the option to interrupt or pass the signal on to the third, and so on. Within each chip, the A data path takes interrupt priority over the B path.

The CPU program sets the PIO up by transmitting information to its control ports C and D. This information indicates whether a port is to be used for input, output, both,

[4]Z80-PIO, Z80A-PIO Technical Manual, Zilog Corporation, Cupertino, CA, 1977.

or control. It also can indicate whether interrupts are to be armed or not for the corresponding data port. Once the PIO has been set up, it can be used for data transmission. The PIO allows a number of options. This book is not intended as a technical manual for any particular device, so we will consider the PIO operation only for simple interrupt-controlled I/O, as this will illustrate most of the important principles.

The PIO has a set of eight data lines for the A and B ports and a pair of *handshaking* lines for each. Handshaking lines are used to synchronize control between an I/O device and the PIO chip. Since the transmission of data between two units (such as the PIO and an I/O unit) requires that one unit take the action to send the data by putting it on the data lines and the other unit take the action to receive the data by copying it from the data lines, it is clear that the two units must stay synchronized. In some systems, this is done by running all devices *synchronously,* using a clock signal to keep them in step. This is not possible with most I/O devices because the speed of, for example, the user typing at the keyboard cannot be controlled by a clock. Instead, the units must talk to each other to determine when they are ready for the next action. This can be done with two signals, one in each direction. Usually one unit is in control and is called the master unit, whereas the other device is called the slave unit. In a computer, the slave is usually the I/O device and the master is its controller, in this case the PIO. In the case of the PIO, the two signals are READY, which goes from the PIO to the I/O unit, and STROBE, which goes in the other direction. READY essentially says that the PIO is ready for the next operation by the I/O unit, and STROBE says that the I/O unit has completed its action. The sequence is discussed in general terms below and is illustrated in Figure 9-15.

There are two cases to consider in handshaking: when the sender is master and when the receiver is master. The operation is as follows.

Sender Master: Output for the PIO The communication between the two units proceeds as follows:

Sender: I have data (READY ON).
Receiver: I am about to take it (STROBE ON).
Receiver: I have taken it (STROBE OFF).
Sender: I am going to change the data (READY OFF).

While the PIO has the READY signal on, it does not change the data on the data lines to the I/O unit and must not change the data until it knows that the I/O unit has completed looking at the data (STROBE OFF). Once the data has been taken, the PIO can raise the interrupt signal if the interrupt is armed. When the interrupt has been serviced and another OUT instruction has been executed to send data to the PIO port, the READY signal can be raised again, indicating to the I/O unit that more data is ready for output.

Receiver Master: Input for the PIO The communication proceeds as follows:

Receiver: I am waiting for data (READY ON).
Sender: I am sending data (STROBE ON).

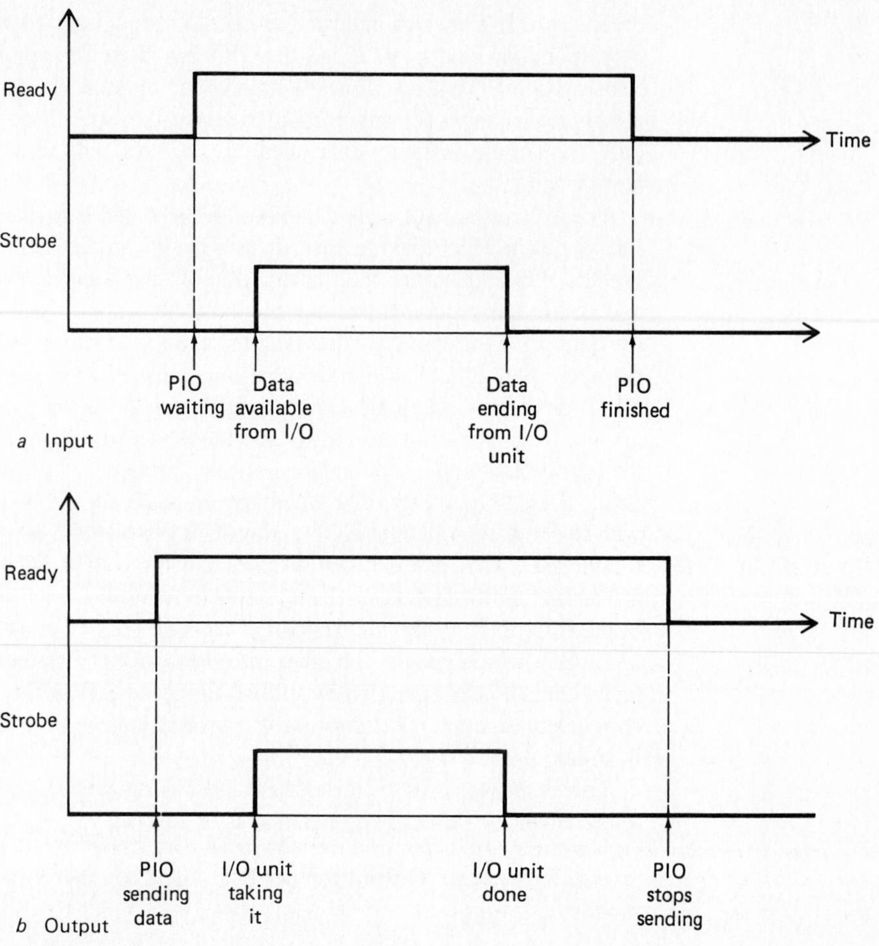

FIGURE 9-15 Handshaking

Sender: I have stopped sending data (STROBE OFF).
Receiver: I am getting ready for next input (READY OFF).

With this form of synchronization, the sender (I/O unit) must keep the data on the data lines while the STROBE signal is on, and it must also be certain that the data is present long enough for the PIO to latch it. These timing considerations are covered in the technical manuals.

Other types of chips are available for I/O control. For example, the Zilog SIO (Serial I/O) chip connects to the CPU in the same way as the PIO chip, but provides for control of bit-serial lines such as telephone connections to terminals.

9.4 SUMMARY AND PROBLEMS

A CPU consists of a set of registers and functional units, such as arithmetic and logical units, interconnected by gates. When a gate is opened, information is copied from one register or unit into another register. There are usually more registers in the CPU than the addressable registers visible to the machine-level language programmer. High-speed machines use many registers operating in parallel to get speed; low-speed machines may use very few registers and a bus to distribute data, so that very few gates can be opened at any one time.

Hardware control is made up of logical circuits that implement the standard logical operations AND, OR, and NOT. Frequently, the actual circuits implement NANDs because they are more natural to the technology used. These elements can be interconnected to form flip-flops, and sequences of control signals for the microsteps can be generated by logical circuits driven by an oscillator that generates a clock signal.

A microprogram control is a device consisting of a memory that stores a representation of the sequences of gate signals. A microcontrol counter sequences through the micromemory, one step after another, until a microbranch step is encountered. This can test bits in the data flow to determine the next microstep needed. Frequently, the microprogram is stored in read-only memory (ROM). It has a wide word to control the many gates. The extreme is to use 1 bit per gate, but the gates are usually arranged in control groups of gates that cannot be opened simultaneously. Some micromachines provide subprogram branch microinstructions and a stack to store the return address.

A microcomputer is simply a small computer that is constructed on a few chips. Chip sets are groups of compatible chips that can be interconnected to form simple computers. The CPU is usually a single chip, and the same chip may also contain some memory. Additional chips contain large amounts of memory and I/O control units.

Problems

9-1 A *full adder* is a logical circuit that adds 3 bits, x, y, and ci (c in), to get a sum s and a carry c. Write the *truth table* that gives s and c in terms of the three inputs. (A truth table is simply a list of all input cases with the corresponding outputs.) Can you design a circuit that gives the sum output using exclusive OR elements? Construct a circuit for the carry output using three AND elements and one OR element. Now construct circuits for the sum and carry using NAND elements only.

9-2 What are the principle advantages and disadvantages of microprogram control?

9-3 Does ROM have any use with programs other than microprograms? Why?

9-4 The handshaking described for input in Section 9.3.3 required that the I/O unit (the sender) keep the data available for a sufficient length of time for the PIO (receiver) to read it. It is possible to rearrange the sequence in which the signals are turned on and off so that there is no time dependency, that is, so that the receiver-master tells the sender when the data has been received. Design and explain such a sequence.

CHAPTER **10**

MULTIPROGRAMMING AND MULTIPROCESSORS

Computer systems are organized to try and meet a number of conflicting goals, including efficiency, short turnaround times, and user convenience. The purpose of this short chapter is to review some of the techniques used to meet these goals. We have already seen that there can be several processes active in primary memory at one time—one process for the CPU and one or more for I/O units. If one of these processes is waiting for another to complete an operation, part of the computer may be idle. Consequently, system designers have organized systems in such a way that many processes are available for execution. Thus, if one process that needs CPU cycles is waiting for an I/O process to complete an action, a different process that also needs the CPU can be serviced for a while. Similarly, one hopes to keep the I/O channels as busy as possible. The set of processes could all be part of a single job if the user were prepared to break the job down into concurrently executable processes. However, that may not always be practical; thus usually several different jobs are loaded at any one time to provide a balance of processes that need I/O channel service and CPU service. This is called *multiprogramming*.

Some systems have special requirements, such as the need to execute certain jobs particularly rapidly or the need for higher than usual reliability. (An example of both is a missile defense system. An example of the latter is an airline reservation system.) In these cases, more than one CPU may be attached to the system to improve the computation speed and to reduce the probability of the system being unable to perform any computation. This is called a *multiprocessor* system. (It is true that most channels can be viewed as processors, but we do not normally use the description "multiprocessor" unless there is more than one CPU.) Several CPUs will increase the total processing capability of the system, often measured in *mips* (millions of instructions per second). Several CPUs, each with its own memory, can be connected via channels, each of which looks like an I/O device to the other computers. This is not multiprocessing, but a multicomputer system, also called a *computer network*. A computer network practices load sharing, passing jobs to the computer that has available processing time on the required facilities. Networks will not be discussed in this book. *Timesharing* refers to the servicing of many customers or other remote terminals, each of whose average instruction rate is low, because interaction between the terminal and the computer slows the execution of the program associated with that terminal. Timesharing service requires a multiprogramming system and makes particularly severe demands on the system because of the large number of user jobs that must be serviced to achieve anything close to full utilization of the equipment.

10.1 MULTIPROGRAMMING

In a multiprogramming environment, several different jobs are loaded into different areas of the primary memory in the hope that they will provide work for most of the equipment that can be run simultaneously. The supervisor program takes care of allocating work to different units by keeping lists of processes that are ready for execution on each of the units. When a unit completes a process, the supervisor can check its lists for new work. In the case of I/O units, completion of a process is indicated by an interrupt that signals the CPU to stop processing the current program temporarily and to allocate more work to the I/O unit if there is any. In the case of CPU, completion is indicated when the CPU program either comes to the end of a job or requests I/O buffers that are not yet available—that is, in the case of input, the system has not yet filled the buffer, or in the case of output, the system has not yet emptied previous buffers so that there is space for new ones.

An important task for the supervisor in a multiprogramming system is scheduling jobs. This involves both macroscopic scheduling (deciding which jobs to load into memory when several are waiting in a job queue) and microscopic scheduling (deciding which process to allocate to a particular unit when there are several processes waiting for programs that are already in memory). No one criterion is used to decide on a scheduling algorithm. Macroscopic scheduling is usually done on some basis of priority—the more important job is loaded before the less important job when space is available. In many systems, microscopic scheduling leans more towards increasing efficiency, although priority information can also be used. The *mix* of jobs loaded in memory at any one time affects efficiency. For example, if every program is *CPU-bound* (that is, spends more time on CPU processing than on I/O work), it is not going to be possible to keep the I/O units busy. For that reason, a system may try to mix CPU-bound jobs with I/O-bound jobs in macroscopic scheduling. Once the mix has been chosen, microscopic scheduling must be used to maintain efficiency. Although at first sight it appears that it is only necessary for as many jobs as possible to be loaded in memory so that there is sure to be work for all units, decisions by the scheduler have a crucial effect on efficiency. Suppose there is one heavily CPU-bound job in memory that does no I/O for a long time. Once that job gets into execution, no more I/O requests will be issued, and eventually activity on all I/O units will cease. A supervisor should interrupt the CPU-bound job periodically to let other I/O-bound jobs execute long enough to create I/O work.

Memory cost is a nontrivial part of a multiprogramming system, because more memory than is needed for a single job must be purchased. Hence a scheduler that can maintain a given degree of activity using less memory is a better scheduler.

It can be seen that a scheduler has to balance several needs, so that there can be no absolute statements made about the correct algorithm to use. The scheduler must reflect the needs of the particular installation. We will not discuss this further here.[1]

The major software and hardware problems caused by multiprogramming are memory allocation, relocation, and protection. When several jobs are in memory simultaneously, each must be able to function as though the others were not present; otherwise, an error in one program could destroy another user's data. That is the problem of protection. When a program is loaded, it must be able to use the available area of memory. This means that it must not depend on using particular addresses. This can be handled with software, which is a loading problem. However, it is more convenient to do it with hardware relocation. The next section will examine a number of schemes that have been used for this.

10.1.1 Memory Allocation, Relocation, and Protection

Relocation was introduced in Chapter 6 as a means of loading preassembled programs into any area of memory. This is called *static relocation*. When the program is loaded, addresses that depend on the program's position in memory are set into the program. This means that the program cannot be moved once it has been loaded unless its relocatable addresses are modified. Let us consider the effect of such a system on multiprogramming.

When there are no jobs in memory, available memory forms a contiguous set of addresses, say from M to $N - 1$. (Usually, the lower-addressed part of memory contains the system programs, such as the kernel and the supervisor. We are assuming that these are in locations 0 through $M - 1$.) Programs can be loaded until the memory is full. These programs can be assigned contiguous sections of memory, say from M to $N_1 - 1$, from N_1 to $N_2 - 1$, etc. A relocating loader can load each program into its place without trouble. Now, suppose programs 1 and 3 are completed, leaving a total of $N - N_4 + N_3 - N_2 + N_1 - M$ words of free storage, as shown in Figure 10-1. Unfortunately, this storage is not contiguous; it has been *fragmented*. If the only programs waiting to be run are larger than either of the separate free areas, problems arise. One of three things can happen: the system can wait until a smaller job arrives or more memory becomes available, a program can be loaded into noncontiguous areas, or some of the programs already in memory can be moved to make the free storage contiguous. The first approach is not conductive to efficiency! The second approach is used in some systems, but it has limited application. If the program to be loaded consists of a number of separately relocatable sections (for example, subroutines and data areas), the loader can try to package them into the available sections of space. Since a good program is segmented into a number of manageable pieces, this is usually

[1]Further information on scheduling can be found in N. Haberman, *Introduction to Operating System Designs,* Science Research Associates, Palo Alto, CA, 1976, chap. 6; and B. Hansen, *Operating Systems Principles,* Prentice-Hall, Englewood Cliffs, NJ, 1973, chap. 4.

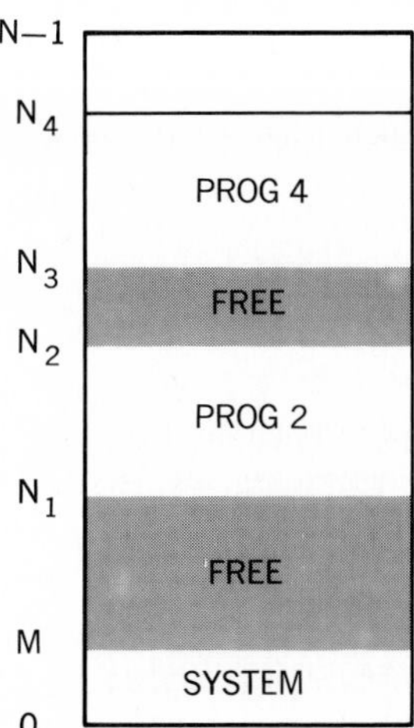

FIGURE 10-1 Fragmentation of free memory

possible. However, if a large data area is needed for a big array, a program may have to wait a long time for a contiguous piece of memory to be available. Alternatively, the scheduler will have to hold on to smaller pieces of memory until several adjacent pieces are free, forming a larger contiguous area. The third solution is not possible unless the program abides by some conventions. Consider a program that puts the address of a memory cell into one register (say, by a subroutine branch instruction) and a constant into another register. If the program were to be moved, the contents of the first register would have to be relocated, but the contents of the second would not. Consequently, the "reloader" that moved the program would have to know which registers to relocate if a program were to be moved in the middle of execution. Similarly, it would have to know which memory cells to relocate. If the program keeps an up-to-date record of which memory and register cells are relocatable, the reloader can move programs, but that puts a burden on the programmer, as the code must be rewritten to keep such records. It could also lead to program errors that would be hard to detect, since failure to keep a correct record causes an error only if a program is moved while the record is incorrect.

Either of the latter two schemes, assigning noncontiguous storage and moving programs, is an acceptable solution if certain hardware features are added. Historically, the first feature added was *dynamic relocation*. This allows code to be moved without the need to relocate addresses, either in memory or in registers. A *relocation register* is added to the hardware. It is set to contain the lowest address of a user's program in memory. Whenever a memory reference is made by that program, the contents of the relocation register are added to the memory address to calculate an actual address. The user's program is assembled and loaded as though it starts in location 0. However, since all memory addresses are displaced by the relocation amount, all memory references are to a contiguous section of memory starting at the address held in the relocation register.

The user cannot change the relocation register. It is set by kernel instructions at the time the user's program is given control of the CPU. Consequently, the relocation register is part of the program state and must be set by the return from interrupt instruction or by related code. (Memory references by I/O instructions must also be relocated. However, if I/O is handled by calls to the kernel, it can perform the relocation by means of software.)

If dynamic relocation is available, the supervisor can move a program simply by copying it from one area to another and by resetting the relocation register. All program references to memory are changed automatically, since no data in the program is dependent on the contents of the relocation register. This is illustrated in Figure 10-2. An example of this organization occurs in the Cyber 175 computer, which has a relocation register (RAC) for CPU programs. The content of RAC is added to all addresses sent to memory. It also has a register, FLC, that contains the number of memory words allocated to the program in execution. All addresses used by the program are checked during execution and must be less than the content of FLC; otherwise the program has attempted to reference beyond the end of memory allocated to it.

The major drawback to using dynamic relocation and moving code is the time spent in the move. In a multiprogramming system in which jobs stay in memory until they have been completed, this is not too serious, as a move will not be necessary more often than each time that a new job is initiated. If jobs take an average time T and there is an average of J jobs in memory, the average time between moves is T/J, which is large as long as T is large and J is small. However, in most modern systems some part of memory is used for timesharing work in which many jobs are being loaded frequently. To overcome the high overhead of moving, hardware has been developed to allow for allocation of noncontiguous memory areas in a way that is transparent to the programmer.

FIGURE 10-2 Effect of dynamic relocation

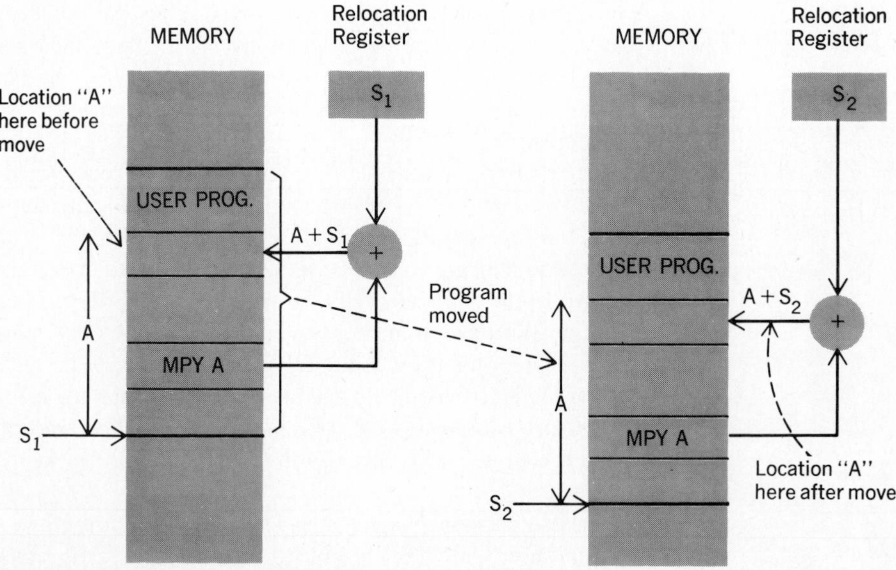

The desirable feature of such a system is that the program can be assembled as if it had a set of L contiguous memory locations, but the memory space allocated to the program is not necessarily contiguous. If L locations are free, it is desirable that the program be executed. Consequently, what is needed is a relocation scheme that relocates different addresses by different amounts, as shown in Figure 10-3.

It is evident that such a *mapping* will be time-consuming and expensive if an arbitrary fragmentation must be handled. Consequently, the memory is usually broken up into pages of 2^p words each, and space is allocated by pages only. In typical systems, p is between 8 and 12. If the address used by the program is $n + p$ bits long, it can address up to 2^n pages of 2^p words each. The leftmost n bits of the address are called the *page address* and determine which page is referenced, whereas the rightmost p bits determine the word address within the page. Suppose that a program refers to an address in the range 0 to $2^p K - 1$. It needs K pages of memory. If that many pages of memory are free, they can be allocated to the program and it can be put into execution. Then a mapping device must convert each of the program's memory addresses so that they refer to the correct physical memory addresses. This can be done by means of a *page table,* which lists the page number and the actual number in memory for each page used by the program. This can be illustrated by an example. Suppose the program refers to addresses 0 to 4095 in a system in which the page size is 1024 words. Suppose memory locations 1024 through 2047, 4096 through 6143, and 8192 through 9215 are free. Consequently, the mapping shown in Table 10-1 should be performed. When the addresses are expressed in binary, mapping shown in Table 10-2 results, assuming that a 16-bit address is used. The 10 x's represent the 10 least significant bits

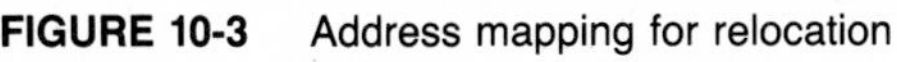

FIGURE 10-3 Address mapping for relocation

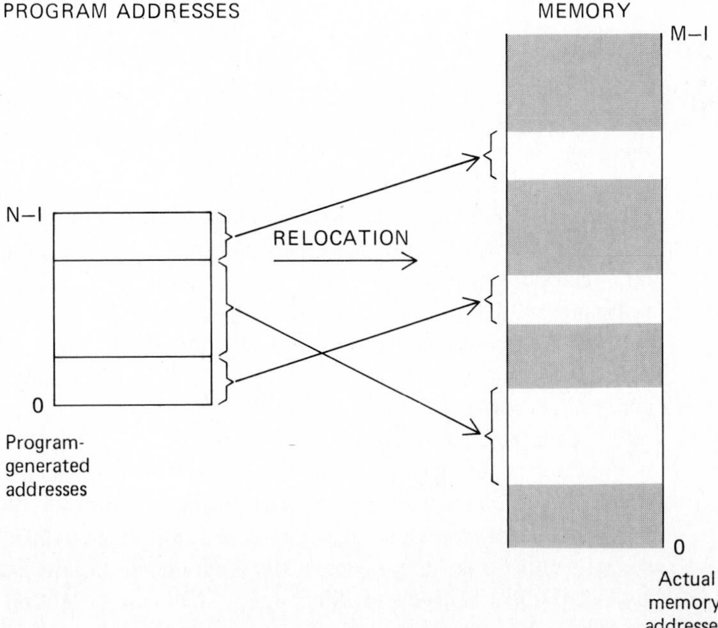

TABLE 10-1 ADDRESS MAPPING

Program address	Memory address
0–1023	1024–2047
1024–2047	4096–5199
2048–3071	5120–6143
3072–4095	8192–9215

TABLE 10-2 BINARY FORM OF TABLE 10-1

Program address	Memory address
000000xxxxxxxxxx	000001xxxxxxxxxx
000001xxxxxxxxxx	000100xxxxxxxxxx
000010xxxxxxxxxx	000101xxxxxxxxxx
000011xxxxxxxxxx	001000xxxxxxxxxx

of the address — the word address within the page. They need not be converted in the address mapping. Consequently, the mapping can be performed by a small *page table memory,* which is 6 bits wide and 64 words long in this example. The leftmost 6 bits of the program address, the page address, can be used to address the page memory. The 6 bits read from the page table can be used to replace those 6 bits in the address sent to main memory. With such a device, the example above could be handled by storing 000001, 000100, 000101, and 001000 in locations 0 through 3, respectively, of the page memory. When address translation of this form is done, the address generated in the program is called the *virtual address* and the final result after translation is called the *physical address*.

Several other benefits can be obtained from this system, which is called *paging*. Additional bits can be stored in the page table to indicate memory protection — whether the program is allowed to access the page for reading, for writing, or not at all. It is also possible to handle *virtual memory*. This is a system in which the program is allowed to "reference" many more memory locations than are physically assigned to it in primary memory at any one time. Space for the user's program and data is assigned on a fast secondary storage device such as a drum or disk, and a complete copy of the program and data is stored there. The page table for that program indicates that the pages are not in the primary memory. When the program starts execution, one or more pages are copied into primary memory, and the page table is set to indicate their physical addresses. The program is executed from primary memory until it attempts to reference a location that is still in secondary storage. This is called a *page fault*. This is indicated in the page table and causes an interrupt to the operating system. The operating system records a request for primary memory to be allocated and for a transfer from secondary storage to that memory. Later, when primary memory has been assigned and the transfer completed, the program can resume execution. Until that time, another process is executed. Since the system cannot rely on primary memory being freed by terminating jobs, it must use a scheduling algorithm to take primary memory pages away from programs that are not currently using them. The contents of these pages can be stored back on the secondary storage device, and the page table can be updated to note that fact. The idea, and hope, of a paging system with virtual memory is that those pages of a memory being used frequently will tend to stay in primary memory, whereas those that have not been used for some time will be banished to secondary storage. A number of scheduling algorithms are in use to decide which pages to move out of primary memory. The LRU algorithm banishes the Least Recently Used page, whereas the FIFO (First-In-First-Out) algorithm banishes the page that has been in memory the longest. These and related topics are covered in a survey article by Denning.[2]

The original purpose of a virtual memory system was to provide a *program address space* (or virtual address space) much larger than the *physical address space,* thus saving the programmer the chore of organizing transfers between primary and secondary memories. It continues to serve that purpose as well as providing dynamic relocation and allocation in a multiprogramming system.

The organization of a user program can affect the efficiency of a virtual memory system. If frequent references are made to a small number of pages, less system time will be spent swapping pages in and out than if references are scattered through memory. This means, for example, that a matrix program in PL/I should index through rows first (second index), whereas the same program in Fortran should index through columns first (first index), because the compilers store arrays by rows in PL/I but by columns in Fortran.

The choice of the size of a page is an important design question. The time needed to transfer a page between secondary and primary storage is almost independent of its length (within reason), because most of the time is the average delay due to latency. This is an argument for larger pages, which also reduce the space needed for the page table. However, larger pages mean that the amount of space needed in primary memory for any one program is larger, and that the amount of wasted space in the last page, which is only half full on the average, is larger. (The incomplete usage of a page is called *internal fragmentation*.)

Paging solves some problems but introduces others. The contents of the page table are part of the program state and must be preserved with the rest of the state when the CPU program is changed by an interrupt. Since it is not feasible to reload the contents of the page table at each interrupt, a different part of the page table is associated with each program. One way of doing this is to use dynamic relocation in the page table. The relative origin of the page table can be held in a relocation register so that only this register need be changed when the program is changed. The easiest way of thinking about this is in terms of page addresses and the page table. Each program is assigned a contiguous part of the page table so that it can address a number of contiguous pages. An address generated by the program is split into a page address and a word address. The page address is relocated dynamically, and the new page address is used to find an actual page address, which is sent to memory with the word address to access the desired data. This is shown in Figure 10-4.

[2]P. J. Denning, "Virtual Memory," *Computing Surveys,* vol. 2, September 1970, pp. 153–189.

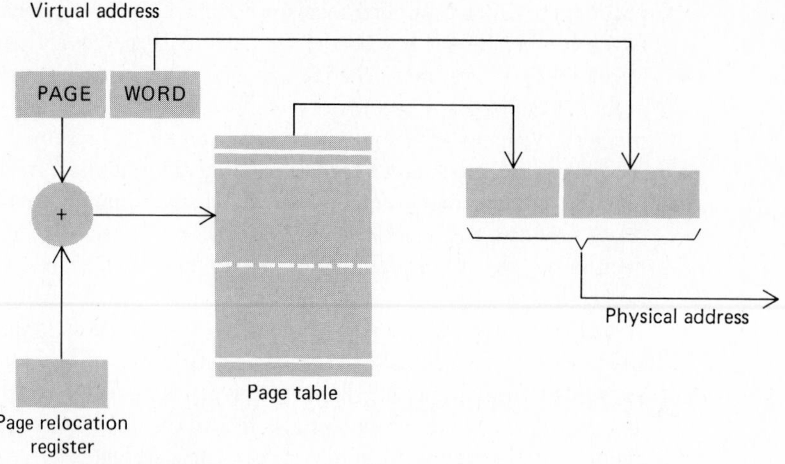

FIGURE 10-4 Relocation and paging

The page table can be kept in a region of primary memory or in a special memory. If it is kept in primary memory, every memory reference will take two references, one for the page address and a second for the data. This is usually unacceptable. However, a second, faster memory for a page table may not be feasible if it has to store all of the page tables for every user in a timesharing system. In that case, an in-between solution is often adopted. A separate, faster page table memory is used to store part of the page tables, whereas all of the page tables are kept in primary memory. The idea is to keep just those parts of the page tables that are currently being used in the page table memory. The hardware must first check to see whether the page address is in the page table memory. If not, it must reference the primary memory copy. This type of page table memory is usually organized as an associative memory. Each entry contains both its address and data. The address is the page table address, and the content is the corresponding physical memory address plus any other information stored in the page table (for example, the secondary storage address of the page, whether the page is in primary memory or not, and, if it is in primary memory, whether it has been changed—the so-called *dirty bit*). The hardware does a comparison of the page table address with all of the entries in the page table memory in parallel (for speed) and fetches the information from there, if present.

This type of memory is called a *cache memory*. Unfortunately, an associative reference to a large memory is slow because of all the comparisons that must be made. Therefore, the page table cache is sometimes organized in blocks of several words associated with consecutive words in the page table. Blocks of consecutive words are moved from the primary memory page table to the cache when any one is needed. Then it is only necessary to associate a page table address with each block, and the page table address stored in the page table cache memory can be shortened. For example, if the blocks are 8 words long, the last 3 bits of the page table address can be ignored when checking the page cache to see whether a block is in it. Another technique that can be used to reduce the cost of checking to see whether the page address is in the page table cache is to identify specific page addresses with specific cache locations. Thus, if we had a cache of sixty-four locations, we could associate page table addresses 0, 64, 128, . . ., with cache location 0; page table addresses 1, 65, 129, . . . , with cache location 1; etc. Various combinations of these techniques are used to decrease the cost of the cache memory while maintaining a high probability that there will not be a *cache fault,* that is, a reference that requires a fetch of a page table entry from primary memory. Clearly, the strategy for filling the page table memory and deciding what to banish to primary memory is related to the strategy for allocating pages to primary memory and banishing them to secondary memory.

A cache memory is not limited to use for page tables. Since it is a fast memory and many computations are limited by speed of access to primary memory, a number of organizations have used a cache memory between the CPU and primary memory. The relationships between this type of cache and primary memory, on one hand, and between primary memory and secondary memory, on the other, are very similar. The only difference is that when a page fault occurs, the process in execution must be temporarily halted, because it will take a long time to load the desired page from disk, whereas when a cache fault occurs, the fetch from primary memory occurs in a very short time. Cache faults are handled by the hardware or microprogram, whereas page faults are normally handled by system programs.

Some machines, such as the Cyber 175, use a form of cache memory called an *instruction stack*. It holds a number of words of instructions so that if a program executes a loop that is completely contained within the number of words in the stack, no further references have to be made to memory for instructions. Some of the PDP-11s have caches. The PDP-11/60, for example, has 1024 words of 16 bits each. In this organization, each memory location corresponds to one word in the cache—the bottom 10 bits of the word address in memory give the cache address. Furthermore, each word in the cache contains additional bits that specify the high-order bits of the address whose contents are in that cache location. For example, if the CPU writes to location 6154(=2(3∗1024+5)), cache location 5 is changed to contain the data being stored and the value 3 is stored along with the data to indicate that the high-order address bits have value 3. Any time that a read from a location whose word address is 5 modulo 1024 is executed, the high-order address bits in cache location 5 are read and compared with the high-order address bits of the word requested. If a match occurs, the data can be read from the cache instead of the slower primary memory. One additional bit is needed in each cache word. This indicates that the data in the cache is not valid. This bit must be set any time an I/O device writes into a memory cell whose data might be in the cache. If this bit is set, no test need be made for a match, as a read from memory must be executed. If a read from memory is executed, the PDP-11/60 will also copy the word into the matching cache location so that if the word is referenced again, a memory read will not be necessary.

Some cache memories are organized so that any cache location can hold the content of any memory location. This means that the full address must also be stored with each word of data and a comparison must be made with the addresses of every word in the cache before a read. This is done in the VAX 11/780 CPU, which uses an 8KB (8-kilobyte) cache for data and instructions operating on units of 8 bytes (double words). That computer has also a 128-word page table cache for the 1 million–word page table. (Virtual addresses in the 11/780 are 29 bits long with a page size of $512 = 2^9$, so 20 bits are the page address. The physical address has the same length.)

Segmentation One of the problems in programming is memory allocation for jobs that use large, varying-size arrays whose size is not known until run time. Examples of these are compiler tables and stacks. If the programmer is presented with a single *linear address space* (that is, a memory with addresses between 0 and $M - 1$), an allocation for each of the arrays must be made by load time. *Segmentation* is a scheme that avoids this. Although, physically, segmentation looks very much like paging, it provides the programmer with several linear address spaces. The program generates a virtual address that consists of a segment address followed by an address within the segment. (We can view this as one very large virtual address if we wish.) Each segment can be used for different data structures or different parts of the program. A segment table is used to keep track of the starting location of each segment in primary memory. This is similar to the way the page table keeps track of the starting location of each page in primary memory. However, the segment table can also keep track of the amount of memory space allocated to each segment; that is, the segment table essentially contains a relocation address and limit address for each segment. Since segments may be very long, paging is still desirable to allow a large virtual memory space, so many systems combine segmentation and paging into a two-level scheme, as illustrated in Figure 10-5. Although the logical structures of segmentation and paging in this figure are identical, their purposes are different: segmentation provides for dynamic memory allocation in several virtual address spaces; paging maps those virtual address spaces onto physical address spaces and provides for automatic use of secondary memory.[3]

[3]For further reading, the student is referred to P. J. Denning, "Virtual Memory," *Computing Surveys,* September 1970, pp. 153–189; and J. B. Dennis, "Segmentation and the Design Multiprogrammed Computer Systems," *Journal of the Association for Computing Machinery,* October 1965, pp. 589–602.

FIGURE 10-5 Segmentation and paging

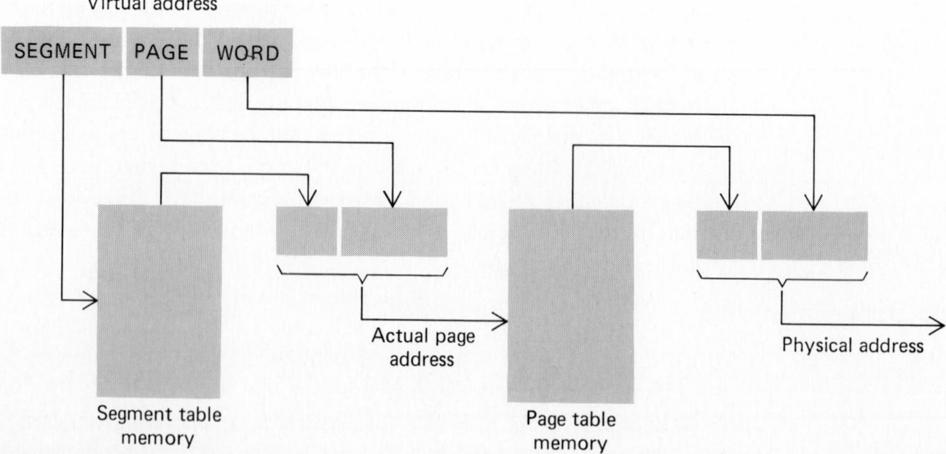

Memory Protection and Shared Programs Segmentation is a valuable tool in memory protection. Each segment can have separate protection codes. For example, some segments can be read only, allowing the program in those segments to be shared by several users. Each segment can have its own bounds register so that references beyond the limits of individual data structures can be detected. Some systems provide protection at the page level instead by putting protection codes into the page table. In fact, a paging virtual memory system with protection can be used to provide the effect of segmentation, on the condition that the virtual address space is big enough. However, this system cannot detect one type of error, that occurs when the addition of an integer to a virtual address produces an address that is outside of the segment containing the original virtual address. In the case of a single virtual address space, the modified address could be in a different segment.

10.2 MULTIPROCESSORS

Two or more CPUs are used in computer systems both to increase the *throughput* and to guarantee *uptime*. The latter is critical in many *real-time* systems that are controlling experiments or handling important allocation problems. For example, if a large processing plant such as a steel mill were under computer control, the cost of a computer malfunction would be high if the plant had to stop production. Similarly, an airline would lose much business if its reservation system did not function while a hardware malfunction was being repaired. The problem can be alleviated by connecting more than one CPU in an organization, which allows the second CPU to continue processing when the first is down for maintenance. When both are running, less critical jobs, such as record production and payroll, can also be processed. These jobs can be delayed when one CPU is down so that the critical work can be performed.

Multiprocessor systems usually also perform multiprogramming, so that there is a list of jobs waiting for CPU service. If the additional CPUs are attached to increase the speed of particular jobs, then multiple processes can be executed for a single job. (An example of a job for which speed is essential is air traffic control. If a program is computing the flight patterns of aircraft at an airport, the computation must be done in time to inform pilots of evasive action necessary to avoid collisions.)

The major additional problem caused by multiprocessors is one of synchronization of related processes. We have already seen this problem in the synchronization of concurrent processes in I/O programming. There we introduced the P and V operations on semaphores. If these are handled by a single CPU running with interrupts disabled, the indivisibility of the operations can be guaranteed. However, when there is more than one CPU or CPU-like processor, it is essential to have some form of synchronization mechanisms. The IBM 370 Test and Set instruction is one such operation that can be used by several processors. A number of mechanisms have been used in systems to achieve synchronization,[4] but many of them are ultimately implemented at the machine

[4]See, for example, B. Hansen, *Operating System Principles,* Prentice-Hall, Englewood Cliffs, NJ, 1973, chap. 3; C. A. R. Hoare, "Monitors: An Operating Structuring Concept," *Communications of the Association for Computing Machinery,* vol. 17, no. 10, Oct. 1974, pp. 549–557; D. R. Reed and R. V. Kanodia, "Synchronization with Eventcounts and Sequencers," *Communications of the Association for Computing Machines,* vol. 22, no. 2, Feb. 1979, pp. 115–123.

level by some variant of the Test and Set instruction. Whatever scheme is used, the designer has to be very careful to avoid *deadlock,* a situation in which a circular list of processes are each waiting for the next one in the list. This can happen in a single processor system when each process is waiting for a resource held by another process, but it is more likely in a multiprocessor system where processors are competing in real time.

10.3 TIMESHARING

When computers were first introduced around 1950, they were slow and were fully occupied by running the program of a single user, who would debug and run a computer by going into the computer room, entering the program via some slow device such as paper tape, and starting the execution by direct manipulation of console switches. When an error was encountered, the computer would simply be stopped while the problem was pondered. The same is true today for small microcomputers, although the size and cost of microcomputer systems have decreased about 1000-fold compared to the early computers. Computer development through the first decade saw the introduction of larger and faster computers, and timesharing was introduced in the early 1960s to make the facilities of these large computer systems available to the user who still wanted to sit at the computer console and interact with a program. This is extremely useful during the debugging phase, when minor errors stop the execution of a program before much information has been obtained, and it is useful when new methods are being explored. Since the amount of computation performed between programmer actions is fairly small, the obvious solution is to share the computer among many programmers, servicing each program for a short period. Multiprogramming provides a mechanism for such a solution, provided that all programs can be loaded into memory simultaneously, but there is no guarantee that the programs will be particularly short, and so a lot of memory space may be required. Since fast memory is expensive, many techniques must be used to implement a system that provides timesharing to a large number of programmers. In this section we mention some of the techniques that are used.

A virtual memory system is one approach to providing a large amount of apparent memory. It has the advantage that all programs in the system are treated equally, so that a program developed in one environment (for example, batch) can be run in an interactive mode later if the need arises.

One of the earliest techniques used was simple swapping of programs between primary memory and fast secondary storage, such as disks or drums. When a program's turn for execution came up, it was loaded into memory and started. When it had used its allocated amount of time, or when it requested I/O that caused a wait, it was stored back on the disk and the next program was loaded. Such a system could be improved by several techniques. For example, if enough memory for several programs were available, one program could be executing while others were being swapped in or out. Swapping is still used in a number of systems. It is reasonably fast if a very-high-speed secondary storage device such as ECS (Extended Core Storage; see Chapter 4) is used.

Some swapping can be avoided if tasks common to many users are handled by common programs. Consequently, the greatest savings in the cost of a timesharing system can be achieved by a careful analysis of user requirements and an effort to provide the common, frequently used processes efficiently. Typical common needs are input and output of data to and from the terminal, storing programs and data from one run to another, editing programs stored in the computer, and checking programs for syntactic accuracy (seeing if they will assemble or compile). The first three of these are provided by almost all timesharing systems. If, for example, a user program wishes to read a line from a terminal to an area of memory, it will request a system input program to perform the read. This will read each character from the terminal until it detects the end of the line, then hand the complete line to the program when it is next in execution. If the program had read each character directly, it would have had to be executed for a few instructions between each character read. This would have created a high overhead because of the need to swap the program into memory after each character.

Timesharing systems designed for large numbers of homogeneous users usually restrict input to a line at a time. Such systems are typically found on IBM and CDC Cyber computers. Smaller systems for computing research environments are usually more flexible, permitting line-at-a-time I/O for efficiency and character-at-a-time (*raw-mode*) I/O for highly interactive operation.

Filing systems are an integral part of a timesharing system. They allow the programmer to input a program, either from a terminal or via other input devices such as card readers, and to leave it on the disk for later use. If a programmer is only typing in a program at a remote terminal, there is no need for a personal input program. A shared program can process all such input and store it on the disk under the programmer's identification. Similarly, if the programmer wishes to edit data or a program that is already stored on the disk, the editing can be done by a shared program.

It is also possible to provide shared programs that check the syntax of programs, either a line at a time as they are typed in or a subroutine at a time as the user requests the check. This type of operation is more feasible in an operating environment in which few different languages are in use. If, for example, users are restricted to one language only, it is probably economical to keep a compiler for that language in memory at all times, as a large number of users' programs can be checked at the same time. If there are many different languages, it is less likely that many users will be requiring a check of programs in the same language at any one time. Timesharing systems have been based on relatively small systems by restricting the use of languages. For example, the early Basic timesharing system allowed only that language and was very effective for a limited class of problems.

It is always dangerous to make predictions, but it appears that timesharing is becoming relatively less important as a mode of operation. The cost of simple computers has dropped drastically in the last few years, so that small computers can be included in a terminal for very little more than the price of the relatively expensive I/O part of the terminal. We can expect these small computers to handle much of the simple work that was previously handled by timesharing systems. The larger jobs must still be sent to a large system, but this is done more as a type of *remote batch* in which a complete job is transmitted and processed and the results returned. The large computers are frequently grouped together as a computer network in which load sharing can be practiced. Further, special-purpose computers can be part of the network, so that users with special problems can get access to the most suitable computer.[5]

[5]For additional information on timesharing systems, the reader is referred to M. V. Wilkes, *Time Shared Computer Systems*, 3d ed., MacDonald/American Elsevier Computer Monographs, London, 1975.

10.4 SUMMARY AND PROBLEMS

Multiprogramming keeps many jobs in memory for efficient utilization of the processors. It is important that context switching among processes be fast, since it happens frequently. A scheduler schedules the jobs loaded to get a balanced mix of compute-bound and I/O-bound jobs and schedules processes to prevent processors from becoming idle unnecessarily. Because there are many jobs, a large memory is needed. As jobs are removed, memory is fragmented; so either programs must be dynamically moved, requiring dynamic relocation registers, or a nonsequential mapping such as paging must be used. Paging not only prevents fragmentation, it can also provide a large virtual memory space to the programmer. A cache memory may be used to store part of the page table and/or to store a small part of the primary memory, thus reducing the number of primary memory accesses. A cache may be fully associative, or some blocking and/or mapping of memory addresses to cache addresses may be used to reduce the associative read time.

Segmentation is used to provide the user with several different linear address spaces for different data and program sections. Segmentation allows different segments to have different protection codes. This allows for shared programs in write-protected memory accessible to several users.

Multiple processors are used to achieve reliability and speed. They introduce more difficult synchronization problems.

Timesharing allows a large number of users to work on-line at human speeds. A timesharing system must be multiprogrammed and requires either a very large virtual memory or fast swapping. Some of these requirements can be reduced by providing shared programs for common actions such as editing.

Problems

10-1 In a multiprogrammed system, would it be better to give priority on the CPU to CPU-bound programs or to I/O-bound programs when both are loaded? What about priority on the channel?

10-2 If ten jobs of equal duration are loaded for processing simultaneously in a multiprogrammed system, and none of the jobs perform I/O until the end of the CPU execution, what is the best scheduling strategy for maximizing efficiency, assuming that there are no other jobs in memory?

10-3 If a user program is in control in a timesharing system, is it sufficient to wait for that program to make an I/O request before switching to another program? Why?

CHAPTER 11

THE ASSEMBLER

This chapter examines the structure of an assembler, both as an example of a program and to understand some of the restrictions imposed by the assembler on the programmer. First we will review the operation of an assembler.

The assembler is a program that accepts input from the user or possibly from the output of a compiler and produces machine language, usually in a relocatable form. The input or source language is frequently in the form of line images. Each line image has four well-defined fields, containing (1) the location identifier (may be blank); (2) the mnemonic instruction, pseudo, or directive; (3) the address field; and (4) the comments field, respectively. Most assemblers allow comment lines to be included at any point. Such lines are usually distinguished by a special character (for example, an asterisk in column 1). We shall not discuss comment lines further, assuming that the section of the assembler that reads the input will arrange to skip over such lines immediately.

The output will be presumed to be in binary format acceptable to the loader. Normally, this output is retained on disk for the loader. It can also be left on disk semipermanently for later reuse. In addition to the binary output, there is usually some form of output listing so that the user can check the input and examine diagnostic messages. This output is also normally left on a disk file so that the user or the scheduler can decide where to send it (for example, to a printer or to a user file). A typical output consists of a listing of the input and an octal or hexadecimal version of the object alongside the input. Since the object is produced in a relocatable form and the assembler does not know where the program will be loaded, the object form is given without relocation. Errors will be indicated on the listing in some form, either at the end of the listing with references back to the program or by means of markers alongside the program line in error.

Most assemblers take two basic passes through the input program to produce the object. The first pass produces a table of all identifiers used and their address values. The second is used to substitute these values into the original symbolic form to get the binary form. If too many complications are introduced, two passes are no longer sufficient, but it is desirable to keep the number of passes to a minimum to make the assembly process as fast as possible. The input for short problems can be kept in primary memory during the translation process, but longer programs would occupy too much space, and so they must be kept on secondary storage. Since such storage is typically much slower than the primary memory, the time spent in each pass is largely determined by the time it takes to fetch the information from secondary storage. Thus doubling the number of passes can effectively double the translation time, although very little actual computation may be done in the extra passes.

11.1 PASS I: THE LOCATION COUNTER

The major task of the first pass is to construct a table of all identifiers used in the program and to associate a memory address with each. To do this, all input lines of code are read, one at a time. If an identifier appears in the location field, it is put into the symbol table (with some exceptions to be discussed later). The assembler assumes that the first instruction to be read is placed into location 0, the next into location 1, and so on. For the moment we shall ignore the problems of pseudos, directives, and macros and just study the two tasks to be performed in constructing the symbol table. In order to know what address value to associate with an identifier in the location field of an instruction just read, an account must be kept of the space used by instructions read so far. We call this the *location counter,* because it contains the address of the location into which the next instruction will be loaded if no relocation is applied. This location counter is maintained during pass I and pass II. After each instruction is handled in either pass I or pass II, the location counter is incremented by the length of the instruction (1 in the case of 1-word instructions and an appropriate integer in the case of multibyte instructions).

When an identifier is found in a location field, it is put into a table along with its address value, which is given by the current value of the location counter. Thus each entry in the table consists of at least two parts: the identifier and its associated address value. Since nothing else need be done with identifiers during pass I, this table could be constructed by simply placing each pair of items in the next free words of an array of pairs of words. If, however, it is decided to check for double definition of identifiers during pass I, then it is necessary to determine whether the identifier just read in the location field is already present in the table. This involves some sort of table look-up procedure. We shall delay discussion of techniques for this until the next chapter and content ourselves with some general comments at this stage. What is actually needed is called an *associative* memory. An associative memory is a memory device that is not addressed in the way we have discussed so far, that is, by a numeric address that refers to a specific location in memory. Rather, an associative memory device is addressed by means of its contents. Initially, an associative memory is assumed to contain no information. That is, there is a state of each word in the associative memory that represents *not used*. When a word is written into an associative memory, no address is given; the memory device stores it in any available (not used) location. When a word is to be read from an associative memory, the contents of part of the word are specified. The memory is expected to locate all words that match the specified contents.

We can see that an associative memory is just what is needed for the symbol and mnemonic tables. When an identifier is first read from a location field, it can be entered into the associative memory along with its address value. (We consider the pair of items as a single entry.) When another identifier is read, it can be checked for double definition by reading from the memory any word whose identifier part agrees with the identifier just read. If the identifier is doubly defined, there will be an entry already in the memory on the second and subsequent occurrences. If it has not been previously defined, it can be entered (stored) into the associative memory.

In this particular use of the associative-memory principle, the same field of the stored information is always used for matching with the identifier in the READ operation. In this case, we call this field a *tag* or *key,* since it is an identifying piece of information that serves as the address for user reference to the memory. Associative memories have been constructed directly from hardware, but they are not economical for most applications. Therefore, we simulate the functions of an associative memory using the CPU and the regular memory. The mechanics of the simulation will be discussed in the next chapter. The specific operations that may have to be provided are

STORE Place a set of information into a new location in the associative memory or table.
READ Locate any entries in the table that match a given tag or key.
CHANGE Locate any entries in the table and change them in a specified fashion.
DELETE Remove an entry with a given tag from the table.

In the remainder of this chapter, we shall assume that these operations are available. In practice, they are provided by suitable subprograms.

If the input lines contain only instructions, then the simple mechanism of incrementing the location counter by the length of the instruction for each line is sufficient. However, there has to be one directive in any code, the END directive.[1] This tells the assembler that the complete deck has been read and that the next pass can begin. (An end-of-file could also be interpreted as an END.) In practice, many other directives must be interpreted, because they affect the location counter in various ways. For example, a BSS 23 should increment the location counter by 23.

In order for pass I to recognize the difference between the instructions, pseudos, and directives, it must examine the mnemonic coding. The mnemonic is usually a string of characters similar to an identifier, so that similar techniques can be used to handle mnemonics.

In this case, the table of mnemonics (in other words, the contents of the associative memory used for mnemonics) is permanent, having been set up by the assembler

[1]Some assemblers use the directive END for several purposes, for example, to end the program, to end conditional expansion groups, and to end macro definitions. In that case, it is necessary to keep track of which is which by keeping the start of each construct in stack. Each END read then matches the top entry in the stack. That entry determines the usage of the corresponding END. The stack entry can be discarded when the matching END is read.

designer. It contains each legal mnemonic together with identifying information. The information needed in pass I tells whether the mnemonic is an instruction (and possibly what type of instruction, if variable- length instructions are allowed) or what pseudo or directive it is. Since pass I will contain a number of sections of code for each instruction, directive, and pseudo type, an easy way to handle the testing for mnemonic type is to store, with the mnemonics, a branch address that gives the address of the code used to handle the mnemonic. This is shown in Figure 11-1. The typical flow of pass I of an assembler is shown in Program 11-1. The input line of code is read and the mnemonic extracted. The mnemonic code is looked up in the mnemonic table. If it is not present, there is an error (unless macros are allowed, as discussed later). If it is present, a branch is made to the address found in the table using a case statement construct. Then the appropriate section of code takes care of the rest of the line. If it is a 1-word instruction, the identifier, if any, is placed in the symbol table together with

FIGURE 11-1 Entry in mnemonic table for pass I

Mnemonic	Branch address

Program 11-1 Pass I outline

```
*LC is location counter
START:  Set LC=0, Set ENDFLAG off
  do while ENDFLAG off
    read next line
    do while column 1='*'
      read next line
      enddo
  extract mnemonic
  table look-up of mnemonic
  case of mnemonic type (handled by branch table)
    instruction:
      extract location symbol
      put in symbol table with value LC if present
      LC ← LC+instruction length
    BSS:
      extract location symbol
      put in symbol table with value LC if present
      extract address field and compute its value N
      if address field not yet defined
        then list error
        else L ← L+N
        endif
    ...
    End: Set ENDFLAG on
    endcase
  enddo
```

the contents of the location counter, and then the location counter is increased by 1. If it is an END directive, pass I is terminated. A BSS directive places an identifier from the location field into the symbol table together with the contents of the location counter, and then it increases the contents of the location counter by the appropriate amount. The code for the pseudos and directives will be discussed in detail in a later section.

11.1.1 Coding the Basic Assembler: Pass I

The manner in which the basic code discussed above is written depends to a large extent on the machine and programming language being used. This section will discuss the general problems that occur and mention typical solutions of these problems. The first step is to read in a new line of program for translation. This is usually a line image from disk. The operating system normally provides a read subprogram that will pass the image of the next line from the input file to the program area. The call to this subprogram has to specify an area sufficient to store the line. The operating system subprogram takes care of buffering the input file, so there is no need for the user to worry about a multiple-buffering scheme for input. However, later passes of the assembler will need to reread the input file, so additional steps depend very much on the source of the input. If the input comes from secondary storage, nothing further need be done; if it comes directly from a terminal, a copy of the input must be created for later use.

When a line image has been read into the program area of memory, the assembler must extract various fields from it in order to form identifiers, mnemonics, and addresses. For example, the address field of an instruction might contain ABCX + 312 in one case and S − 21 in another. The assembler will have to extract the identifier ABCX in one case and S in the other and the numbers 312 and 21. These numbers start in different columns and are of different lengths. If the machine is character-oriented or possesses instructions and addressing with these properties (such as the IBM 370 and INTEL 8080 systems), then it is fairly simple to work a character at a time. If the machine does not have these properties, then it is usually easier to construct a subprogram that extracts characters one at a time from the input line. The characters from the line must be examined, one at a time, to determine where each field and the various subfields and elements of subfields start and finish. This is usually done by a *lexicographic* scan, which looks only at the type of the characters that appear and does not concern itself with more detailed meaning. Most assemblers separate fields and subfields by means of *break* characters, also called *separators*. For example, the blank character and the comma are used as break characters in the IBM 370 assembler, whereas the colon, comma, semicolon, and sometimes the blank character are used in the 8080 assembler. The logic of a lexicographic scan can often be most easily described by a *state diagram*. This shows the state of the program in terms of what it is doing and indicates how the state is changed when certain characters are read. Partial state diagrams for the IBM 370 and INTEL 8080 assemblers are shown in Figures 11-2 and 11-3, respectively. States are shown in circles, whereas the arrows leaving the circles indicate the control path to be followed when a character in the indicated class is read as the next character. These state diagrams are incomplete, as the address field must be broken down into its basic components by looking for the separators allowed. The valid separators may change as the state of the scan changes. For example, once the character used to define a string has been read, all characters are part of the string until the character terminating a string has been read. The assembler rules make many character combinations invalid; for example, a plus sign is a separator between elements in an address field, but it is an invalid character in either the location or the mnemonic field in most assemblers. Consequently, the lexicographic analysis is a substantial piece of code for most assembly languages and should therefore be separated from the rest of an assembler as a subprogram.

The lexicographic subprogram should extract one item at a time from the input line and return to pass I with the result. These items are called *tokens*. For example, it might extract the following list of tokens:

Location field identifier (or a mark that there is no identifier)
Mnemonic
First element in address field
Second element in address field
. . .
Last element in address field
End of line

The determination of location and mnemonic fields is indicated in Figures 11-2 and 11-3 for two particular assemblers. Breaking up the address field is much more complex, as the types of separators allowed and the number of different possible constructions vary with the instruction. Generally speaking, numbers and identifiers can be easily recognized, as numbers always start with a digit and contain only digits, and identifiers always start with an alphabetic character and contain only alphanumeric characters after that. Hence the first character of the wrong type can be used as an indication that the number or identifier has been completely read. Most other characters, except for blanks, are separate elements that will have to be passed on to the pass I program for more analysis. For example, the input

```
ABCD        LOAD        3+R,W21   COMMENT
```

might be analyzed to get

```
ABCD
LOAD
3
+
R
,
W21
end-of-line
```

The comments would be skipped, as they are not relevant to pass I processing. Pass I would analyze this output to see whether it was a valid assembler statement; if so, it

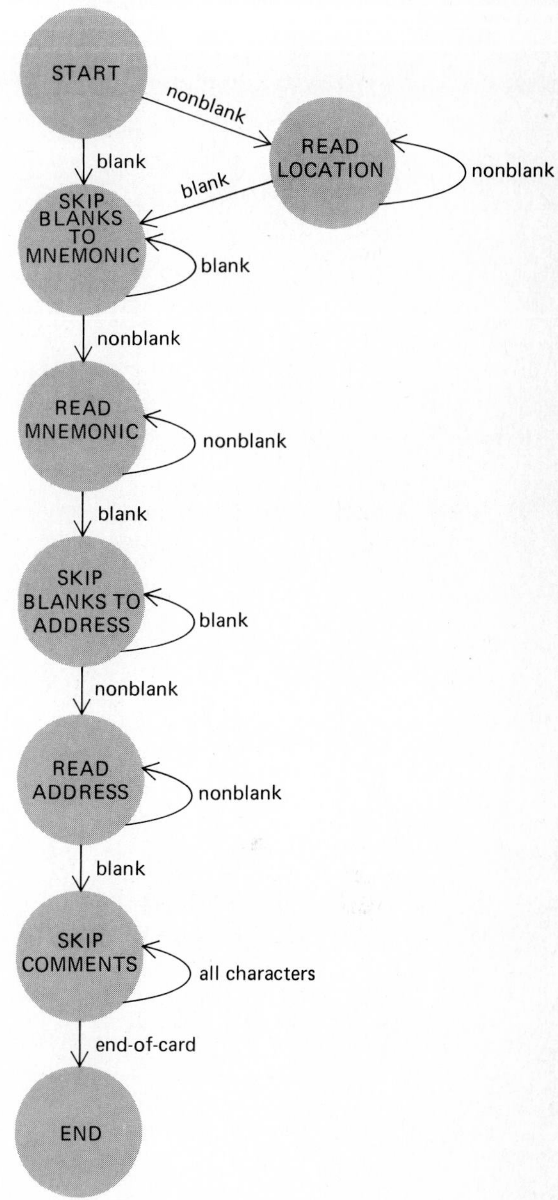

FIGURE 11-2 Partial state diagram for IBM 370 assembler

would define the location field and suitably change the location counter, depending on the mnemonic. In many cases, the address field does not have to be analyzed completely in pass I, as its value is not necessary for determining the amount by which the location counter should be changed. However, instructions whose addresses determine their length and some pseudos have address fields that must be analyzed in pass I. For this reason, it is common to analyze the address field completely in pass I and to try to avoid repeating the analysis in the second pass. Ways of avoiding a second analysis

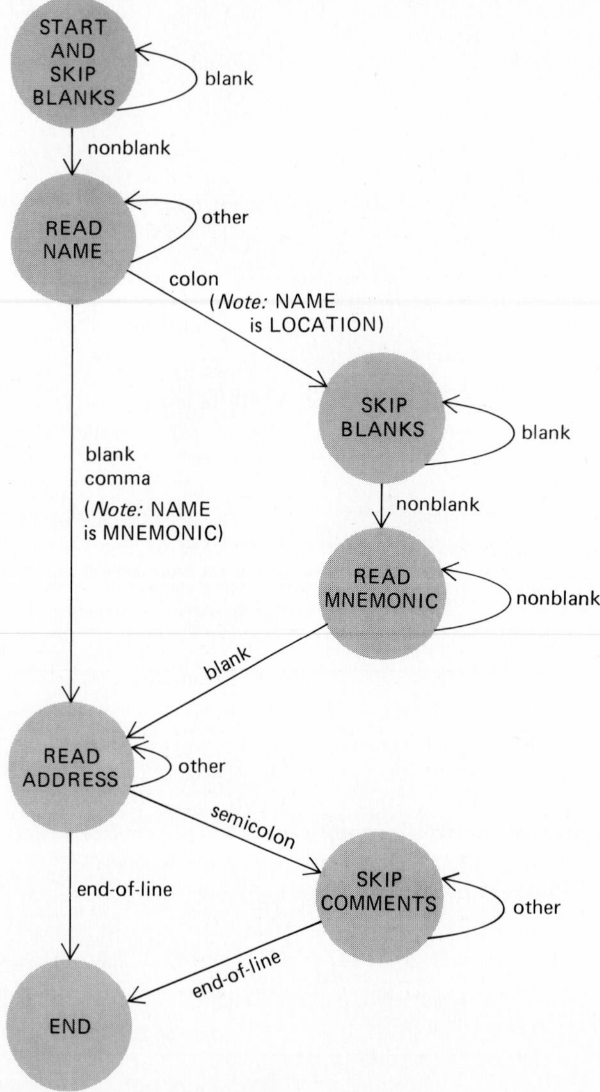

FIGURE 11-3 Partial state diagram for INTEL 8080 assembler

will be discussed in Section 11.4. In the next few subsections we will mention some techniques that are useful for programming the analysis.

11.1.2 Programming Techniques

The lexicographic analysis program has to examine the type of character just read to determine which state to go to next. A bad way of doing this is to test for all cases of interest. Thus, if it is necessary to find out whether the next character is alphabetic, 26 or 52 comparisons must be made, although the character code used may make it possible to use fewer tests. However, it is desirable to write the program in a way that is independent of the particular coding used so that alternative character sets can be accommodated without rewriting. A fast way of performing the test is to construct a character table that contains an entry for each character. Since characters are 6 to 8 bits in most systems, there need not be more than 256 entries. These can be arranged in such a way that they can be indexed using the binary value of the character as the index. The entries in the table can consist of several fields, each only a few bits long. For example, one field of 1 bit can be used to indicate whether the character is an alphabetic character or not, another 1-bit field can be used to indicate whether it is a numeric digit or not, and a 4-bit field can be used to hold the value of the character if it is a numeric digit.

Using such a technique, a test to see whether a character is in a certain class can be executed using an indexed LOAD, an AND with a mask, and a test for 0. For example, suppose the 8-bit character code for 2 is 11110010. This has the numeric value 242. The 242d entry in the table would indicate that the character is a numeric digit, not an alphabetic character, and that its value is 0010 in binary. Other 1-bit fields can be used to indicate whether the character is a separator for location fields, for mnemonic fields, for address fields, etc. A possible format and the entry for the character 2 are shown in Figure 11-4.

In the scan of the location and mnemonic fields, it is known that the only valid element is an identifier, at least in the assemblers discussed here. Consequently, the lexicographic scan need only check for identifiers in those fields. However, many other forms are possible in the address field, so the lexicographic scan must test for many cases there. The problem is to take a string of characters such as A123+123*123−B123 and recognize that A123 and B123 are identifiers and that 123 is a number. In other words, we would like to break up the string into A123, +, 123, *, 123, −, and B123. This recognition can be performed very simply by scanning from left to right and noting the following:

1 Names start with a letter and contain letters or digits.
2 Numbers start with a digit and contain only digits.

FIGURE 11-4 Format for a character table and entry for 2

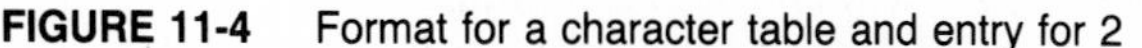

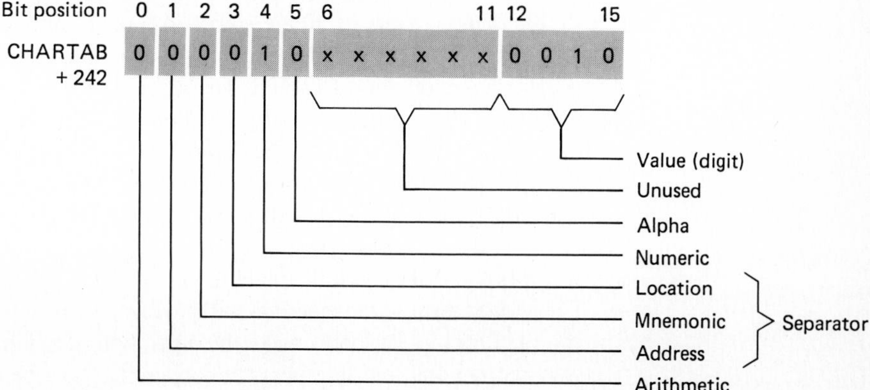

Starting from the left, the next character is examined. If it is a letter, then an identifier is recognized. A subscanner called an *identifier recognizer* examines consecutive characters until a nonalphanumeric character is read. This signals the end of the identifier. (There may have to be a check for excessive length if identifiers are restricted to a maximum length.) After the string of characters representing the identifier has been scanned, control returns to the basic recognizer. Similarly, if the first character is a digit, a subscanner for recognizing numbers can be used to read the characters constituting the number. Most arithmetic operations are single-character tokens, although, if exponentiation is allowed (it seldom is) using the notation ** for the operator, the appearance of the first asterisk must cause a check for a second. Character strings in the address field also call for a special recognizer, as all characters inside a character string are valid except for the terminating character, and there is usually also a special convention for allowing that.

Because there is usually very little uniformity among different instruction types and different pseudos and directives, it is usually easiest to code a separate recognizer for each possible address structure.

Converting Numbers to Binary The principles of this were covered in Section 2.2.6. The number recognizer scans the characters, testing to see if they are numeric digits. If they are, the value of the digit is taken from the table and used in the conversion process. The steps are

```
Set N to value of first digit
do while next character is digit (test "digit" bit from table)
N ← N*10 + next digit value (value obtained from table)
enddo
```

If floating- or fixed-point numbers have to be recognized, additional characters must be accepted. One of the better ways of converting floating-point decimal numbers to binary is to convert the mantissa to an integer using the above process. The position of the decimal point should be noted when it is read. This can be computed by counting the number of digits after the decimal point. The count is subtracted from the exponent given by the user, and the integer form of the mantissa is multiplied by the resulting power of 10. If the powers of 10 are stored in a table, only one rounding error need occur, as the initial conversion of the mantissa to an integer will be exact. An example of this is the conversion of 64.572E+8. The recognizer will convert the mantissa to get the integer 64572 represented in binary. It will record the value 3 for the count of digits after the decimal point. The character E causes the exponent to be read as an integer. When 3 is subtracted from the exponent, the result, 5, is used to get the fifth power of 10 from a table. This will be multiplied by the mantissa currently stored as an integer to get the result 6457200000. The powers of 10 will have to be stored in floating-point binary form, because they will be too large or small for integer representation in most cases. The integer form of the mantissa will have to be converted to floating-point form before the final multiplication to make this operation possible. Some computers have conversion instructions, but in others the conversion must be done using logic operations and shifts. The integer can be shifted to an appropriate part of a word and an exponent can be inserted. For example, if the mantissa is 24 bits, the mantissa can be stored in these 24 bits and the exponent set to 24. Alternatively, the arithmetic for the calculation of N can be done in floating point if the arithmetic is fast and sufficiently accurate.

Packing Names The identifier-recognizer subprogram gathers the characters forming a single identifier and packs them into a single datum for storing in the symbol table or for search in the mnemonic table. Many assemblers either restrict the length of an identifier or examine no more than the first n characters, where n is usually between 4 and 10. In this case, the identifier can be packed as if it always has n characters by extending it with blanks if it has fewer than n characters. For example, if eight-character identifiers are allowed, and each is represented in an 8-bit byte, one 64-bit double word can be used to represent each identifier. The identifier A1234 would have three trailing blanks. (The extra blanks should be on the right if one wants to sort the identifiers alphabetically prior to listing for the user.)

Assemblers that limit the length of identifiers do so for the simplicity of dealing with fixed-length quantities, and the maximum length is chosen to fit into a convenient data unit such as a double word. In fact, packing using the standard character code representation (8 bits in ASCII) is not efficient in space, although it is usually convenient for coding. If upper- and lower-case letters are allowed, each character in an identifier can take no more than $52+10+1$ values (that is, one of the fifty-two letters, ten digits, or blank). These could be packed into 6 bits, so a 10-character identifier could be packed into a 64-bit double word. If such a scheme is used, the 6-bit representation of the character can be obtained from a character table of the sort shown in Figure 11-4. If no distinction is made between upper- and lower-case characters, the number of possibilities is reduced even further to thirty-seven possibilities for each character. These cannot be represented by less than 6 bits individually, but as a group of six-character identifiers, there are less than $37 \times 37 \times 37 \times 37 \times 37 \times 37 = 2{,}565{,}726{,}409$ different identifiers. Since the first character is restricted to be only a letter and blanks cannot appear in the middle of an identifier, there are actually fewer.

Since $2^{32} = 4{,}294{,}967{,}296$ is greater than $37^6 = 2{,}565{,}726{,}409$, 32 bits can be used to represent all possible six-character identifiers; the only problem is how. The representation has to be such that the conversion in either direction is straightforward. One simple method is to consider a six-character identifier (with blanks on the right if it is shorter than six characters) as a base-37 number representation. Each character, 0, 1, . . . , 9, A, B, . . . , Z, BLANK, is assigned a unique value between 0 and 36, say, 0, 1, 2, . . . , 36, in the order given. The integer represented by the base-37 number is converted into binary. It will necessarily occupy fewer than 33 bits. For example, the identifier CAD31 is equivalent to

$$\text{C} \times 37^5 + \text{A} \times 37^4 + \text{D} \times 37^3 + 3 \times 37^2 + 1 \times 37 + \text{BLANK}$$

which is equal to

$$12 \times 37^5 + 10 \times 37^4 + 13 \times 37^3 + 3 \times 37^2 + 1 \times 37 + 36 = 851{,}531{,}763$$

This number, stored as a binary integer, can be used to represent the identifier CAD31 in the table. It can be converted back to the alphanumeric form by converting back to base 37 and then recoding the characters into the standard form used in the machine. If this representation of identifiers is used, six characters are packed into 32 bits for an average of 5.33 bits per character, which is not too much more than the minimum possible. In fact, there are 1,617,038,380 identifiers of six or less alphanumeric characters that start with a letter. Therefore, they can be represented by a minimum of 31 bits. A conversion such as this will slow the assembler slightly, especially on microcomputers with no hardware multiplication instruction; thus, unless memory space is critical, the conversion should not be used.

If identifiers can have an unlimited length, it is usually easier to store the character string in contiguous bytes and to enter the address and length of the string into the symbol table. This will be discussed in Chapter 12.

Evaluating Expressions in the Address Field The final problem to be taken care of in the address field is to convert a string of identifiers, numbers, and operators into a single number represented by the expression if it is a legal one, if it is illegal, to find that out. When an expression is to be evaluated in pass I, it must normally be well defined, that is, all of the identifiers must have been previously defined in the symbol table. Therefore, we assume that each identifier has been looked up in the symbol table and replaced with a numeric value. The problem is to combine a string of numbers and operators. $123 + 456$ can be handled from left to right, as can $123 * 456 + 789$, but $12 + 34 * 56 + 78$ can be handled neither from left to right nor from right to left, that is, its value is neither $((12 + 34) * 56) + 78$ nor $12 + (34 * (56 + 78))$. The reason is that the *hierarchy* of the multiply is *higher* than that of the plus operator, so that the multiply must be done before either plus.

Many standard techniques for translating arbitrary expressions are used in compilers. We can use one of the simplest of these for this case. Using the concept of hierarchy of operations, note that an operation should be performed if it is flanked by operators of no greater hierarchy. In this problem, there are only two hierarchies, the lower for plus and minus and the higher for multiply. Thus in $12 + 34 * 56 - 78$, the multiply can be done to get $12 + 1904 - 78$, since it is flanked by the lower hierarchies of plus and minus. Now both the plus and the minus operators are flanked by operators of no greater hierarchy (we can think of beginnings and ends of expressions as operators of lowest priority). In the case of equal hierarchies, the convention usually followed is *left to right*. Thus $1 - 2 + 3$ is $(1 - 2) + 3 = +2$ rather than $1 - (2 + 3) = -4$. The successive steps in reducing $12 + 34 * 56 - 78$ are

$$\begin{aligned} 12 + 34 * 56 - 78 &= 12 + 1904 - 78 \\ &= 1916 - 78 \\ &= 1838 \end{aligned}$$

It is not necessary to examine the complete string at every step. It can be scanned from the left until an operator can be performed. This can be sensed by comparing an operator with the operator on either side. Initially, we know that the first operator *(beginning of expression)* is not higher than the next one, so that we know that the next operator (+ in 12 + 34 * 56 − 78) need only be compared with the following (*). If the following operator does not have a higher hierarchy, the plus can be performed. In this example, the multiply operator has a higher priority than the plus, so we continue the scan over the multiply. The fact that the scan continued indicates that the operator (+) preceding the one currently being tested (*) has a lower hierarchy. Hence it is only necessary to compare the following operator (−) with the current one. (In the case of address expressions, we know that there is no higher hierarchy than multiply, so that this test is not strictly necessary.)

In the course of this scan, we passed over one operand (12) completely, and continued over the second (34) in order to look at the multiply operator. This can best be implemented using a stack technique. The basic recognizers extract numbers and operators one at a time from left to right. At any time, we wish to compare an operator with operators on either side. If the incoming items are placed in a stack when they are skipped over, the last items read will be the ones immediately available. Initially, a mark meaning " beginning of expression" is placed in the stack. Items are recognized in turn and compared with the top two entries in the stack. Depending on the result of the comparison, either the items in the top of the stack are manipulated and a new comparison is made, or the incoming item is placed on the stack and a new item is recognized. The comparison with the top items on the stack is to determine whether the last operator has a hierarchy at least as great as the incoming operand, this being the condition for execution of the last operator, which is in one of the top two levels of the stack (because of the last-in-first-out operation of a stack). Let us follow an example through to see what sort of comparisons we must make. Suppose the string B 3 + 4 * 5 B is to be converted, where B stands for "beginning of expression" or "end of expression." The pairs of lines below indicate the state of the string as items are removed from it, followed by the state of the stack where the top of the stack is on the right.

String Stack	3 + 4 * 5 B B	The first element has been moved to stack. The next element is a number, so move it.
String Stack	+4 * 5 B B 3	The next element, +, is higher than B in the stack, so move it to the stack.
String Stack	4 * 5 B B 3 +	The next element is a number, so move it.
String Stack	* 5 B B 3 + 4	* is compared with + in the second stack level. * is higher; move it to stack
String Stack	5 B B 3 + 4 *	The next element is a number; move it.

String Stack	B B 3 + 4 ∗ 5	The next element, B, is lower than the operator ∗ in the stack. Perform ∗.
String Stack	B B 3 + 20	The next element, B, is lower than the operator + in the stack, so perform +.
String Stack	B B 23	The beginning-of-expression and end-of-expression operators B match, so we are done.

We notice that the operations were generally in the second stack level when they were compared with the incoming operation from the string. This would not be true if there were errors in the expression or if other operators such as unary minus or parentheses were allowed. Therefore, the comparison should check both the second and the top levels. When an operand (number) is sensed as the input, it is put directly into the stack, since it is to be saved for use in a later operation. The rule to follow is to examine the next item in the input and the top two levels of the stack and to perform the steps indicated in Tables 11-1 and 11-2.

TABLE 11-1 STACK COMPARISONS

Input	Top-stack entry	Second-stack entry	Action
Number	—	—	Move input to stack.
Operator	Number	Operator	Compare the hierarchies of the two operators. If the input hierarchy is higher, move the input to the stack. Otherwise perform the operator in the stack according to Table 11-2.
or			
Operator	Operator	—	
Operator	Number	Number	Error

TABLE 11-2 STACK OPERATIONS

Operation	Action
Beginning-of-statement	Terminate the computation; the answer is in the stack.
+	If the first and third levels are numbers, add them, discard the top three stack levels, and push the result on top. If the second level is a number, discard the unary plus in the top level.
−	As for plus, except a unary minus must negate the new top level.
∗	If the first and third levels are not numbers, there is an error. Otherwise, as for plus.

This scheme is more complex than necessary for the simple address expressions that cannot involve parentheses, because there are only three hierarchies in total. If, however, we introduce parentheses, the scheme can be extended to cover the situation by adding to the second table. A pair of parentheses indicates that the expression inside the parentheses is to be evaluated and then used as an operand in another operation. Therefore, when a left parenthesis "(" is sensed in the input string, it should indicate that all of the following input up to the matching right parenthesis has a higher hierarchy than anything currently in the stack. Hence a left parenthesis should be placed into the stack immediately, as if it has a higher priority than any preceding operations. However, when another operation from the input is compared with a left parenthesis in the stack, the parenthesis must be given lowest priority so that the input operation will be placed in the stack for future execution. When a right parenthesis is read from the input, it should be assigned the same hierarchical level as the left parenthesis in the stack, so that any operations in between will be performed.

The additional line needed in Table 11-2 must handle the left parenthesis, which can get into the stack. Since it is given a low priority while in the stack, the only operations in the input string that can appear with it are right parenthesis and the end-of-statement. The latter is an error caused by too many left parentheses. The beginning-of-statement may pop up to the top of the stack when too many right parentheses are present. Therefore, we must also change the first line of Table 11-2, as shown in Table 11-3.

The numerical hierarchical level assigned to operators is shown in Table 11-4. The greater the number, the higher the hierarchy. Consider the example 3∗(4 + (5 + 6) ∗7) + 1. The successive states are:

```
String    3 * (4 + (5 + 6) * 7) + 1 B
Stack     B
```

TABLE 11-3 CHANGES TO TABLE 11-2 FOR PARENTHESES

Operator	Action
Beginning-of-statement	If the input is end-of-statement, the answer is in the top of the stack. Otherwise, too many right parentheses.
Left parenthesis	If the input is a right parenthesis, discard both. Otherwise, too many left parentheses.

TABLE 11-4 HIERARCHY LEVELS

Operator	Input hierarchy	Stack hierarchy
Beginning	—	0
End	0	Never in stack
(	3	0
)	0	Never in stack
+	1	1
−	1	1
∗	2	2

String	∗ (4 + (5 + 6) ∗ 7) + 1 B	
Stack	B 3	∗ is higher than B.
String	(4 + (5 + 6) ∗ 7) + 1 B	
Stack	B 3 ∗	'(' is higher than ∗.
String	4 + (5 + 6) ∗ 7) + 1 B	
Stack	B 3 ∗ (	
String	+ (5 + 6) ∗ 7) + 1 B	
Stack	B 3 ∗ (4	+ is higher than '('.
String	(5 + 6) ∗ 7) + 1 B	
Stack	B 3 ∗ (4+	'(' is higher than +.
String	5 + 6) ∗ 7) + 1 B	
Stack	B 3 ∗ (4 + (	
String	+6) ∗ 7) + 1 B	
Stack	B 3 ∗ (4 + (5	+ is higher than '('.
String	6) ∗ 7) + 1 B	
Stack	B 3 ∗ (4 + (5 +	
String	) ∗ 7) + 1 B	
Stack	B 3 ∗ (4 + (5 + 6	Now perform addition.
String	) ∗ 7) + 1 B	
Stack	B 3 ∗ (4 + (11	Now eliminate '(' and ')'.
String	∗7) + 1 B	
Stack	B 3 ∗ (4 + 11	∗ is higher than +.
String	7) + 1 B	
Stack	B 3 ∗ (4 + 11 ∗	
String	) + 1 B	
Stack	B 3 ∗ (+ 11 ∗ 7	Now perform ∗.
String	) + 1 B	
Stack	B 3 ∗ (4 + 77	Now perform +.
String	) + 1 B	
Stack	B 3 ∗ (81	Now eliminate '(' and ')'.
String	+1 B	
Stack	B 3 ∗ 81	Now perform ∗.

String	+1 B	
Stack	B 243	+ is higher than B.
String	1 B	
Stack	B 243+	
String	B	
Stack	B 243 + 1	Now perform +.
String	B	
Stack	B 244	Here is the answer.

11.2 PASS II

The purpose of pass II of the assembler is to convert the source language into binary, using the symbol table constructed in pass I to convert the addresses and a mnemonic table to convert the instructions. To do this, a copy of the source program must be read, a line at a time, and many of the steps of pass I must be repeated. The location field can be ignored because it was completely handled in pass I. The mnemonic field must be examined and a table look-up performed. In this pass, the mnemonic table must provide both a branch address or other indication of the type of instruction or pseudo and, when instructions are to be converted, the binary code.

The address subfields must be converted into binary numbers for packing into the instructions or for use in pseudos. The code used in the pass I handling of pseudos and directives can be reused for this process. A location counter must be maintained in a manner identical to that of pass I. In this case, it is used to determine where to place the binary output (for load-and-go assemblers) or what location address to provide to a binary loader. Pass II is also terminated when the END is read. In many assemblers, the END can involve an address field that is used to provide the starting address at execution time. In the case of a load-and-go assembler, the last instruction executed is a transfer to the address evaluated from the END. If the output of the assembler is input to a loader, this address is provided to the loader.

The second pass can best be coded by breaking up the job into a number of subprograms to perform the basic tasks, such as "read the next line," "extract the mnemonic," "search for the mnemonic in the mnemonic table," " convert an address subfield to binary," and "accept a word of output for the location specified." Program 11-2 gives an outline of pass II of a typical assembler. The result of one pass around the instruction loop is to construct one instruction and hand it to the output subprogram.

11.3 PSEUDOS AND DIRECTIVES

Pseudos and directives are contained in the mnemonic table in passes I and II and cause a branch to an appropriate program to handle each separately. This section will discuss the methods used and the restrictions that these methods place on the assembler user.

Program 11-2 Pass II outline

```
* LC is location counter
START:  Set LC = 0, Set ENDFLAG off
  do while ENDFLAG off
    read next line
    do while column 1 = *
    read next line
      enddo
  extract mnemonic
  table look-up of mnemonic
  case of mnemonic type (handled by branch table)
    instruction:
      insert op-code in partially assembled word
      evaluate address field
      insert in partially assembled word
      output assembled word to object code
      LC ← LC + instruction length
    BSS:
      extract address field and compute its value N
      L ← L + N
    . . .
    END:  Set ENDFLAG on
      evaluate address field
      save value as starting address
    endcase
  enddo
```

11.3.1 Data Loading Pseudos

Typical data loading pseudos include forms of WORD, BYTE, and CHAR. The identifier in the location field is placed in the symbol table in pass I just as for an instruction. The address value stored with the identifier is taken from the location counter. (In some assemblers it may be necessary to adjust the location counter to a word boundary first for the WORD pseudo. This is necessary if the hardware requires that multibyte data such as full words in a byte-addressable memory be aligned. If that is so, we expect the WORD pseudo to align data by incrementing the location counter to the start of the next word if it is not already on a word boundary.) It is necessary to determine how many words of storage will be occupied by the data given in the pseudo so that the location counter can be incremented accordingly during pass I. In WORD and BYTE pseudos, this requires that the field be scanned to determine the number of data words by counting commas. A typical character-conversion pseudo is CHAR. Its address field must be scanned to determine the number of words needed by counting the number of characters present.

If a simple pseudo such as DATA is used for all data entry, the address field must be scanned in detail in pass I to determine the amount of space used, because the type of data is determined by the format of the address field, not by the mnemonic.

During pass II, the location field can be ignored, but the address field must be converted into binary according to the rules for the particular pseudo. At the same time, the location counter must be increased once for each word or byte produced. Conversion of character strings is straightforward, since the code used either is identical to the incoming code or can be converted by a character-table look-up. Octal or hexadecimal conversion can be done on the same basis, since each character supplies 3 or 4 bits, or it can be treated as an ordinary base-8 or base-16 conversion problem similar to decimal conversion.

11.3.2 Directives that Affect the Location Counter

A number of directives affect the location counter and possibly cause identifiers to be entered in the symbol table in pass I. The programs used to modify the location counter in pass I and pass II can be identical; the program used to handle the entry of the identifiers in pass I need not be used in pass II. Typical of these directives are BSS and ORG. BSS causes the address-field value to be added to the location counter and any identifier present in the location field to be entered in the symbol table with the value of the location counter before it was incremented. ORG causes the address-field value to be set in the location counter directly.

As long as the addresses in the address field are purely numeric, there are no problems. However, if a symbolic address is involved, then a value has to be assigned to it so that the numeric value of the address can be calculated. In pass I, only those identifiers that appeared before the line currently being examined are in the symbol table with numeric values. Therefore, if this method is to be used, identifiers must be defined before they are used in any directives that affect the location counter in a manner dependent on their address field. For example,

```
A        BSS      N
S        LOAD     A
N        EQU      10
```

could *not* be assembled because the value of the address N in the BSS directive is not known at the time it is read in pass I.

11.3.3 Directives that Affect the Symbol Table

It is desirable to be able to define identifiers in the symbol table directly rather than by equating them to the current value of the location counter. Many identifiers are not used as symbolic locations but as absolute integers or as identifiers for index registers, etc. For example, a program may be written to process records of information coming in from a magnetic tape. It could be programmed so that the record size is fixed in the program. Blocks would be defined by BSS directives with an absolute address. On the other hand, the program could, and should, be written so that the block size is a symbolic address—say, BLKLG. This program would be assembled with two addresses defined by use of the EQU directive. If the length of the block were 128,

```
BLKLG      EQU      128
```

would have to appear in the program. Since BLKLG appears as the address field of a BSS directive, the EQU that defines it must appear earlier in the input. Therefore, it is conventional to put all the definitions at the front of the program.

During pass I, the identifier in the location field of an EQU must be put into the symbol table, together with the address calculated from the address field. The identifier itself may contain identifiers, so they must be defined prior to their use. That is,

```
A          EQU      B+1
B          EQU      10
```

is illegal, whereas

```
B          EQU      10
A          EQU      B+1
```

is allowed.

The SET directive is handled similarly, except that the existence of the identifier in the location field in the symbol table is not an error for SET; rather the value is reassigned.

11.3.4 Other Directives for Special Purposes

Particular machines often have a number of directives intended to assist the programmer in coping with some of the unfortunate features of the machine. (Do not look for "unfortunate features" in the index of your programming manual; they will probably be listed under "advanced features.") A common example of this type of directive arises in machines that have either a subword structure (such as two instructions or more per word) or a multiple-word structure for some instructions. There are frequently restrictions in the hardware that make it essential that some instructions appear in a special position within the word, such as at the start. In that case, a pseudoinstruction is needed that guarantees that the next instruction is located in this privileged position. Similarly, if multiple-word items are involved in operations—for example, double-word arithmetic or transfers of blocks of a given size—there may be restrictions requiring that multiple-word items have to start in special positions such as on an even-word boundary or at a multiple of 2048 characters.

The purpose of an assembler is to save the programmer the details of specific addresses, so it must take care of such problems at the same time. Therefore, there may be directives that force the location counter to the next even value if it is odd currently, or that do the same for block structures. In the IBM 370, the DS and DC pseudos can be used for this purpose. For example,

```
DC        0F
```

would force the location counter to a fullword boundary, while

```
DS        0D
```

would force it to a doubleword boundary. Since these cause no data to be loaded into any locations skipped over, they must not be used in the instruction stream. The directive CNOP is proved for this in the IBM 370 assembler.

```
CNOP      b,4
```

forces the location counter to the next fullword ($b = 0$) or the next middle of a fullword ($b = 2$). It assembles a *no-operation* instruction to fill up unused locations.

```
CNOP      b,8
```

moves the location counter to the zero, second, fourth, or sixth byte of a doubleword when b is 0, 2, 4, or 6. This is done at assembly time by testing the bottom bits of the location counter. However, note that the loader must not relocate program in a way that would change the alignment. In the IBM 370, this restricts relocation to multiples of doublewords.

A related problem occurs in the Cyber 170, which has up to four instructions per word and yet can branch only to the first instruction in a word. Because of this, the appearance of any identifier in the location field "forces upper" (that is, fills out the partially assembled word with no-operation instructions and starts a new word) in case the identifier is used in the address field of a branch instruction elsewhere.

11.4 INTERMEDIATE LANGUAGE

In the brief discussion of pass II, it was noted that it is almost identical to pass I except for the job of outputting the binary object code and listing the translation. If the second pass is I/O-limited, this is an advantage, since pass II can be written by taking pass I, discarding the symbol-table construction section, and adding the output section. However, if computation time is significant, we should consider the fact that the steps of reading, converting, and doing table look-ups on the mnemonics are repeated in both sections, as is the work on the address fields of pseudos. Usually the most time-consuming part of the computation time is the symbol-table searching, followed by the mnemonic-table searching. The former cannot be reduced below one search per occurrence of an identifier; the latter can be reduced to one search per line of code, rather than the two presently used. In order to avoid a second search in pass II, enough information must be extracted from the table in pass I and saved for pass II use. The information required by pass II includes the actual binary code for the instruction and an indication of how to treat the address field. This means that a string of information must be generated in pass I and saved (on secondary storage) for rereading in pass II. This string of information is a partial representation of the input code, and so we call it an intermediate language — that is, intermediate between the assembly-language source and the binary object language.

If an intermediate language is to be used, it is worth exploring the possibility of translating everything from the input into an intermediate form so that the speed of subsequent passes can be improved. This can prove particularly valuable if either more than two passes are used (the additional passes will not have to reread the original input, which is neither densely packed nor especially rapidly retranslated) or it is not necessary to list the original input during pass II, in which case we can save rereading the original input completely.

If the input is to be translated into an intermediate language completely, then in addition to replacing the mnemonic with its binary equivalent and identifying information, it is necessary to convert the address field into a more convenient form for internal manipulation. To do this, numbers should be converted into binary and all identifiers in the address field should be converted into a form that is more convenient to handle. If the identifier has already been defined, then it can be replaced by its address. In fact, there is no reason why the line should not be translated completely during pass I if the information is available. In general, however, there will be forward references to identifiers not yet defined, so the identifier cannot be converted to a number. To avoid re-searching the table in pass II, the identifier can be replaced by the address of the entry in the symbol table corresponding to the identifier. (This means that identifiers must be entered when they are first encountered, although they may not be defined until they are encountered in the location field.)

The practical assembler will contain many features tailored to the particular environment. In many cases it is difficult to analyze the situation sufficiently to determine which of several ways are better, but typically the I/O considerations are the determining factors, so they should be examined first.

11.5 RELOCATION, ENTRIES, AND EXTERNAL VARIABLES

The foregoing discussion has not taken the problems of relocation into account. We recall from Chapter 4 that the assembler is expected to produce relocation information with each address — information that tells the loader whether the relocation used for that program at load time is to be applied to that particular address. In general, numeric addresses are taken to be absolute, whereas symbolic addresses may be absolute or relocatable. An address is determined to be relocatable if it "moves" with the program, that is, if it is defined by content of the location counter. First we will discuss a simple relocation scheme in which the address in each instruction is flagged as relocatable or not by a bit. In addition to the value of the identifier, the symbol table must also contain a bit that indicates whether or not an identifier is relocatable. When an identifier is put into the table, this bit must be set. Any identifier appearing in the location field of an instruction is relocatable, as are identifiers in the location fields of the pseudos BSS, WORD, BYTE, CHAR, and similar pseudos. This means that we always assume that the location counter is relocatable. (This is not essential, but allowing the locations to be absolute rather than relocatable would mean that information would have to be given to the loader so that it could determine whether to relocate a section of code or not. This would allow the programmer to place code absolutely in memory, a facility that can cause problems.) A directive that can define a nonrelocatable identifier is the EQU directive. N EQU 20 should set N to be the nonrelocatable value 20, since it may be used in a position where a nonrelocatable address is needed, for example, as an initial count for loading into an index register. In order to determine whether the symbol in the location field of the EQU directive is relocatable, it is necessary to find out whether the value of the address field is relocatable. This problem must also be solved for the address field of an instruction. Therefore, a set of rules is needed that can be used to determine the relocatability of an expression used as an address. When this has been determined, it can be used to determine the relocatability of the object address of an instruction and of the location field of an EQU, and to determine whether the other directives are valid. BSS should have nonrelocatable addresses; otherwise the loader will not be able to handle the object. ORG could be allowed either relocatable or nonrelocatable addresses, although normally we want code that can be relocated, so it should contain a relocatable address.

An absolute (nonrelocatable) address can be constructed from any allowable expression involving numbers and absolute-value symbolic addresses. Thus $23 * 3 - 4 * C$ is a valid absolute address if C is an absolute identifier. A relocatable address can certainly be formed by adding to or subtracting from a relocatable identifier any absolute amount. Thus, if B is a relocatable identifier, then $B - 34$ is also relocatable. Some assemblers restrict constructions to just those forms: absolute expressions and relocatable identifiers plus or minus absolute expressions. However, it is convenient to allow combinations of relocatable addresses for some purposes. A particular example occurs when a table of words is to be input through the assembler and it is necessary to know how many items there are in the table, perhaps to set an index register for counting purposes. If the address of the first entry is C and that of the last is B, then the expression $B - C + 1$ is the number of entries. If more entries are added to the middle of the table by adding lines, it is not necessary to further modify the program, only to reassemble it. This is shown in the following example:

```
C        WORD     1
         WORD     5
         WORD     9
         ...
B        WORD     63
N        EQU      B-C+1
```

Changing the first or last lines when an additional first or last entry is to be made can be avoided by the coding

```
C       BSS     0
        WORD    1
        ...
        WORD    63
B       BSS     0
N       EQU     C-B
```

Thus we would like to arrange for the difference between two relocatable-address expressions to be an absolute expression. In this way, the expression A − B + C would be legal unless A and C were relocatable and B was absolute or vice versa. Although the address A + C may be meaningful to the programmer in some situations where both A and C are relocatable, it is not possible for most loaders to handle it, as they allow single relocation at most. If, in assembly, A and C are given the values 23 and 34, respectively, then A + C will assemble as 57. However, if the program is relocated by 100 so that A and C have the values 123 and 134, then A + C will have the value 257, which is doubly relocated. Even with single relocation, it is feasible to allow expressions such as 2 * A − B, where both A and B are relocatable, since the total relocation is single. However, not all assemblers allow such constructions.

In addition to program relocation, which adjusts addresses as the program is moved around in memory, other forms of relocation are desirable. The need for them arises from various sources. One is the use of common variables in subprograms that are translated into binary separately. This can be handled by using common variables such as those provided in Fortran. The assembly-language equivalent of labeled common requires that several different location counters be established, one for each labeled section. A different relocation is associated with each location counter. If it is possible for a large number (more, say, than 8 or 16) of location counters to be established, it begins to become inefficient to associate relocation bits with each different location counter. Instead, a small field in the symbol table can be used to indicate which location counter should be used to relocate the identifier, if any. If up to 255 location counters were possible, 8 bits could be used in the field. The 256th possibility would indicate no relocation. Under those conditions, the 8-bit field could also be passed to the loader so that it knows how to relocate an address, but it is probably more efficient to pass a list of the program words that have to be relocated by each location counter, since the majority of addresses do not need relocation in the instruction sets of modern computers. This requires a linking loader (see Section 6.4.2). If this method is used, multiple location counters, labeled common, and external symbols can be handled by the same mechanism. The assembler can generate a list for each location counter, each labeled-common section (and blank common), and each external symbol. When an address in an instruction such as

```
LOAD    A+B*2-C+10
```

is assembled, the relocations must be calculated. For example, if A has been declared as an external via the pair of directives

```
          EXTRNL   Z
A         EQU      Z+20
```

and B and C are addresses within the current program segment (perhaps declared by the directives

```
C         BSS      N
B         BSS      N
```

where N is an absolute address), the address field A+B*2−C+10 is relocatable by the external Z and the current location counter; therefore, the location of the instruction should be placed in the lists for Z and the current location counter.

When an EXTRNL declaration is encountered, the identifiers declared must be placed in the symbol table with an indication of the appropriate relocation. As suggested above, this can be handled by keeping a separate table of external variables (including labeled-common identifiers and program-section identifiers) and putting a pointer from the symbol-table entry to the external table. For example, the sequence

```
          EXTRNL   Z
A         EQU      Z+20
```

would place Z in the symbol table and the external table. The definition of Z in the symbol table would give a value of 0 with a relocation of Z—the latter indicated by a pointer to the Z entry in the external table. When the EQU was processed in pass I, it would put A in the symbol table only and give it a value of 20 relocated by Z. If this technique is used, symbols are restricted to single relocation.

When an ENTRY directive is processed, identifiers in its address field must be placed in a list. Then, after pass I, the assembler can pass on the external and entry information to the loader in two lists. The first is the list of entry points and their addresses within the program. The second is a list of external identifiers (plus labeled-common and program sections). The latter consists of a set of sublists, each containing an external identifier and the program addresses to be relocated by that external identifier. The information provided by the user to the assembler consists of source-language statements such as ENTRY and EXTRNL. Entry statements tell the assembler that the identifiers in the address field are to be passed on to the loader, together with information telling the loader where the corresponding address is located relative to the code being translated. For example, the statements

```
          ENTRY    A,B
A         LOAD     =2
B         ADD      =3
```

at the start of a program indicate to the assembler that the identifiers A and B are to be given to the loader with the relocatable addresses 0 and 1, respectively.

11.6 MACROS

Macros were introduced in Chapter 7. There are two important phases in the processing of a macro: the definition phase, when the set of statements defining the macro are read and stored in a suitable form, and the expansion phase, when the identifier of a macro is replaced with the set of statements representing that macro. This section will examine some of the methods that can be used to process macros. It will also mention some additional features that can be added to the macro facility.

Macros are usually handled as part of the assembler, since macros are most often used in assembly language. Macro expansion schemes have been defined for higher-level languages, but their use in such environments will not be covered here.[2] Their utility in higher-level languages is less than in assembly language because higher-level languages are supposedly adapted to the type of problems being solved, and hence macros are likely to achieve less compression of the source and little additional clarity. Assembly language is difficult to follow and lengthy to write, so macros can reduce the size of the source language and increase the clarity tremendously in long programs. The clarity can be improved even if a macro is used only once.

Macros can be expanded during pass I of the assembler so as to retain a two-pass assembler, or they can be expanded prior to pass I in what is called a *prepass*. In the latter case, expansion can be made optional, so that users not requiring a macro expansion will not be penalized for the time of the extra pass. We shall discuss macros as though they are to be processed in pass I. This will introduce some restrictions of predefinition similar to the restrictions on the use of symbolic addresses in the EQU directives. Finally, we shall consider ways of removing these restrictions by using prepasses.

We recall that the definition of a macro is accomplished by preceding it with the directive MACRO and following it with the directive MEND. The macro definition may contain parameters that are identifiers separated by commas. When the macro is used, its identifier appears in the mnemonic field, and the address field contains strings of information to be substituted for the parameters. The location field may contain an identifier that is to be assigned the current value of the location counter. Some macro assemblers—for example, the IBM 370—allow the location field of a macro to be another parameter. However, it is confusing to place anything in this field except a symbol that will qualify the first instruction of the macro expansion, because the user normally looks at a listing without a listing of the macro expansions.

The translator must save the set of statements that makes up each definition, recognize the use of a macro identifier in place of a regular instruction, expand the macro so that the expanded form is available during both pass I and pass II, and make the substitutions for the parameters during the expansion. Whereas most parts of assembly are I/O-limited, so that we can usually use simple techniques for the computations and ignore speed problems, macros provide a facility for generating large amounts of code from a few input statements. The translator will not be input-limited during these sections, and it may not be I/O-limited during pass II if the listing is not too verbose.

[2]For a general description of macro processors, see P. J. Brown, *Macro Processors and Techniques for Portable Software*, John Wiley & Sons, New York, 1974; or A. J. Cole, *Macro Processors*, Cambridge University Press, Cambridge, 1976.

Therefore, we need to be concerned about the speed of expansion methods used. In particular, we must decide whether to perform the expansion during pass I and pass on an expanded form to pass II or to reexpand during pass II. Decisions of this type inevitably depend on many factors and are very difficult to make. For example, if we decide to use a prepass technique to avoid some restrictions, the expansion must be done prior to pass I, and there is no decision to make. If we decide to run pass II from the original copy of the source language, then we have to reexpand in pass II. The benefit of the latter decision is that the source is typically shorter; the benefit of the former is that pass II processing time is saved. Generally, it is better to pass the expanded form to pass II, because the macro expansion code is then limited to one place.

This decision is also influenced by the available storage space for the macro definitions during assembly. If large amounts of primary memory are available, then most programs can be expected to be such that the macro definitions will never spill over into secondary storage. Although a limit on the number of lines of macro definition could be set, it is better to allow any program to be assembled that can be run within the system; thus provisions will have to be made for a program that contains more macro definitions than can be saved in the primary memory. The additional macros will have to be saved on secondary storage devices. Accessing them may be slow, depending on the type of device available. If the available devices are too slow, it is probably better to expand in pass I to avoid taking up the time in pass II.

11.6.1 Expansion Methods

During the first pass, the appearance of the directive MACRO must cause the assembler to stop the regular assembly process and enter a mode in which a copy of the input is kept for later use. The line images must be copied, one at a time, into a storage area until a MEND directive is encountered. The MACRO and MEND directives themselves need not be copied, but the information from the line following the MACRO must be saved in an index of the macro definitions. The macro identifier must be entered into this index, which is a subsidiary mnemonic table. The parameter identifiers must also be saved, either in the index or at the front of the definition. After a MEND card has been read, the assembler returns to its normal state of examining each card for mnemonic type and handling it appropriately.

When the assembler checks the mnemonics, it must also check for the presence of a macro. We must decide whether the user is allowed to redefine existing mnemonics or their names are permanent. In the latter case, the mnemonic table is scanned. If the mnemonic is found there, that definition is accepted; if not, the index of macro definitions is scanned. If the identifier in the mnemonic field is not found in mnemonic table or the macro index, an error exists; otherwise, expansion must take place. Note that this means that macros must be defined before they are used. If the user can redefine existing mnemonics as macros, the macro index must first be searched. If the identifier is not there, the mnemonic table is scanned in the regular way. (If the user is allowed to redefine macros that have been previously defined, the search through the macro index must be done in the reverse of the order in which the defined macro identifiers are added to the index.)

When an identifier is located in the macro index, the expansion starts. The macro index must contain a pointer to the storage location of the macro definition. Simply stated, all that has to happen is that the read section of pass I must switch over and read the definition instead of the source input until the end of the definition is reached, at which time the read section must switch back to the original source.

Perhaps the simplest way to program this is to provide a subprogram that reads the next source-language statement and to put a switch in this program, which reads either from the actual source or from the definition. In this way, the remainder of pass I is not affected in any way. This subprogram must also take care of substituting the actual parameter values provided by the user in the use of the macro. This can be a slow operation, since it is a character-string manipulation problem. Consider the macro definition

```
COPY      MACRO     B,C
          LOAD      B+1,C
          STORE     B,C
          MEND
```

and the use

```
          COPY      W+7,XSPEC
```

The definition contains the two statements LOAD and STORE, with address fields. These address fields must be modified so that the result reads

```
          LOAD      W+7+1,XSPEC
          STORE     W+7,XSPEC
```

That is, the character strings W+7 and XSPEC must be substituted for B and C, respectively.

This can be done by analyzing the definition when it is first read or by reanalyzing it each time. In the former case, the definition must be scanned when it is first read, and any occurrences of the parameters must be noted by replacing them with indicators showing which parameters they are. At expansion time, these indicators must be replaced with the character strings provided by the user. In the latter case, the definition must be read at expansion time, and every identifier (including location and mnemonic fields) must be checked against the list of parameter identifiers. If the identifier is found in the parameter list, the string provided by the user must be copied in its place. Since the program is not input-limited during the expansion phase, it is preferable to do as much of the analysis as possible in the definition phase. A number of tricks can be used to speed up the processing during the latter phase. We shall examine one possible technique in more detail.

When the definition is read, the identifiers of the parameters are placed in a table at the head of the definition. As each line of the macro is read, it is scanned to the end of the address field, starting from the location field. Names are extracted by doing a lexicographic scan looking only for *break* characters. These are characters that cannot be legitimate parts of identifiers (for example, plus, minus, comma, multiply, blank, etc.). Each group of characters between break characters is compared with all of the parameter identifiers. If there is agreement, that character string is replaced with a parameter indicator constructed by using an internal code that is not a legal character followed by the number of the parameter (in the example above, B would be 0 and C would be 1). (Since there are fewer printing characters than bit combinations in most machines, there are non-printing-character bit combinations. One of these combinations is used as the internal code. To save processing time during the expansion phase, those statements containing parameters can be marked. At expansion time, the character strings provided by the user (delimited by commas and blanks) are placed in a parameter value table in positions corresponding to the matching parameter. As each statement is read from the definition, those not marked as containing parameters are copied directly to the assembler; otherwise they are copied one character at a time. When the code indicating parameter use is sensed, the number following it is used to extract a character string from the parameter value table. This is copied in place of the parameter indicator. This process continues until the end of the statement is reached. The length of the line image can change during expansion, so the latter parts of the assembler must accept variable-length lines. As an example, the macro given above would appear in the macro definition table as

```
LOAD        &0+1,&1
STORE       &0,&1
```

where & (ampersand) has been used to represent the special code. When it is used by the statement

```
COPY        W+7,XSPEC
```

the two character strings W+7 and XSPEC are listed in the actual parameter value table as entries 0 and 1, respectively. As the definition is read, the appearance of & causes the entry corresponding to the number following to be copied in its place, to get

```
LOAD        W+7+1,XSPEC
STORE       W+7,XSPEC
```

During the expansion process, the output from the subprogram that gets the next statement is processed by the assembler to control the location counter and build up the symbol table. It is possible that the assembler may encounter another macro identifier in the mnemonic field, since the definition has not been checked to see whether it contains only legal mnemonics. This is normally allowed, and it is called *nested macro use*. One macro may be defined in terms of others. The mechanism is quite straightforward. The assembler recognizes the use of a macro in the usual way, so that it conditions the read subprogram to read from the macro instead of from the input. Unfortunately, it was already reading from a macro definition, although a different one. Since it should return to reading from the first macro when the expansion of the second has been completed, it is necessary to use a stack to save the state of the read section when a macro is encountered by the assembler. Each time a macro is encountered, the address field of the macro is copied into the parameter value table of character strings (this itself may involve parameter replacement if a macro is currently being expanded). Then the current state of the read section is placed in a stack and reading of a new definition commences. When the expansion of a macro is complete, the previous state of the read section is restored. This includes restoring the state of the macro parameter value table.

An example may help to clarify the picture. Suppose the input is

```
19    A    MACRO    X,Y,Z
20         LOAD     X+4
21         Z        X,Y-1
22         STORE    X-4
23         ADD      =1
24         B        123,Y
25         STORE    R
26         MEND
27    B    MACRO    W,V
28         ADD      S+W,V
29         MEND
30         A        J,K,LOAD
```

(These lines are numbered for reference in the text below.)

When the assembler has finished processing line 29, the macro index table contains two entries, A and B. The definitions stored for A and B are

	Definition		Parameter use mark
A1	LOAD	&0+4	1
A2	&2	&0,&1-1	1
A3	STORE	&0-4	1
A4	ADD	=1	0
A5	B	123,&1	1
A6	STORE	R	0
B1	ADD	S+&0,&1	1

The current entry in the push-down stack of the read section is

"Reading line 30, Source."

When the assembler reads the next line via the read section, it finds that the mnemonic field contains the macro A. Its parameters are J, K, and LOAD. It places these in a parameter value table and changes the state of the read section so that the macro A is being read. The state of the push-down stack for the read section is now

Top	"Reading line A1, macro A."
Second	"Reading line 31, source."

The parameter value table contains

Entry	Contents
2	LOAD
1	K
0	J

As the read section passes on line images to the main assembler, the parameters are replaced by the entries in the parameter value table. Thus the images

```
LOAD     J+4
LOAD     J,K-1
STORE    J-4
ADD      =1
B        123,K
```

are generated. When the last statement is processed by the assembler, it recognizes the use of the macro B. The parameters are placed in the parameter value table (this can be done in a push-down fashion so that the previous entries are available later), and the read section is changed to a new state. The push-down stack for the read section is now

Top "Reading line B1, macro B."
Second "Reading line A6, macro A."
Third "Reading line 31, source."

and the table of parameter values is

Entry	Contents
1	K
0	123
(separation between levels)	
2	LOAD
1	K
0	J

The next use of the read section causes the image ADD S+&0,&1 to be replaced by ADD S+123,K. Since that is the end of the macro B, the stack pops up, so that it now reads

Top "Reading line A6, macro A."
Second "Reading line 31, source."

and the table contents revert to their previous state with the three entries shown above. The last line of the macro A is passed on immediately from the read section to the assembler since it contains no parameters, and now processing of macro A has been completed. Control pops up again, so that the read section is back on the source stream.

Keyword parameters can be implemented by adding a small symbol table to the front of each macro definition. At the time that the macro is used, the key words can be constructed in the correct order. Undefined parameters can then be specified by the default definition, which should also be in the symbol table.

11.6.2 Macro Expansion in a Prepass

If macros are to be expanded during pass I, it is necessary to define each macro before its use. If this restriction is to be removed, it is necessary to add at least one extra pass in order to first accumulate all the macro definitions and then expand them. If nested definitions are not used, it is possible to locate all the definitions in a prepass and then perform the expansion during pass I, as discussed earlier. However, nested definitions can cause additional definitions to appear as the result of expansion, requiring yet another pass. Therefore, it is simpler to complete the expansion prior to the first pass of the assembler, and to view the macro expander as a separate translator that accepts macro language as a source language and outputs assembler language as its object. Since the checking for valid assembler language is most easily accomplished by the assembler, the macro expander will not check for validity of the object program and should be viewed as a character-string manipulation program.

The macro expander can be implemented in much the same way that a macro assembler is implemented. Statements from line images are read one at a time, and the mnemonic field is checked. Any time that a macro definition is encountered, it is copied into a definition storage area and entered in a definition macro index. Any time that the use of a macro is sensed, the definition is copied, substituting for the parameters as above. If, during one pass, no new definitions are encountered, it is known that the expansion has been completed. If new definitions are encountered, then it is possible that they were used in an earlier section of the source; thus additional passes may be necessary. These passes are made over the expanded version output from the last pass, using the macro definitions that have been accumulated thus far. It is highly desirable to minimize the number of passes in a translator, since the input read time accounts for most of the translation time. The solution proposed above requires at least two passes if any macros are used—one to find the definitions and the other to expand. This is similar to the two-pass assembler; one pass is used to find the definitions of the symbols and the other is used for replacement.

We commented early in the discussion of assemblers that it is possible to have a one-pass assembler if all identifiers are predefined, and that some assemblers make provisions for a one-pass option. A similar technique can be used in a macro expander. If the program defines all macros before use, it should not be penalized for the flexibility available to other users. The translator can recognize that there are no earlier uses of the defined macros and avoid the extra pass. This is accomplished by constructing a table of all different mnemonics read in a pass over the source. Initially this is empty, and as each mnemonic is placed into the output from the translator, its mnemonic field is entered into a table (unless it is already there). When a definition is encountered, it is copied into the definition storage area in the usual way, and the table is checked to see whether it has been used previously. If it has, a switch is set. At the end of the pass, this switch is tested. If it is off, then no macros were defined that had not been defined previously; therefore, no additional passes are necessary. (This technique would be worthwhile only if processing were I/O-bound.)

11.7 SUMMARY AND PROBLEMS

During pass I, a location counter keeps track of the future locations of all words to be assembled so that symbol values can be defined. The symbol table is used to store identifiers and their associated values. This table functions as an associative memory. A mnemonic table is another associative memory that is permanently assigned values by the assembler designer. The usual structure of pass I is a loop to read lines and branch to one of a set of subprograms—one for each instruction type and one for each directive and pseudo. The branch address is one of the pieces of information held in the mnemonic table. Some address fields have to be analyzed during pass I because their value affects the location counter.

The first stage in pass I is a lexicographic scan of the input line to break it into tokens. A character table is used to make rapid decisions. Numbers are converted to binary by multiplication, and identifiers are packed into some suitable form. Expressions are evaluated using precedence and a stack.

Pass II can repeat much of the code of pass I, but in addition it must generate the binary object code. It can ignore the location field of input lines.

Each directive and pseudo is handled by a separate block of code or subprogram in passes I and II. Data loading pseudos must be analyzed to determine their length in pass I and their binary form in pass II. The address fields in BSS, ORG, and EQU directives must be evaluated in pass I to keep track of the location counter. This implies predefinition. Because many of the address fields have to be at least partially analyzed in pass I, an intermediate language can be used to avoid a reanalysis in pass II. The intermediate language contains a compact form of the input with numbers converted to binary and symbols converted to binary pointers (addresses) to the symbol-table entry.

Relocation information is also placed in the symbol table. It can consist of a bit for each relocation base, or, if many bases are to be allowed, a field specifying the base. The latter limits each symbol to single relocation, although addresses can still be subject to multiple relocation. Pass I builds up tables of Entry identifiers and External identifiers. These are output for the linker-loader after pass I.

Macros can be expanded in pass I (which requires predefinition of all macros) or in a prepass. Expansion speed is important, because large amounts of code can be generated from few input lines. We may choose to generate an intermediate form that has been expanded or to reexpand in pass II.

Macro identifiers are entered into a subsidiary mnemonic table when their definitions are first encountered. Each operation field mnemonic is looked up in this table first if redefinition of operation mnemonics is allowed. Each definition is stored, usually after some processing to replace parameters with simple numeric codes that can be handled rapidly during expansion. When a macro call is encountered, the actual parameter values are placed in a table, and the assembler input switches to reading from the definition. When the parameter codes are encountered, the values from the table can be substituted. Keyword parameters can be handled in the same way as position parameters by entering the actual values or the default values in the table just prior to the expansion. Nested macro use is allowed by using a stack to store the actual parameter value table and information about the current input position prior to the last macro call.

If predefinition of macros is not required, two prepasses may be needed—one to collect definitions and one to perform expansions.

Problems

11-1 Suppose that multiple positive or negative relocation is to be allowed by a single relocation address, perhaps the program start address. Discuss how the expression evaluator in Section 11.1.2 could be extended to calculate the relocation factor. It should be able to determine that the address

```
3*A-B
```

is doubly relocatable if A and B are relocatable singly, for example. What restrictions could be put on expressions in order to keep the problem reasonable? Would the address

```
N*A-(N-1)*B
```

be allowed, where A, B and N are relocatable? What if A and B were relocatable but N was absolute?

11-2 Show that there are 1,617,038,306 identifiers of six or fewer characters that start with a letter and contain only letters or digits. Suggest an algorithm for converting between such identifiers and the integers between 0 and 1,617,038,305 such that if the identifiers are in alphabetical order, their numeric equivalences are in numerical order.

11-3 Is code of the form

```
N BSS 1
A BSS N
```

valid? Why?

11-4 How would you handle conditional assembly (directives IF, THEN, ELSE)?

11-5 Suggest a mechanism for handling conditional assembly inside a macro definition.

11-6 Some assemblers permit repeated assembly with directives such as WHILE and ENDWHILE. How would you handle these in pass I and pass II?

CHAPTER **12**

SEARCHING AND SORTING

An associative memory is a device that lets the user retrieve information when part of the information is specified. The need for associative memory devices is common to many applications. Some examples in the data processing field include associating account information with a customer known by name (or account number), associating the address information with the symbolic identifier in assemblers and compilers, and associating employee statistics such as age, marital status, and wage rate with employees' names. Outside the computer, we meet two very common examples in the phone directory and the dictionary, both associating a set of information with a given word.

Because the associative memories that have been built are fairly expensive and relatively small, other techniques must be used in practice to simulate the associative memory, just as the numbers of all telephones cannot be stored in an associative memory. The human head can store a few phone numbers and apparently operate as an associative memory, but that is an expensive memory and a slow device. Instead one uses a telephone directory and performs a search for the name in order to get the number. It is often fruitful to bear this example in mind as searching techniques are discussed, since a number of the techniques used to find a name in the telephone directory of a large city have their counterpart in computer techniques.

The basic operations needed in an associative memory are as follows:

1 Enter an item.
2 Remove an item.
3 Add to or modify an item already there.
4 Read an item to obtain additional information when part of the item is known.

The frequency with which each of these actions is taken and the size of the total amount of information serve to determine the best way to simulate the associative memory. In some cases, such as the telephone directory, only one action is normally taken by the user—that is, to find additional information when the name is given. Hence the alphabetic ordering technique is the best. Anybody who has tried to find the phone number of a common entry such as Smith in a very large city, knowing the address but not the initials, is aware that the telephone directory is not efficient for uses other than an alphabetic search.

The set of entries in an associative memory is called a file. Each item (record) in the file contains a set of information, such as name, address, and telephone number. If one piece of information (a *field*) in a record is used to identify that record when the file is to be interrogated, that field is called a *key*. In come cases there can be more than one key for each item. If we wished to find the name of a person with a given phone number, then the phone number would be the key. Obviously, the phone directory does not offer a good way of performing this operation, although it could be so used. Since the phone company needs to determine who has been assigned a particular number, it usually keeps an *inverse* file in which the entries are sorted in order of phone number. The phone company also needs a list of phone numbers arranged by addresses. This means three directories, or possibly three times the memory space for the files. This is a case of *multiple keys*. The amount of information can be reduced by keeping only one complete directory, sorted, say, by name. The other two can contain the phone number and name and the address and name, respectively, and they can be sorted by phone number and address, respectively. The amount of storage space is reduced, but it now requires two look-ups if the reference is by phone number or address. The second look-up in the name directory can be simplified if the reference to it is an index number (for example, page, column, and row) so that no search is necessary.

Sometimes each record contains a fixed number of fields or can be conveniently arranged to have this form. We then talk of fixed-length records. The alternative is variable-length records. (For example, the file of people who have books checked out from a library may be variable-length. Each record could consist of the user's name—the key—followed by a variable number of fields representing the books checked out to that person.) In general, variable-length records require more careful planning for efficient handling.

Requirements such as these must be examined in planning the simulation of associative memories. This chapter will discuss some of the simple techniques for programming associative memories, with specific reference to their use by the assembler symbol table. Some of the methods discussed will not be valuable for most assembler implementations, but the reader is invited to consider their application to other problems.

12.1 SEQUENTIAL SEARCHING

Perhaps the simplest technique that can be applied to the symbol table problem is the sequential method. A table is constructed sequentially in memory, using as many words as necessary per entry. For example, 3 words may be needed for the assembler symbol table, with the first containing the coded identifier, the second containing the address

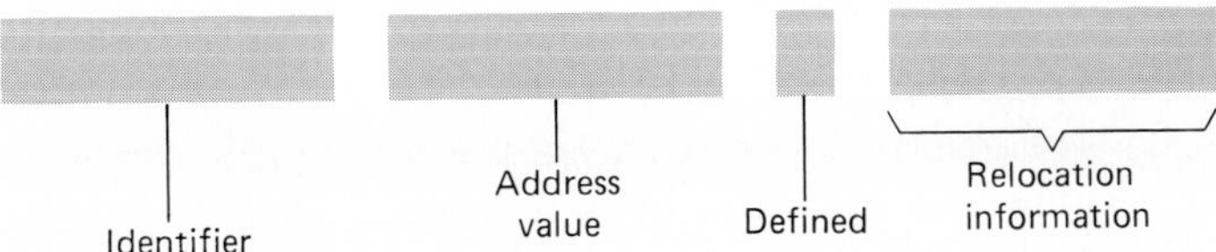

FIGURE 12-1 Symbol table entry

value (when it is defined), and the third containing flags and relocation information. This is shown in Figure 12-1. A table of N entries would then occupy $3N$ consecutive locations.

The four basic operations would be performed as follows:

Enter a new entry. A count of the number of entries N is maintained. The incoming entry is added to the bottom of the table (the next three words in memory) and N is increased by 1.

Remove an entry. This cannot be done without either leaving holes or moving other information, so it is not generally allowed in this scheme. (It is not necessary for the assembler symbol table.)

Modify an entry. The table of items is searched for the key, that is, each identifier (the first word of the group of 3) is compared with the key in turn until a match is found or the end of the table is reached. This is the search part of the process. It yields the address of the 3 words of the entry or the fact that there is no matching record. Using the address, the other parts of the record can now be changed.

Locate an entry. This is done by searching on the key as above.

If deletion is to be allowed, then the hole left should be filled by moving the last entry in the table to the space and reducing N by 1.

This technique should only be used when tables are relatively small; otherwise the search time will be too long. Techniques exist to make this method faster by small factors, but not by enough that one should consider searching a table the size of a phone book a record at a time.

12.1.1 Expected Length of Search

Consider an assembly-language source program with N different identifiers and suppose that each is used M greater than 1 times. If the definitions and uses are distributed evenly but no identifier is used before it is defined, then at the stage where K identifiers have been defined, we can expect a search to take about $K/2$ comparisons ("on the average," the seach goes halfway down the table). This will be done M times before the next identifier is defined, or a total of $M * K/2$ comparisons will be made. Thus the total expected number of comparisons is about

$$M/2 + 2M/2 + 3M/2 + NM/2 = M(1 + 2 + 3 + \cdots + N)/2$$
$$= MN(N + 1)/4$$

We say that the length of time is *asymptotic* to $MN^2/4$ (that is, the important or fastest-growing part of the time is $MN^2/4$). Thus, if we double the number of identifiers, the search time is quadrupled.

The estimate is not exact, but it is a good approximation. It is too small because identifiers are used before they are defined, and therefore the number of entries in the symbol table increases very rapidly as the first part of the program is read. On the other hand, many programs refer most frequently to identifiers that are defined near to the point at which they are used (branches, for example). It is therefore a better practice to search backward through the symbol table, since the chances are good that the identifier is a recent entry and therefore near the bottom. This serves to lower the expected time of search, and the two effects may cancel each other out.

12.2 BINARY SEARCHING TECHNIQUES

The length of time used in the sequential search technique is the result of a lack of information about the order of the items in the table. The phone book is ordered alphabetically, which gives us this very important facility; if a name is compared against an entry in the table and it does not match, then it is possible to tell immediately if the name should appear before or after the referenced entry in the table. This means, for example, that it is possible to eliminate half the entries in one step by simply comparing the name with the middle entry. If the name is larger (alphabetically), then the name will not be found in the first half of the table, so that the first half need not be searched further.

This technique is comparable to flipping open the phone book in the center and then deciding which half to concentrate on. Most people do not use this method directly because they have some idea from the name where it might be. For example, in looking up Brown, they know that they must start about one-twentieth of the way through. Such considerations can be taken into account in computer methods, and they will be discussed in the next section. In this section we wish to explore the advantages and disadvantages of *binary searching techniques,* which are the extension of the idea above.

Initially we start with a large table, T, of entries—say 1024 entries, as an example. We suppose that the keys in the table are sorted into order. When we wish to look up identifier S in this table, we compare it first with the middle entry (the 512th). (See Figure 12-2.) If the identifier S happens to match the middle entry, we are lucky and have completed the process. If not, then S is either larger or smaller than entry 512. If it is larger, we need look only at the top half of the table; if it is smaller, we need look only at the bottom half. In neither case are there more than 512 entries left to examine, and in both cases the half that is left is itself a sorted table T1. Therefore the same technique can be applied again. That is, identifier S can be compared with the middle entry of the remaining table T1 (that is, with the 256th or 768th entry of the original table). Again, we can tell whether it is in the top or bottom half of table T1, so, after two comparisons, we have narrowed the possibilities down to one-fourth of the original table. This process can be repeated until there is only one entry in the table to be searched, in which case a direct comparison will determine whether it is identifier S or not. The example of a 1024-entry table will take 10 or less steps, as can be seen in

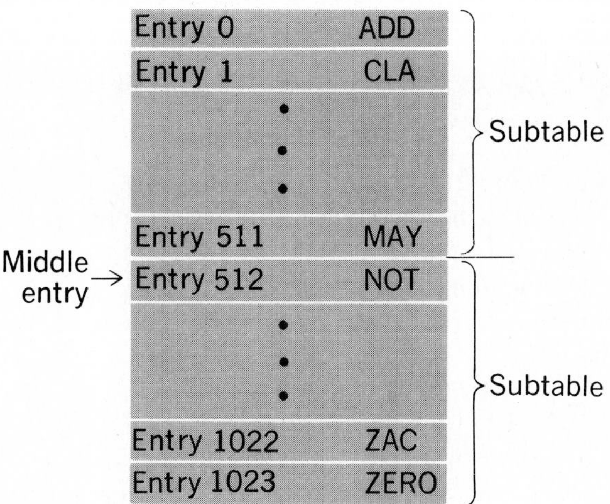

FIGURE 12-2 Binary searching

TABLE 12-1 NUMBER OF STEPS FOR BINARY SEARCH

Number of steps	Number of entries remaining in table
0	1024
1	512
2	256
3	128
4	64
5	32
6	16
7	8
8	4
9	2
10	1

Table 12-1. It is obvious that each additional step doubles the number of entries that can be taken care of. Thus, if a total of n steps were to be taken, 2^n entries could be accommodated in the table. We need not restrict ourselves to tables that have numbers of entries exactly equal to a power of 2. Other tables can be handled. The technique calls for the construction of the address of the middle entry of the remaining table. Consequently, if we save the addresses of the first and last entry in the remaining table, we can form the average. Its integer part is the middle address. The procedure is shown in Program 12-1. In this program, L is the address of the lowest entry in the remaining table, and M is the address of 1 beyond the highest entry. This saves a small amount of arithmetic.

Many computers have three-way compares so that equality can also be detected. It might appear that checking for equality would save a number of passes through the loop and speed the process up. In fact, for random data, it only reduces the average number

Program 12-1 Binary search

```
Set L = address of bottom table entry
Set M = address of one higher than top entry
do while L < M − 1
  Set I = integer part of (L + M)/2
  if C(I) ≤ searched name
    then Set L = I
    else Set M = I
    endif
  enddo
either C(L) is name, or name is not in table
```

Program 12-2 Binary search using three-way compare

```
Set L = address of one below bottom table entry
Set M = address of one higher than top entry
do while L < M − 1
  Set I = integer part of (L + M)/2
  case of comparison of C(I) with searched name
    C(I) smaller: Set L = I
    C(I) larger: Set M = I
    equal: exit loop
    endcase
  enddo
If L = M − 1 then name is not in table, otherwise it is C(I)
```

of passes around the loop by about one,[1] and each pass is possibly more expensive. Therefore, the decision is strongly influenced by the nature of the computer used. A form of the revised algorithm is given in Program 12-2. In this case, the address L points to the entry before the start of the remaining table.

Example Suppose that we have a table with thirteen entries that, for simplicity, we shall suppose are the letters A through M. Let us consider the problem of looking up entry H in the table. (Remember that we do not know that the entries are of this simple form, so H might be anywhere.) Suppose that the table starts in location T and takes 1 word per entry, as shown in Table 12-2. Initially, $L = T - 1$ and $M = T + 13$ if we use the method of three-way comparison. The steps are shown in Table 12-3. The entry H is found on the third pass through the loop. If the letter K had been looked up, then four search steps—the maximum for this table—would have been taken.

[1]For a thorough analysis of this and all searching and sorting methods, see D. E. Knuth, *Searching and Sorting: The Art of Computer Programming*, vol. 3, Addison-Wesley, Reading, MA, 1973.

TABLE 12-2 EXAMPLE DATA FOR BINARY SEARCH

Location	Entry
T+12	M
T+11	L
T+10	K
T+9	J
T+8	I
T+7	H
T+6	G
T+5	F
T+4	E
T+3	D
T+2	C
T+1	B
T	A

TABLE 12-3 STEPS IN EXECUTION OF PROGRAM 12-2

Pass through loop	
1	L < M − 1, therefore continue.
1	I = (M + L)/2 = T + 6
1	Entry at T + 6 is G, less than H; therefore, set L = I = T + 6.
2	L < M − 1
2	I = (L + M)/2 = T + 9
2	Entry at T + 9 is J, greater than H; therefore, set M = I = T + 9
3	L < M − 1
3	I = (L + M)/2 = T + 7
3	Entry at T + 7 is H. Exit loop, having found it.

12.2.1 Application of the Binary Search Method to the Assembler Symbol Table

The prerequisite for the use of the binary search technique is that the table be sorted into order. Keeping the table in order as it is generated is a slow process, since it is necessary to move existing information. On the average, half the table will have to be moved for each new entry; hence the techniques discussed for the assembler are not directly applicable. What must be done is to first gather together a set of all entries to be made in the table. This can be done in pass I of the assembly. During pass I the table is unordered, so that no search of identifiers used in address fields can be made and no check on double definition or nondefinition can be made. Between pass I and pass II, the defined identifiers must be sorted into order. At this stage, double-definition errors will be caught when two entries with the same key are found. The identifiers used in the address fields can be looked up by the binary search technique during pass II at the time of final translation. Because no table look-up is possible during pass I, pseudos such as BSS and EQU must either have absolute addresses or be delayed until after pass I. Use of this method obviously makes it less desirable to translate into an intermediate language during the first pass. Only the instruction mnemonic can be replaced by its binary form, and any location field identifiers (which have already been processed) can be omitted.

12.2.2 Comparison of Binary with Sequential Search

If the number of different identifiers is N and each is used an additional $M - 1$ times, then the sort at the end of pass I will take order of $N \log_2 N$ operations if a binary (two-way) internal merge is used. (This will be shown in the section on sorting that follows.) The searching during pass II for $(M - 1)N$ identifiers will take order of $(M - 1)N \log_2 N$ operations with a binary search technique. Thus the total is $MN \log_2 N$ operations. This compares with $MN^2/4$ operations with a sequential search method. In addition, the comparison loop for the binary sort-and-search method is about twice as complex; thus we wish to compare $2MN \log_2 N$ with $MN^2/4$. Suppose that $M = 4$. The result is shown graphically in Figure 12-3. It can be seen from this figure that as N increases, the binary search method becomes preferable.

12.3 SORTING

Much work has been done to find efficient methods of sorting, since sorting is an important part of many large business data processing problems. Our intent is not to go over this work in detail, but rather to highlight some features.[2]

Two related processes that are very important in data processing are sorting and merging. Sorting is the process that starts with a random file and finishes with a completely ordered file. Merging is the process that starts with several ordered files and produces a single ordered file. In practice, both processes are needed to do a given job. For example, a bank that is updating its ordered file (on tape or disk) of customer accounts with the day's transactions may first sort the day's transactions into order and then merge this file with the file of the month's transactions to date to get an updated file. This will make it unnecessary to read through the month-to-date file more than once. If the month-to-date file is much larger than the daily transaction file, this approach has obvious advantages. The use of large, semirandom access devices such as disk files, which make the customer records available on-line, allows other techniques, but this is the most straightforward. Sorting itself may involve merging, particularly if the number of entries is larger than can be accommodated in high-speed store. Typically, groups of entries that can be held inside the primary store are sorted by some technique and then written onto secondary store. When the whole file has been processed, the result is a collection of smaller sorted files. These are now merged. The first stage of this is called *internal sorting*. It is convenient to examine internal sorting

[2]The most complete reference for sorting is D. E. Knuth, *Searching and Sorting: The Art of Computer Programming*, vol. 3, Addison-Wesley, Reading, MA, 1973. Survey articles include W. A. Martin, "Sorting," *Computer Surveys*, vol. 3, no. 4, pp. 147–174, December 1971.

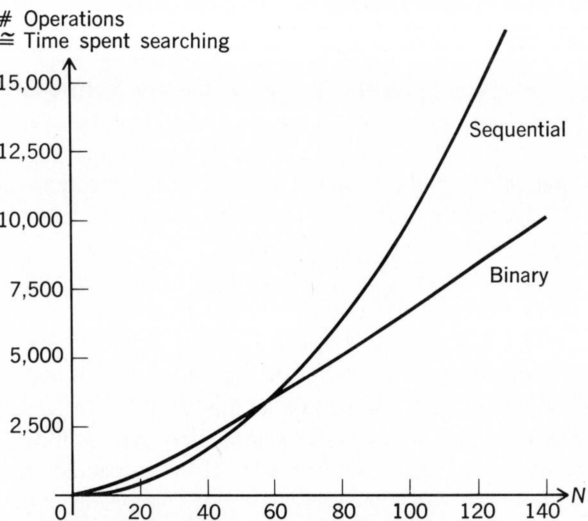

FIGURE 12-3 Comparison of sequential and binary search times

separately, because the class of methods that can be considered is larger than the class that can be used efficiently when a secondary store is used.

Internal sorting can be categorized in a number of ways. Three important classes of methods are those based on sequential searching, those based on merging, and those based on the radix representation of the key or some translation of it. In addition, there is a very important technique called *hash addressing,* which can be used in a form of sorting that makes searching very fast.

12.3.1 Sequential Methods

A typical method in this category is the example invariably given in introductory Fortran texts. The first item in the file is moved to a location reserved for the smallest. It is then compared with each of the others in turn. If a smaller item is found, it is placed in the cell reserved for the smallest. When all of the keys in the file have been compared in this way, the smallest member is known. It is exchanged with the first member of the file and then attention is restricted to the remaining $N - 1$ members. The smallest of the reduced file is the second smallest of the whole file, so it is exchanged with the second member, and so on. After M passes, the file would contain the first M members in order. After $N - 1$ passes, a file of N entries would be in order. The number of operations is proportional to

$$(N - 1) + (N - 2) + \cdots + 3 + 2 + 1 = N(N - 1)/2$$

which is approximately $N^2/2$ for large N. All of the sequential search methods use KN^2 operations for some value of K. (We express this by saying that they are $O(N^2)$ methods—read *order of* N^2 methods.) Thus, as N increases, the time for sequential methods increases very rapidly for both sorting and searching.

It is often convenient to sort a table *in place,* that is, without using additional storage space. This can be done sequentially by interchanging the nth entry with the nth largest, $n = 1, 2, \ldots, N - 1$. An alternative is to compare each entry with its neighbor in order, exchanging the two if they are in the wrong order. The largest will "float" to the top in this process. The same process can then be applied to the remaining $N - 1$ unsorted elements. After at most $N - 1$ applications, the table will be in order. If the table is already partially sorted, this method will take fewer passes. This method is called the *bubble sort.*

12.3.2 Merging Methods

There are combination methods utilizing the sequential sort for smaller files and then merging techniques. One example of this is called the *quadratic selection process.* The original file of N records is broken into $\sqrt{N}$ subfiles, each with $\sqrt{N}$ records (or the nearest integer to $\sqrt{N}$). The subfiles are sorted into order by a sequential method (using approximately $(\sqrt{N})^2/2 = N/2$ comparisons each on $\sqrt{N}$ files, for a total of approximately $N^{1.5}/2$ operations). The N subfiles are now merged by comparing the smallest of each to find the overall smallest (this takes $\sqrt{N}$ comparisons). This smallest is placed in its final position, and the process is repeated with it removed from its subfile. Since there are $\sqrt{N}$ records, this merging process takes $N^{1.5}$ operations, for a total of $1.5\ N^{1.5}$ operations. We can therefore say that this is an $O(N^{1.5})$ method. The quadratic selection process is a special case of the *P-way merge.* In a P-way merge, the original file is split into P subfiles of N/P elements each. Each of these subfiles is sorted by some method, and then the P-ordered files are merged as in the quadratic selection process. This last operation takes order of $N * P$ operations. The subfiles of N/P elements could be sorted by any method. For example, another P-way merge could be used by breaking each subfile into sub-subfiles of $N/P/P$ elements. This subdivision can be repeated until the sub-sub- . . . subfiles are small enough to be sorted sequentially.

How many passes of merging are needed for a file of N elements? Assume that the number of records that are to be sorted initially is fixed at Q. Then, if N is less than Q, only the initial sort pass is needed. If N is between Q and PQ, then one additional pass is needed. For each factor of P, one additional pass is needed. Hence the number of passes is the smallest integer at least as large as

$$1 + \log_P \frac{N}{Q}$$

The amount of work in each pass is proportional to NP, so the total work is proportional to

$$NP(1 + \log_P \frac{N}{Q}).$$

As N increases, this increases at a rate of $N \log N$. For a given N and Q, the optimum value of P can be calculated by differentiation. It can be seen that as N/Q becomes large (which is the case of interest when merging techniques are being discussed), then the value of P for which the total merge time is minimum is $\varepsilon = 2.71828\ldots$. Since P must be an integer, 2 or 3 is optimum. In practice, merging from secondary storage devices is likely to be I/O-limited, so that the computation time is not as significant as I/O time. As P increases, the number of passes decreases, but the computation time increases. Ideally, P should be increased until the computation time is equal to the I/O time. If magnetic tapes are being used, then it is probable that the physical number of tape drives available will be the limiting factor, so the crudest rule of thumb is to use all tape drives available. When disks are being used, buffer space is usually the limiting factor.

Merging techniques can be used from an internal sort by starting with files of length 1 that are necessarily sorted and performing P-way merges. Since the internal sort is not I/O-limited, a P of 2 or 3 should be chosen. In fact, a more careful analysis of the time for a given machine will usually suggest that P should be 2. This is called a binary merge, or binary sort.

12.3.3 Radix Methods

The key is usually expressed in some radix. For example, it may be expressed internally in binary, it may be a decimal number, or it may be an alphabetic identifier, which is radix 26. A radix method is a method that takes account of the representation of the key in order to do the sorting. It can be likened to the method of alphabetizing a list of identifiers by first sorting them into 26 piles, or *buckets,* according to the first letter, and then treating each pile separately, alphabetizing them according to the second letter, and so on. This technique can be adapted to computer use. For internal sorting, there is no limit to the radix that could be used except that of the storage space required to provide at least 1 word for each bucket. It is not necessary to provide space for more than one entry in a contiguous location of memory, since subsequent entries in the same bucket could be chained together. If this technique is used for sorting files from secondary storage, then there must be at least as many output-file storage devices (for example, magnetic-tape units) as there are buckets, so the radix used is limited. In addition, at least one input-file device is needed, and if unnecessary file-to-file copies are to be avoided, there should be as many input files as there are output files, so that on the next pass their roles can be switched. Methods based on this idea are sometimes called *bucket sorts*.

The number of operations is proportional to the number of passes and the number of items N. The number of passes K is determined by the radix that can be used and the length of the key. To some extent, K is independent of the number of entries, except that it should be realized that the maximum number of entries is limited by the radix R and the number of passes K, because it is not possible to have more than R^K different keys consisting of K digits base R. Radix sorting is not very efficient unless the ratio of the number of keys used to the maximum possible number is large (close to 1). Roughly speaking, this is because the method is going through the motions of distinguishing between many more different keys than are actually present unless the ratio is large.

A sort using radix 2 called *radix exchange* has been developed for internal sorting. It has the property that very little temporary storage is required. Since the radix is 2, it is useful for binary machines in which the key is a fixed-point number. The unordered set of keys is scanned from the first entry, looking only at the most significant bit. When a 1 bit is found, the scan starts backward from the last entry until a key with a 0 first is encountered. The two entries are exchanged, and the scan continues. Two address pointers are used during this scan to remember where the forward and backward scans have reached. When the pointers meet, the file is in order on the first bit; that is, it has been divided into two subfiles based on the first bit. Each of these two subfiles can be sorted on the second bit to get four subfiles in order on the first 2 bits, and so on. If the key contains K bits, K address pointers will be needed for temporary storage.[3]

The radix exchange method described above is slow if the keys are long, because the number of passes is proportional to the number of bits in the keys. *Quicksort* and *Quickersort* are the names of two similar methods that overcome this problem.[4]

The first step in the radix exchange is to divide the table into two by putting all keys less than 1000000 . . . 0 at the top of the table and all entries greater than or equal to this number below. This is done by scanning simultaneously from the top and bottom of the table so that keys can be exchanged when they are in the wrong relative order. Quicksort chooses one of the keys at random and uses this for the comparison instead of 100 . . . 0. Each key is examined, starting from the first, and is compared with the random key chosen. When a larger key is found, the scan starts from the bottom of the table looking for a smaller key. When one is found, the larger and smaller are exchanged and the scan continues. This step is called *Partition* by Hoare.

The result of applying Partition to an array $A(K), K = M, \ldots, N,$ is to break it into three subarrays of elements: less than or equal to, greater than or equal to, and equal to the randomly chosen element. These are arranged in ascending blocks; a call to Partition (A,M,N,I,J) rearranges A so that the blocks are between M and J, J and I, and I and N. Partition also guarantees that the middle block will contain at least one entry, so the first and third blocks will be at least one smaller than the input block. Hence it can be used in the recursive procedure quicksort shown in Program 12-3. This first checks to see whether the table contains one or fewer elements, in which case it is already sorted. If not, quicksort partitions the table into smaller tables and applies quicksort to those recursively. The procedure Partition is shown in Program 12-4.

At first sight it appears that no extra storage is used in this sorting method. That is not strictly true, because execution of recursive procedure uses memory space proportional to the number of levels of recursion. In this case, there are a minimum of log n levels of recursion, although the worst case is n levels, in which case the execution time is proportional to n. However, Quicksort is one of the best all-around sorting techniques for medium-size tables, having the best average execution time.

[3]This method is described in P. Hildebrandt and H. Isbit, "Radix Exchange," *Journal of the Association for Computing Machinery,* vol. 6, no. 2, April 1959, pp. 156–163.

[4]Described in C. A. R. Hoare, "Algorithm 64," *Communications of the Association for Computing Machinery,* vol. 4, July 1961, p. 321, and R. S. Scowen, "Algorithm 271," *Communications of the Association for Computing Machinery,* vol. 8, no. 11, Oct. 1965 pp. 669–670.

Program 12-3 Quicksort

```
Quicksort: subprogram (A, M, N)
  array A
  integer M, N, I, J
  Quicksort is a recursive procedure that sorts the array A(I), I = M,..., N
  if M < N then
    call Partition(A, M, N, I, J)
    call Quicksort(A, M, J)
    call Quicksort(A, I, N)
    endif
  endsubprogram
```

Program 12-4 Partition called by quicksort

```
Partition: subprogram (A, M, N, I, J)
  array A
  integer M, N, I, J, R
  The elements of A are arranged and the integers
  I and J are computed such that, for some random
  element F of A(R), M ≤ R ≤ N, we have
    M ≤ J < I ≤ N provided M < N
    A(K) ≤ F for M ≤ K ≤ J
    A(K) = F for J < K < I
    A(K) ≥ F for I ≤ K ≤ N
  Set R to be a random integer between N and M inclusive
  Set F = A(R) (F should be same type as A)
  J ← N
  do while I ≤ J for I ← M to N
    Now A(K) ≤ F, M ≤ K < I.
    if F < A(I) then
      do for J ← J to M by −1 while F ≤ A(J) enddo
      Now A(K) ≥ F, J < K ≤ N.
      if I < J
        then switch A(I) and A(J)
          J ← J − 1
        endif
      endif
    enddo
  if I < R
    then switch A(I) and A(R)
      I ← I + 1
    else if J > R
        then switch A(J) and A(R)
          J ← J − 1
        endif
    endif
  endsubprogram
```

12.3.4 Internally Sorting Long Records

In many business applications and in some system applications, the record is very long compared with the size of the key. Since the sorting methods discussed involve the movement of records from one part of memory to another several times, it is desirable to look for methods that avoid this movement or minimize it. The schemes that can be used depend on the way in which we need to access the file after it is sorted. There are three possible needs: either sequential access is sufficient, adjacent elements in the file must be contiguous in memory, or we need to index to the ith element.

If sequential access suffices, it is only necessary to provide a link from one entry to the next. This can be done by allocating an extra field to each record stored to contain the address of the next entry or the end-of-file mark (usually indicated by a 0 address). As the file is sorted, only these addresses have to be changed.

Suppose, for example, that the six records in Table 12-4 were stored in the locations indicated (occupying 20 words each). The link address is shown as it would be set up originally. Table 12-4 gives the file in the sequential order in which it was created. A sorting process, such as a three-way merge, might start by creating three ordered files of two records each. These files start in locations 120, 160, and 200 (this information must be saved), and the records are modified to those shown in Table 12-5. The three-way merge is now performed by comparing the keys in locations 120, 160, and 200. BROWN in 120 is found to be smallest, so it is put at the start of this final chain. The first file now has a starting address of 100, since the earlier entry was removed. The next comparison shows that BRYAN is the smallest of the three keys compared. Thus the entry in 200 is placed in the output file chain by putting 200 in the address link of the record 120. The result at the completion of the merge is shown in Table 12-6, which tells us that the order of the file is 120, 200, 160, 100, 180, 140.

TABLE 12-4 DATA FOR CHAINED-SEARCH EXAMPLE

Location	Key	Content	Link address
100	JONES	DATA.A	120
120	BROWN	DATA.B	140
140	SMITH	DATA.C	160
160	DAVID	DATA.D	180
180	PETER	DATA.E	200
200	BRYAN	DATA.F	—

TABLE 12-5 DATA SORTED INTO THREE SUBFILES

Location	Key	Content	Link address
100	JONES	DATA.A	—
120	BROWN	DATA.B	100
140	SMITH	DATA.C	—
160	DAVID	DATA.D	140
180	PETER	DATA.E	—
200	BRYAN	DATA.F	180

TABLE 12-6 DATA AFTER FULL SORT

Location	Key	Content	Link address
100	JONES	DATA.A	180
120	BROWN	DATA.B	200
140	SMITH	DATA.C	—
160	DAVID	DATA.D	100
180	PETER	DATA.E	140
200	BRYAN	DATA.F	160

It is necessary to save the starting address, 120, of the chain in the memory. This file can now be accessed sequentially, starting from the first member.

It may be necessary to place the successive records of a file in contiguous locations so that the file can be written onto an output device. This means that the records must be moved. To avoid moving them during the sort process, a technique such as the one above can be employed. When the file has been alphabetized, it can be physically moved. This movement need not take more than one move of each record, which is an improvement over the number of moves that would have been used if the records had been moved in the sorting process.

If the file is to be indexed, some set of information has to be kept in order in contiguous memory cells. However, it is not necessary to move the records; instead, an array of pointers to the records can be sorted. When keys are to be compared for sorting, they can be accessed by indirect addressing from the pointer array. If this is done with the records in Table 12-4, the pointer array will be as shown in Table 12-7 after sorting.

12.4 HASH ADDRESSING

The previous section explored techniques that depend on the table being ordered in memory but that do not require a knowledge of where a given identifier appears in the table. This contrasts with the technique that a person uses in a phone book search. One knows, for example, that the entry for Brown will appear about one-twentieth of the way through the book. The strategy used could be to open the book at this point and then to scan forward or backward, depending on the result of a comparison of the name Brown with the entry found at the one-twentieth point. The corresponding computer

TABLE 12-7 SORTED ARRAY OF POINTERS TO TABLE 12-4

Entry	Contents
1	120
2	200
3	160
4	100
5	180
6	140

technique would be to construct an address based on an estimate of where the identifier being searched is likely to appear and then to start a sequential search forward or backward from that point. Let us illustrate this with an example. Suppose that the keys are 3-digit decimal numbers between 000 and 999 and that there are 100 entries in the table. If they are evenly distributed (that is, one key lies between each of 0 to 9, 10 to 19, . . . , and 990 to 999), then the address of the entry in the table is given by the address

$$A = T + (K/10 \text{ Truncated to an integer})$$

where the table is assumed to start in location T and require one location per entry, and where K is the key.

Unfortunately, the keys of a table will not be so evenly distributed in general, but the more that they approximate this distribution, the faster the method will be. In the worst possible case, the method will not be worse than the sequential search method, except that there is an additional calculation of a starting address and at some point the table has to be ordered. If it is a fixed table, such as the mnemonic table, then the sorting does not have to be done for each assembly. Therefore, this is a better method than the sequential method, and yet it retains most of the sequential method's simplicity.

If this method were to be used for the symbol table, then either the entries would have to be sorted between passes I and II (which means that no references to the table could be made in pass I unless a sequential technique were used) or the table would have to be constructed in order. Constructing a table in order can be a time-consuming job if it has to be reordered after each new identifier is entered, because up to half of the entries in the table will have to be moved in order to make space for each new entry. This can be partially avoided if the table has blank spaces in it originally, so that there is a strong possibility that there will be a space for the next entry. The more spaces that are available in a table of given size, the faster the entry process is likely to be. Let us return to the previous example where the keys are between 000 and 999. Suppose that there will be as many as 100 entries in the table, although initially there are none. Suppose that we allocate 200 locations for the table, so that it never becomes more than 50 percent dense. In this case, the probable address for an entry will be given by

$$A = T + K/5$$

When an entry is to be placed in the table, this address is calculated from the value of the key. If the addressed location is empty, the entry is placed in the table at that point. If the location is full, then we have a *collision*. There are many methods for collision resolution, one of which we will describe now. The key is compared with the entry already in the table. If the table entry is larger, the next lower address $A - 1$ is examined. If this is empty, it is used to make the new entry. If its contents are larger, another step to the next lower address is taken. If it is smaller, then it is necessary to open up a space by moving everything, from this point down to the first blank space, down one position. If the original comparison showed that the table entry was smaller, then a similar process is followed in the upward (increasing address) direction. This process ensures that the table remains ordered. Let us examine the process when

TABLE 12-8 HASH ADDRESSING—FIRST VERSION

Location	Key	After step 1	After step 2
T+40	201	201	201
T+41	203	203	203
T+42			
T+43	215	215	215
T+44	216	216	216
T+45			217
T+46	231	231	231
T+47			
T+48		247	246
T+49	246	255	255
T+50	255	256	256
T+51	257	257	257
T+52			
T+53	266	266	266

the entries 256 and 217 are added to the table after it already contains some entries. In Table 12-8, the left-hand column gives the memory location, the next column contains the keys already entered, and the subsequent columns show the states of the table after the next two entries are made.

In step 1, entry 256 is added to the table. The probable address of the key 256 is $T + 256/5 = T + 51$. Unfortunately, location $T + 51$ is already occupied by the key 257, which is larger than 256. Therefore, the entry in the next smaller location $T + 50$ is checked. It contains the key 255, which is smaller than 256. Therefore, 256 is entered into $T + 50$ and all entries from $T + 50$ down are moved one location lower until the next blank in $T + 48$ is found. In step 2, the key 217, corresponding to the probable address $T + 43$, is entered. The present entries in $T + 43$ and $T + 44$ are both smaller than the key 217. However, the next table entry, $T + 45$, is empty. Therefore, 217 is entered into $T + 45$.

A table search process can be viewed as a means of calculating a function of an argument. The argument of the function is the key that is to be looked up, and its value is the address of the entry. If this function is known, that is, if for each key K we can calculate the address A by means of a function F such that $A = F(K)$, then there is no need to perform a search through the table. In the technique discussed above, an approximation to F was formed by using a linear function F. It was linear because the table was to be ordered. However, if we ask what use was made of the ordering property, we see that it was used only to determine whether to search backward or forward from the probable address when the entry and the searched identifier did not agree. We could just as well always search in the same direction, say in the direction of increasing address, in which case the ordering would not be necessary. This has an additional advantage. Since the table does not have to be in order, it is not necessary to move previous entries. The method for finding an identifier by searching is now as follows: a new entry is placed in the table by executing the search process above and placing the new entry at the blank location found. (If the searched value X is found in the table already, the search must continue for a blank location if equal entries are to be permitted.)

This process will be illustrated by repeating the earlier example using the new entry method. Refer to Table 12-9. In step 1, the entry 256 is added to the table. Since the approximate address function gives location T + 51, which is not empty, the first blank location with a higher address is used, namely, T + 52. Note that the table is now out of order. When the entry 217 is made in step 2, the process also has to search forward two cells until a blank location is found. Note that, in this unordered technique, it is never necessary to move items already in the table; hence the entry time is faster. However, the search time will be slower when the table becomes fairly dense, since it is necessary to search until an item is located or a blank location is found, whereas in an ordered table it is only necessary to search until either a blank location or a larger (or smaller if the search is backward) entry has been found. The unordered technique will never be slower than a sequential search.

In the above example we calculated an approximate address by means of a linear function of the key. In applications of this technique to assemblers and compilers, there is a high probability that the keys will not be distributed in anywhere near a uniform fashion over the range of possible keys. This will cause bunching in the table and slow down the search-and-entry process. Many assembly-language programs, for example, contain identifiers that start with the same three letters, because these three letters serve to identify that section of code to the programmer. Since the ordering is not important, there is no reason why the approximate address function should be a monotonic function of the key. (A *monotonic function* is a function whose value changes only in one direction, up or down, as the value of the argument is increased.) Therefore, we should try to use an approximate address function that spreads the keys used fairly evenly over the locations used in the table. If the table is fixed, as the mnemonic table is, then various address functions can be tried until a reasonably good choice in terms of speed of calculation and speed of search is achieved. If the table changes, as happens

TABLE 12-9 HASH ADDRESSING—SECOND VERSION

Location	Key	After step 1	After step 2
T+40	201	201	201
T+41	203	203	203
T+42			
T+43	215	215	215
T+44	216	216	216
T+45			217
T+46	231	231	231
T+47			
T+48			
T+49	246	246	246
T+50	255	255	255
T+51	257	257	257
T+52		256	256
T+53	266	266	266

in the case of the identifier table, an address function must be chosen without prior knowledge of the entries. The idea generally used is to mix up or *hash* the key in some way so that keys assigned in any routine fashion are unlikely to fall in the same part of the table. Such an address is called a *hash address*.

Some examples of hash addresses that could be used in an assembler symbol table include packing the identifier into a word (using, say, ASCII), multiplying that representation by a constant, and extracting a certain number of bits from the result, or dividing the packed form by a suitable integer and using the remainder. (The integer should have no common factor with the number of bits per character. For example, if 8-bit characters are used, the integer should not be divisible by 2.)

The problem of collisions, which occur when the space in the table is already occupied, is frequently solved by calculating a second hash address and trying that location. One common technique is to use for the first hash address the remainder from a division by a prime p, dividing the quotient from that division by another prime to get a second remainder for the hash address, and so on as necessary. Another solution to the problem of conflicts is to create a chain of additional entries with the same hash address and to search this chain sequentially.

12.5 CHAINING TECHNIQUES

In the previous sections, it has generally been assumed that the record positions in memory were in contiguous locations. This was necessary in methods that used address calculations, such as the binary search method and the hash addressing technique. However, in sequential searching, it was only necessary that the successor of an entry be accessible directly. This was exploited in the discussion on sorting long records, where they were chained together in order to avoid moving them in memory. Chaining techniques can be exploited to advantage in a number of methods. This section will discuss various chaining techniques that can be used.

12.5.1 Sequential Search with Deletions

The method of sequential searching has a number of drawbacks. One is its inherent slowness, which is only offset by its simplicity. In some situations, it is desirable to replace identifiers with the table address containing the related information. This means that deletion is not possible unless blank entries are permitted, since other entries may not be moved. Permitting blank entries slows down the entry process. If the entries are chained together in memory, the speed is not improved, but it is possible to remove entries from the chain without leaving blank entries in the table. This is shown in the following example. If the original data has the form shown in Table 12-10, and the address 110 is indicated as being the start of the table, then the order of the table can be seen to be SAM, BETTY, PAT, JOHN, BOB, ... Suppose that the entry PAT is to be removed. We note that this entry is preceded by BETTY and followed by JOHN in locations 114 and 112, respectively. In order for the successor of BETTY to be JOHN, the chain link from BETTY must be changed to the address of JOHN. That is, the chain address in location 114 must be changed from 118 to 112. The data now has the form shown in Table 12-11.

TABLE 12-10 DELETION FROM A CHAINED LIST—BEFORE

Location	Key	Link to next entry
110	SAM	114
112	JOHN	120
114	BETTY	118
116		
118	PAT	112
120	BOB	

TABLE 12-11 DELETION FROM A CHAINED LIST—AFTER

Location	Key	Link
110	SAM	114
112	JOHN	120
114	BETTY	112
116		
118	PAT	112
120	BOB	

It was not necessary to remove the key PAT in any way; it is omitted from any search process because the chain of link addresses does not pass through it. In this particular example, the first entry in the chain is also the first location of the table. If this entry were to be removed from the table, the first member of the chain would be in location 114. Therefore, there must be a cell in memory that is used to hold the address of the first entry in the table.

If a new entry is to be added to the table, then it can be placed on the beginning or end of the chain. In the latter case, it is necessary to save the address of the last entry in the chain, so it is simpler to add a new entry to the beginning of the chain, unless there are reasons for preferring the end.

When an entry is added to the chain, it is necessary to find an empty place in memory for recording the new record. Since the present records are not in contiguous locations, there may be holes in the table. Since we did not blank out a record when it was removed from the chain, it is not possible (or desirable) to scan through all locations looking for an empty position. Therefore, a method that will allow us to find empty positions must be introduced. This method must allow the positions made free when an entry is removed to be reallocated. A chaining principle can also be used for this by constructing a chained list of all free positions. The starting address of this chain must be kept in a known memory cell. When an item is to be added to the table, the first entry in the *free chain* (sometimes called the *free list*) is removed from that chain and used as a location for the new entry. When an item is removed from the table, its address can be added to the beginning of the free chain. Suppose our data is in the state shown in Table 12-12. The free chain contains locations 118 and 116. The 0 link in location 116 is used to indicate that it is the end of the chain. (This rules out location 0 as a

TABLE 12-12 USE OF A FREE CHAIN

	Key	Link
Table start		110
Free-chain start		118
Location		
110	SAM	114
112	JOHN	120
114	BETTY	112
116		0
118	PAT	116
120	BOB	0

possible table address.) The table contains locations 110, 114, 112, and 120. Location 118 contains a nonblank key because it was previously used, but this key is not in the table because it is not in the table chain. If the key TOM were to be added to the table, then the procedure would be as follows. The new entry TOM is placed into the location given in the start of the free chain (118). Thus location 118 now contains TOM. The start address for the free chain is set to the link in location 118, the link in location 118 is set to the contents of the start of the table chain, and the new value of the start of the table chain is made equal to the old value of the start of the free chain. Thus the data has the form shown in Table 12-13.

If the entry BOB is now removed, the procedure is as follows. BOB is located in the table by a search. It is found in location 120. It is also noted that the preceding entry was in location 112. The link from location 120, namely 0, is copied into the link of the preceding location, 112. The start of the free chain (116) is copied into the link of 120, and the address of the item being removed (120) is copied into the free-chain start-storage cell. Thus the data takes the form shown in Table 12-14.

12.5.2 Binary Tree Method

The binary search method is inflexible because it is necessary to order the information so that the address of any particular entry can be calculated. However, the information is only accessed in a particular sequence: first the middle entry, then the entry one-

TABLE 12-13 FREE CHAIN AFTER ADDITION OF TOM

	Key	Link
Table start		118
Free-chain start		116
Location		
110	SAM	114
112	JOHN	120
114	BETTY	112
116		0
118	TOM	110
120	BOB	0

TABLE 12-14 FREE CHAIN AFTER DELETION OF BOB

	Key	Link
Table start		118
Free-chain start		120
Location		
110	SAM	114
112	JOHN	0
114	BETTY	112
116		0
118	TOM	110
120	BOB	116

quarter or three-quarters of the way up, and so on. If the table is stored so that the middle entry is in a fixed position, and if from that position it is possible to get to either of the next two entries required and from each of those to their two successors, etc., then the information need not be ordered. This suggests storing two pointers, or chain addresses, with each entry. The search mechanism consists of comparing the desired identifier with the entry in the fixed position reserved for the middle entry. If the desired identifier matches, there is nothing further to do. Otherwise, the search continues to the entry pointed to by the appropriate one of the two pointers. Let us refer to these as the left pointer for entries that are less than the middle entry and the right pointer for entries that are larger. Part of such a table is shown in Figure 12-4. This structure is an example of a *tree*. It is drawn upside down in that the *root* of the tree is at the top of the figure. A tree consists of a set of *nodes* connected to each other by *branches*. It is such that there are no *closed circuits* in the branch connections, so that there is one and only one path between any two nodes. The nodes may be labeled, as they are in the example. One node is special and is called the root of the tree. The branches extend from this root to each of the nodes. A node that is connected to only one other node below it is called

FIGURE 12-4 Binary tree

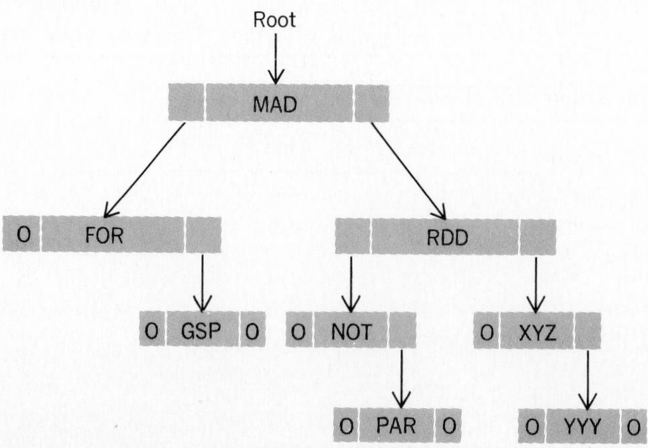

a *terminal node*. In this particular example, there are exactly two branches from each node to lower nodes, although either of these branches can be empty (called *null*). The branches are identified as the left and right branches. Such a tree is called a *binary tree*. Storing the information this way for a binary search has the advantage that it is no longer necessary for the entry at the root of the table to be the middle entry. Whichever entry is used, it is only necessary that all other entries be to the left or right of it, according to whether they are smaller or larger than it. Thus, in the figure, MAD is not the middle entry, but the search method would still work. If, for example, we were to look up PAR, we could check it against MAD. Since PAR is larger, we would check with the right-hand neighbor of MAD. PAR is less that RDD, so we would check it against NOT. The latter is larger, so the right-hand branch would be taken, which would lead to a match.

The search process can be handled easily with a recursive procedure. Suppose that each element is stored in a group of 3 words in an N-by-3 array A. Let A(n,1) contain the integer form of the key, A(n,2) contain the left pointer (that is, the index of the group of 3 words containing the node to the left), and A(n,3) contain the right pointer. An outline of the search procedure is shown in Program 12-5. Zero is assumed to be an invalid index, so it represents a null pointer and is returned if the entry is not found. The program is called with POINTER set to the index of the tree root. This method has the advantage that entries can be added to the table at any time. If a new identifier is to be entered, a search process is followed that will finally come to the end of a chain, indicated in the figure by a 0 link address. If the identifier is found in the search, then it obviously should not be reentered. When the end of a chain is reached, the new entry can be added. This makes the method very suitable for assembler use if the space for the links is available. It has the additional advantage that it is trivial to print the table in alphabetical order when the time comes. It is not simple to remove an entry from the

Program 12-5 Binary tree search

```
Search: subprogram (A, KEY, POINTER, RESULT)
  array A
  integer KEY, POINTER, RESULT
  Search for KEY in A(i, 1). A(i, 2) and A(i, 3) contain
  the left and right pointers of a binary tree.
  RESULT is such that A(RESULT) = KEY if such exists;
  0 otherwise.
  if POINTER = 0
    then RESULT ← 0
    else if KEY < A(POINTER,1)
      then call Search(A,KEY,A(POINTER,2),RESULT)
      else call Search(A,KEY,A(POINTER,3),RESULT)
      endif
    endif
  endsubprogram
```

table, since—unless the entry is the last in a chain—it is necessary to replace the entry with another for comparison purposes in searching. If the identifiers entered are in alphabetic order, the method is very bad because the tree is one-sided. It is then as slow as a sequential search and takes up more space.

The fact that a random tree may turn out to be a simple list and be as slow for searching and sorting as sequential methods has led to a number of modifications. One important form of tree is a *balanced tree*. This, as its name suggests, is not too lopsided. Formally, the distances from any node to the furthest terminal nodes on its left and right subtrees should not differ by more than 1. This complicates the tree-building process, but it can be shown that an additional entry can be added at a cost proportional to that of the same tree if balancing is not enforced (proportional to log N steps, where N is the number of nodes). It also guarantees that the searching process will be reasonably efficient (again, proportional to log N).

12.5.3 Heapsort

This algorithm, first described by Williams,[5] is a binary sort. It is a little slower than Quicksort (Section 12.3.3) on the average, but has the advantage that the worst case time is also proportional to $N \log N$, whereas Quicksort can be proportional to N^2 in the worst case (the same as sequential methods). The idea is based on the following important representation of binary trees: If a node is in location J, let its left and right offspring be stored in locations 2J and 2J + 1. Figure 12-5 shows a binary tree (not sorted) stored in this fashion. The tree shown in Figure 12-5 has the property of being *complete* (every node has two subnodes or is terminal) except for the missing terminal nodes in the last three locations. A tree with this structure has the advantage that there

[5]J. W. J. Williams, "Algorithm 232, Heapsort," *Communications of the Association for Computing Machinery,* vol. 7, June 1964, pp. 347–348. See also R. W. Floyd, "Algorithm 245, Treesort," ibid., December 1974, p. 701.

FIGURE 12-5 Tree stored in contiguous locations

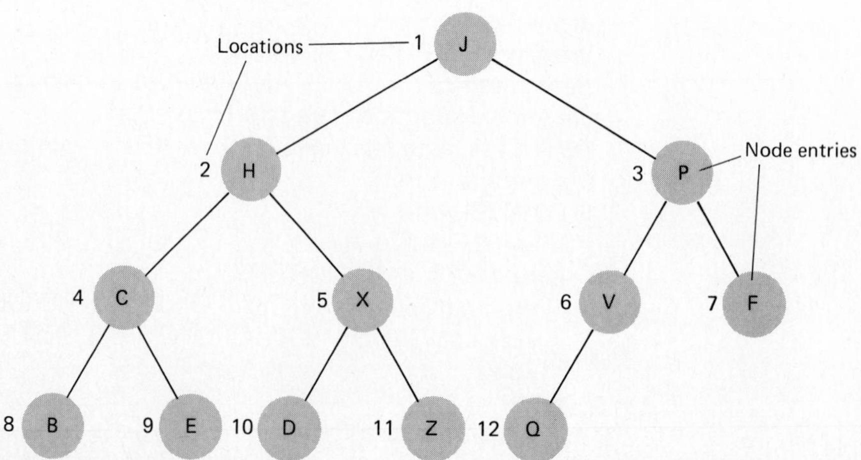

is no wasted space. If we know the size of the tree, we can determine the offspring of any node by calculation. For example, node 6 has an offspring in location 12 (2 * 6), but no offspring in location 13 (2 * 6 + 1) because 13 is beyond the storage area of the tree. The first stage in heapsort is to transform the information into a *heap*. A heap is a binary tree stored in the fashion above such that the value in any node is larger than the value in either of its offspring. At the moment, this is satisfied by very few nodes in Figure 12-5 (just the node in location 6 and the terminal nodes that have no offspring). If we start scanning back from the node in the largest location that is not terminal (location 6 in Figure 12-5), we can rearrange at most one pair of parent-offspring for each node to convert the data structure to a heap. Node 6 is OK, so we move to node 5. Of its offspring, node 11 has the larger element, and it is larger than node 5; thus we switch the contents of nodes 5 and 11. After examining node 4, we switch nodes 4 and 9. Now the structure is in the state shown in Figure 12-6

The scan continues to node 3. This time, nodes 3 and 6 must be switched. Because 6 is changed, we must now check 6. Clearly, we must switch 6 and 12 to maintain the heap relationship for node 6. When node 2 is checked, it is switched with node 5, which in turn is switched with node 11. Finally, node 1 is checked. It causes switches of nodes 1 and 2, and 2 and 5. The resulting heap is shown in Figure 12-7. A program to do this is obtained by calling the subprogram shown in Program 12-6 with the code

```
do for I ← integer part of N/2 to 1 by −1
  call Sift (A,I,N)
  enddo
```

where N is the number of elements in the array A. The subprogram Sift (A, I, N) examines node I, determines whether its offspring need to be switched with the parent, and continues down to the bottom of the tree for each offspring that is switched. (This is at most order of log *N* steps.)

FIGURE 12-6 Intermediate stage of heap formation

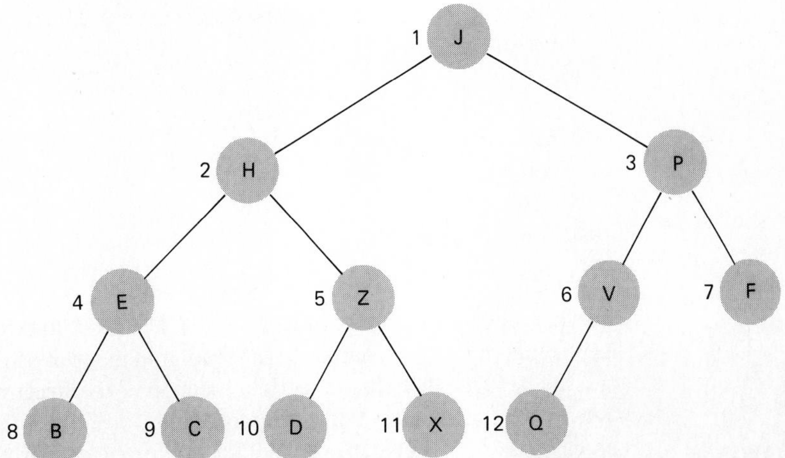

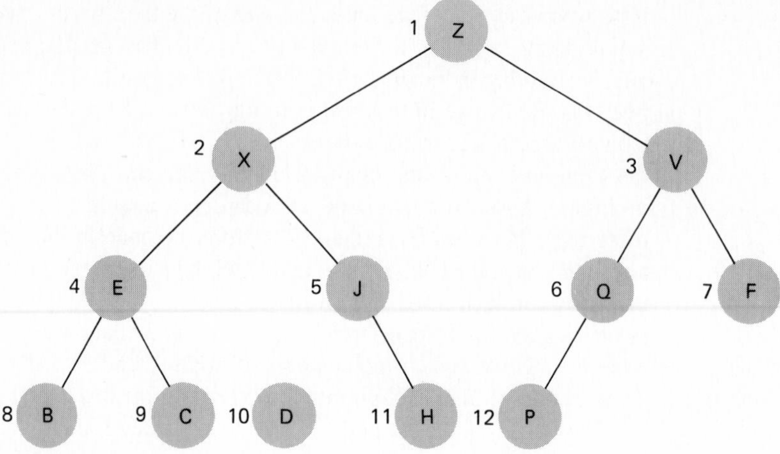

FIGURE 12-7 A heap

Program 12-6 Sift subprogram for heapsort

```
Sift: subprogram (A,I,N)
  array A
  integer I, N, J, K
  This procedure ensures that all nodes below node I are
  a heap provided that all nodes below node I's offspring
  are heaps.
  J ← I
  do forever
    K ← J
    J ← 2*J
    if J > N then exit loop endif
    if J < N
      then if A(J+1) > A(J) then J ← J − 1 endif
      endif
    if A(K) ≤ A(J)
      then switch A(K) and A(J)
      else exit loop
      endif
    enddo
  endsubprogram
```

Now that we have a heap, what do we do? The most important fact we need from the heap is that the largest element is in location in the root position. In this method of storage, the largest element is in the first location of the structure. If we switch it with location N, we can consider converting locations 1 to N − 1 to a heap again. Clearly, this process can be repeated. However, when we consider forming a heap in locations

Program 12-7 Heapsort

```
Heapsort: subprogram (A,N)
  array A
  integer N, I, M
  First convert the N elements of A into a heap, then
  sort them by moving the largest element to the end
  and reheaping the remaining elements. Apply this
  procedure iteratively.
  do for I ← integer part of N/2 to 1 by −1
    call Sift(A, I, N)
    enddo
  do for M ← N − 1 to 2 by −1
    switch A(1) and A(M+1)
    call Sift(A, 1, M)
    enddo
  endsubprogram
```

1 to N − 1, we see that the only element that needs to be considered is the element just moved into location 1. Hence we can apply Sift (A, 1, N−1). Thus the final algorithm is as shown in Program 12-7. (Note that this code and Sift both indicate that elements should be switched. Examination shows that consecutive switches involve the same element; thus, in practice, one of the elements can be kept in a register until a chain of switches is complete.)

12.6 SUMMARY AND PROBLEMS

Searching and sorting involve files of records. We want to be able to add, change, reference, and delete records by specifying the key. Sequential search is simple, but it takes time proportional to N for each reference. Binary search is faster for large values of N because it takes time proportional to log N. However, it requires a sorted file.

Sorting is important for presentation of information and for organizing it so that fast retrieval is possible. Internal sorting is done in primary memory. If larger files have to be sorted from I/O units, internal sorts are performed first on the largest blocks that can be held in primary memory. Sequential methods of sorting take $0(N^2)$ time, whereas P-way merging methods take $0(N \log N)$ time. For internal sorts, a P of 2 (two-way merge) is usually best, but for sorts from secondary storage, P should depend on the availability of I/O devices and/or buffer space.

Radix methods are based on the representation of the key. They are only efficient if the number of keys is a reasonable percentage of the number of possible keys. A method related to the radix two sort is called Quicksort, which is the best all-around method for internal sort. Its average time is $0(N \log N)$.

When long records have to be sorted, they should not be moved, but pointers to the records should be manipulated.

Hash table techniques are the fastest if the approximate size of the table is known in advance so that enough space can be allocated to leave some space free. As long as collisions occur infrequently, the average time to enter an item or search for it is independent of N.

Chains are used when we want to delete items from tables without leaving "holes." Chains can be used with sequential methods or binary methods. In the latter case, a tree is used. The advantage of these methods is that the structure can be built as the items are received and accessed for a search at any time. A heap is a binary tree structure that has the property that it can be built very rapidly and has the largest element in the root. Because of this, it can be used in a sorting process. By storing a complete binary tree in consecutive locations where the address of a subnode can be calculated from the address of a node, a sorting method called heapsort can be constructed, that uses no additional storage and has worst case time to $N \log N$. It is a little slower than quicksort, on the average.

Problems

12-1 Program a binary search for a table of length N.

12-2 Program a sequential search for a table of length N.

12-3 Write a program to build up a table of length N containing the integers 1 through N. Use the programs from problems 12-1 and 12-2 as subroutines to search, in turn, for each entry in the table. Use the system clock to find the total time for all references in the two cases. Run the program for various values of N (5, 10, 15, etc., stopping when too much computer time has been used) and plot the time of each method as a function of N.

12-4 Sketch a graph of the way in which the merge time for a P-way merge of a large file depends on P. Show the compute time and the I/O time separately. If I/O and compute are overlapped, indicate what P would be optimum. If I/O and compute are sequential rather than overlapped, what P is optimum on the basis of the sketch?

12-5 What are the best case data and the worst case data for quicksort; that is, what form of data leads to the fastest sort, and what form to the slowest?

12-6 Write a recursive subroutine that will make a new entry in the binary tree described in Section 12.5.2.

12-7 Rewrite Program 12-5 so that it is iterative rather than recursive.

12-8 Rewrite programs 12-6 and 12-7 to avoid unnecessary data movement in the switches.

INDEX